THE RAINBOROWES

By the same author

Historic Houses of the National Trust
Country Houses from the Air
Life in the English Country Cottage
Visions of Power: Ambition and Architecture
The Polite Tourist: A History of Country House Visiting
The Arts & Crafts House
The Art Deco House
His Invention So Fertile: A Life of Christopher Wren
By Permission of Heaven: The Story of the Great Fire of London
The Verneys: A True Story of Love, War and
Madness in Seventeenth-Century England
Pirates of Barbary: Corsairs, Conquests and Captivity in the
Seventeenth-Century Mediterranean

THE RAINBOROWES

Pirates, Puritans and a Family's Quest for
the Promised Land

Adrian Tinniswood

Jonathan Cape
London

Published by Jonathan Cape 2013

2 4 6 8 10 9 7 5 3 1

Copyright © Adrian Tinniswood 2013

Adrian Tinniswood has asserted his right under the Copyright, Designs and Patents Act 1988 to be identified as the author of this work

First published in Great Britain in 2013 by
Jonathan Cape
Random House, 20 Vauxhall Bridge Road,
London SW1V 2SA

www.vintage-books.co.uk

Addresses for companies within The Random House Group Limited can be found at: www.randomhouse.co.uk/offices.htm

The Random House Group Limited Reg. No. 954009

A CIP catalogue record for this book is available from the British Library

ISBN 9780224091480

The Random House Group Limited supports the Forest Stewardship Council® (FSC®), the leading international forest-certification organisation. Our books carrying the FSC label are printed on FSC®-certified paper. FSC is the only forest-certification scheme supported by the leading environmental organisations, including Greenpeace. Our paper procurement policy can be found at www.randomhouse.co.uk/environment

Typeset in Bembo by Palimpsest Book Production Limited,
Falkirk, Stirlingshire
Printed and bound in Great Britain by Clays Ltd, St Ives, PLC

For my wife

Contents

A Note on Names

I've encountered more than a dozen spellings of 'Rainborowe' – everything from 'Rainbow' to 'Rainsborough' to 'Raynesburrow'. I have settled on 'Rainborowe' because this is how the Rainborowes always spelled their name. It seems presumptuous to correct them.

List of Illustrations

St Katharine by the Tower and Wapping, seen from the south bank of the Thames.

An early view of Sallee from the west. (© Courtesy of the National Library of Israel, Shapell Family Digitization Project and The Hebrew University of Jerusalem, Department of Geography – Historic Cities Research Project)

William Rainborowe senior's fleet stationed at the mouth of the Bou Regreg.

William Rainborowe senior's last command: the *Sovereign of the Seas*. (© National Maritime Museum, Greenwich, UK)

Travel between England and Massachusetts took anything between five weeks and five months. (© Courtesy of the Thomas Fisher Rare Book Library, University of Toronto)

Several dozen Puritan settlements sprang up around Boston Harbour in the middle decades of the seventeenth century. (© Getty Images)

John Winthrop, the authoritarian governor of Massachusetts and the second husband of Martha Rainborowe. (© Peter Newark American Pictures/The Bridgeman Art Library)

The Irish rising of 1641 spawned a new genre of hate literature. (© Courtesy of the National Library of Ireland)

Stephen Winthrop, husband of Judith Rainborowe and 'a great man for soul liberty'. (Courtesy of Harvard Art Museums/Fogg

Museum, Harvard University Portrait Collection, Gift of Robert Winthrop, representing the Winthrop family, to Harvard University, 1964, H606; Imaging Department © President and Fellows of Harvard College)

Thomas Rainborowe: 'a joy to the best, and a terror to the worst of men'. (© Thomas Rainsborough (engraving), English School, (17th century)/Private Collection/The Stapleton Collection/ The Bridgeman Art Library)

The signature of Thomas Rainborowe.

Laying siege to a town. (© Courtesy of the National Library of Ireland)

Hugh Peter, one-time minister of Salem and the Puritan that English royalists loved to hate. (© National Portrait Gallery, London)

Sir Thomas Fairfax chairs a meeting of the Army Council, 1647. (© The British Library Board/G.3861)

The deaths by firing squad of Sir Charles Lucas and Sir George Lisle after the fall of Colchester in August 1648. (© British Library, London, UK/The Bridgeman Art Library)

The Glorious day of the Saints' Appearance, the sermon preached at Thomas Rainborowe's funeral by his old chaplain, Thomas Brooks. (© The British Library Board/E.474(7))

Major William Rainborowe's battle standard, depicting the severed head of Charles I. (Reproduced by kind permission of the Trustees of Dr Williams's Library, London)

The 'damnable and diabolical opinions, their detestable lives and actions' of the Ranters fascinated Commonwealth England and proved the ruin of Major Rainborowe. (© The British Library Board/E.618.(8))

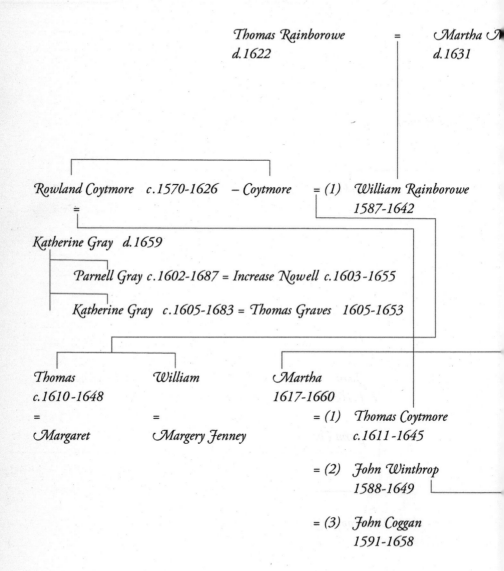

Thomas Rainborowe
d.1622

= Martha N
d.1631

Rowland Coytmore   c.1570-1626   – Coytmore   = (1)   William Rainborowe
    =   1587-1642

Katherine Gray   d.1659

Parnell Gray   c.1602-1687 = Increase Nowell   c.1603-1655

Katherine Gray   c.1605-1683 = Thomas Graves   1605-1653

Thomas   William   Martha
c.1610-1648   1617-1660
=   =   = (1)   Thomas Coytmore
Margaret   Margery Jenney   c.1611-1645

                                       = (2)   John Winthrop
                                               1588-1649

                                       = (3)   John Coggan
                                               1591-1658

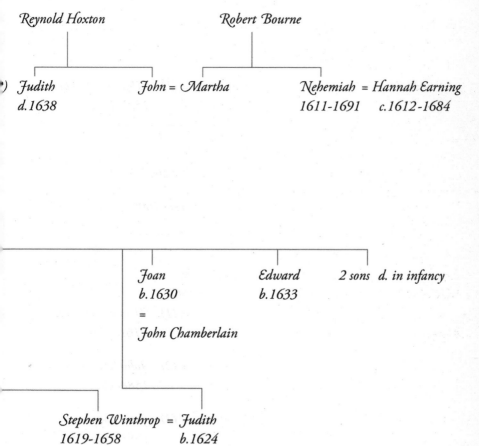

Reynold Hoxton   Robert Bourne

) Judith   John = Martha   Nehemiah = Hannah Earning
d.1638   1611-1691   c.1612-1684

Joan   Edward   2 sons   d. in infancy
b.1630   b.1633
=
John Chamberlain

Stephen Winthrop = Judith
1619-1658   b.1624

THE BRITISH ISLES

Atlantic

Ocean

Shetland
Islands

Orkney
Islands

Hebrides

North

Sea

SCOTLAND

Edinburgh

ENGLAND

Newcastle

Belfast

IRELAND

Isle of
Man

Irish

York

Galway

Sea

Pontefract

Hull

Dublin

Doncaster

Lincoln

Chester

Limerick

Nottingham

Crowland

Cork

Norwich

Saffron
Walden

WALES

Oxford

Abingdon

London

Cardiff

Bristol

Reading

Gravesend

St. George's Channel

Bridgwater

Putney

Deal

Taunton

Sherborne

English   Channel

0   100 mi

0   100 km

FRANCE

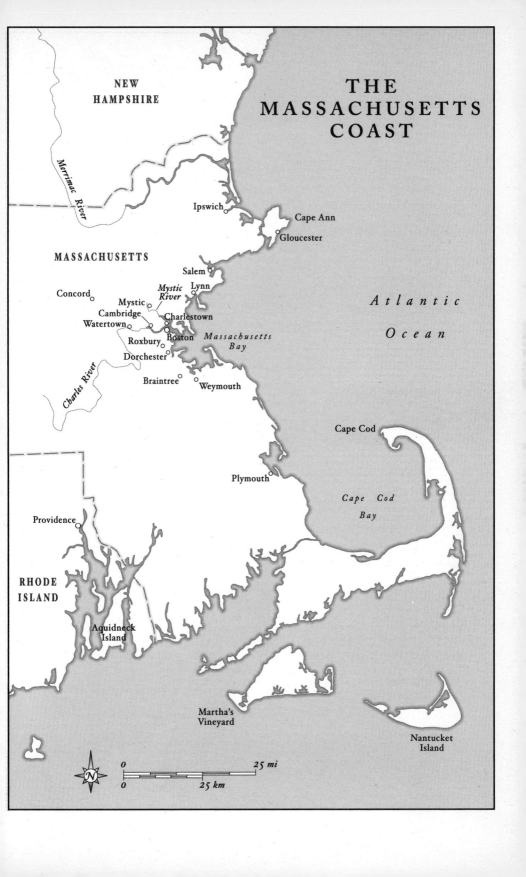

THE
MASSACHUSETTS
COAST

NEW
HAMPSHIRE

Merrimac River

Ipswich

Cape Ann

Gloucester

MASSACHUSETTS

Salem

Mystic River Lynn

Concord Mystic

Cambridge Charlestown

Watertown Boston

Roxbury

Charles River

Dorchester

Braintree Weymouth

Massachusetts Bay

Atlantic

Ocean

Cape Cod

Plymouth

Cape Cod Bay

Providence

RHODE
ISLAND

Aquidneck
Island

Martha's
Vineyard

Nantucket
Island

0   25 mi

N

0   25 km

Two worlds.
One dream.
A new England.

Preface
Their Earthly Canaan

It started, as these things often do, with a couple of lines in someone else's book.

I was leafing through an old edition of John Winthrop's journal of the beginnings of the Massachusetts Bay Colony, when I came across this entry from 1645, three years into the English Civil War:

> Mr Israel Stoughton, one of the magistrates, having been in England about merchandise, and returned with good advantage, went for England again the last winter, with divers other of our best military men, and entered into the Parliament's service. Mr Stoughton was made lieutenant colonel to Colonel Rainsborow, Mr Nehemiah Bourne, a ship carpenter, was major of his regiment, and Mr John Leverett, son of one of the elders of the church of Boston, a captain in a foot company.

I already knew a little about the Rainborowe family. The father, William Rainborowe, was a powerful figure in English naval circles in the 1630s, an adviser to Charles I and the leader of a spectacular raid to free captives from a Moroccan pirate base in 1637. His eldest son Thomas, the 'Colonel Rainsborow' in Winthrop's journal, was well known to students of the English Civil War as a brilliant siege-commander on the Parliamentarian side, and a man of advanced political views. His passionate speech in favour of universal male suffrage – 'I think that the poorest he that is in England hath a life to live as [much as] the greatest he' – is frequently quoted as a landmark in English political history. But why should a bunch of New Englanders, a merchant, a shipwright and the son of a church elder, travel 3,000 miles to fight for Thomas Rainborowe? Was the English Revolution of the 1640s nourished by radicalised Americans?

That chance encounter with Governor Winthrop's journal led back and forth across the Atlantic, as I tried to track the lives of the Rainborowes and their clan. They drifted in and out of history, sometimes standing right at the heart of things, sometimes hovering in the shadows. I discovered that when Winthrop made that entry in his journal, one of the Rainborowe girls was living in his house, the wife of his own son Stephen; that in 1647 John Winthrop himself would marry another Rainborowe girl; that so many members of the Rainborowes' extended family emigrated to Massachusetts from their Thames-side homes in Wapping, that the place where they settled in Charlestown was named Wapping Street. All enthusiastic Puritans, the Rainborowes belonged to the first generation of New England settlers. They helped to build the city on a hill.

And then they built it all over again in the land of their birth, seizing the freedoms that were being held out to Puritans in the old England of the 1640s. The Rainborowe clan epitomises an unfamiliar side of early colonial life: the unsettled nature of settlement, the willingness of so many New Englanders to leave their brave new world in search of something better.

As I delved into the complex web of relationships which defined the Rainborowes and their friends and relations, watching it stretch from Salem and Charlestown to the battlefields of the English Civil War and beyond, to the deserts of North Africa and the islands of the Mediterranean, it became obvious that the middle decades of the seventeenth century are perceived very differently on each side of the Atlantic. In England, the period is dominated by the violent struggle for power between King Charles I and his Parliament. Even now, 370 years later, mention the English Civil War and most Brits will declare an allegiance. Everyone is a Cavalier or a Roundhead, wrong but romantic or right but repulsive. Everyone still takes sides in the English Revolution.

America, on the other hand, is not quite sure what to *do* with the seventeenth century. Once the Pilgrims have landed and the remnants of the first Thanksgiving have been cleared away, colonial history fast-forwards to the Sons of Liberty and the Boston Tea Party, intent on the glorious cause of forging a nation, a little uncomfortable at the repression and intoler-ance which shaped and informed the New England way (unlike old England, where distance lends enchantment and historic repression and intolerance are celebrated as part of life's rich pageant).

That's a travesty, of course, and it neglects the insightful research on early colonial America and the Atlantic world which has been carried out by historians on both sides of the Atlantic in the past ten years or so. But the sense persists that for America, the seven-teenth century was a prelude, while for England it was a defining moment.

And this masks a different truth. In both Massachusetts and England the period 1630 to 1660 was a quest for identity, a time when both communities sought to define the nature of govern-ment, the nature of representation and – most importantly of all – the rights of the individual in relation to the state. No matter that the journey would last for centuries. This is where it began.

The Rainborowes witnessed these events. Some of them played leading roles. If things had turned out differently, they might have lived out lives indistinguishable from those of thousands of hard-working, God-fearing entrepreneurs and artisans who made their homes by the Thames in seventeenth-century London. Just another English sea-captain and his wife, with a gaggle of children and a tribe of like-minded relatives.

But something in the Rainborowes' make-up set them apart, turned them into adventurers, made them pirate-hunters and revolutionaries, visionaries and pioneers. The Thames was not wide enough, the London sky was not big enough, England was not good enough for them. So the Rainborowes went in search of the promised land. They built new societies. They were ordinary men and women, and they did an extraordinary thing.

In their own small way, they changed the world.

1

Between Worlds and Worlds

*E*leanor Roe watched from the deck of the *Sampson* as four sleek war-galleys slipped through the narrow entrance to the harbour and rowed out to meet them. They flew the distinctive red and white colours of the Order of St John of Jerusalem, and that should have reassured Lady Roe. From their base on the tiny Mediterranean island of Malta the Knights of St John waged a crusade against Islam, attacking Muslim shipping, raiding villages along the North African coast, enslaving the Turk wherever they found him. In theory, as defenders of the faith they protected all Christians whose business took them into the dangerous waters of the eastern Mediterranean.

In theory.

It was ten o'clock on the morning of 8 August 1628. The *Sampson* was making its slow way home to London from the Levant with a cargo of silks and wool and a passenger list which included Lady Roe and her husband, Sir Thomas, who had just served a grim six and a half years as English ambassador at Istanbul. The ship had left the Ottoman capital on 1 June and, after putting in at Smyrna for a month, she was now bound for the Tuscan port of Livorno, where the Roes and their household planned to continue their homeward journey overland while the *Sampson* and its valuable cargo – 'goods to the value of half a million', according to Venetian intelligence sources – sailed on to England.[1]

On this particular morning the *Sampson* found herself becalmed a few miles off the coast of Malta. The sea was 'as smooth as glass', recalled Sir Thomas later; 'not a breath of wind'.[2] It must have been with some trepidation that the Roes watched the four Maltese galleys take formation and advance towards their ship; the more so when they were near enough for the couple to make out that in addition to their complements of oarsmen the galleys were crowded with hundreds of armed men.

Shortly after midday, without any warning, the leading galley opened fire. It was a ranging shot from a cannon mounted on a fighting platform in its prow, and it fell short. The galley edged closer and fired another, which almost reached the English ship. A third shot from one of the other galleys went high, whizzing over the Roes' heads and passing between the *Sampson*'s masts. Then the Knights of Malta stopped and waited.

If they expected the Englishmen to strike their colours and surrender, they had made a big mistake. The *Sampson* was a large ship of 500 tons, and she was well armed for a merchantman, with thirty-two iron guns. Six at least were culverins, heavy cannon capable of throwing a 40 lb ball more than a quarter of a mile.

But the *Sampson*'s most potent weapon was its master, the London merchant-mariner William Rainborowe. Forty-one years old and with more than a decade of experience in these waters, Captain Rainborowe had fought off pirate attacks before.[3] And he had a lot to lose if he yielded to the Knights of St John – not only the Levant Company's vast and vastly valuable cargo which, because he had been trading with the Turks, the Knights would consider fair game; but also his ship. And in a very real sense it *was* his ship; he was co-owner of the *Sampson* as well as her master.

There was a standard procedure to follow when you were facing an attack at sea. If you were carrying bales of cloth, as the *Sampson* was, you dragged them out and positioned them so they would absorb the impact of the enemy's shot and take the lethal splinters of wood which flew around the deck like shrapnel. Rope netting was suspended above the deck to entangle boarders; canvas drabblers were laced to the bottoms of the sails to give extra speed when the ship was manoeuvring or, in the *Sampson's* case, if the wind got up and Rainborowe was able to manoeuvre her. Small arms and swords were distributed among the crew and handed to any passengers who cared to join in. Cannon were lashed into place, and gunners organised everything that was needed to use them: powder measures and ladles and rammers and sponges, baskets to carry the shot to each gun, barrels to carry the powder, wedges to adjust the elevation of the guns, fuses to fire them.

Captain Rainborowe ordered this done as soon as he realised that the galleys were making for his becalmed vessel. Their appearance, recalled Roe, was enough for him 'to fit sails and selves for fight, not knowing their purpose'.[4] So he was ready for them. After their final ranging shot he ordered his gunners to return fire. A cannonball from one of the *Sampson's* heavy guns grazed their captain general's starboard bow; and the fight began.

The Maltese galleys – all painted a bright red except for the captain general's, which was a sinister black – lined up facing the *Sampson's* starboard side. Mediterranean war-galleys had their heavy armament mounted in the prow, usually with wooden fighting platforms above where members of the fighting crew stood at swivel-mounted anti-personnel guns. They thus presented the smallest possible targets to the *Sampson's* guns, while the merchant-man's broadside presented a sitting target.

The captain general's galley had a demy-cannon, two demy-culverins and five smaller cannon mounted in the prow, and when they were loaded and ready she rowed up to within 150 or 200 yards of the *Sampson* and blasted away at her with all eight pieces at once. Then she fell back and another galley took her place, turn and turn about. In all the smoke and confusion it was hard for the Knights' gunners to see what impact their salvoes were having, so each vessel kept a man hanging out on the end of one of their oars to observe where their shots fell.

For three hours Captain Rainborowe exchanged fire with the Knights, taking hits and giving them. A passenger was killed when a ball from a demy-cannon smashed through the cabins next to the *Sampson's* main mast. A shot went through the forecastle and into the 'furnace', where the cooking was done, and hurt two men, while another hit in the same area killed two sheep, and two more went through the great cabin and killed a parrot, perhaps William Rainborowe's pet.

Eleanor Roe remained remarkably composed throughout. According to her husband she sat on the deck among the guns and watched the action, except every now and then when that action came a little too close for comfort and she was forced to retreat to the other side of the ship. 'She showed no fear nor passion', said Sir Thomas proudly.[5] Great shot fell around her and she remained unmoved. Only once, when her husband came to see how she was faring and he was knocked to the deck by a falling timber, did she show any emotion; and even then 'when I rose, and had no harm but pain, she said the chance of the day was past' and the bullet that had Sir Thomas's name on it had missed him.[6]

In mid-afternoon a gentle breeze got up, enough for Rainborowe to take the *Sampson* round so that she presented a smaller target to the Maltese galleys, and could bring her stern guns into play. Still the battle raged on, until around five o'clock, when the Knights decided they would board the *Sampson* or sink her. All four galleys came up abreast until they were within pistol-shot. Their men crowded on deck with swords drawn and trumpets sounding, and called on Rainborowe to lower his topsail in surrender. His response was to invite the Knights to come aboard if they dared, and he ordered one of his crew to beat the point of war on his drum from the poop deck. The galleys came on until they were only yards away from the *Sampson*, pouring shot into it all the time, but Rainborowe held his nerve and held his fire.

It wasn't until they were almost under the ship that he gave the order. 'And then', said Sir Thomas, they 'poured in two culverin, and two demy-culverin, and one saker with a round shot and a case, that raked them fore and aft'.[7] The captain general's black galley lost its poop, which was blown into the sea. Another shot from the *Sampson* snapped off his foremast at the deck and a third pierced his bow and came out of his stern, causing carnage among the banks of rowers. He fell back and played no further part in the battle. After another desultory bombardment the other galleys followed his example, and all four hoisted sail and retired to Valletta harbour to lick their wounds.

It was half-past six in the evening; the battle had lasted nearly seven hours, and the *Sampson* had received more than 120 hits in her hull, masts, yards and rigging. Her main mast was shot through, and she was hit in eight places between wind and water, some of the balls passing through nineteen inches of plank and timber and burying themselves in the bales of silk and wool. The Knights' final parting shot had been one of the most damaging, coming into the *Sampson*'s gunroom and injuring three sailors. But casualties were miraculously light, with fatalities confined to that single passenger, the two sheep and the parrot.

Rainborowe got his battered ship to the tiny island of Lampedusa, a hundred miles west of Malta. His crew spent the next five days making running repairs to the sails, the masts and rigging and, of course, to the damaged and leaking hull. 'The carpenter', said Roe, 'was forced to hang like a tortoise upon the water, and drive many nails under the sending of the sea, washing him over continually.'[8] The *Sampson* eventually reached Livorno eighteen days after the attack. While they were there, reports came in that the captain general of the galleys had been killed in the battle (he hadn't), and that thirty-six Knights had died with him, and 264 slaves, oarsmen and soldiers.

Sir Thomas Roe praised the *Sampson*'s captain as a man 'who behaved himself with brave courage and temper'; and, ever the diplomat, celebrated his miraculous deliverance from the Knights of St John with a letter to England about the need to maintain peaceful relations with all the nations of the Mediterranean, or 'our poor merchants suffer'.[9] His wife Eleanor, when she reached her parents' home at Stanford in Leicestershire after an absence of seven years, commemorated 'God's great mercy, goodness and protection in a long and dangerous voyage' by donating a Book of Common Prayer and a carpet for the Communion table to her parish church.[10]

Captain William Rainborowe took his courage and his temper back to his wife in the close-knit little community by the Thames which was his home. His voyage was over. But the adventure had only just begun.

2

That Proud City

$\mathcal{S}$ tand with your back to the Tower of London, so you have the brown waters of the Thames to your right. You're at the eastern edge of the City of London. The shadow of Tower Bridge flicks out across the cars as they flash by. The curving glass bubble of City Hall gleams on the opposite bank and the corporate high-rises of Canary Wharf puncture the distant skyline.

Now walk east, following the Thames Path past the ugly bronze and concrete hotel complex in St Katharine Docks, and in ten minutes you'll find yourself on Wapping High Street, zigzagging in and out between canyons of nineteenth- and early twentieth-century warehouses, reinvented as fashionable riverside apartment buildings. To the north is Whitechapel, where tour companies vie with each other to offer the most ghoulish Jack the Ripper walk. To the south, the occasional container barge chugs past, weaving its purposeful way through the armada of sightseeing cruisers which waddle up and down between the Houses of Parliament and Greenwich.

Now retrace your steps and take that journey again. Your starting point is the same place, but a different time. Say it is early

November 1628, when William Rainborowe and the *Sampson* reached home after their bloody encounter with the Knights of Malta. The only tall buildings for miles around are the White Tower, popularly (and wrongly) said to have been built by Julius Caesar; and the medieval St Paul's Cathedral, whose massive outline had been more massive still until 1561, when its spire was struck by lightning. William Rainborowe's London is a low-rise city, with the exception of these two buildings – and the towers and steeples of 109 churches which cluster together so closely that they seem to fill the sky.

There is no Tower Bridge, of course. In William Rainborowe's day the only fixed crossing over the Thames for miles is the medieval London Bridge, a few hundred yards upriver. Its stone arches are built over with 200 shops and houses, and above the gatehouse on the south bank there is a cluster of thirty or so skulls and withered heads on pikes, a warning to the curious that treason against the state rarely ends well.

The Thames Path now runs through St Katharine's by the Tower, the densely packed neighbourhood immediately to the east of the Tower of London. This tiny suburb of around twenty-four acres is home to nearly 4,000 people – 'more in number than in some cities in England', according to John Stow's *The Survey of London* in 1603[1] – and they have come from all over England and Protestant Europe, drawn by the fact that St Katharine's lies just outside the jurisdiction of the City of London, so they can trade and work unhindered by the authorities and unencumbered by the restrictions imposed on artisans by the livery companies who control commerce and manufacture within the city walls. But there are also plenty of sailors and river-watermen here; and that means there are hundreds of lodging-house keepers and tavern-keepers and whores who offer their services to mariners and take their money.

Within a few hundred yards St Katharine's gives way to Wapping High Street, dismissed by Stow as a 'filthy strait passage, with alleys of small tenements, or cottages'.[2] Wapping is a comparatively new hamlet in 1628. For several centuries it was the traditional place of execution for pirates, who were hanged by the low-water mark and left until three tides had washed over them as a warning to others. But towards the end of Elizabeth

I's reign the gallows were moved upstream, and after that clusters of cottages and tenements sprang up to house the sailors, shipwrights, chandlers and victuallers who make their living from the port. No doubt there are plenty of small tenements and cottages, as Stow says, some of them scarcely more than one-room lean-to shacks; the fact that apprentice-boys could pull down four houses at Wapping during a riot in 1617 suggests a certain impermanence. But there are also some substantial houses with ten or twelve rooms, the homes of prosperous merchant-mariners. William Rainborowe owns several houses in one of the dozens of little alleys and courts which lead north off Wapping High Street, and this is where he lives.

The marshes of Shadwell, to the east of Wapping, have been drained in William's lifetime; and as a result this area is also developing into a sizeable community, with marine industries, smithies, roperies and wharves (thirty-two along a 400-yard stretch of waterfront by the mid-century). Next door to Shadwell is Ratcliffe, another Thames-side hamlet which is growing rapidly; 'of late years', says Stow, 'shipwrights, and (for the most part) other marine men, have built many large and strong houses for themselves, and smaller for sailors'.[3] Ratcliffe is the first landfall downriver from London to have a decent road leading into the City; as such it is a popular embarkation point for travellers and mariners. William Rainborowe sometimes leaves his ship twenty miles downriver at Gravesend and travels the last leg of his journey by barge or lighter. When he does, Ratcliffe is where he will come ashore, if he can't persuade the barge to land him at one of the dozens of busy wharves in Wapping itself.

Spenser's 'silver-streaming Thames' is everything. It defines the landscape. It provides a living. It carries people away, and sometimes it brings them home again. It is a highway, the biggest and most reliable in England. And it is busy. 'Here for almost two miles', wrote a German visitor to Wapping in 1609, 'we saw an infinite number of ships on the river, gallant in their beauty and loftiness.'[4] Above London Bridge there might be fifty or more vessels in sight at any one time: wherries and ferries and rowing boats, fishing skiffs and eel-ships, barges carrying everything from civic dignitaries to bales of hay. Below the bridge in the Pool of London there are all of these vessels; but this is the heart of the busiest port in the kingdom, and they are joined by a fleet of heavy two- and three-masted ocean-going craft, dozens of vessels riding at anchor in midstream, or working their way slowly down towards the lower reaches of the river, or tied up at the wharves while their cargos are loaded or unloaded. The clerks and comptrollers in the Custom House welcome and inspect and charge duty on goods from almost every part of the known world – pitch, tar and hemp from the Baltic to supply the naval dockyards, timber and tobacco from the plantations of Virginia, raw cotton and sugar from the Caribbean and spices from the Dutch East Indies. And every one of the vessels that ply their trade out of London need crew, they need ropes and sails and masts, they need victuals and munitions.

The extramural neighbourhoods of St Katharine's by the Tower, Wapping, Shadwell, Ratcliffe; Limehouse and Poplar a little further east; Rotherhithe on the south bank of the Thames; these riverside hamlets form a tight community of interests, with the making and fitting and supplying and sailing of ships at its core. Between them, they house 80 per cent of London's population of seamen, watermen and fishermen, and 86 per cent of the capital's shipmasters.[5] Small though it is, Wapping is home to more than 370 mariners, Ratcliffe to over a thousand. And this world, contained within a mile or so of riverbank and quays and wharves, warehouses and taverns and cottages, this is the world that made William Rainborowe.

Rainborowe was an Elizabethan, born the year before the Spanish Armada and baptised on 11 June 1587 at St Mary's Whitechapel, since Wapping was then part of Whitechapel parish. His parents, Thomas and Martha, had been married at St Mary's five years earlier; his younger brother and his three sisters would all be baptised there after him.

William's father called himself a mariner, but he was rather more than that. For one thing, he was co-owner of four merchant ships, all of which operated out of London: the *Liley*, the *Barbara Constance*, the *Rainbow* and the *Royal Exchange*. The last three, certainly, and the *Liley* possibly, sailed to and from the eastern Mediterranean, the Aegean and the Sea of Marmara carrying goods for the Levant Company, which had a monopoly on the trade. The bales of West Country cloth, dyed bright red, violet, burgundy or green, which were sought after all over the Ottoman Empire, had to travel in Company ships, or the merchant must pay a prohibitive 20 per cent surcharge; so did the return cargos, Persian silks, Turkish mohairs and currants from the Greek islands.

Old Thomas Rainborowe's status as a shipowner needs a little qualification. He actually had a sixteenth part of the *Barbara Constance*, the *Rainbow* and the *Liley* (and of their tackle, sails, guns and other equipment); and a forty-eighth share in the *Royal Exchange*. This reflects a general change in patterns of ship-ownership during the first half of the seventeenth century; as vessels grew bigger and more expensive, single ownership gave way to partnerships as a means of spreading the cost, especially in London. (The smaller coastal outports maintained the habit of single ownership for rather longer.) The advantage to Thomas Rainborowe of having a relatively small share in several ships is obvious: the more baskets he put his eggs in, the less he stood to lose if one of his investments foundered. Sixteenth shares were usual in the larger ships, although they were sometimes combined, so that one investor might have a quarter – powerful Levant Company merchants in the City were the chief owners of the *Barbara Constance*, for example, and William Rainborowe's *Sampson* – while other shares were bought by syndicates, so that four people might have equal shares in a sixteenth. Thirty-secondths and forty-eighths weren't uncommon. More often than not a master would hold a share in the vessel he commanded, as well as taking wages.

Like many successful merchant-mariners, Thomas Rainborowe also had interests in property, which paid fair returns without the risks involved in sea voyages. At his death in 1623 he owned a house in Greenwich, having moved from Wapping; and he had a lease on an estate at Claverhambury in Essex, the rents from which were worth £220 a year.

At the time of his father's death William was an experienced sea-captain in his mid-thirties. Details of his early life are sketchy: in 1618, he was the captain of a Levant Company ship and performing good service against pirates in the Mediterranean, for which the Company offered him a reward of £25; he turned it down and asked instead to be admitted to membership, which would allow him to trade on his own account. Two years later, in 1620, he sailed to Istanbul as captain of the *Castle*, another Levant Company ship; and towards the end of 1625 he took command of the powerful 500-ton *Sampson*, newly built in one of the yards at Limehouse.

The Rainborowes' social networks revolved around ships and shipping. William married the daughter of another Wapping owner-mariner, Rowland Coytmore, who was prominent in both the Virginia Company and the East India Company. Neither her name, nor the date of their wedding, nor even the date of her death is known. The only evidence for the marriage is a passing reference in Coytmore's will to William as his son-in-law. It is probable that William's eldest son Thomas was the product of this marriage, and possible that his second son, William junior, was too. Again, no one knows their dates of birth, only that both were over the age of twenty-one in 1638.

This mysterious, anonymous first wife died sometime before 23 January 1615, when twenty-seven-year-old William married Judith Hoxton at St Edmund's Church in Southwold, on the Suffolk coast. Judith, who was in her teens, was the daughter of a prominent Wapping shipwright, Reynold Hoxton. The couple had six children: Martha, born in April 1617; Judith (September 1624); Samuel (July 1628); Joan (birth date not known, but probably around 1630); Reynold (June 1632); and Edward (October 1633).

The already tortuous Rainborowe pedigree took another twist in the 1630s, when daughter Martha married Thomas Coytmore, the sea-captain son of Rowland. That meant Martha Rainborowe married her own step-uncle, if such a title exists.

One of William's sisters married a Rotherhithe sea-captain who was a part-owner of the *Rainbow* and the *Exchange*. And William's own marriage to Judith brought a link to another important Wapping family. In 1627 her brother John Hoxton, a shipwright with a yard in Wapping, married Martha Bourne, the sister of Nehemiah Bourne, another shipwright and a near neighbour of the Rainborowes in Wapping. To complicate this already complicated social network, Rowland Coytmore was referred to by the Bournes as their kinsman, because one of his wives (he was married three times) had been the widow of a cousin's father-in-law.

Family mattered in the seventeenth century. So did community. When, for example, a Wapping gunner's mate was captured by Barbary pirates on a voyage to the Strait of Gibraltar, leaving his wife and three children destitute, Nehemiah Bourne's father Robert petitioned Trinity House for their relief. When a Wapping shipowner fell on hard times after one of his ships was wrecked in a storm coming from Norway and another was lost on the North African coast with all hands, Rowland Coytmore, in his capacity as churchwarden of St Mary's Whitechapel, helped organise a collection for him in the City.

The most important instrument of community for sailors like William Rainborowe was Trinity House, which began life in 1514 as a fraternity of mariners, the Guild of the Holy Trinity. The guild was granted a charter by Henry VIII 'so that they might regulate the pilotage of ships in the King's streams'.[6] By the early seventeenth century it had moved to Ratcliffe from its original home by the naval dockyards at Deptford, to be more accessible to the City and the marine population of East London; and had taken on new responsibilities, including the provision of ordnance to merchant ships, advice on the construction of the king's ships and sea defences, the conservation of the Thames and the licensing of indigent seamen and their wives and widows to beg without being prosecuted for vagrancy. The majority of the corporation's members were masters of ships, and they were divided into two classes: thirty-one elder brethren, who formed the governing body; and 254 younger brethren. An inner caucus of master, four wardens and eight assistants was chosen from the elder brethren, and elected by the whole membership.

William and his ex-father-in-law Rowland Coytmore were both elder brethren, and both members of the inner caucus. Coytmore was particularly active, helping to arbitrate on matters as diverse as the definition of the Levant Sea (it began within the Strait of Gibraltar and extended to the coast of Syria), the erection of dwelling houses for seamen at Blackwall and the construction of a bridge over a creek in Maidstone, Kent.

Trinity House also provided important advice on ships for the king's navy. In 1621 the navy commissioners wrote to say that a Scotsman, John Dove, had recently built a ship, the 300-ton *Mayflower* of Leith, and had brought it down to Shadwell to offer it to the king, claiming she was built as a man-of-war and that 'her strength and goodness at sailing is inferior to no other ship in the kingdom'. Coytmore and his comrades went aboard, surveyed the *Mayflower* and declared her 'unfit for the King's service'.[7] That was that.

Being an elder brother of the corporation, and particularly being on the court of assistants, brought power, influence and opportunities to help one's friends. Robert Bourne, Nehemiah's father, requested permission to extend his 'wharf or building place for ships' at Wapping another fourteen or fifteen feet into the Thames, 'because ships are now built of greater burthen and length than formerly'. Coytmore, who was his kinsman, was one of those who recommended a licence for the work. When Trinity House inspected the new wharf the following year and discovered that Bourne had actually carried it out twenty-five feet, Coytmore was one of those who recommended that it should stay, declaring it 'in no way hurtful to the bridge or the city'.[8] And when an anvil-maker on the river complained that his next-door neighbour had built out a new wharf to the detriment of his business, and some elder brethren went down to inspect it, they decided there were no grounds for complaint. No doubt it was coincidence that the neighbour of whom the smith complained was Rowland Coytmore.

William was elected an elder brother of Trinity House in or before 1625, and made a member of the court of assistants soon afterwards. He was master in 1633. Until 1635, when the surviving Trinity House transactions for the period came to an end, he frequently appeared in the corporation's minutes, arbitrating on everything from the shares in a prize due to officers of a man-of-war (the captain should have the best piece of ordnance and the lion's share of captured clothing), to the best method of dredging the Thames.[9] The advantages, besides the warm glow of altruism and the exercise of power, lay in extending his network of contacts to the heart of government. Admiralty court judges conferred with William over maritime precedent; the principal officers of the Royal Navy asked his opinion on the seaworthiness of the king's ships. The Privy Council at Whitehall asked his advice on making collections for the ransom of sailors who were being held by Barbary pirates.

Alongside Trinity House and the informal networks – family and neighbourhood, the taverns and wharves and shipyards where men who earn their living from the sea always congregate – the life of the community revolved around the church. Wapping was in the parish of Whitechapel; but as the hamlet grew, its inhabitants felt the need for their own place of worship, both because St Mary's was a mile away and also, perhaps, because their sense of identity required it.

The result, consecrated by the Bishop of London in July 1617, was St John's on Wapping High Street, a square brick box in an uneasy mixture of Gothic and Tuscan. It cost the community £1,600; a century later Edward Hatton's *A New View of London* still remembered that 'the building was procured by the special care of Mr Rowland Coytmore, Mr Robert Bourn[e] . . . and other inhabitants of this hamlet'.[10] Coytmore, who had sailed for Surat as master of the East India Company's *Royal James* before the work was finished, helped to organise a shipboard collection of £180, which funded 'a pretty gallery of the Tuscan order' on which was painted a commemorative inscription and an uncompromising message of welcome: 'Know ye that the Unrighteous shall not inherit the Kingdom of God.'[11]

If the preambles to their wills are anything to go by, William's parents leaned towards an earnest Protestantism. His father was sure he would be 'freely pardoned all my sins', and that 'after this transitory life I shall remain with [Christ] in glory for ever more'; and his mother looked to be made 'partaker of the kingdom of heaven, with the blest in Christ'. The same holds true for the East London milieu in which the Rainborowes moved: the Coytmores and the Hoxtons and the Bournes all lined up with the godly on the Puritan side of the Anglican Church. There was a definite flavour of Calvinism about Rowland Coytmore's will, as he assured himself that he was, 'through the merits, bitter death and passion which my Saviour suffered for me, to be one of God's elect in heaven'.[12]

So it seems fair to assume that the Rainborowe household also leaned towards the Puritan wing. But the very word 'Puritan' – a term of abuse which first appeared in Tudor times – is liable to cast more darkness than light. 'Concerning the name *Puritan*', declared a hostile Oxford cleric Giles Widdowes in 1630, 'it is ambiguous, and so it is fallacious.'[13]

He had a point. Puritanism was not so much a fixed theological position in early seventeenth-century England, more a
spectrum. Almost all English Puritans operated within the
Anglican Church, even though they disapproved of its hierarchies,
its rituals and its love of uniformity in worship. Very few indeed
contemplated a spiritual life outside it, even those who argued
for a form of governance which centred on the congregation as
a unit rather than archbishops and bishops and clergy. Some
things they agreed upon: they stressed the teaching function of
the church; and they disapproved of the wearing of surplices by
ministers, the singing of psalms, the slavish adherence to the
prayer book. Such things smacked of popery, and no matter
where Puritans saw themselves on the Protestant spectrum, they
were united in their loathing of the Catholic Church.

However, they were less likely to agree on the role of bishops
or the personal experience of God's grace as a prerequisite for
salvation. Giles Widdowes satirised ten different types of Puritan,
from the Perfectist and the Sermonist to the Presuming
Predestinatist, who presumed to be saved 'by God's absolute
election'.[14] It was parody, but it hovered at the edge of truth.

The eastern suburbs where the Rainborowes and their kin lived
had a tradition of religious independence stretching back to the
1550s, when as many as 200 Protestants who were opposed to
Mary Tudor's reintroduction of Catholicism would meet at
Wapping, at a house by the waterside. Eighty years later, a group
broke away from an independent church in the City and moved
to Wapping, where they formed the first Particular Baptist congregation in England. In the neighbouring parish of Stepney a Puritan
minister got rid of the organ in 1585 – church music was one
of the many, many things that Puritans disapproved of – and
Stepney didn't get another for nearly a hundred years. The same
congregation also ejected one vicar 'for being a proved prelatical
innovator of Romish ceremonies and a desperate malignant'.[15]

There are good reasons for this predilection for reformed religion in the Thames-side hamlets. More than most, the mariners
who lived in them were exposed to new ideas on their travels;
and at the same time, the incomers from the Low Countries who
settled around St Katharine's by the Tower introduced their own
reformed worship. It isn't hard to imagine men like William

Rainborowe subscribing to what have come to be seen as traditional Protestant values – self-reliance, a mistrust of arbitrary authority, a strong work ethic. And a resistance to authority manifested itself in the neighbourhood in all kinds of ways, political as well as theological: when Charles I tried to raise money without recourse to Parliament through the Forced Loan of 1626, for example, locals refused to pay up. His commissioners reported ruefully that 'it was commonly said in Wapping, Ratcliffe and Limehouse, that if it were done by Parliament they would pay . . . but by this course they would not do anything'.[16]

Wapping's choice of minister for St John's says something about the religious temper of the congregation at a point when cracks were widening in the Anglican consensus. Richard Sedgwick, the forty-three-year-old son of a Norfolk clothier, came with a long record of causing trouble. Educated at Peterhouse College, Cambridge, he had taken up a series of posts before coming to St John's, and each time, according to his biographer and fellow Puritan Samuel Clarke, 'the Devil . . . raised up persecution against him'.[17] He must take some of the credit for that himself. He was dismissed from Canterbury after preaching against the corruption of the cathedral clergy. He was dismissed from a living at Battersea, 'because he freely reproved sin, and boldly spake against the corruptions that were then in the church'.[18] He was very nearly dismissed from a preaching post with the Merchant Venturers at Hamburg after one of the English merchants in his flock took exception to his teaching and threatened to have him summoned back to England; 'but before that day came,' said Clarke with satisfaction, the merchant 'was summoned by death to another place'.[19]

After being called to Wapping in the spring of 1617, Sedgwick spent the rest of his life there, 'being holy and exemplary in his life and conversation, and abundant in labours, preaching constantly thrice a week, and catechising on the *Lords-day* besides'.[20] He was a popular minister, mentioned approvingly by local shipwrights and mariners as a preacher of God's word; and his only published work, an admirably brief discussion of the articles of faith, the Ten Commandments and the Lord's Prayer, he dedicated 'to my loving and beloved brethren and neighbours, ordinary auditors in the new chapel at Wapping'.[21]

Richard Sedgwick must have been a powerful influence on the young Rainborowes, preaching three times a week and catechising on Sundays. William had limited opportunities to hear him, of course. Although Sedgwick preached that the long absence of a husband was a sin, except 'in the unavoidable necessity of extraordinary employments, or of men's particular callings', the sea-captain's occupation certainly involved the unavoidable necessity of extraordinary employments, and he spent most of his time in the 1620s and early 1630s apart from Judith and his children.[22] Even if he only took the *Sampson* out for the Levant Company once a year, the annual 5,000-mile voyage to Istanbul, Smyrna or Aleppo might last up to three months, with a stop at Livorno to take on fresh provisions. And that was one way. Add another couple of months while the Company's factors or agents shifted the incoming cargo and bargained for goods for the return journey, and perhaps another month while William sailed from one Levant port to another; and a single voyage could easily involve an absence of eight or nine months.

In the autumn of 1628 the eldest Rainborowe boys, Thomas and William junior, were in their mid-teens and old enough to go to sea or to be put out to learn a trade. But Martha was only eleven, little Judith just four and Samuel only three months.

Responsibility for their upbringing and education rested with their mother. Like everyone in their social group the Rainborowes would keep servants – at least a couple of maids – and neighbours played an important part in the extended support network which helped to define domestic life in the early modern world. Baby Samuel may have been handed over to a local wetnurse, although Puritan teaching disapproved of the practice and urged women to suckle their children themselves. 'God hath given to women two breasts fit to contain and hold milk; and nipples unto them fit to have milk drawn from them', wrote the male author of one manual on domestic duties. 'Why are these thus given? To lay them forth for ostentation?'[23] Within the more immediate family circle we would expect to find Judith's mother and mother-in-law taking significant roles, although that wasn't so easy in practice: old Martha Rainborowe now lived on the other side of the City, in the parish of St Bride's Fleet Street; while Judith's mother and father, Joan and Reynold Hoxton, had moved a hundred miles away to the coastal town of Southwold in Suffolk. Judith had no sisters of her own, but she did have Rainborowe sisters-in-law; perhaps they involved themselves in her children's upbringing.

In later life the two older boys were well able to express themselves in writing (as was their father), which points to their having some formal education, probably to grammar school level. Neighbour Robert Bourne wanted his son Nehemiah to study at Cambridge, 'if God shall fit him with gifts in that behalf'.[24] God didn't; instead of going to university he followed in his father's footsteps and became a shipbuilder in Wapping.

The three Rainborowe girls are a different matter. They were taught their letters in a local petty school or at their mother's knee. One of the virtues of the Protestant cultural climate in which the Rainborowes lived was a recognition of the value of literacy for both boys and girls. Men had died to make God's word freely available to everyone; and it behoved the godly to ensure that their children were equipped to benefit. Elizabeth Jocelin's *The Mothers Legacie, to her unborne Childe*, which went through many editions after its posthumous publication in 1624, expresses the aspirations of a moderate Puritan mother for her daughter:

> I desire . . . her bringing up may be learning the Bible, as my sisters do, good housewifery, writing and good works: other learning a woman needs not . . . But where learning and wisdom meet in a virtuous disposed woman, she is the fittest closet for all goodness. She is like a well-balanced ship that may bear all her sail.[25]

One of the duties of the Protestant household was the inculcating of godliness, by ensuring regular church attendance and through daily instruction within the home. 'The family is the seminary of the church and common-wealth', wrote the theologian John Downame in 1622. It is 'as a private school, wherein children and servants are fitted for the public assemblies . . . to perform, when they meet together, all religious duties of God's worship and service'.[26] Families were encouraged to confer together about the sermon they had just heard as soon as they got home from church, the older children sometimes taking notes while the minister was preaching. Communal prayers were said every day; and Protestant household manuals urged parents to 'call every morning all thy family to some convenient room; and first, either read thy self unto them a Chapter in the Word of God, or cause it to be read distinctly by some other'.[27]

Invoking texts such as Ephesians 5:22, 'Wives submit yourselves unto your own husbands as unto the Lord', the same manuals took it for granted that the responsibility for ensuring that one's children hear and understand God's Word rested with the father as head of the household. 'In the family a parent is all in all over his child: a king, a priest, and a prophet. Therefore that which a minister is to do for matter of instruction in the church, a parent must do at home.'[28] In households like the Rainborowes', where the man might be absent for long periods, the woman was often the primary educator, always assuming she was literate herself, helping the young children with their letters and hearing their catechism.

William Rainborowe's homecoming in 1628 was marred by problems over the *Sampson*'s cargo. He spent most of November trying to arrange for merchants who had goods aboard to come and collect them. But word had spread about the ship's epic fight with the Knights of Malta – and the damage her cargo had sustained in the course of it – so that a number of merchants refused to accept their goods. That meant William couldn't discharge his crew.

Eventually he petitioned the Privy Council, and at the end of the month they issued an order from Whitehall acknowledging that he was 'at great charge every day for the maintenance of his men' and authorising him to deliver the leftover goods to Custom House Quay, where they were to be kept in safe custody until their owners came to collect them.[29]

The homecoming was marred by something else. The new son whom William met for the first time when he arrived back at Wapping after his voyage would never learn his letters, never say his prayers. Never go to sea, like his brothers. On 24 November, three months and twenty-six days after being baptised in his father's absence at St John's, Samuel Rainborowe was buried there.

Do you not know me? Well, I'll tell you then,
'Tis I that conquer all the Sons of Men.
No Pitch of Honour from my Dart is free;
My Name is *Death*, have you not heard of me?[30]

3

Whom Shall We Send?

*I*t was an ancient piece of fiscal legislation which gave William Rainborowe a new career. In October 1634 Charles I revived a medieval device whereby in times of national crisis the Crown could require coastal and maritime counties to pay for building and equipping a fleet. 'You in the sea-coasts, to whom by sea as well great dangers are imminent, and who by the same do get more plentiful gains', announced the king's writ, 'are chiefly bound to set to your helping hand.'[1] This first levy of ship money raised about £80,000. The following year the notion that only the coast should pay was dropped, and the levy was extended to inland counties.

So what was the crisis? Ostensibly it was the pirates of Barbary. The first writ of 1634 explained that the money was needed

because we are given to understand that certain thieves, pirates, and robbers of the sea, as well Turks, enemies of the Christian name, as others, being gathered together, wickedly taking by force and spoiling the ships, and goods . . . and the same, at their pleasure, have carried away, delivering the men in the same into miserable captivity.[2]

In private, the king's advisers had other reasons for the levy. Sir Francis Windebank, one of his two Secretaries of State, saw a strong fleet as a bargaining counter in a future alliance with Spain against the Dutch Republic. The other Secretary, Sir John Coke, was more concerned with the disruption to trade and fisheries caused by Dutch privateers, Dunkirkers and warring navies in the four seas which England traditionally claimed as her territorial waters – the Channel, the North Sea, the Irish Sea and St George's Channel. While Spain, France and the United Provinces all had large and powerful navies, England in the early 1630s defended her coasts with half a dozen warships. The ship money would enable Charles to enforce the sovereignty of the British seas without having to pay for it himself, and without having to summon Parliament to raise taxes – something he had not done since he dissolved the last disobedient Parliament in a fit of pique in 1629. A stronger navy would also act as a deterrent against over-mighty neighbours.

One of the ship money levy's unlooked-for consequences was a new role for William Rainborowe, already one of the most respected merchant seamen in England. When the Lords of the Admiralty sought advice on manning His Majesty's ships, they consulted William. When the navy needed someone to inspect new vessels being built at Deptford and Woolwich, it was William they turned to. He was prosperous, with a family that was growing in every way: his eldest son Thomas had followed him to sea; his eldest daughter Martha was being courted by Thomas Coytmore, the Cambridge-educated sea-captain son of William's former father-in-law Rowland Coytmore; and after bearing and losing another boy, Reynold, wife Judith gave birth to Edward in 1633. William had been elected master of Trinity House that spring, and in June 1634, just after his term came to an end, he was described approvingly in the Admiralty as one of only two professional seamen 'that have the command as captain and [have] performed good fight at sea in merchant ships'.[3] William Rainborowe was doing well.

There was more to come. In 1635, keen to demonstrate the benefits of the ship-money levy, Charles's government ordered to sea a powerful fleet consisting of nineteen ships of the Royal Navy and six merchant vessels, including the *Sampson* and the *Royal Exchange*, in both of which Rainborowe had an interest. The fleet's admiral was the Earl of Lindsey, a nobleman with plenty of experience of naval matters, if rather less experience of success: he had been vice admiral of the fleet which went with the Duke of Buckingham on his disastrous 1627 expedition to the Île de Ré, and admiral of the fleet which tried and failed to relieve the Huguenots of La Rochelle in 1628.

On 30 March 1635, the Lords of the Admiralty signed an order appointing William captain of Lindsey's flagship, the *Merhonour*. Lindsey came aboard on 26 May, and the fleet set out at the beginning of June, causing William to miss his daughter's wedding: Martha was married to Thomas Coytmore at St John's, Wapping, a week later.

This first ship-money fleet spent the summer and autumn cruising up and down the Narrow Seas, as England's territorial waters were known. Lindsey's orders were to protect fisheries and trade routes, to look for pirates, and to chase away anyone who presumed to keep a guard on British territorial waters. As for exactly how he might do this, the king left it to Lindsey's discretion, 'who, with the advice of a well-chosen council of war of experienced commanders, will be best able to resolve upon emergent occasions what is fittest to be done'.[4] In the event there were no emergent occasions, and when the fleet arrived back in the Downs at the beginning of October it had seen no action.

Although William was part of the well-chosen council of experienced commanders, his appointment as Lindsey's flag captain caused resentment among gentlemen officers of the navy who weren't accustomed to having a Wapping mariner promoted over them. And he didn't trouble to ingratiate himself with them once they were ashore. On 23 November he fired off a single-page proposal to the Lords of the Admiralty explaining just why the navy's cherished practice of having galleries around the sterns of their larger warships was a big mistake. These covered walks, built out from the captain's cabin and extending around the port and starboard quarter to provide private promenades for the captain, were usually carved and gilded or painted, external and very public expressions of their user's status. As far as William was concerned, they were a dangerous waste of space. A gallery was an easy target, he said, 'being made of elm timber and very much dried in the sun and very apt to take fire'.[5] If the enemy was in musket range, then quenching that fire put men's lives at unnecessary risk, and if it spread it could destroy the entire vessel. A gallery was heavy, it made a ship leaky and rotten, and it reduced the number of guns that could be placed in the stern.

And what could be said in its favour? Two things: 'the grace of the ship, and the commodity [convenience] and pleasure of the captain'. But a ship could be graceful without a gallery; the guns that replaced it would be just as beautiful. As for the captain's comfort, said William, 'I believe all men that know the sea will acknowledge that if the galleries be taken away there will be commodity and pleasure sufficient for the captain.'[6] A *real* mariner didn't need such fripperies, in other words.

It says something for William's reputation that the Lords of the Admiralty took his proposal very seriously. It was presented to them in early December, and they immediately consulted with the Navy Board, a separate body responsible for building and repairing the king's ships and for the administration of the dockyards. The officers of the Board sent the proposal to several master shipwrights, and to William's fellow elder brethren at Trinity House. On 15 January 1636 the Board reported back, advising compromise: when a warship was brought into dry dock, shipwrights should take the opportunity to rebuild its gallery so that it didn't project out too far beyond the stern, and replace the side galleries with guns. This would reduce the risk of fire and make the stern quarters more defensible. But as to removing galleries altogether, said the members of the Navy Board, 'we are of opinion . . . that it will much diminish the beauty of His Majesty's ships'.[7]

So galleries were kept. The same couldn't be said for Rainborowe's admiral. When the second ship-money fleet went out on the cruise in May 1636, the Earl of Lindsey had been replaced (much to his distress) by a man completely inexperienced in naval matters, the courtier Algernon Percy, tenth Earl of Northumberland. William kept his place as flag captain, transferring to the *Triumph* (a ship which boasted a positively 'exorbitant' gallery, according to a fellow officer).[8]

The 1636 fleet was the most powerful ever fitted out from England. There were twenty-four warships and three merchantmen, carrying nearly 4,700 men and a formidable array of weaponry. Unlike the previous year's expedition, Northumberland was provided with detailed and hierarchichal instructions on how to proceed against the enemy in the event of a sea fight: 'The admiral to join fight with their admiral, the vice admiral with their vice admiral, and the rear admiral with their rear admiral'.[9] Within each of the fleet's three squadrons, the orders stipulated who was to provide support, and what support they must provide.

The authoritative tone of Northumberland's fighting instructions wavered a little at the end, when after pages and pages detailing exactly who was to do what to whom and in what order, the unknown author slipped in the admission that 'the uncertainty of a sea fight is such that no certain instructions can be given'.[10] Which must have left the inexperienced Earl of Northumberland a little confused. But not his flag captain, who knew better than to rely on theory when it came to the practice of war at sea.

William took the *Triumph* down towards the Scilly Isles, where Northumberland received word that a French fleet was off the coast of Brittany, and decided to intercept it. But instead of the French, they found stormy weather. Viscount Conway, who was aboard the *Triumph*, described to a friend with gleeful relish how the ship's chaplain 'endures the sea like an apostle', while their apothecary was trying to bribe the crew to put him ashore somewhere, anywhere, he didn't care where as long as he could stand on dry land again. 'We were one night sitting down to supper', Conway told his correspondent, 'when a tumble of the ship flung all the dishes on the ground. Dowse [a colleague] let go the hold of a post to take up a shoulder of mutton, but his unsteady footing made him sit down in the sauce of one dish with his feet in the buttered meat of another.'[11]

By the beginning of July William and the *Triumph* were back in the Downs with the rest of the fleet. There was no sign of the French and the weather was still awful. There they waited for several weeks, their days enlivened by the occasional visit from the shore. 'Came six or seven wenches of the country aboard this ship,' wrote Conway from the *Triumph*, 'and by foul weather were kept here two days.' They were accompanied by three or four men 'that took great care of their maidenheads', he went on, commenting wrily that no one thought to protect the girls from their gallant guards.[12] Another of the ships received two or three boatloads of women, all in their best clothes and oblivious to the wind and rain, who feasted and danced with the sailors all day.

Eventually the fleet weighed anchor and sailed up along the east coast towards the great North Sea herring fisheries. One of Northumberland's objectives was to force the Dutch herring fleets, which were reckoned to take a catch worth £1 million a year off the English coast, to accept that they required licences from the English Crown, and that they had to pay duty, in acknowledgement of the king's 'sovereignty and hereditary dominion in his seas'.[13] The English fleet was quite successful, dishing out over a hundred licences, intimidating the Dutch men-of-war who guarded the herring busses, and generally reminding the world that England was reclaiming its territorial waters. 'We shot one day so many cannon', wrote Conway, who was still aboard Rainborowe's ship, 'that the noise in blowing up of the Parliament house [by Guy Fawkes] would have been but bastard brother to it.'[14] Charles I reckoned the exercise a great success, and three days after the fleet put in to Yarmouth the third ship-money writ was issued to fund the 1637 fleet.

The Earl of Northumberland immediately prepared a list of the navy's faults. His plan was to show this to the king, but before he did so he circulated it for comment to some of his officers, including his flag captain. It is hard to believe that William wasn't involved in helping his admiral to draw up the original list – Northumberland's second article argued for taking away galleries from His Majesty's ships, for example – but whether he was or not, his comments on the list have survived, and they show the same professionalism as his earlier memorandum to the Lords of the Admiralty.

Northumberland's articles covered everything from the poor state of the king's ships, the inadequacy of their masts and cordage and the bad quality of their victuals, to the abuses of pressmasters and the fact that large sums of money had been 'borrowed' from the Chatham Chest, established by Elizabeth

I to provide pensions for disabled seamen. William agreed with most of these points, but his response was measured. The cables and landing ropes he had seen were very good, but the running ropes were 'as bad as ever I saw used in ships'.[15] The victuals aboard the *Triumph* were generally good, apart from the butter and the beer; but the bread supplied for the previous year's cruise was so bad 'that it did fetch the skin off many mouths'.[16]

He was businesslike about impressment. No one in the navy objected to the practice as such, just to the inefficient and corrupt way it was managed. Sir Henry Mainwaring, an experienced sailor who captained the *Unicorn* in Northumberland's squadron during the 1636 cruise, was furious that his crew was made up of thatchers and glovers and men with no knowledge of the sea at all, while it was well known that there were plenty of unemployed seamen around, who were somehow overlooked by the pressmasters. William, who had overseen the press in Dorset before the cruise set out, shed light on the reasons for this:

> I have heard of many that have taken money to discharge good men that they have pressed, and taken bad in their room; and I myself being our Pressmaster for Dorsetshire had 6 pieces [i.e. coins] put into my hand by a man to clear him, yet I made him crew, and I was extraordinary railed at, because I would not clear men for money.[17]

His solution was to hand over responsibility for impressment to local officials, justices and mayors, instructing them to supply the fleet with a quota of able men along with a list of their names; if any man failed to turn up for duty, 'then certificate of their names be returned down, and so that punishment be inflicted accordingly'.[18]

William's stolid reasonableness shook a little when it came to the question of those exorbitant galleries. He told Northumberland, 'I do believe none that hath seen a sea fight, but will acknowledge they being taken away, and ordnance placed in their room, will be a great force added either for defence or offence.'[19]

Northumberland took his ideas straight to the king, together with the comments of his officers. The Lords of the Admiralty were unimpressed, both at the way he sidestepped their authority and at the implication that they were to blame for the failings he listed. Nor did they show the slightest inclination to rectify them.

In the meantime, some remarkable plans were being made by the king and the Admiralty for William Rainborowe's future. Coastal communities in the south and west of England in the mid-1630s were up in arms at the threat posed by Barbary pirates. In September 1635 the governor of Pendennis Castle, Sir Nicholas Slanning, reported that six Turkish warships stood off Land's End, lying in wait for the return of the Newfoundland fishing fleet. A few days later the mayor of Dartmouth reported that two ships on the way home from Newfoundland had been taken by Turkish pirates less than ten miles off Cornwall's Lizard Point. A thousand poor women petitioned Charles I to send an ambassador to the pirate base of Sallee on the Atlantic coast of Morocco to plead for the release of their husbands, who were, they complained, in 'woeful slavery, enduring extreme labour, want of sustenance, and grievous torments'.[20]

By 1636 there was panic among the merchants and fishing fleets who operated out of the south-coast ports. Shipowners from Exeter, Dartmouth, Plymouth, Barnstable, Southampton, Poole, Weymouth and Lyme Regis got together and complained to the king that over the past few years they had lost an alarming eighty-seven vessels to piracy, which, along with their cargos, were worth £96,700. In addition, 1,160 English seamen were kept in captivity; and the burden of caring for the wives and children of those captives was becoming intolerable.

The raiders were back that summer. Another forty-two seamen were captured off the Lizard, and two fishing boats were taken by a Turkish man-of-war in full view of the fort at Plymouth. In September 1636, with the Newfoundland fleet due home at any time, merchants petitioned the king, complaining there were so many pirates about that 'seamen refuse to go [to sea], and fishermen refrain to take fish, whereby customs and imposts are lessened, merchandising is at a stand, petitioners are much impoverished, and many of them utterly undone'.[21]

The pirates causing such havoc for West Country merchants and shipowners were the Sallee rovers of Morocco. In 1613, during the last Spanish expulsion of the Moriscos, a group of Muslims from Extremadura in western Spain found their way to Sallee, where the Moroccan ruler Mawlay Zidan allowed them to settle in a decrepit old fortress at the mouth of the Bou Regreg river. Taking their name from their home town of Hornacha in Extremadura, the Hornacheros repaired the fort and came to an informal arrangement with Mawlay Zidan whereby they took care of his defences along that particular stretch of the North Atlantic coast in return for being allowed to make their living as privateers. Within a decade the Morisco settlement at 'New Sallee', named to distinguish it from the original town on the opposite bank of the Bou Regreg, had attracted several thousand Muslim exiles and several hundred European renegades and outlaws, and when Mawlay Zidan died in 1627, the Hornacheros decided they were powerful enough to dispense with the patronage of his ineffectual successor, Abu Marwan Abd al-Malik. Encouraged by a charismatic religious leader named Muhammad al-Ayyashi, who was simultaneously waging a holy war against the Spanish and making a play for control of the north-western corner of Morocco, they broke away and set up their own small republic, presided over by a Grand Admiral and his council.

In 1626, Trinity House had reckoned there were between 1,200 and 1,400 English captives at Sallee, all or mostly taken in the English Channel. 'When the ships are full of the king's subjects', the elder brethren reported to the Privy Council, 'the pirates return to Sallee, sell the captives in the common market, and then return for more.'[22] Ten years later, a ransomed English sailor reported that ten Sallee men-of-war were preparing to set out for the English coast, and the authorities at Plymouth were told that 200 Christian captives were landed at Sallee on a single day. 'In times past,' complained West Country merchants, 'only the pirates of Algiers sometimes came into the English and Irish channels; now the pirates of Sallee are become so numerous, strong, and nimble in their ships, and are so well piloted into these channels by English and Irish captives' that no one dared put to sea.[23]

In June 1636, Captain Giles Penn, a Bristol merchant who traded regularly with Morocco, approached the Chancellor of the Exchequer, Sir Francis Cottington, and suggested the king mount an expedition against 'the heathen moors of Sallee'.[24] Penn was well acquainted with the complex political scene in Morocco – he may have been acting at the behest of the sultan in Marrakesh, who saw an English naval blockade of Sallee as an inexpensive way of bringing down the Hornachero rebels – and Cottington gave him enough encouragement for him to take his proposal further. In October 1636 he wrote to Sir Francis Windebank, and in December to the Lords of the Admiralty, each time setting out the requirements for a successful venture. The expeditionary force should consist of 800 men in four ships and two pinnaces, with 'able surgeons, doctors of physic, and good divines'.[25] Shirts and jackets should be provided for the poorer seamen, and the force should take some captured Moors along as exchange prisoners. Penn sketched out the political situation on the Bou Regreg: there was growing tension between the rovers in their fortress at New Sallee and their erstwhile ally, the holy man Muhammad al-Ayyashi, who was based across the river in Old Sallee. He also urged the Admiralty to make him commander of the expedition – and 'surveyor of all goods taken in reprisal during the voyage'.[26] Self-interest was never far away when the Stuarts spoke of the public good.

The political will to suppress the activities of the Sallee pirates and to secure the release of their English captives was there. So was the cash to fund an expedition. As resistance to the ship money began to grow, it would do the king no harm to produce a very public demonstration of how well that money was being spent. But Penn was not the man to lead it. In November, the month after the season's ship-money cruise had put in at Yarmouth and disbanded, Charles I was acquainted with the plans for the Sallee expedition, told what ships the Admiralty thought fit to send, and asked for his approval. He gave it, writing in the margin of the memorandum, 'Rainborowe to be employed.'[27]

England's record on sending punitive expeditions to Barbary wasn't good. Her only previous attempt, Sir Robert Mansell's 1620 expedition to Algiers, had taken three years to finance and organise and then ended in farce as the Algerians, far from being fazed by the appearance in their waters of an English battle fleet, simply ignored it. After a while, Mansell went home.

This time was different. The ship money meant finance was already available; and William Rainborowe was made of sterner stuff than Mansell. He received the news of his appointment while he was at Southwold, and immediately fired off a letter of reply to Edward Nicholas, secretary to the Admiralty, telling him of his 'extraordinary willingness' to lead the Sallee expedition and promising to be up in London as soon as he was able.[28]

He was at the Admiralty within days, and preparing two 600-ton warships, the *Leopard* and the *Antelope*, for service. Trinity House supported Penn's view that the expedition should consist of four ships and two smaller pinnaces; William began negotiating with the owners of two merchantmen, the *Hercules* and the *Angel*, to hire their vessels. In the meantime the Lords of the Admiralty authorised the building of two brand-new pinnaces at yards in Bermondsey. The *Providence* and the *Expedition* were vital to the mission's success: they were small, fast and lightly armed but crucially, they had a shallower draft than the warships, and so could operate much closer to shore; and they were equipped with fifteen banks of oars to a side, so they could be manoeuvred to gain tactical advantage without being dependent on the winds. One of the reasons for the failure of Mansell's expedition had been that his heavy men-of-war were powerless to intercept small pirate vessels as they slipped in and out of Algiers harbour, hugging the shoreline.

By January 1637 William was back home in Wapping and in a frenzy of activity – attending the Lords of the Admiralty in Whitehall, visiting the Bermondsey yards to inspect the progress of the pinnaces, recruiting men to serve with the fleet. He proposed that he should captain the *Leopard* and act as admiral of the expedition. Brian Harrison of Wapping, a cousin of Nehemiah Bourne and hence a distant kinsman of the Rainborowes, was to be captain of the *Hercules* and rear admiral; and George Hatch, a Trinity House elder brother who had served on the court of assistants with William, would captain the *Great Neptune*. Hatch had been master of the *Barbara Constance*, one of the ships part-owned by William's father; and part-owner of another, the *Royal Exchange*. The pinnaces were captained by two more neighbours of William, Thomas White and Edward Seaman. The maiden name of William's mother-in-law was Seaman.

So five of the six captains belonged to the same Thames-side community of mariners; they knew each other, and they shared family and business interests. The odd man out was George Carteret, William's vice admiral and commander of the *Antelope*. Born into an ancient Jersey family, Carteret was young – about twenty-six – and his experience at sea had been gained with the Royal Navy rather than in trade.

William paid attention to every detail of the preparations. Each vessel must be furnished with twenty pairs of pistols or carbines. There should be enough victuals to last eight months, and they should include sugar, rice and oatmeal for sick men and an allowance of vinegar for cleansing the ship.

There were problems. Work on the pinnaces was proceeding too slowly, and one of the builders had to be ordered to replace rotten timbers. The *Great Neptune* broke her moorings in a storm and ran aground at Woolwich, causing so much damage that George Hatch had to transfer to another merchantman, the *Mary*. This was frustrating: the fleet had to set sail by the end of February or early March at the latest, or by the time they reached Sallee they would find their prey had gone out on the cruise for the summer. Yet when William left Wapping to go aboard his flagship at Tilbury on 21 February, the pinnaces were still not finished. And there was no sign of George Carteret and the *Antelope*. Rainborowe wrote to the Admiralty asking them to replace him.

Then he took the *Leopard*, the *Hercules* and the *Mary* to the Downs and waited at anchor, growing ever more impatient. On 1 March the *Antelope* showed up, but Carteret wasn't aboard her; and three days later William gave the order to sail, leaving a cross little note in which he told his absent vice admiral he had put his reputation at stake by waiting so long. Now he was going to Falmouth and then he planned to sail direct for Sallee 'where with God's blessing you shall be sure to find me'.[29]

The Lords of the Admiralty's instructions to William and his own to his officers both survive. The former were straightforward: in essence, they told him to sail straight to Sallee, suppress the pirates and liberate Christian captives. There were a few other clauses which he incorporated into his own instructions to the fleet. For example, because no enterprise could hope to succeed without the blessing of God, prayers were to be held twice every day according to the 'liturgy of the Church of England'.[30] Many of the other orders concerned practical matters such as the signals to use when communicating from ship to ship:

> If you chance to discover any shipping at sea by day which you think I see not, you shall give me notice by shooting off a piece of ordnance, and putting your flag into the mainstay, letting it fly so many times as there be sails. If in the night you discover any, to shoot off a piece and put a light in the main-stay; and if they appear to be Turks, pirates, or sea rovers, you shall shoot twice or thrice to warn the rest of the fleet to put in order for fight or pursuit. When you are in chase, if I shoot off a piece and strike my foretop sail, you are to give over the chase and to retire to me.[31]

Sometimes, William's instructions offer a glimpse into everyday life on board. He ordered his men to exercise every day if the weather was good enough, and practise with their muskets and other weapons. In a fight, officers were not to allow their men to board the enemy 'till the smoke of their ordnance be cleared'. They must take special care to guard against fire: no one was allowed to carry powder uncovered during a battle, and buckets of saltwater must be kept in readiness.

The fear of fire didn't come and go with the noise of battle. Because 'many fearful accidents have happened by fire', William urged his captains to ensure that every night, after the setting of the watch, all candles were extinguished, and two men deputed to check that the fire in the galley was out. 'And that you do likewise strictly forbid the taking of tobacco in any place but upon the upper deck, and that sparingly too.'[32]

Several of William's orders (there were twenty-nine in all) dealt with what to do in a crisis – if a ship was driven aground, or separated from the fleet, or forced to run for a harbour in foul weather. They proved useful all too soon. After midnight on 12 March, eight days after leaving English waters, the fleet hit a storm off the Portuguese coast and the *Hercules* lost her main mast. The *Leopard* and the *Mary* stayed close by her all night, and at daybreak it was obvious that Captain Harrison was going to need a new mast. He limped off to Lisbon to find one, leaving just two ships in the Sallee fleet.

Carteret finally turned up a few days later, when the *Leopard* and the *Mary* were off Cape St Vincent and about three-quarters of the way through their 1,500-mile voyage. By now, with the *Hercules* in port for repairs and no sign of the two new pinnaces, William was just grateful to see him. In his published account of the mission John Dunton, the master of the *Leopard* and a man who had escaped from captivity in Algiers, wrote a rather optimistic description of the fleet's arrival off Sallee at four o'clock on the afternoon of 24 March: 'And our captain and general having the command of all the ships, sent some unto the southward, and some unto the noreward; and we riding in the middle right against the castle, and before the harbour's mouth . . . so we dispersed all our ships all over the road of Sallee.'[33]

Dispersing 'all our ships' might have been grammatically correct, but the statement disguised the fact that William was having to do the best he could with pathetically thin resources. No matter how he disposed the *Leopard*, the *Antelope* and the *Mary*, they constituted a nuisance to the pirates rather than a blockade. True, the pirates' bigger ships were kept in harbour – and William's anxiety to get to Sallee as quickly as possible was justified by the fact that around fifty vessels were there preparing to set sail, some for the coast of England. But the smaller rovers continued to come and go with impunity, keeping in close to the shore. When the English shot an arrow into the New Town with a stern letter demanding the release of all Christian captives and compensation for ships and goods taken, the pirates didn't even bother to reply. Their leader, an Andalusian Muslim named Abd Allah ben Ali el-Kasri, was so puffed up with thieving, William reported to the English agent in Madrid, that he 'thinks himself able to brave all the princes in Christendom'.[34]

4

Such An Enemy We Have

*B*rian Harrison and the repaired *Hercules* sailed into Sallee Road on a wet and windy April afternoon, twenty-five days after the rest of the little fleet. Their arrival made no difference; without the pinnaces, William couldn't prevent the pirates of the New Town from slipping in and out under cover of darkness. He tried sending out some men in boats; el-Kasri despatched two carvels to intercept them and, after a fight which lasted three hours, the English had to retreat. William lost his coxwain and eight other seamen were injured, one so seriously that he wasn't expected to survive. The *Antelope* gave chase to another small pirate ship coming down from the north, but despite Carteret firing twenty shots at her she was still able to get into harbour.

And still there was no sign of the pinnaces. 'I am so much grieved that they do not come that I am almost out of heart', William wrote.[1]

But help was at hand, and from an unexpected source. When the fleet arrived in Sallee Road, the simmering tension between the followers of the holy man Muhammad al-Ayyashi in the Old

Town and the pirates across the river in the New Town had just erupted into open conflict. Al-Ayyashi, whom the English called 'the Saint', was determined to oust the Hornacheros from their citadel at New Sallee, but he had no heavy guns and the walls of their town were strong. The two sides gathered regularly on their respective banks of the Bou Regreg and hurled insults, arrows and bullets at each other, and the Saint made forays across the river to burn the crops in the fields around the New Town. It didn't take him long to realise that he shared a common purpose with Rainborowe's fleet; and he swiftly sent an emissary aboard the *Leopard*, handed over all his Christian captives (there were only seven, plus another ten who had swum across the Bou Regreg from New Sallee) and concluded articles of peace and mutual assistance with England.

The tactical advantages of the alliance with the Saint were enormous, and William was a willing friend. The Old Town stood to the north of the mouth of the Bou Regreg, set back from the river and facing the New Town on the south bank. Between the two lay 1,000 yards of scrub, tidal mudflats and deep water. The New Town's harbour nestled on the estuary just behind a protruding headland, out of sight of the English ships. If William had access to the north bank, he could build fieldworks there and bombard the pirate fleet, who would be caught between the Devil of his land-based guns and the deep blue sea of the *Antelope*, the *Leopard* and the others as they waited offshore.

He wasted no time. On 3 May, the day the Saint's representative came aboard the *Leopard* to discuss a treaty, he sent one of his gunners into the Old Town. The next day he recorded in his journal that 'we shot at their ships from the Old Town and tore them so that they broke up two for firewood'.[2]

In the meantime, the *Hercules* and the *Mary* were plying back and forth between Sallee and the harbour at Fedala (present-day Mohammedia), forty miles down the coast, hoping to pick up any pirates who were waiting to come in, acting on intelligence fed to them from their new friends in the Old Town. Aboard the *Antelope* George Carteret seems to have been doing his best to undermine his admiral's reputation back in London. Sir John Pennington, in whose squadron Carteret had sailed as part of the 1636 ship-money fleet, wrote to Secretary Nicholas at the

Admiralty with a warning: 'An enclosure from Captain Carteret will unfold that business at large. I perceive he neither dares write to you nor me, but covertly . . . You will find that all things are not true that Rainborowe writes.'[3]

Carteret's letter is lost, so one can only guess at its contents. In William's despatch to the Admiralty of 20 May, the one to which Pennington refers, he gave an accurate picture of the situation at Sallee, explaining how and why he had made peace with the Saint on the king's behalf, estimating the number of captives in the New Town fairly at around 300, and making it quite clear that he wasn't able to prevent some of the smaller pirate ships from leaving the harbour. 'If the pinnaces had been here,' he told the Admiralty, 'we had taken them and all that we have had sight of and had taken as much wealth as would have paid the charges of the voyage; but without pinnaces it is not possible to take any of them because they row from us with their oars.'[4]

The Saint confirmed the treaty with Rainborowe on 10 May, and William sent him a barrel of gunpowder as a present. He also sent eleven carpenters and a gunner ashore to make and repair field carriages for the Saint's cannon. They were there for three months, scouring the interior in search of suitable timber, working in the heat of summer with nothing to drink but unwholesome stinking water and constantly vexed by mosquitoes. Sailors who had seen service on land were sent to survey the Saint's defences, and to act as military advisers to his army. Under their direction earthworks were dug on the northern shore, facing the New Town harbour; and on the first day of June Rainborowe noted in his customary matter-of-fact style that his men had fired from the 'trench' and sunk three ships. Two days later 'we sunk 5 ships more in the harbour from the trench'.[5] John Dunton's description of the assault was intended for publication and was rather less succinct:

> When the trench was made and their guns hauled down into the trench, our general [i.e. Rainborowe] sent for all the best gunners of every ship, and appointed every gunner and his company his day, and to take powder and shot with them, and so to go to work with their ships to sink and burn them all, and as they were shooting at their ships and barks, the Moors

in the new town did shoot at our men in the trench and did
shoot off one of our men's legs, but he is well again, God be
praised for it, for we did so torment them in sinking and
burning of their ships, that they were stark mad, and at their
wits' ends, for we did every day sink some of their ships, and
kill some of them in the new town with the great guns, with
shooting out of the trench at them, and shooting through their
houses and from the walls and forts of the old town.[6]

On 10 June the *Expedition*, the first of the two new pinnaces,
finally made its appearance, followed the next day by its sister
ship, the *Providence*. Now Rainborowe's grip on the New Town
tightened. When the pirates saw the pinnaces, 'and did see them
row with oars after one of their ships they were stark mad',
claimed Dunton.[7] And well they might be. Over the next few
weeks the fleet forced four pirate ships on to the shore, with the
loss of more than a hundred lives. On one occasion a ship with
a mixed crew of Moors, Spanish slaves and French renegades (and
one English youth) which tried to slip into the Bou Regreg was
forced on to the rocks, where she foundered. Most of the crew
were drowned, or killed by the Saint's men as they came ashore:
the English saved the Spaniards, the Frenchmen and the English
boy: William was pursuing a policy of taking Europeans and
leaving the Moors to the mercy of the Saint.

He also enforced a strict embargo on outside trade with New
Sallee. Captains of French, Spanish and English ships that arrived
to trade were politely but firmly told to take their goods elsewhere. A 140-ton merchantman from Amsterdam appeared,
carrying a mixed cargo of linen, iron, timber – and fifty-one
barrels of powder. When challenged, her master claimed he was
really bound for Santa Cruz (present-day Agadir), 300 miles south;
William prudently confiscated most of the barrels.

With their crops burned in the fields, and their land and sea
supply lines cut off by the Saint and the English, the Sallee rovers
seemed doomed. They retreated behind the walls of their citadel
and dismantled a bridge of boats and boards they had built upriver
to allow them to harass the Old Town, for fear William's men
would use it to establish gun positions on the south bank, within
their outer defences. Even their smaller ships were now confined

to the harbour by the presence of the pinnaces, but still they held out. William sent in a fire-boat to burn their small ships at their moorings, although the mission was upset by a barking dog which raised the alarm; the sailors had to swim for their lives through a hail of musket-shot. With food running short, the Saint was confident that the New Town would fall any day, assuring William that 'he will not be long before he finish the business'.[8] And still the pirates held out.

Behind their battered walls, they argued over the best way to extricate themselves from their predicament. Surrender to William was favoured by some. A second faction wanted to hand New Sallee over to the Spanish, who had a base at Mamora (present-day Mehdia) twenty miles up the coast. A third talked of trying to make terms with the Saint. A fourth pushed for an alliance with the new sultan at Marrakesh, the eighteen-year-old Mohammad ech-Cheikh el-Ashgar, hoping that because they were at war with the Saint, whom he was determined to oust from Old Sallee, he would regard his enemy's enemy as his friend and come to their relief. They may not have been aware, in the labyrinthine world of Moroccan politics, that the Saint was ahead of them. He had already sent word to Marrakesh that he was besieging the New Town and that he planned to hand it to the sultan when he took it.

One thing the rovers were all agreed on – their over-mighty governor, Abd Allah ben Ali el-Kasri, was the author of their misfortunes. He had to go. On the night of 22 June, under cover of one of the dense fogs which descend on the Atlantic coast of Morocco in the summer months, el-Kasri was sent in chains to Marrakesh as a sacrificial peace offering. While they waited to hear from the sultan, the New Towners sued for peace with the fleet; but William insisted they must not only give up all their captives, but also compensate the English Crown for every ship they had ever taken. That was too much. 'Those words made them in a dump', said Dunton.[9] They sent a delegation to treat with the Saint, although William was convinced this was a device to buy them time, in the hope that his supplies would run out and he'd have to abandon his blockade. They also sent to the Spanish at Mamora: the fact that the Hornacheros could even contemplate giving up their base to their sworn enemies says a great deal about just how desperate they were.

By the middle of July William was losing his patience. 'I have great confidence in the Saint,' he told his allies in the Old Town, 'but I verily believe he is deluded by the Andaluzes [i.e. the Hornacheros of the New Town, who were still in talks with him].'[10] He had to do something to move the business forward, he said, and concluded that he was willing to risk his men and his ships to take the New Town.

A seaborne assault on the citadel of New Sallee wasn't a thing to be undertaken lightly. Neither the Saint nor the English gunners had managed to breach its walls; and the idea of rowing into range of its shore batteries and ramparts in a flotilla of small boats was brave indeed. But it turned out to be unnecessary. A few days later a Spanish ship arrived from Mamora carrying Don John de Toledo, 'an understanding gentleman', according to William, who allowed him ashore to open negotiations with good grace – it was no part of his orders to take and hold New Sallee for the Crown, simply to free Christian captives and disable the pirate fleet. If the Spanish helped him to do that they were welcome to the town. They were in any case already proving useful by allowing his fleet into Mamora to fetch supplies of fresh water.

The New Towners agreed without much fuss to give up their citadel to the King of Spain, and Don John told them he would go back to Mamora to confirm their terms and return with 500 Spanish soldiers. New Sallee was poised to become another Spanish base on the African Atlantic. However, the sea was so rough that Don John coudn't get off from the citadel for several days; and while he was waiting to leave, a ship came in with a surprising message from the sultan. He had decided to pardon the Hornacheros for all their previous rebellions, and was sending the penitent and rehabilitated el-Kasri to receive the town on his behalf.

That changed the New Towners' minds about surrendering to the Spanish. They reneged on their treaty, sent Don John back to Mamora empty-handed, and awaited the arrival of their newly reinstated governor – with some trepidation, presumably, since they had last seen him the month before when they waved him off in chains to what everyone believed would be a grisly end at the sultan's court.

Morocco had a history of good relations with the English Crown, not least because it regarded England as an ally against the Spanish: when news of the defeat of the Armada in 1588 reached Marrakesh, bonfires were lit in the streets in celebration. By the time of the Sallee expedition, William was fully aware that his political masters were looking anxiously at recent attempts by the French and the Dutch to establish bases on the Atlantic coast, cutting English traders off from access to Morocco's rich natural resources, the gold mines of the south, the dates, figs, olives, honey 'and sundry sorts of hides and skins', enthused *The Merchants Mappe of Commerce* in 1638, 'especially that excellent sort of cordovant [tanned goatskin] from this Kingdom of Morocco called Maroquins, famous throughout Spain, France, and Italy'.[11]

A Spanish occupation of New Sallee would meet all William's immediate objectives; but an alliance with Sultan Mohammad which suppressed piracy, liberated Christian captives, cemented relations between England and Morocco *and* opened up new opportunities for trade was infinitely preferable to handing another Atlantic base to the King of Spain. El-Kasri came into Sallee Road on 28 July aboard an English merchant ship accompanied by the sultan's Morisco representative and Robert Blake, an Englishman living in Marrakesh who had come as interpreter. William ordered them all aboard the *Leopard*, where he dealt civilly with them 'by reason of the ancient league and amity between my sovereign and the King of Morocco'.[12] But he still had to make sure those immediate objectives would be met.

So he told el-Kasri he was keeping him as a hostage while the others went ashore. And that he would hang him if anything went wrong, 'at which he trembled very much', said Dunton.[13] Blake and the Morisco *caid* went off to put the sultan's offer to the New Towners, after William made it clear that the release of all Christian captives without payment of any ransom was non-negotiable. Later that same day Blake was back aboard the *Leopard*, bringing with him thirteen English captives as a token of the New Towners' good faith, and a request that William would repatriate any Moors he was holding in return. William sent a note to Carteret telling him to ask around among the prisoners held on the *Antelope*. If any said they were Moors, by which he meant Muslims, he should release them; if they claimed to be Christians they must be kept.

The New Town accepted the sultan's terms; and over the next few days they released all their Christian captives. There were fewer than the fleet had hoped for when it set out – around a thousand had been shipped off to the markets of Algiers and Tunis earlier in the year – but William still managed to liberate 302 of the king's subjects from England, Ireland, Scotland and Wales, together with twenty-four Frenchman, nine Spaniards and eight Dutch – a grand total of 343 captives released.

His journal of the Sallee expedition was always succinct, and the entries for 1 and 2 August are typical: 'The wind at so: west. We had 180 Christians came aboard.' 'The wind at so: west. We had 73 more came aboard.'[14]

Usually it is possible to put flesh on these bare bones from other sources. John Dunton, for example, wrote that the New Towners hurried to bring out their captives because they were so eager to have the fleet gone. The purser of the *Providence* wrote that English renegades who had turned Turk (that is, converted to Islam) were offered their liberty if they would come back to the faith of their fathers. 'And many do, both men and women.'[15] A faded paper in the British National Archive headed 'The names of the captives released' is a litany of loss and liberation, but the columns of names and home towns raise more questions than they answer. How did James Lawe of Edinburgh come to be captured by the Sallee rovers? Or Edward Broomfield of Weymouth? What calamity befell the sailors of Dungarvan in County Wexford that twenty-seven of them almost ended their days in a Moroccan fortress on the edge of the Atlantic? How did Katherine Richards and Grace Greenfield and Rebecca May come to be in Sallee? Were they among the women who turned Turk and then turned back again?

And what was it like for them when they got home? Did James and Edward and Katherine slip effortlessly back into normal life, avoiding questions that could never be asked aloud? Did they think back to Barbary as they lay in their beds at night? Did they hear the muezzin's call in their dreams?

William was more loquacious than usual when he reported back to the Lords of the Admiralty on 8 August. He may have been conscious that although his instructions had included a command to send regular despatches back to London, he had only managed two since arriving in Sallee Road twenty weeks earlier. Now he gave a blow-by-blow account of everything that had happened since his last despatch of 20 May. But his purpose was less to inform the Admiralty about past events than to let them know his plans for the future. The expedition had freed all the Christians in the place, as it had set out to do; and it had saved many more, he said, who would have been taken on the high seas that summer if the pirates had been able to get out. But he wasn't convinced that the New Town would keep to its word when he left for home; so he had decided to sail down to Safi and negotiate articles of peace with Sultan Mohammad, articles which would commit the sultan to answering for the behaviour of the Sallee rovers in the future.

> And although they be as wicked fellows as any be, and nothing else but a den of thieves [he went on], yet I am persuaded they will keep the peace with us, first because we have brought them to such extremity . . . and our ships are terrible to them. And secondly, they fear if they perform not that the King of Morocco will besiege them by land and that His Majesty's ships should again besiege them by sea. So I doubt not but there will be much quietness upon His Majesty's coasts.[16]

William was exceeding his authority in trying to negotiate a treaty with Marrakesh. But it made perfect sense, and for exactly the reasons he put forward. If New Sallee were able to rebuild its fleet and set off on the cruise next year, or the year after, the mission would be a failure. Ship money or no ship money, Charles I didn't have the resources to send a fleet to Morocco on a regular basis: William's expedition cost around £40,000, or £117 for every captive freed, and if their release was all that was achieved, it would have been cheaper to pay their ransom and have done.

The freed captives were distributed around the fleet and William ordered Carteret to take the *Antelope*, the *Hercules* and the two pinnaces and patrol the coast of Spain for Algerian pirates, and to take any they found and exchange them for some of the several thousand British slaves currently being held in

Algiers. He would take the *Leopard* and the *Mary* down to Safi. In a turn of events which well illustrates the logistical and communication problems inherent in conducting a long-range mission in the seventeenth century, as he was preparing to leave Sallee two English ships, the *Mary Rose* and the *Roebuck*, arrived with supplies, reinforcements – and orders to hold New Sallee for the English Crown.

It was too late for that, although with all those extra mouths to feed the victuals were welcome. On the morning of 21 August, after more than a week of heavy seas and fogs, the *Leopard* sailed out of Sallee Road with the *Mary* and the two supply ships. William's little fleet came into Safi at noon two days later.

5

From Afric Shore

The port of Safi had once been an outpost of the Portuguese. Their sixteenth-century governor's residence loomed over the harbour, and the *medina* was still dominated by the incongruous Gothic choir of a cathedral, unfinished when the Portuguese pulled out in 1541. More recently – in William Rainborowe's lifetime, in fact – the town had been a favourite haunt of English renegades, men who, having made a career out of privateering against the Spanish, turned to outright piracy when James I brought the war with Spain to an end in 1604, and drifted down to Barbary. In different circumstances William might have been one of them.

Sultan Mohammad's court lay at Marrakesh, eighty-five miles inland. It was four or five days' hard ride, and for some reason William decided he was going to stay with the *Leopard*. His journal entry for 23 August reads simply, 'The wind at north-north-west. At noon I came into Safi. Mr Blake and the king's alcaide went ashore with my lieutenant and my son whom I sent to the King of Morocco.'[1]

'My son'? This is the first and only intimation that one of William's boys was on the Sallee expedition. There are no clues as to whether he arrived with the supply ships, or if he was there all along. No clues, even, to his identity. He can't have been the youngest boy, Edward, who was less than four years old and safe at home in Wapping with his mother; but Thomas, the eldest, was in his mid-twenties by this time and married with a child; and Thomas's brother, William, was only a couple of years younger. Either could have sailed with their father. Either could have made that journey with Robert Blake and the Morisco *caid* to the sultan's court in the fabled capital city of Morocco.

Their road led south-east from Safi across red earth and green, cultivated plains; past ancient salt mines and more ancient forts, deserted now and half-buried in their own ruins. The young Rainborowe's first sight of Marrakesh, 'accounted to be one of the greatest cities in the whole world', according to Leo Africanus' *Historie of Africa*, would have come through the summer haze as the riders approached the peaks of the High Atlas.[2] The vast city of 100,000 houses was enclosed by a battlemented wall of red mud four miles in circumference and surrounded by a rich plain. In front of those walls rivers of men and camels and mules and dogs flowed in and out of twenty-four gates, and behind the walls rose the minaret of the Koutoubia mosque, already 500 years old when the Englishmen first saw it, and so tall, claimed Leo Africanus, that 'it would make a man giddy to look down . . . for men walking on the ground, be they never so tall, seem no bigger than a child of one year old'.[3]

Making their way in past the walls and turrets and defensive trenches which protected the city, the Englishmen found themselves in a labyrinth of streets and lanes and narrow passages, once teeming with people, now in decay as a result of the civil wars of the early seventeenth century. 'One third part', wrote John Ogilby in 1670, 'is destitute of inhabitants, by reason of many ruins, between which it is planted with groves of dates, vineyards, and other trees.'[4]

The only lodging house that would accept Christian travellers was on the main square and run by a Provençal named Amalric, who kept rooms on the first floor of a huge courtyard building, while European merchants bought and sold goods on the ground floor and in the courtyard itself. The delegation's objective was an audience with the sultan at El Badi palace, the enormous royal complex put up by one of Sultan Mohammad's predecessors in the sixteenth century. There were halls and chambers, 'on all sides within and without furnished richly with all sorts of imagery, and appointed for places of contemplation and study', said Ogilby, with sunken gardens, a pool nearly a hundred yards long and a white marble fountain at the centre.[5] El-Mansour, the sultan who commissioned the palace, was said to have brought craftsmen from all over the Mediterranean to build it, importing the marble from Italy and paying for it in sugar. He even set up crèches for the workers' children so that the artisans could devote themselves to their work without being distracted.

A Dutchman who visited Marrakesh in 1640 declared that El Badi should not only be regarded as the Eighth Wonder of the World, but as the Wonder of Wonders. There was a high tower with a stair that the sultan could ride up on his horse, and every day at noon falcons, vultures and other birds would cluster round its summit to be fed. The sultan, attended by European renegades and black Africans, all in elaborate robes and heavy decorated belts, greeted foreign delegations with an ostentatious display of luxury. After the initial introductions, when visitors knelt and presented themselves, everyone sat on brocade cushions to exchange pleasantries and listen to the court poets declaiming verses in praise of their master. The air was heavy with scents of amber and aloe, and guests were kept cool by being sprinkled with rose water and orange-blossom water from myrtle branches dipped into cups of gold and silver.

Quite an experience for a young Puritan from Wapping. The Englishmen stayed in Marrakesh for two weeks, while the sultan considered William's articles of peace. On 12 September he agreed them, having made a few minor changes. Four days later Blake, William Rainborowe's son and his unnamed lieutenant were back in Safi and preparing to board the *Leopard*, bringing with them the modified draft treaty.

And that wasn't all. Sultan Mohammad had decided to send an ambassador to London, a Portuguese eunuch named Djouder ben Abed Allah. He arrived in Safi with Blake and the others, along with an entourage of twenty-eight servants and presents for Charles I — sixteen freed English captives, four hawks, four Barbary horses and two saddles with gold-plated bridles and stir-rups, each worth £1,000. In his usual laconic manner, William didn't even bother to mention the ambassador's arrival at Safi (or indeed, the safe return of his son) in his journal. On 16 September he simply noted, 'Mr Blake came from Morocco.' And two days later, 'Calm. A great sea. We took in the horses.'[6]

The *Leopard* sailed on 21 September. News of William's coming had already reached England with the arrival into Falmouth harbour of the *Hercules* and the *Expedition* the previous day. The *Antelope* and the *Providence* weren't far behind – Carteret hadn't taken his admiral's order to patrol the coast of Spain for Algerian pirates very seriously. The West Country had suffered badly from the depredations of Barbary pirates, and nearly half the freed captives came from that part of the world: as soon as Brian Harrison of the *Hercules* brought word of their success at Sallee ashore, the vice admiral of Devon and Cornwall wrote to Secretary Windebank to say that 'these news are most joyfully taken in these parts, and will much forward upon all occasions His Majesty's service'.[7]

This was the real point. The Sallee expedition had succeeded on many different levels: William and his comrades had subdued a hostile regime and rescued hundreds of Christians from captivity; they had initiated a peace treaty with the sultan of Morocco, which would bring new commercial opportunities in Barbary. They had achieved a remarkable tactical victory for the Royal Navy after decades of failures, and sent a signal to Barbary – and to other European maritime powers – that England was a force to be reckoned with once again: as a pamphleteer wrote nearly ten years later, William's fleet 'performed the best service that any part of England's navy hath achieved in the forty-four years which have last past'.[8] Most importantly of all, William handed a domestic propaganda coup to the government by demonstrating to the nation the validity of Charles I's ship-money levy in a 'fashion which was so much more glamorous than serving fishing licences to Dutch herring busses. And the government was standing by to exploit it to the full. When the new writs for ship money went out at the beginning of October, the Privy Council stressed that the Sallee expedition 'has not only kept in from sea those enemies to Christianity, but has been a means to redeem some of His Majesty's subjects'.[9]

The *Leopard* made Land's End on the afternoon of 5 October, and the next day William sent the *Roebuck* into Torbay to put some of the West Country captives ashore. He dropped anchor in the English Channel between Deal and Dover a day later and sat down to explain his actions to Sir John Coke, arguing that the treaty with Morocco would help 'to keep them thieves of Sally the better in awe'.[10] But he was touchingly anxious about his next step. Fighting pirates was fine. So was mounting a long, hard blockade, or sending fireships into an enemy harbour, or coordinating an artillery bombardment. The negotiating of diplomatic niceties was a different matter. What exactly was he meant to *do* with Djouder ben Abed Allah? 'I have in my ship given him the respect of an ambassador,' he wrote to Coke, 'but what belongs to him when he is landed and how far he shall proceed in his journey to London I am altogether ignorant of . . . I beseech your honour to take order for him, being unacquainted with the course of ambassadors.'[11] This social anxiety extended to his own future – was it necessary for him to go straight to the king at Hampton Court to report on the expedition, or would it be all right for him to wait until the king returned to London?

Coke's reply hasn't survived. In any case it didn't matter. The following day, before he could have expected to receive an answer, William took matters into his own hands and set the ambassador ashore, along with his entourage, Robert Blake, the captives, the four hawks and the four Barbary horses. They made their way to Gravesend to await an official welcome from the king's master of ceremonies, Sir John Finet. William left the *Leopard* at Rochester on 12 October and the following day it arrived safely into Chatham dockyard, 241 days after leaving.

Finet's first clue that a Moroccan embassy had arrived in England came when a group of merchants turned up at Hampton Court with the news on 10 October, and he immediately rushed over to Gravesend to make the necessary arrangements for his reception. The master of ceremonies found Djouder ben Abed Allah lying sick with a fever. This was unfortunate, but at least it gave Finet time to make proper preparations – and to establish exactly who was to pay for them. After a swift game of pass the parcel in which the comptroller of the king's household insisted that merchants with interests in Morocco ought to pay, and the merchants countered that they were not rich and that in any case 'the ambassador's employment to His Majesty tended rather to matter of state, than to commerce', Charles I finally stepped in and said that because of the importance of the treaty 'and the rare bravery of his present' he would allow the Moroccans a house in London and a daily allowance of £25, but only until the day after a royal audience.[12] Then the ambassador was on his own.

It was a week before Djouder ben Abed Allah was well enough to travel, but on 18 October he arrived at Tower Wharf, a few hundred yards from the Rainborowes' house – surely they must have come out to watch? – where he was helped into the king's coach and conducted to his lodgings by one hundred aldermen and other prominent citizens in their scarlet gowns and chains of gold, all on horseback, the way lighted by 600 flaming torches. 'There is an ambassador come from the King of Morocco, and is received with great pomp', wrote Viscount Conway. 'The reason of all which is the shipping money.'[13]

As Anglo-Moroccan negotiations began, the government pressed ahead with its campaign of celebration and self-justification, in spite of – indeed, because of – mounting opposition in the country to the ship-money levy. After a break of three years, the king decided to resurrect the Twelfth Night masques which had lapsed when he commissioned *The Apotheosis of James I* from Rubens to decorate the ceiling of the Banqueting Hall at Whitehall, and it was feared the paintings might suffer from the candle smoke. Over the winter a wooden masking house was put up in the palace precincts, and on the Sunday after Twelfth Night, 1638, Charles and Henrietta Maria and the rest of the court were treated to a performance of William Davenant's *Britannia Triumphans*, with sets by Inigo Jones. Djouder ben Abed Allah and Robert Blake were seated in a box just behind the king, who later chided Finet for not having given them more prominent places. The Moroccan ambassador was not just meant to see the show; he was part of it, a tangible reminder of Britain's rediscovered naval prowess.

Davenant's masque told how Britanocles, 'the glory of the western world, hath by his wisdom, valour, and piety, not only vindicated his own, but far distant seas, infested with pirates'.[14] Fame, with a pair of wings and a golden trumpet, hovered in the air while singing a paean of praise to the king, whose sceptre was changed, she argued, to a trident, and whose power commanded the unruly seas. The masque closed with the sea nymph Galatea floating by on a dolphin, and a great fleet, presumably on a painted backcloth, entering safely into harbour. There was also a giant Saracen who capered round the stage with a dwarf, and some tactless anti-Islamic jokes. One wonders quite how Robert Blake interpreted them to the ambassador.

William Rainborowe, in the meantime, was a hero. The poet Edmund Waller eulogised his exploits at Sallee – 'One squadron of our wingéd castles sent,/O'erthrew their fort, and all their navy rent'[15] – and King Charles offered him a knighthood, which he declined, accepting instead a gold chain and medal. His pay for the mission to Sallee amounted to £500, and he invested it in property rather than shipping: by the summer of 1638, besides houses in Wapping, he owned new-built property across the river in Southwark.

In early December the king, having considered the damage being caused to English shipping by the pirates of Algiers, referred the Algerian problem to a committee of advisers, asking them to consult with the Levant Company and Trinity House. In response, over the winter of 1637–8 William began to sketch out a proposal for a second expedition, against a more formidable enemy even than the Sallee rovers. For nearly thirty years the pirates of Algiers had preyed on European shipping inside and outside the Strait of Gibraltar, taking merchantmen, selling their cargos on the no-questions-asked black market which operated all over the coast of North Africa and in European ports like Genoa, Livorno and Marseilles; and selling their crews into slavery in the *bedistan* of Algiers. An English sailor who was held in the city in 1637 guessed that there were some 60,000 Christians 'groaning under the yoke of Turkish tyranny' there; and William was told that hundreds of Christian captives had been sent to Algiers from Sallee before his expedition arrived.[16]

The Algerians' depredations weren't confined to the Mediterranean, either. In 1631 Algerian corsairs landed at Baltimore, Co. Cork, and kidnapped 107 Protestant settlers; and in the summer of 1636, when the ship-money fleet was out, they took a bark on its way from Bristol to Ireland with thirty passengers aboard. The same pirates also took five Cornish fishing crews; the government was told their comrades had found their boats 'floating upon the sea with never a person in them, nor sail to their yards'.[17] The Earl of Northumberland had dispatched two ships to hunt for them, but without success. Writing from aboard the *Triumph*, when William was his flag captain, he freely admitted to the Lords of the Admiralty that he couldn't see how to prevent such raids, 'for the Turks can see the king's great ships at a further distance than they can discern them, and being good sailors, avoid them at pleasure'.[18]

Sir Robert Mansell's failed expedition of 1620 was the last time – in fact the only time – that England had attempted to take the fight to Algiers. Since then, apart from patrolling coastal waters and occasionally convoying the Levant Company's ships through to Aleppo and Smyrna in the eastern Mediterranean, English efforts to suppress Algerian piracy had focused on making representations to the Ottoman court in Istanbul, since as a *sanjak* or province of the empire, Algiers was in theory subject to the articles of peace in force between Istanbul and England.

William had first-hand experience of just how much the articles were worth. During one of his voyages to the Levant he had been at Smyrna, preparing to leave for home with his ship fully laden, when a fleet of nineteen Algerian warships arrived in the bay under the command of the notorious Italian renegade Ali Bitshnin, 'one of the greatest slave-merchants that Barbary ever produced' according to an eighteenth-century *History of Algiers*.[19] Ali told William he would take him if he put out to sea, to which William pointed out that England was at peace with the Ottoman Empire. 'His answer', said William, 'was that if he could take so rich a ship he would dispense with the peace.'[20]

On 25 January 1638 William submitted a proposal for redeeming the captives in Algiers to the Lords of the Admiralty. Since the pirates wouldn't obey the commands of the Grand Seignior in Istanbul, he argued, they were hardly likely to treat with England. If the government tried to procure English captives by paying ransom, 'they will cost that way at least £100,000 and besides, if they [the Algerians] find them redeemed for money they will be greedy to take more in hope to have them likewise redeemed for money which will never have an end'.[21] The only answer was to blockade Algiers as he had blockaded Sallee. A fleet of ten good ships and six pinnaces should do it; and if the blockade continued for three or four years 'their ships will be worm-eaten and rotten in that time and so unserviceable', he claimed, 'which I conceive will make them give up the captives'.[22]

This was ambitious. Maintaining such a large fleet for so long might, as William urged in his final paragraph, be very much to the king's honour 'in all the maritime parts of Christiandom'. On the other hand, it might also be regarded with deep suspicion by maritime nations such as Spain and Holland, who had their own interests in the Mediterranean; and, as William realised, a blockade risked upsetting Istanbul and provoking reprisals against English merchants elsewhere in the empire. It would be massively expensive: keeping four ships, two pinnaces and two supply ships at Sallee over the summer had cost around £40,000. Double the size of the fleet and extend the blockade from four months to four years, and there wouldn't be much left over to keep the ship-money fleet in the Narrow Seas.

The mission would also be very, very difficult to accomplish, even for a commander as able as William. Algiers was heavily fortified, with a system of towers and blockhouses around the bay and a well-defended harbour. England would need the co-operation of Spain so that the fleet could resupply at Alicante or Majorca. And there was no Saint to foment internal unrest or to cut off access to the city from the land.

The committee for considering the Algiers problem submitted its report to the navy commissioners in February 1638, but nothing more was heard of William's plan, perhaps because the king had more pressing concerns: large numbers of Scots signed the Covenant that same month, rejecting English moves to impose uniformity of worship and setting the two nations on a course which would lead to the Bishops' Wars of 1639 and 1640.

Djouder ben Abed Allah and Robert Blake sailed for Morocco in May, taking with them presents for Sultan Mohammad, including a gilded coach painted with flowers and five Denmark horses to draw it, some fine linen and portraits of the king and queen, copied from Van Dyck's originals. They also carried the articles of peace agreed between the two nations – and a separate agreement which had been deftly brokered by Blake, and which gave him and a syndicate of English merchants a monopoly of trade with Morocco, on the understanding that they would not deal with rebels.

Neither the treaty nor the trade agreement were exactly a wild success. Fighting had already broken out again between Old and New Sallee, with Abd Allah ben Ali el-Kasri reneging on his promises to the sultan. The Saint, who seems to have been adept at finding friends in his war with the New Town, entered into an alliance with some dissident Moriscos; el-Kasri was killed in the fighting, and his son, who succeeded him, repeated history by immediately recognising the authority of the sultan as the only way to preserve New Sallee from the Saint and his friends. The sultan's attempts to restore order ended in disaster when his army was routed by hostile mountain tribesmen before he even reached Sallee and he had to flee for his life.

Blake's trade monopoly had an equally unhappy time. English merchants ignored it and sold guns to the rebel tribes; the sultan objected to its terms, which were weighted heavily in favour of Blake and his friends; and excluded competitors back in London lobbied against it. Blake's trading company was wound up in 1639 and replaced with a looser association of merchants.

The sultan, whose grasp on power in Morocco was much less secure than even he realised, was unable to prevent the Sallee rovers from regrouping and resuming their attacks on Christian shipping outside the Strait. But it was on a much smaller scale than before. If William's expedition didn't have the long-term results that he had hoped for, the fault lay with others. He at least had shown the world that the English navy was once more a force to be reckoned with.

And his reward was to be given command of the most powerful ship which that navy had ever seen.

According to Phineas Pett, the shipwright who designed the *Sovereign of the Seas*, the king first mentioned 'his princely resolution for the building of a great new ship' to him during a royal visit to the yards at Woolwich in June 1634, to view the frame of the half-built *Leopard*, which would become William's flagship on the Sallee expedition three years later.[23] Pett took the king at his word, coming up with a scheme for a vessel which at 1,500-tons burden, and with guns ranged over three decks, would dwarf every other ship in the navy. Like the ship-money fleets and the Sallee expedition, the *Sovereign of the Seas* was meant to assert royal power both abroad and at home.

News of the project was greeted with scepticism at Trinity House. She would be too big. She would cost too much. Her armaments would pose huge problems. If she was to carry ordnance in proportion to her bulk, she would need three tiers of guns, with the heaviest ordnance on the lowest tier. In any but the lightest winds all the ports on this bottom tier would have to be shut fast against the sea, 'or else the ship will . . . sink as did the *Mary Rose* in King Henry VIII's time at Portsmouth'.[24]

The elder brethren concluded by advising the king to abandon the idea. For the same cost he could build two ships of 500 or 600 tons, and fit them both with forty pieces of good ordnance. 'And these two ships will be of more force and for better service and will beat the great ship back and side.'[25]

The advice went unheeded. The keel of the great new ship was laid at Woolwich in the presence of the king on 16 January 1636, after Pett had personally travelled to the forests of north-east England to supervise the felling and preparing of 2,500 trees required for her.

At first it seemed that the critics were right. Phineas Pett (or rather his son Peter, who was largely responsible for building her) was six months behind schedule in delivering the *Sovereign*, and at £13,680 his estimate of costs was so far out that it is hard to see how he arrived at it. The amount eventually spent on her was £40,833 8s. 1½d. – excluding the cost of the 102 guns, which was reckoned by the Officers of the Ordnance at £24,447 8s. 8d. And in September 1637 the first attempt to launch her ended in fiasco when, in the presence of the king, the queen, 'and all the train of lords and ladies [and] their attendants', the ship stayed resolutely on its slipway.[26] A second attempt was more successful, but equally embarrassing: it was scheduled for the morning of Sunday 14 October, but the tide came in so fast and high on the Saturday night that the Petts decided not to wait, so that when dignitaries (who mercifully didn't include the king) assembled the next day, they were disappointed to find her already launched and at her moorings in the middle of the Thames.

William's return from Sallee with his cargo of captives and diplomats coincided exactly with the launch of the *Sovereign of the Seas*. He may even have sailed right past her on the Sunday morning following her premature torchlit launch of the previous night, while men still clambered over her vast bulk, inspecting her timbers for signs of leaks and making sure her cables held. When Sir John Finet conducted a wobbly Djouder ben Abed Allah up the Thames to Tower Wharf four days later, he was careful to pause at Woolwich, 'where they saw His Majesty's new great ship (the Eighth Wonder of the World) with pleasing and much contenting admiration' – a deliberate display of English naval power.[27]

Over the following weeks, as William settled back into home life with Judith and their family at Wapping, Pett's workers set up sheer legs and tackle and lifted the *Sovereign*'s masts into place; they fitted her rigging and sails. While he waited over the hard winter to hear the response to his proposal for an Algiers expedition, she lay at anchor at Erith and her guard of a hundred men bashed away at the encircling ice to keep her safe. At the end of January the Lords of the Admiralty ordered the officers of the navy to prepare the ship-money fleet for sailing in April. The *Sovereign of the Seas* was to lead it, and William was appointed as her captain at ten shillings a day, more than any other captain in the fleet.

This was a little optimistic – she 'has much work as yet unperfected', the officers of the navy reported at the beginning of March;[28] and by the middle of June, several months after the fleet had sailed – without her – the king's gunfounder was demanding payment before he cast her final guns, four 12½ ft-long demy-cannon weighing 5,300 lb apiece, and costing £1,700 for the four. In the meantime William's duties seem to have consisted of being a tour guide and showing guests over the ship. While she was moored at Erith, for example, the City merchant and shipowner Sir Marmaduke Rawdon, who had a party of relatives down from Yorkshire 'seeing those rarities that were to be seen about London', hired a barge and went aboard the *Sovereign*. 'The commander of her then', wrote Rawdon's seventeenth-century biographer, 'was Captain Rainsbery, an acquaintance of Sir Marmaduke's, who entertained them with the best things he had aboard.'[29]

The king also went aboard to inspect his great new ship; and on 6 June, after she had been moved downriver to Greenhithe to take on provisions and some of her ordnance, he visited again, accompanied by Henrietta Maria, the Duke and Duchess of Lennox and 'divers other lords and ladies more, [who] came on board the ship at Greenhithe, where they dined to their great content', wrote Phineas Pett.[30] In July, when the glittering gold and black leviathan was moved down to Gravesend, the delighted Charles came aboard once again. They gave him a seventy-two-gun salute when he went ashore.

At the beginning of March 1638 William's wife Judith died; Richard Sedgwick buried her in the chapel of St John, and William was left a widower for the second time.

Judith Rainborowe is a cipher. There is nothing known about her, save for the stark list of names and places and dates already listed elsewhere. Her family, the Hoxtons, came from East London and from Suffolk. She bore her husband six children and buried two of them. She was in her late thirties or early forties when she died. And that's all. Not much to say for a life. No sad songs sung. No elegy. No trace of tears. Just a reminder that the past forgets so much more than we can ever know.

His wife's death, and the fact that he was about to take the *Sovereign* out on sea trials, prompted William to consider his own mortality. His will was signed on 16 July 1638. Aside from a bequest of £50 to Trinity House, with the condition 'that they give to poor seamen or their widows of the hamlet of Wapping every St Thomas Day [21 December] forty shillings', it reads like that of a prosperous property owner rather than a mariner. 'All those my houses in Southwark . . . some of them lately built', go to his eldest son, Thomas. 'My houses in Gun Alley in Wapping purchased of my father-in-law Hoxton' go to his second son, William, who also gets £1,000. The youngest boy, Edward, still under five years old, is given £1,200. Of the three girls, the two youngest, Judith and Joan, receive £1,000 apiece, while Martha has £700 'if she be alive at the time of my death'. Including a number of smaller bequests – to an army of relations and in-laws, to the poor of Whitechapel, to his only grandchild, the son of Thomas – William leaves the grand total of £5,570, excluding the value of the property. That sum represents more than £600,000 at today's prices, and fifteen times that amount if we base the computation on average earnings. Either way, William Rainborowe was a rich man, with enough personal wealth to build and equip from scratch a forty-gun warship. By way of comparison, an ordinary seaman in the Royal Navy earned £9 a year before stoppages.

The residue of William Rainborowe's estate was to be divided equally between the two eldest boys, Thomas and William, whom he appointed as his executors and charged with bringing up the three younger children, Judith, Joan and Edward, seeing to their education and paying for their 'meat and drink and clothes'.

The *Sovereign* was ready for her sea trials that summer. She was taken to Margate, and then to Dover – 'neither the town nor Castle took notice of us', said Phineas Pett ruefully – and finally, after several false starts caused by bad weather and lack of wind, William set sail from the Downs, with both of the Petts aboard, on Wednesday 15 August. 'I hope she will prove a brave, stout, serviceable ship', wrote Admiral Sir John Pennington, who watched her go.[31]

The trials lasted until Saturday afternoon when, with victuals running low, the *Sovereign* returned to the Downs. Pennington sent up to London William's report, 'that she works very well, and steers exceeding yarely'.[32] The king was delighted, and William was tired. He never went to sea again.

6

In Freedom Equal

Within weeks of Martha Rainborowe's marriage to Thomas Coytmore in June 1635, she was pregnant with their first child. The baby, named Katherine after Martha's mother-in-law, was baptised in the little church at Wapping on 13 April 1636, and buried there six days later. Before the year was out the Coytmores had decided to leave England for ever. To look for a new life in a new world.

By the mid-1630s subjects of Charles I had settled in dozens of outposts in the Americas, from the little settlement of Marshall's Creek in the tropical rain forests of Suriname, to the snowy wastes of Avalon in Newfoundland. Some of these colonies consisted of vast tracts of land still unexplored by Europeans, like the seven million acres around the Chesapeake Bay and north of the Potomac river which were so generously bestowed by Charles I upon the second Lord Baltimore in 1632, and named Maryland after Henrietta Maria. Others were tiny: the colony on Providence Island, established off the Mosquito Coast in 1629 by a group of prominent Puritans as a haven for the godly and a base from which to harry the Spanish, is just four miles long by two and a half miles broad.

The literature of colonialism in the seventeenth century is filled with seductive descriptions of paradise; the reality was harsh. Prospective settlers in England were told that in Virginia 'there is great plenty', and 'there wants nothing for the settling of that Christian Plantation, but more hands to gather and return those commodities which may bring profit'.[1] That rosy assessment was in 1617, where seven years earlier starving settlers had eaten the corpses of their dead comrades.

For many settlers, life in the Americas was frightening, brutal and brief, cut short by death, or by despair and a return passage. There is a story told of twenty-three-year-old Dorothy Bradford, one of the original Pilgrims. Dorothy and her husband William boarded the *Mayflower* at Southampton in August 1620, leaving their only child behind. When their leaky, battered ship finally dropped anchor at the eastern end of Cape Cod on 11 November, after a crossing filled with storms and fear, Dorothy looked out on this unknown coast, which even her hopeful husband described as 'a hideous and desolate wilderness, full of wild beasts and wild men' – and threw herself overboard.[2]

The story is uncorroborated. But in a way that's irrelevant. It contains a deeper truth, a glimpse into the existential angst that swept over so many settlers at their first contact with the hideous and desolate wilderness. Depressive anxiety, disorientation and an intense and agonising sense of loss at the thought of what had been left behind were common responses to the experience of migration. 'Most give themselves over, and die of melancholy', George Sandys told his brother in 1623, after two years spent among the settlers of Virginia.[3]

There was plenty at which to despair: harsh climate, disease, a shortage of food, intermittent contact with home and the ever-present threat of violence. 'I came to build, and set, and sow, but I am fallen to fighting with Frenchmen', said an exasperated Lord Baltimore in 1628, as his dreams of a haven for Roman Catholics in Newfoundland sank beneath a wave of tit-for-tat raids by French privateers in retaliation for English attacks against French settlements on the St Lawrence.[4] One of the greatest threats came from Native Americans, whose response to having to share their lands with English settlers was unpredictable and frequently savage. At one end of the spectrum was the coordinated assault by Powhatans on the fifty or so English farmsteads and plantations along the James river on the morning of Friday 22 March 1622, in which some 340 English men, women and children – around a quarter of the European population of Virginia – were slaughtered in a massacre which, as one planter said at the time, 'killed all our country; beside them they killed, they burst the heart of all the rest'.[5] At the other end was the sudden, isolated ambush with consequences which were less dramatic for the young settlements, but no less appalling for its victims. John Winthrop, the governor of Massachusetts whose journals and papers provide so much information about life for the first English settlers, described one such encounter in 1636:

> About the middle of this month, John Tilley, master of a bark, coming down Connecticut river, went on shore in a canoe, three miles above the fort, to kill fowl; and having shot off his piece, many Indians arose out of the covert and took him, and killed one other, who was in the canoe. This Tilley was a very stout man, and of great understanding. They cut off his hands, and sent them before, and after cut off his feet. He lived three days after his hands were cut off; and themselves confessed, that he was a stout man, because he cried not in his torture.[6]

In spite of the harshness, the brutal violence, the shortages and uncertainties, by the end of the 1630s around 50,000 citizens of England, Scotland, Wales and Ireland were making new worlds in twenty-four distinct settlements on the other side of the Atlantic. Fifteen of these outposts were less than ten years old. Why did so many men and women make that voyage? Why did Martha Rainborowe and her husband Thomas decide to emigrate?

These are different questions. The answer to the first depended on where in the English Atlantic a colonist chose to go, since those twenty-four settlements were widely different in character; they didn't share a unifying centralised system of government; they didn't offer the same opportunities, the same familiarities, the same communities.[7] The economies of the cluster of English colonies scattered around the coast of Newfoundland, for example, were based on fishing; Providence Island and the Bermuda relied on seafaring in all its forms, from fishing to trading to out-and-out piracy. Settlers on the Leeward Islands – Montserrat, St Christopher, Antigua, Nevis – were small-scale tobacco farmers, although they also grew indigo, ginger and cotton. The main export of densely populated Barbados was tobacco, but it was Virginia and Maryland which dominated that market; they were the main contributors to a trade which imported more than one million pounds of tobacco into England every year by the end of the 1630s. In their early years the New England colonies depended heavily on the fur trade.

As important as their economies – more important, in that it defined the character of each colony – was their brand of Christianity. The little island of Montserrat was settled by Irish Catholics. Avalon in Newfoundland had been established by George Calvert, the first Lord Baltimore, as a haven for English Catholics like himself: 'It is of great importance to the Holy Church and to Christianity that it be inhabited not by heretics but by Catholic Christians', said a priest in a clandestine report to Rome.[8] After Avalon failed, Lord Baltimore's son moved the dream to Maryland. Neighbouring Virginia pledged allegiance to the Church of England, with the law of the land mandating that 'there be an uniformity in our church as near as may be to the canons of England; both in substance and circumstance'.[9] The religious complexion of Plymouth Colony was determined by the Protestant zeal of the separatists who made up around 40 per cent of the original *Mayflower* Pilgrims, and whose determination to worship outside the constraints of the Anglican Church had led them from England to Leiden in Holland, and then to America.

Thomas and Martha decided to make their new home in the youthful Massachusetts Bay Colony – seventeen towns, villages and hamlets scattered around Massachusetts Bay and along the banks of the Mystic and Charles rivers. Although English adventurers had made sporadic attempts at settling the Bay in the past (Captain John Smith led three expeditions in 1614 and 1615, naming the region 'New England' but failing to establish a colony), it had only been in the late 1620s that settlement began in earnest, with the grant of a royal charter to the Massachusetts Bay Company and a concerted effort by a group of English Puritans to relocate to a more congenial place where they could pursue their own

Calvinistic brand of Protestantism away from the disapproving eyes of the Anglican establishment. In 1630, when there were already townships established at Salem and Charlestown, an expeditionary fleet of four ships set sail from Yarmouth on the Isle of Wight carrying 700 men, women and children to Massachusetts. Their leader and the governor of both the company and the colony was John Winthrop, a disgruntled member of the Suffolk gentry with a strong commitment to Protestantism and a growing feeling that the Church of England could not or would not supply his spiritual needs. His personality would help to define the culture of New England, and his life would connect with the Rainborowes in ways which neither he nor they could imagine.

In a lay sermon given to his fellow colonists as they were about to set sail for Massachusetts, Winthrop spelled out his own vision for the colony as a community of saints, a commonwealth. 'We must bear one another's burdens. We must not look only on our own things, but also on the things of our brethren.'[10] By working together and following God's commands, the colonists could create a new society which would be the envy of the world:

> We shall find that the God of Israel is among us, when ten of us shall be able to resist a thousand of our enemies; when He shall make us a praise and glory that men shall say of succeeding plantations, 'may the Lord make it like that of New England'. For we must consider that we shall be as a city upon a hill. The eyes of all people are upon us.[11]

Winthrop and his fellow saints were uniquely placed to make this dream come true because, unlike all the other colonies on the English Atlantic, Massachusetts was neither owned by a handful of well-connected proprietors nor controlled from London by a board of stockholders. The fact that it was self-governing may have appealed to Thomas and Martha. That it fitted with the kind of Puritanism which was practised by both the Coytmores and the Rainborowes mattered more.

But what mattered most of all was the presence in Massachusetts of members of their extended clan of relations. They were accompanied on their voyage by Martha's widowed sixty-one-year-old mother-in-law Katherine Coytmore. Parnell, one of Katherine's

daughters from a previous marriage, was already settled at
Charlestown, Massachusetts, having married one of the colony's
most prominent citizens, Increase Nowell, and coming over with
him in 1630. Increase was a magistrate, an elected member of the
Court of Assistants who governed the company, and a moving
force in the Charlestown church. In May 1636 he became secretary of the colony, a post he held until 1650. He also had some
knowledge of ships, it seems: in 1629 the minister of Salem, Francis
Higginson, advised friends in England who were thinking of
coming over that 'if any be of the mind to buy a ship my cousin
Nowell's counsel would be good'.[12]

Even more expert in maritime matters was another of Katherine
Coytmore's sons-in-law, Thomas Graves, a Wapping sea-captain
and neighbour of the Rainborowes who regularly crossed the Atlantic
bringing colonists and supplies to Massachusetts. In the same letter
of advice, Higginson included 'one Mr Graves the master's mate
dwelling in Wapping [who] may herein stand you in stead'. In June
1635 John Winthrop noted in his journal that Graves, who arrived
in Boston Bay with a cargo of cattle and passengers, 'had come
every year for these seven years'.[13]

By now it will come as no surprise to find that Graves was
also related to the Rainborowes and the Bournes: his father John,
a shipbuilder with a yard in Limehouse, married Susan Hoxton,
who was Martha's aunt and whose nephew, John Hoxton, was
married to Nehemiah Bourne's sister. This may be the moment
to consult the family tree.

In 1638 Graves and his wife joined Increase and Parnell and
Thomas and Martha and settled in Charlestown. So did Thomas
Coytmore's full sister Elizabeth and her husband, William Tyng;
and Nehemiah Bourne and his wife Hannah. A year later, Martha's
own half-brother, William Rainborowe, arrived. The street where
Martha and her husband and mother-in-law settled in Charlestown
was called Wapping Street; the wharf beyond it was called Wapping
Dock. If the environment they lived in was alien, the community
was comfortable and familiar.

When they moved to Massachusetts, Thomas Coytmore already
knew the place from his commercial activities, plying back and
forth between old and New England: in March 1634, for example,
he replaced Thomas Graves as master of the *Elizabeth Bonadventure*

when she sailed for New England with passengers and a mixed cargo including wheat, malt, parcels of clothing and one ton of iron pots. He knew from personal experience the opportunities that were available to an entrepreneurial ship's captain in Massachusetts, and Martha knew of them not only from her husband but also from brother-in-law Graves, from letters home written by Parnell, from stories told at St John's and in the stalls and streets of Wapping. By its nature, their neighbourhood looked outward, beyond the City of London, beyond England. The men of Wapping made their fortunes and lost their lives all over the known world, from the East Indies to the West Indies. They saw sights that most English men and women could hardly imagine: the camel trains of Aleppo, five miles long and laden with silks and spices, appearing out of the desert like wraiths; the shimmering waters of the fabulous Blue Caves of Zante and the minarets of the Ottoman sultan's palace at Istanbul; mountains so high that their peaks were lost in the heavens, and seas so deep they reached down to hell.

So Thomas Coytmore was better prepared than, say, a Puritan lawyer from Suffolk or a dissident minister from the Midlands. And Martha was too, if the stories of ocean voyages that had been part of her life for ever could prepare her to make one of her own. But the mechanics of migration were still daunting. What should they take to New England? How much would it cost? How were they going to live when they got there?

The cost of passage varied from ship to ship, but it remained pretty close to the rates which were set out by the Massachusetts Bay Company in 1629: £5 a head, and £4 a ton for goods. (The ton referred to here is the space occupied by a tun cask of wine, the unit used in measuring the carrying capacity of a vessel.) There was a sliding scale for children according to age: under-twelves travelled for £3 6s. 8d., under-eights for £2 10s. and under-fours for £1 13s. 4d. 'Suckling children not to be reckoned.'[14]

It was vital to go prepared. In the first years of the colony, prospective settlers were constantly being reminded to bring foodstuffs, tools, everything they might need to sustain life, in fact. 'For when you are once parted with England,' warned Francis Higginson, 'you shall meet neither with taverns nor alehouses, nor butchers, nor grocers, nor apothecaries' shops to help what things you need

. . . nor when you come to land here are yet neither markets nor fairs to buy what you want.'[15] Migrants were advised to bring meal for bread, malt for brewing beer, shoe leather, linen and woollen goods, glass for windows and locks for doors.

The situation was easing by the time the Coytmores went over. A Thursday market was established in Boston in 1634, and the town boasted at least one shop, run by the Devon merchant John Coggan; and a tavern. Its owner, Samuel Cole, is described at different times as an inn-holder, a confectioner and a comfitmaker, all of which titles imply that life's little luxuries were making their appearance in New England.

Everything came through Boston, the gateway to the colony, the point of entry not only for settlers but also for goods from home. Each spring men would start to gather in the town from all over Massachusetts, waiting for the arrival of the first of the year's ships; and as soon as a sail was sighted there was a mad rush to buy on the quay, or even on deck before the vessel had come into harbour. Periodic attempts were made to regulate these quayside auctions, which forced up prices and brought the life of the community to a standstill; in 1635 the General Court, which governed the colony, appointed a merchant from each township to buy for all, and to sell at no more than 5 per cent profit. The law was repealed four months later, partly because the designated merchants didn't have enough ready money to buy in such large quantities, and partly because English sailors, who customarily brought over goods of their own to sell, circumvented the system by bringing those goods ashore and making private sales.

Chaotic quayside auctions were still part of life in the Bay when the Coytmores arrived, but their importance was diminishing as merchants like John Coggan established networks of their own, obtaining supplies directly from contacts back home and selling them on to shopkeepers in other townships. Soon, anything from gold buttons to a bag of nails was available, and if little enough in the way of manufactured goods was produced in the colony itself, merchants were able to function quite happily by combining the export of beaver and timber with the credit they could obtain from friends on the other side of the Atlantic.

All the same, prices were high in New England, and it made sense for the Coytmores to take over as much as they could.

William Wood, in *New Englands prospect*, a promotional tract of 1634, gave the prospective migrant clear advice: take as much as you can of meal, malt, beef, butter, cheese, good wines, vinegar, strong waters – 'whosever transports more of these than he himself useth, his over-plus being sold will yield as much profit as any other stable commodity'.[16] Woollens and linens were in demand, everything from blue calico and sailcloth to fine green serge 'for housewives' aprons'. Advising settlers to carry hats, boots, shoes and stockings, Wood warmed to his theme, urging them to take over items which combined utility with resale value:

> All kinds of grocery wares, as sugar, prunes, raisins, currants, honey, nutmegs, cloves, &c. Soap, candles, and lamps, &c. All manner of household stuff is very good trade there, as pewter and brass; but great iron pots be preferred before brass, for the use of that country. Warming pans and stewing pans be of necessary use, and good traffic there. All manner of ironwares, as all manner of nails for houses, and all manner of spikes for building of boats, ships, and fishing stages: all manner of tools for workmen, hoes for planters, broad and narrow for setting and weeding; with axes both broad and pitching-axes.[17]

Fish-hooks and nets, saws and drills and wedges, guns and powder: his list goes on. But the theme remains the same. Glass will be easy to sell, and iron goods. 'Sea coal, iron, lead, and millstones, flints, ordnances [i.e. cannon], and whatsoever a man can conceive is good for the country, that will lie as ballast, he cannot be a loser by it.'[18]

Coal? Millstones? Lead? William Wood didn't envisage that migrants to Massachusetts would be travelling light. But he wasn't alone, to judge from the modest request that John Winthrop sent over to Thomas Graves in London in the summer of 1634: 'Mr Graves, I pray bring me a pair of mill stones, peak stones [i.e. grit-stones from the Peak District of Derbyshire] seven foot broad and of thickness answerable. They are for a windmill.'[19] And although Winthrop didn't say it, they probably weighed around five tons each. In a postscript, he also mentioned that one of his fellow magistrates would like 'six chalder of sea coal'. A chalder or chaldron of coal weighed nearly one and a half tons.

Some writers offered very specific advice. A checklist from 1630, *A Proportion of Provisions Needfull for Such as Intend to Plant themselves in New England, for one whole year*, itemised everything the new colonist was likely to need and gave it a price: six pairs of shoes, 16s., for example; two hatchets, 2s. 8d.; one mackerel line and twelve hooks, 10d.; and so on. Its author reckoned a year's provisions would cost £17 7s. 9d., plus freight charges, of which £7 11s. 8d. was accounted for by foodstuffs. He helpfully marked the items which 'the poorer sort' could manage without – malt, since 'they can content themselves with water in the heat of summer', salt, handkerchiefs, boots.[20]

Given the mercantile milieu in which both Martha and Thomas moved, it is easier to imagine them investing in glass and mill-stones for resale in the New World than skimping on salt and handkerchiefs. As we saw earlier, Martha's father William left £1,000 each to his two unmarried daughters, Judith and Joan, and only £700 to her as the eldest daughter. This probably reflects the fact that he had already paid out for her dowry, but it just may be because he had advanced the capital for the young couple – she was nineteen, her husband was twenty-four – to invest for their voyage. It would also have been normal practice for William Rainborowe to ship manufactured commodities of his own over with them, a private venture with Thomas Coytmore sending back the profits on a later ship in the shape of goods or bills of exchange.

Having made the decision to emigrate, Thomas couldn't simply take Martha by the hand and board the next ship for New England, even if his father-in-law was a prominent figure in naval circles and half his friends and family owned their own ships. Controls on citizens leaving the kingdom – particularly if they were leaving to go to Massachusetts – were on the increase. In February 1634, after Archbishop Laud was informed that two ships were preparing to set sail from Ipswich in Suffolk, each carrying 120 passengers who were either in debt or discontented with Anglicanism, the government took steps to delay the depar-ture of the Atlantic fleet that month, enforcing an existing require-ment that all passengers had to take the oath of allegiance, which acknowledged Charles I as 'lawful king of this realm, and of all other His Majesty's dominions and countries'.[21] They had also to take the oath of supremacy, which acknowledged Charles as head of the Anglican Church; and the masters of every vessel had to promise to hold daily services during the crossing, using the Book of Common Prayer; 'and that they cause all persons on board these said ships to be present at the same'.[22]

The regulations were tightened in 1635, when in addition to enforcing the oaths, the government made it compulsory for anyone wishing to emigrate to obtain a testimonial from their local minister as to their orthodoxy in religious matters, and a certificate from a justice of the peace confirming their financial solvency.

So Martha and Thomas needed a certificate, either from Rev. Sedgwick at St John's or from another local minister. They needed another certificate from their local justice. And both documents had to be shown to customs searchers who came aboard their ship and went through the passenger list, checking everyone's paperwork. Richard Mather, who sailed for New England from Bristol in the spring of 1635, described the process in his journal:

> This day there came aboard the ship two of the searchers, and viewed a list of all our names, ministered the oath of allegiance to all at full age, viewed our certificates from the ministers in the parishes from whence we came, approved well thereof, and gave us tickets, that is, licences under their hands and seals to pass the seas, and cleared the ship, and so departed.[23]

There was usually a fee. The searchers at Gravesend, for example, charged sixpence apiece to issue the clearance licences.

It remained for the Coytmores to gather their possessions and buy supplies for the voyage itself. The price of passage included food and drink for the voyage – as long as you were happy to live for six or eight weeks on a diet of salt beef, pork, salt fish, butter, cheese, dried peas, soup, gruel, biscuits and beer. Most passengers chose to supplement this with a few luxuries: lemons to guard against scurvy, prunes, sugar, meat pies, eggs and bacon, perhaps even live poultry and sheep to slaughter aboard ship. Olive oil was reckoned to be good for seasickness, as were hot spiced claret, conserve of wormwood and pills containing powdered cinnamon, ginger and musk.

Most of the seafarers' goods were packed in casks and chests
and stowed in the hold, along with all those millstones and baskets
of sea coal. William Wood advised migrants to keep out small
skillets and frying pans 'to dress their victuals in at sea';[24] and
suggested they bring their own bedding, and suitable clothing:
'the oldest clothes be the fittest, with a long coarse coat, to keep
better things from the pitched ropes and planks'.[25]

For most migrants to New England, the ocean was an alien
environment, more frightening in its power and its vastness than
the unknown lands on its far shores. 'The waters compassed me
about, *even* to the soul', said Jonah; 'the depth closed me round
about, and the weeds were wrapped about my head.'[26] The godly
might put their trust in the Lord, but it was a devout man or
woman indeed who felt no qualms at all at the prospect of consigning
themselves not only to God, but also to a captain they didn't know
who was prepared to cram a hundred or more passengers with all
their worldly goods, a crew of forty or more and all manner of
commodities, including five-ton millstones, into a vessel perhaps
thirty feet wide and a hundred feet from stem to sternpost.

Martha Coytmore was better prepared than most. Even though
she had never experienced an ocean voyage herself, her father had
been going to sea since before she was born. Her husband was a
mariner, like his father before him. Her eldest half-brother was
a Levant trader, plying back and forth between England and the
eastern Mediterranean. In fact all the men in Martha's life – friends,
neighbours, relations – had either sailed the oceans or built the
ships that took men across the world. There was no shortage of
advice on what to take, what to wear, how to combat seasickness.
No need for her to pore over the printed checklists and pamphlets
which aimed to help pioneers to avoid the more obvious pitfalls
of transatlantic travel. Even so, there was the anxiety of uprooting
and separating from family and familiar surroundings. And the voyage
itself must have been a daunting prospect, bringing to mind tales
of tempests and shipwrecks, of enchanted islands and sea monsters.

7

Safe Towards Canaan

*L*ike so many of those who left England in the Great Migration of the 1630s, the names of Martha and her husband appear in none of the surviving passenger lists. Thomas's inclusion on a 1636 list of Charlestown inhabitants, and a grant of cow commons to him in the summer of the following year, are the first indications of their arrival in the brave new world which was to be their home for the rest of their lives.

But it is possible to reconstruct the pattern which their voyage took. By the mid-1630s transatlantic travel was big business (the reason, no doubt, why so many Wapping shipmasters were involved in the trade). In 1635, for example, a year for which a particularly good set of passenger lists exists, fifteen London ships sailed for New England with settlers aboard, while nearly forty more went for Virginia and Barbados, St Christopher, Providence Island and the Somers Isles. And that's not counting the ships that went from Bristol and Ipswich and the south-coast ports.

Thomas and Martha's possessions might well be put aboard below London Bridge, but the passengers themselves usually gathered to embark twenty miles downriver at Gravesend or, for those who were determined to keep their time aboard ship to the absolute minimum, at Portsmouth or Southampton or the Isle of Wight. Once they reached their embarkation point, it was a question of waiting: waiting for the searchers to clear the ship, waiting for other passengers and cargo to arrive and, most crucially, waiting for a fair wind and the right tide.

Passengers didn't dare to move too far from the harbour, because the master of their ship might decide to weigh anchor at very short notice. Henry Winthrop, John Winthrop's son, missed the *Arbella* in 1630 because he wasn't paying attention to the guns which signalled its departure. Nearly eighty years later Rev. John Barnard made a badly timed excursion to the Isle of Wight while he was waiting for his ship to depart from Portsmouth. As a result he missed hearing the signal guns for sailing being fired. 'What should we do now?' he recalled later. 'Our clothes and effects were all on board ship, the wind fair and strong, the fleet under sail, and no boat to carry us to them.'[1] He ended up commandeering the Isle of Wight ferry in a mad dash through heavy seas to catch up with his ship as it reached the open sea.

Even setting sail was no guarantee that a voyage had really begun. Having waited in Bristol for a month and a day for his ship to be made ready, Richard Mather went aboard the *James* on 23 May 1635, where he was forced to wait for another twelve days for a fair wind. The *James* finally sailed for New England on 4 June; eight days later she had gone no further than Milford Haven, just a hundred miles away on the west coast of Wales, where she stayed for another twelve days while the strong westerly winds turned. Mather arrived in Boston on Monday 17 August – 116 days after arriving in Bristol ready to board the *James*.

Ships bound for New England often aimed to sail in April or May, to reach their destination in early summer; colonists would be able to establish themselves and settle in before the fierce Massachusetts winters hit them. Journey times varied wildly. In 1635 Thomas Graves sailed into Boston harbour five weeks and three days after leaving Southampton. The following year John Winthrop recorded the arrival at Boston of a London ship full of men, women and children which had been at sea for a full eighteen weeks, 'their beer all spent and leaking out a month before their arrival, so as they were forced to [drink] stinking water (and that very little) mixed with sack or vinegar, and their other provisions very short and bad'.[2]

There was no such thing as a typical crossing. But if there were, the experience of John Josselyn is perhaps as typical as it gets. Josselyn, who published an account of his 1638 voyage, sailed for New England with his father aboard the 300-ton *Nicholas*. She carried twenty guns, forty-eight crew and 164 aspiring colonists. The merchant who organised the voyage was Edward Tyng, whose brother was married to one of Thomas Coytmore's sisters. The English maritime world really *was* small in the seventeenth century.

The *Nicholas* moved out into the Thames estuary at six o'clock on the evening of Thursday 26 April 1638, and over the next nine days made its way slowly round the coast towards the Isle of Wight. In the process she picked up one of the master's mates at Dover, sending the skiff ashore for him; and lost two crewmen to a press gang which came aboard in the Downs. By 8 May they were out of sight of land and in an alien environment. 'Two mighty whales we now saw', wrote Josselyn, 'the one spouted water through two great holes in her head into the air a great height.'[3] These spouts were so huge they would sink the ship or suck her down to the bottom of the ocean – or so the sailors told Josselyn, a gullible chap. They were also coping with more tangible threats – disease and indiscipline and damage to the ship. The disease was smallpox, the scourge of long-distance sea travel: one of the passengers came down with it when the *Nicholas* was only a few days out. He died nine days later, and 'we buried [him] in the sea, tying a bullet (as the manner is) to his neck, and another to his legs, [and] turned him out at a port-hole, giving fire to a great gun'.[4] Minor offences were met with savage penalties: a servant got drunk on his master's brandy and was ducked at the yardarm for it; another was whipped naked at the capstan for stealing lemons out of the surgeon's cabin.

When the *Nicholas* was well out into the Atlantic, the mainmast was found to be twisted and split; so was the fore-topmast. Both had to be bound tightly with rope to keep them intact. By the middle of May many of the passengers were sick with smallpox or fever. In mid-June, as they neared the Newfoundland Banks in heavy fog and temperatures as cold as January back home, they saw an iceberg looming out of the mist, 'an island of ice . . . three leagues in length, mountain high, in form of land, with bays and capes like high-cliffed land, and a river pouring off it into the sea'.[5] They were close enough to see 'two or three foxes, or devils skipping upon it' before they were safely past.[6]

It is tempting to picture every ship that sailed to Massachusetts during the Great Migration being full to the gunwhales with the godly, with messianic ministers preaching stern salvation from the quarterdeck to a kneeling assembly of saints. But by no means everyone who set out for New England was eager to build that city upon a hill: even the *Mayflower* carried several dozen 'strangers' alongside the Leiden Pilgrims, men and women who did not share the Pilgrims' religious enthusiasms. John Josselyn was an Anglican: he noted with wry amusement how when passengers and crew cast their hooks for cod off the Newfoundland Banks one Sunday morning, 'the sectaries aboard threw those their servants took into the sea again, although they wanted fresh victuals'.[7] Aspiring colonists are best viewed as occupying different points on a spectrum of religious belief, with hierarchically established institutions at one end – Anglicans and Catholics, primarily – and extremist separatists at the other. According to this model, the non-separating congregationalists who dominated the governance structures of the Massachusetts Bay Colony in the 1630s would themselves occupy more than a single point on the spectrum, with some being a great deal more non-separating than others.

Yet even among the less-committed Protestants who went over in the 1630s, the presence on board ship of a devout minister must have had an impact. Although the master of the ship was supposed to ensure that daily prayers were held, using only the Book of Common Prayer, there was no way the authorities could enforce the rule; and Puritan preachers tended to take charge of the spiritual side of the voyage without being asked. Richard Mather and his fellow minister Daniel Maud took it in turns to lead prayers every day aboard the *James*, and both preached on Sundays, one in the morning and the other in the afternoon. The sight of these godly men worshipping day after day without the paraphernalia of the Anglican liturgy prefigured the forms of worship which passengers would encounter in America, even if they hadn't been familiar with them in England; and when Mather or Maud led them in prayer and called on God to save them as the *James* was being tossed around the ocean in a storm or drifting in heavy fog or lying becalmed a thousand miles from nowhere, and they were indeed saved, it didn't take much for frightened, disoriented men and women to look into their hearts and find God's purpose there.[8]

But not everyone. Having survived icebergs and storms, John Josselyn arrived in Massachusetts Bay still hanging on resolutely to his Anglicanism, two months and one week after leaving Gravesend. He was unimpressed with Boston, calling it 'rather a village, than a town, there being not above twenty or thirty houses'.[9]

The Coytmores' new home lay a short ferry ride across the Charles river. Now little more than a suburb of Boston, Charlestown predates its more eminent neighbour by several years (as its inhabitants have been pointing out for nearly four centuries). In 1628 a group of men from Salem, twelve miles to the north-east, were exploring the area when they found a neck of land on the north bank of the Charles river, bounded on the east by the Mystic river. There was a good natural harbour and Wonohaquaham, the leader of the small population of native Wampanoag, was friendly.

The Salem men were not the first Europeans to settle at Mishawaum, as the Wampanoag called it. When they arrived they found a thatched cottage, occupied by an illiterate smith, Thomas Walford, and his family. To this day no one is altogether sure how he got there; but there were others like him scattered around the Bay, refugees from the world, leading hard, unfamiliar lives among the Wampanoag. Across the Charles river in Shawmut was the cottage of William Blackstone, a Cambridge-educated minister who had left England years earlier 'because I did not like the Lord Bishops'.[10] Out in the Bay on Noddle's Island was the fortified homestead of Devon-born Samuel Maverick, a committed Anglican who made a living trading in timber and furs.

The records of Charlestown's early development are muddled and fragmentary. Its English name, given by the Salem settlers, derives from its position at the mouth of the Charles river, which had been named in honour of Charles, then Prince of Wales and now King Charles I, back in 1614. An historical narrative of its origins written in the 1660s states that in 1629 the Salem group

appointed an engineer called Thomas Graves (no relation to the
Wapping sea-captain and Coytmore relation of the same name)
to 'model and lay out the form of the town, with streets about
the Hill'. Graves built a 'great house' and according to this
narrative, laid out and fenced a crescent street of two-acre lots
on which the Salem men built their homes.[11] Roger Clap, who
saw Charlestown in May 1630, told a rather different story. He
remembered finding only 'some wigwams and one house', in
which was a man, presumably the smith Thomas Walford, who
offered his visitors a boiled bass to eat.[12] There were no other
Englishmen to be seen.

Perhaps it just took rather a long time to lay out and build
the town, in which case it was still in its early stages when close
to 700 men, women and children from the Winthrop Fleet
descended on it in the summer of 1630. They intended only a
temporary stay while Governor John Winthrop and his deputy,
Thomas Dudley, argued over the best location for their city upon
a hill.

But the long journey, the scarcity of supplies and the humid
Massachusetts summer took their toll on the new settlers. There
were outbreaks of dysentery and scurvy; 'almost in every family
lamentation, mourning, and woe was heard, and no fresh food
to be had to cherish them'.[13] There were rumours that the French
were planning to attack the settlement. When the ships that had
brought them left on their return journey to England, upwards
of a hundred colonists gave up and went home.

The remainder scattered, deciding their best chance for survival
was to disperse. Winthrop took some across to Shawmut on the
south bank of the Charles river, to a site they had christened
'Trimountain' on account of the three peaks which dominated
the marshy peninsula. In September they rechristened it 'Boston'.
Others moved up the Mystic and the Charles, until by the end
of that month there were six encampments in the Bay: Boston,
Watertown, Roxbury, Medford, Saugus – and Charlestown, where
the Coytmores' kinsman Increase Nowell and a small group
decided to stay. In November 1632, after the church the settlers
had founded in Charlestown was transferred across the Charles
to Boston, Nowell and some others – nineteen men and sixteen
women in all – received permission to break away and form a

church of their own, which gathered in the great house. The first to sign the covenant at Charlestown church were Increase and Parnell Nowell.

When Thomas and Martha arrived at Charlestown, the town was small by English standards, with around a hundred families. By way of comparison Wapping, which still called itself a hamlet, had thirteen times as many homes. But despite its small size, Charlestown was already a diverse and thriving community. In 1635 Robert Long had bought the great house and turned it into a tavern, while the townsfolk had built themselves another meeting house to the north-west of the town. Richard Sprague and his wife Mary ran a shop in the square selling dry goods, hardware and haberdashery; and a market was held every Friday, also in the square. Thomas Carter was the local blacksmith; Thomas Lynde was the maltster. There were plenty of farmers, of course, but there were also men in the building trades – masons, carpenters, a brickmaker, a glazier. There were coopers, a butcher, a glover, a fuller, a furniture-maker. The town had its own physician, Dr Richard Palgrave, who had been a neighbour of the Rainborowes in East London; and its own barber-surgeon, Abraham Pratt. A ferryman, Edward Converse, charged twopence to take people across the quarter-mile-wide strait that separated Charlestown from Boston.

The little community came from all over England: from the Puritan heartlands of Bedfordshire and East Anglia, from Kent and Dorset and, of course, from London, particularly the neighbourhoods of Stepney, Whitechapel and Wapping that the Coytmores knew so well. Charlestown offered a good natural harbour, 'which hath caused many seamen and merchants to sit down there', noted one citizen in the 1650s.[14] At least four other Wapping mariners settled there, including Thomas Coytmore's brother-in-law, Thomas Graves, who lived across the street with his wife. There was another native of Wapping, too: John Hodges, who found it hard to fit into life in the colony. Hodges already had one conviction for drunkenness when, in March 1639, he was hauled before the magistrates in Boston and fined 'for swearing God's foot, and cursing his servant, wishing a pox of God take you'.[15] This didn't prevent him from earning another conviction for drunken behaviour in September. And another in the following

July. And another the following January. One suspects that if Thomas and Martha had known John Hodges back in Wapping, they would be quite eager not to renew the acquaintance.

Charlestown was burned in 1775 during the Battle of Bunker Hill (named for George Bunker, whose land stretched across the top of the hill in the 1630s). Scarcely a trace of the seventeenth-century townscape survives today, except for the post-holes from the 1629 great house and the foundations of the tavern which succeeded it, both of which were discovered in the 1990s and preserved as the centrepiece of City Square Park. Standing on the site today, surrounded by a sea of intersections and freeways, with the criss-cross cables of the ten-lane Zakim Bridge snaking across the sky, it is all but impossible to see that first Charlestown, a huddle of houses grouped in an oval which encircled the slopes of Town Hill. The great house stood in the marketplace to the south of the hill. Thomas and Katherine Graves lived opposite, on Crooked Lane, which wound round the western slopes; their house backed on to the wharves of the Charles river. Increase and Parnell Nowell's house was on the eastern side of the hill, on a road called simply 'the highway' or 'the street way'. And across the street way from the Nowells were the Coytmores, their two-acre plot defined by the Charlestown Book of Possessions as 'butting to the south-east upon Wapping Dock . . . [and] bounded on the south-west by Wapping Street'.[16]

Dugouts and wigwams and other shelters put up by new settlers on their arrival were always intended as temporary dwellings, to be replaced by something sturdier, something more English, as soon as weather, money and the supply of skills and materials would allow. Edward Johnson, who lived on Crooked Lane in the 1630s, wrote a little later in the century of how 'the Lord hath been pleased to turn all the wigwams, huts, and hovels the English dwelt in at their first coming, into orderly, fair, and well-built houses, well furnished many of them, together with orchards filled with goodly fruit trees, and gardens with variety of flowers'.[17] Charlestown's marketplace was 'comely and fair', he said, its two streets were 'orderly built with some very fair houses, beautified with pleasant gardens and orchards'.[18]

Oak-framed and sturdy, some of these houses were still quite humble, consisting of a single multi-purpose 'hall' perhaps sixteen feet by eighteen, with a sleeping platform or chamber above, reached by a narrow stair or even, in the poorest homes, a ladder. More common was the two-room groundplan, in which a central entrance led to a hall on one side and a parlour on the other; two or more chambers above them were reached by a staircase that led off the entrance porch. A development of this arrangement involved the addition of a single-storey lean-to at the back of the house, containing a kitchen, a dairy or pantry and a spare chamber which could be used for sleeping or storage or both. Roofs were steep-pitched and covered with thatch or wood shingles; walls were clapboard; windows were small and sometimes unglazed, due to the high cost of glass and the difficulties of importing it from England – oiled paper or wooden shutters were used instead.

The defining feature of these early New England houses was a massive central chimneystack, perhaps ten feet by twelve, which served four fireplaces, two on each floor – or five, if there was a lean-to kitchen. The largest heated the hall, which was the main living area, with the parlour reserved for special occasions and important visitors. The floor was of plain oak boards, and the furniture – home-grown pine, maple or oak, which was often painted, even the oak – might consist of a table and un-upholstered stools and benches. Thomas and Martha's home, however, was furnished with a number of luxury items, imported from Europe or farther afield. We know from an inventory of 1647 that they owned a dozen leather chairs and a single wicker chair, and chests and trunks of spruce, cypress and sealskin. As well as pewter, they had some silver and a set of china plates and saucers. One of the two feather beds in their house – they also owned two trundle beds which were kept underneath the standing beds and a 'hamacho', a hammock – was hung with striped silk curtains and covered with a red and green silk quilt. This, the best bed, was presumably their own. Their fire furniture was brass, their tableware was linen and damask. They owned books which the inventorists valued at £7 8s. 8d. while infuriatingly neglecting to mention their titles. And Martha's possessions included '1 silver girdle & silk jacket' – a startling reminder, if a reminder were needed, that not every Puritan in New England wore black.[19]

8

Better Thou Belong

*S*trangers in a strange land, Thomas and Martha made use of their family connections and, instead of building from scratch, they moved straight into the house on Wapping Street, having bought it along with the two-acre plot on which it stood from Thomas James, who also sold them five acres of woodland on the banks of the Mystic river.

Too much can be made of the virtues of the extended family living under the same roof. Katherine Coytmore didn't live with her son and daughter-in-law: wisely, she bought a house of her own and seven acres in the high field, to the north-west of Town Hill, together with five acres of meadow in Mystic marshes, from a trader and Charlestown merchant who had come over in 1629.

Thomas James had been the minister of Charlestown since the church separated from Boston in 1632; and his departure provided Thomas and Martha with an introduction to the realpolitik of religious life in New England, where Puritan preachers may have been safe from interfering bishops, but not from interfering congregations. James was 'a very melancholic man, and full of causeless jealousies', according to John Winthrop.[1] By early 1634 his attitude was proving so difficult that Increase Nowell and some of the other members of the church began to ask quite loudly if they might not be better off rejoining the Boston congregation, where the preaching of pastor John Wilson and teacher John Cotton was drawing worshippers from all over the colony. The other churches sent elders to arbitrate and it was agreed in March 1636 that Rev. James and any followers should be allowed to leave Charlestown; but that if he refused to go of his own free will, then as John Winthrop put it, 'the church should cast him out'.[2]

The bitterness between Nowell and Thomas James was gone, if not forgotten, by the time Thomas and Martha arrived in Charlestown. James was gone too, taking his melancholic disposition and his causeless jealousies with him; which is how they came to move into his house. But they landed right in the middle of a religious controversy which dwarfed the petty squabbles between Nowell and James, and almost tore apart the entire colony – even though, as Cotton Mather said sixty years later, 'multitudes of persons, who took in with both parties did never to their dying hour understand what their difference was'.[3]

It revolved around Anne Hutchinson, a devout and godly woman with an enormous family who came to Boston from Lincolnshire in 1634 with her husband William and quickly became a prominent if challenging member of the Boston church. Anne's piety was unquestionable. So was her intellect. And so, more ominously, was her refusal to defer to authority. Soon after arriving in the colony she started to hold private religious meetings in her Boston home, encouraged by Henry Vane, a twenty-two-year-old diplomat's son whose dissatisfaction with Anglicanism led him to come over in October 1635, and whose social status and social skills brought him the governorship of the colony just seven months later; and by Anne's brother-in-law John Wheelwright, a minister who, like Anne herself, encouraged those seeking assurance of salvation to find it through a charismatic experience of the Holy Spirit.

Anne taught that salvation came through God's grace alone, and not through works. Innocent enough, one might think: but the leaders in the Bay realised the implications of Anne's ideas. A covenant of grace meant there was no point in doing good works: you were already saved, and whether or not you obeyed the law or loved your neighbour was irrelevant. This went to the heart of one of the great Puritan dilemmas, inherited from its Calvinist roots: if you were one of the saints not by virtue of anything you did or even of anything you believed, but through the grace of God, unmerited and unearned and preordained, then your spiritual journey involved recognising this fact, rather than doing anything or behaving in any way which could lead you to salvation. And nothing you could do or say would alter your destiny.

Most of the colony's ministers recognised that salvation was not about external things, and realised the need to guard against too great an emphasis on externals like good behaviour and a reformed liturgy. But ironically enough, considering their history of dissent, they also understood the need for conformity and for a strict adherence to the law. In March 1636 the General Court tried to put a stop to the establishment of new congregations without prior permission, declaring that

> this Court doth not, nor will hereafter, approve of any such companies of men as shall henceforth join in any pretended way of church fellowship, without they shall first acquaint the magistrates, & the elders of the greater part of the churches in this jurisdiction, with their intentions, & have their approbation herein.[4]

While the settlers of the Massachusetts Bay Colony defined themselves by their relationships with God and with their homeland, history has tended to define them rather differently – by their relationship with the Native American tribes whom they ultimately displaced. Perspectives on that relationship have ranged from the arrogant to the sentimental, from cold callousness to fluffy warm foolishness. The white supremacism of the nineteenth century is eloquently expressed by the Connecticut historian and philosopher John Fiske who, writing in the 1880s, justified the Puritans' slaughter of 700 Pequot men, women and children in a single night in 1637 by explaining 'the world is so made that it is only in that way that the higher races have been able to preserve themselves and carry on their progressive work'.[5] Since the appearance in 1975 of Francis Jennings' iconic and iconoclastic masterpiece, *The Invasion of America: Indians, Colonialism and the Cant of Conquest*, that kind of racist imperialism has been consigned to the dustbin of history, although the odd diehard lifts the lid and tries to climb back out every once in a while. But following Jennings' revisionist critique, which recast the Puritans of New England not as a 'higher race' come to civilise the savage, but as calculating and exploitative, the pendulum has swung so far in the direction of the Rousseauesque Noble Savage, at one with nature and in touch with the earth, that criticising any aspect of Native American culture is tantamount to heresy.

The fact is that while bad things were undoubtedly done to the Narragansett, the Pequot, the Mohegan, and the other groupings of the American north-east, they did some rather horrible things to each other as well. And to Europeans. They tortured captives as a matter of routine, dismembering them while they were still alive, roasting them over fires. It is also true that the first settlers, while unthinkingly imposing their own imported cultural values and, more subtly, defining the interaction between native and settler in terms of those values, nevertheless did their best, most of them, to behave decently. The capacity of each side to misunderstand the behaviour of the other was of course enormous – and even to talk of two sides is to muddy the waters, since at different times Massachusetts, like its neighbours Plymouth and Connecticut, forged alliances with one tribe in order to exclude or subdue another, as did the Native Americans themselves.

The Pequot War which erupted soon after Thomas and Martha arrived in the colony was the first serious conflict between natives and Europeans in New England. It had its roots in a series of tit-for-tat killings which began in 1633, when the Pequot murdered some Narragansett who were on their way to trade at a Dutch post in present-day Hartford, Connecticut. This violated a treaty with the Dutch, which stipulated that all Native Americans, no matter what their tribal affiliation, should be allowed to come to their trading post; and the Dutch retaliated by kidnapping and killing the Pequots' *sachem* or chief. In return, the Pequot killed an English trader, John Stone, while his ship lay at anchor on the Connecticut river, later saying they had thought he was Dutch.

(Stone, an unpleasant man with a reputation for drunkenness, violence and even cannibalism, had taken two Pequot captive, and it seems likely that the primary reason for attacking him was to release his prisoners.) They offered restitution to the Massachusetts Bay Colony, but refused to hand over the men who had killed Stone, offering wampum (the shell beads used as currency) to Boston instead – an act which they believed atoned for the murder. The colonists disagreed, remaining suspicious of the Pequots; and when several Englishmen were killed on Long Island, they disregarded the advice of a trader who told them another tribe was responsible and accused the Pequots of being involved. In 1636 the mutilated body of a second English trader, John Oldham, was found in his ship on the coast of Block Island; the Block Islanders weren't Pequot, but the colonists believed that the Pequot were sheltering them and what a recent historian has called 'conglomerations of error-reactive gestures of revenge' turned into a war.[6]

It was won by the English in a series of ruthless raids on Pequot settlements. Huts were burned, women and children were burned with them, or shot, or taken captive and enslaved. The Pequot leader, Sassacus, fled to what he hoped was the safety of Mohawk territory; the Mohawks, mindful of English force of arms and recent English tactics, decided it would be impolitic to offend them. So they cut off the old man's head and sent it to Hartford as a token of good faith. 'Thus did the Lord scatter his enemies with his strong arm!' exulted one of the English combatants.[7]

The Pequot War was a resounding victory for the English at a surprisingly low cost. There were just three English fatalities, although some of their Narragansett and Mohegan allies were hurt by friendly fire, 'because they had not some mark to distinguish them from the Pequots'.[8] Against that, their enemies were indeed scattered, while neutral tribes were reluctant to offend them and friendly tribes became a lot friendlier, sending in the heads and hands of Pequot captives as tokens of their good faith. At the end of August 1637, John Winthrop recorded that 'the Narragansetts sent us the hands of three Pequots – one the chief of those who murdered Captain Stone'.[9] (What did they *do* with all these body parts, one wonders?) Fifty women and children were sent back to Boston. Israel Stoughton, one of the leaders of the English expedition, asked

Governor Winthrop to reserve one for him, 'the fairest and largest that I saw amongst them, to whom I have given a coat to clothe her'.[10]

So to say Thomas and Martha Coytmore's first year in New England involved some readjustment is putting it mildly. One half of the promised land was in dispute with the other over a theological point so abstruse that most people weren't sure what they were arguing about. The Coytmores' Charlestown neighbours were at loggerheads over the same half-comprehended thing. The entire territory was awash with terrible stories of killing and retribution, and Native Americans walked the streets of Boston carrying body parts removed from their enemies. This wasn't Canaan. This wasn't milk and honey. It wasn't Wapping, either.

And still the infighting continued, in a religious controversy grown so bitter that it made Archbishop Laud's drive for uniformity of worship seem like a child's game. On 30 August 1637 a synod of the colony's ministers met at Newtown to condemn eighty points of doctrine which were held by Hutchinson, Wheelwright and their followers.

The upshot was that Anne Hutchinson and John Wheelwright were banished from the colony. That winter Wheelwright took 175 men, women and children, largely from the Boston congregation, to what would become the town of Exeter in New Hampshire, which was founded on land bought from the Pennacook. Mrs Hutchinson secured a stay of sentence over the winter on compassionate grounds, but while she was under house arrest in Roxbury she expressed such extreme views that she was brought before the church at Boston in March 1638 and accused of heresy. She recanted some of her opinions but failed to convince her judges of her sincerity. She was, said Thomas Shepard, 'a very dangerous woman to sow her corrupt opinions to the infection of many'.[11] It was left to John Wilson, the Boston pastor whom she had criticised and undermined throughout her four years in Massachusetts, to deliver her sentence:

In the name of our Lord Jesus Christ and in the name of the Church I do not only pronounce you worthy to be cast out, but I do cast you out and in the name of Christ I do deliver you up to Satan, that you may learn no more to blaspheme, to seduce and to lie, and I do account you from this time forth to be a heathen and a publican and so to be held of all the brethren and sisters, of this congregation, and of others. Therefore I command you in the name of Christ Jesus and of this church as a leper to withdraw yourself out of the congregation.[12]

A terrible thing. But not, perhaps, as terrible as the fate that eventually befell Anne Hutchinson. She and her family took themselves off to Rhode Island, where they helped to set up a new colony at Aquidneck. When her husband died and Massachusetts seemed to be on the verge of annexing the colony in 1642, she moved again, to a remote spot on Long Island Sound. In the late summer of 1643 she and five of her children were murdered by an Indian raiding party.

Martha Coytmore's response to the uncertainty and upheavals of her first years in Massachusetts was commitment. Undeterred by the Pequot War and the Hutchinson conflict, by the banishments and the parades of body parts, she was admitted to full communion at Charlestown church on Sunday 3 June 1639.

By now, the colonists' particular brand of non-separating congregationalism, as the practice of remaining technically within the Anglican communion while rejecting most of its tenets has become known, was turning into a distinctly separating form. 'Here is a muttering of a too palpable separation of your people from our church government', an English correspondent had already warned the colony in November 1631; and that palpable separation was encouraged during the 1630s by an influx of militant ministers.[13] Thomas Weld, pastor at Roxbury, had been excommunicated from the Church of England. Thomas Shepard of Newtown had been barred from preaching in a personal interview with William Laud, then Bishop of London, who told him 'I will have no such fellows prate in my diocese'.[14] John Cotton had been in hiding to escape prosecution for nonconformity before he sailed for New England in 1633, convinced that he could 'offer a much clearer and fuller witness in another land than in the wretched and loathsome prisons of London'.[15]

Before he became minister of Salem, Hugh Peter had his licence to preach suspended by the authorities in England and was gaoled twice after he tactlessly prayed for the Catholic queen Henrietta Maria to 'forsake the idolatry and superstition wherein she was and must needs perish if she continued in the same'.[16] His predecessor at Salem was Roger Williams, whose extreme views on church government had proved too much even for Massachusetts, leading to his banishment. Among other things, Williams had caused offence by criticising the Boston church 'because they would not make a public declaration of their repentance for having communion with the Church of England';[17] and rejecting the validity of the Massachusetts Bay Company's charter on the grounds that the King of England had no right to grant Indian land to his own subjects.

Martha's application to join Charlestown church was no mere formality. Candidates could be and were rejected, as the story of Susanna Bell demonstrates. Susanna and her husband arrived in New England a couple of years before Martha and Thomas and applied to join the church at Roxbury. He was admitted; she was not because, having asked her what promise the Lord had made to her, the members were dissatisfied with her response:

> I answered them, 'Jer[emiah] 31:3, "Yea, I have loved thee with an everlasting love, therefore with loving kindness I have drawn thee."' But they told me this was a general promise; that I must look to get some particular promise made home in power upon me, and persuaded me to wait a little longer to see what God would further do for my poor soul.[18]

The rejection affected Susanna deeply. She scoured the colony for spiritual guidance, talking with John Cotton at Boston, listening to sermons by Thomas Shepard at Newtown, reading the Scriptures and praying for proof that she really knew what it was to have grace in her heart, 'to have union with Christ'.[19] When the Roxbury congregation eventually took pity on her, 'seeing me in this sad condition', and invited her to come in and be a member with them, she refused. She still wanted to belong to the church, to feel a part of her new community; but she was no longer sure that Christ was working in her, that she was saved.

Only when she was convinced of that was she able to accept the church's offer of fellowship. 'And soon after I was admitted a babe in Christ among them.'[20]

Perhaps it was this need to be certain about one's spiritual state that delayed some settlers from applying to join their churches as full members, and which no doubt deterred others completely. 'Here', wrote a visitor to the colony in the early 1640s, 'is required such confessions, and professions, both in private and public, both by men and women, before they be admitted, that three parts of the people of the country remain out of the church.'[21] The proportions were an exaggeration, but the arduous nature of the admission procedure was not. Although Martha's mother-in-law Katherine was admitted nine months before her, in September 1638, husband Thomas waited until February 1640. It was common for husbands and wives to join on the same day – Thomas and Katherine Graves were admitted to Charlestown together, in October 1639 – and perhaps Thomas Coytmore's delay was due to doubts on his part or on the part of the church elders. Perhaps he was just away at sea in the summer of 1639 and Martha didn't want to wait. Either way, Martha's decision suggests an independence of mind, a determination.

The more extreme Separatist churches in Europe had practised an exclusionary policy since the end of the sixteenth century, and in the colony's first few years the gathered churches of Boston, Charlestown and the other towns adopted a similar model. Applicants for membership had to demonstrate a sound knowledge of the Scriptures and a relatively blameless personal life. They had also to subscribe to the covenant, a written agreement which varied slightly in its wording from church to church, but which in Charlestown's case ran as follows:

In the Name of our Lord God, and in obedience to his holy will and divine ordinances.

We whose names are here written being by His most wise and good providence brought together, and desirous to unite ourselves into one congregation or church, under our Lord Jesus Christ our Head: In such sort as becometh all those whom He hath redeemed and sanctified unto Himself, do here solemnly and religiously as in His most holy presence, promise and bind ourselves to walk in all our ways according to the rules of the Gospel, and in all sincere conformity to His holy ordinances; and in mutual love and respect each to other: so near as God shall give us grace.[22]

This contract was considered binding. Members of the church who wanted to leave had to ask the congregation for written permission to be released from the covenant; they had, in theory at least, to show these letters of dismission or testimonial to their new church, although in practice the elders of that new church often turned a blind eye. Thomas Weld, the minister at Roxbury, admitted it was 'a constant and usual thing . . . to accept members of other churches upon their desire, without any letters testimonial'.[23]

By the time Martha joined Charlestown church, the nature of the tests for membership had become even more rigorous. Martha had almost certainly been confirmed into the Church of England back in London, having to earn her place by showing an ability to recite the Articles of Faith, the Lord's Prayer and the Ten Commandments, and learning her catechism as set down in the Book of Common Prayer. Now, not only did she have to subscribe to Charlestown's covenant, show that she was acquainted with the principles of the Protestant faith as evinced in the Scriptures, and prove to the satisfaction of the congregation that she led a good life; she and the other candidates for admission also had to show, in John Cotton's words, 'how the Lord hath won them to deny themselves and their own righteousness, and to rely on the righteousness of Christ'.[24] Martha had to stand up in church and provide her listeners with details of her spiritual journey. Of how it had pleased God to work in her to bring her home to Christ.

And she had to convince them, as Susanna Bell's experience demonstrates. It was a daunting task. Minister John Cotton asked that his wife Sarah's confession should be heard by the Boston elders in private, since a public confession was 'not fit for women's modesty'.[25] His request was refused. It was neither surprising nor unusual that Martha waited for several years after arriving in Charlestown before putting herself through the ordeal. Non-members weren't barred from attending church, and the delay gave her time to get to know the Charlestown congregation and to decide for herself how she met their requirements before she committed – an important factor since the people, rather than the priest, held the reins of power in the gathered churches of Massachusetts Bay, a point made by John Winthrop in 1634: 'Our churches are governed by pastors, teachers, ruling elders and deacons, yet the power lies in the whole congregation.'[26] The people had the right of admitting or not admitting new members, the job of evaluating their professions of faith and deciding whether or not they were genuine in claiming the working of Christ within them.

But no matter how long she waited, how much preparation she undertook, it was still a trying experience for Martha to stand before her neighbours and discuss her past, her inadequacy, the moment when she realised that the grace of Jesus saved her in spite of her unworthiness. It could be trying for the audience, too: Rev. Thomas Shepard complained that it wasn't at all appropriate to treat a congregation to 'relations of this odd thing and t' other, nor hear of revelations and groundless joys, nor gather together the heap, and heap up all the particular passages of their lives, wherein they have got any good'. Far better, he said, to be businesslike and succinct: 'Thus I was humbled, then thus I was called, then thus I have walked, though with many weaknesses since . . . and thus the Lord hath delivered me.'[27] Amen to that.

9

Dispersed in Foreign Lands

*I*n 1639 Martha and Thomas Coytmore were joined in New England by Martha's half-brother, William Rainborowe junior.

William makes his first appearance in this story when he and Coytmore join the Military Company of Massachusetts, a by-product of the expeditions against the Pequot. The fretful and controlling John Winthrop thought this was a perilous development, worrying 'how dangerous it might be to erect a standing authority of military men, which might easily in time overthrow the civil power'.[1]

As new members of the Military Company, still in existence today and better known as the Ancient and Honourable Artillery Company of Massachusetts, William and his brother-in-law assembled for drill on the first Monday of every month (unless it was raining). They joined more than one hundred volunteers, dressed in an odd assortment of steel helmets, body armour, buff coats and long cavalry boots (on account of the fact that they often had to march through prickly briars), and weighed down with the other accoutrements of war – heavy musket, forked rests,

bandoliers and shoulder belts, priming horn, match case, ball
pouch and short sword. Every month the Company paraded
through the streets of Boston in scarlet plumes, led by the
Company drummer beating the colours, before crowding first
into the meeting house for prayers and a sermon from Rev. John
Wilson, and then into the adjacent tavern for a good dinner. Only
then did they march off to Boston Common to engage in their
core purpose, described by their charter as 'the advancement of
the military art and exercise of arms'.[2]

William, who was single and in his twenties, lived a little way
out of town. On 26 November 1639, the clerk at Charlestown
noted that 'Mr William Rainsborough pays for the old meeting
house that stands between the town and the neck, £100 to Mr
Increase Nowell and Thomas Lind towards building the new
meeting house, newly built in the town, on the south side of
the Town Hill.'[3] There's a puzzle about this: Charlestown's
original meeting house was the great house put up for the first
colonists and sold to Robert Long in 1635. It sounds as though
the settlers built another meeting house a little way out – the
'neck' in the records refers to the narrow Charlestown Neck to
the north-west which connected the peninsula to the mainland.
Presumably they soon found it unsatisfactory and built another,
their third in a decade, in the centre of town.

Two more members of the Rainborowe clan arrived in the
late 1630s: Nehemiah and Hannah Bourne, who came over in
the summer or autumn of 1638. Nehemiah was a real son of the
Atlantic, forever moving back and forth between the Old World
and the New and never quite finding the peace he sought. His
shipwright father Robert had died in 1625, leaving the fourteen-
year-old a house 'commonly called by the name of the sign of
the Pewter Platter' in Gracechurch Street in the City of London,
along with the unfulfilled injunction that he study at Cambridge
'if God shall fit him with gifts in that behalf'.[4] The Bourne family
shipyard, Bell Dock just off Wapping High Street, was leased to
John Hoxton, the Rainborowes' cousin, who married Nehemiah's
sister; it seems safe to assume that Nehemiah learned his trade
there. And he learned it well: by the time he and Hannah, the
daughter of a Limehouse mariner, were married in Stepney in
January 1630 – he was eighteen or nineteen and she was about

seventeen – he was described as 'of Wapping in Whitechapel shipwright'.[5] Hannah bore him two sons while the couple were living in Wapping; both died young and were buried at St John's by Rev. Sedgwick.

On 6 April 1638, the day that the English government prohibited 'merchants, masters, and owners of ships' from sailing for New England without a licence, Nehemiah applied for a pass to leave for America. It was granted four days later, and soon after that he and Hannah went over. They had a piece of land in Charlestown, and they may have stayed there briefly with the rest of the Wapping clan; but they soon moved on to Dorchester, five miles to the south of Boston, where Nehemiah set up in partnership as a merchant with another Wapping shipwright, Thomas Hawkins, whose landholdings included a farm that stretched down to the water, and was thus ideal as a shipyard.

Nehemiah and Hannah were admitted to full membership of Dorchester church at the beginning of September 1639, and that month he began to prepare for a voyage home. He and Hawkins were co-owners of the fifty-ton *Sparrow*, which they planned to take over to England, bringing back a cargo of goods and emigrants. He arranged for a letter authorising Hannah to receive debts and conduct business while he was away. (He also left her carrying their child, although neither of them would have known it yet – she gave birth to a son, Nehemiah, the following June.) And he paid his respects to Governor Winthrop in Boston, asking him if there were any service he could do for him on the other side of the Atlantic.

There was, as it happened: Winthrop had a live otter which he asked Nehemiah to present to Charles I. Just why the governor thought the king would want an otter, history does not record: there was a plentiful supply in English rivers, but perhaps this was a special otter, a regal otter, an otter fit for a king.

The *Sparrow* sailed in early October, with the special otter kept safe in the hold. Nehemiah made land at Plymouth in Devon about six weeks later, and immediately wrote Winthrop a long letter full of the latest news. Massachusetts was eager to hear news of the war of words between Scotland and England over Charles I's clumsy attempts to force the Book of Common Prayer on Scottish Presbyterians, which had boiled over into open conflict that summer. The First Bishops' War (there was to be a second in 1640) had worked to the colony's advantage, absorbing so much of the English government's time that, as Winthrop noted with relief, 'they had neither heart nor leisure to look after the affairs of New England'.[6] As Nehemiah was setting sail, however, rumours of a rapprochement were reaching America, and now he could confirm that those rumours were true. The war with the Scots was over, he reported, 'but what the issue will be we know not but it's much feared, it will break out afresh again'.[7]

Of less relevance to New England, but much more newsworthy, was a recent fight between the Spanish and Dutch fleets in sight of the English coast. In September a massive Spanish armada had been on its way to relieve the Spanish-held port of Dunkirk on the French coast when it was intercepted by a Dutch squadron commanded by Maarten Tromp, and forced to take refuge in the Downs between Deal and Dover. This led to a tricky diplomatic stand-off in which a small English squadron tried to keep the peace and assert England's claims of sovereignty over the Narrow Seas, while the Spanish appealed to the king for protection and the Dutch mounted a blockade and took to searching English ships crossing the Channel on the grounds that they were ferrying Spanish troops into Dunkirk. Suspicious Puritans like Nehemiah muttered darkly about Spain's real motives in sailing so close to England with a force of 24,000 men. 'What their intentions were God knows', he wrote; 'but it's not without suspicion that their ends were worse they hearing how things stood between the 2 kingdoms [i.e. England and Scotland].'[8] In the event, the English squadron decided that discretion was the better part of valour and stood aside as the Dutch and Spanish fell to it in the Battle of the Downs, which resulted in a crushing defeat for Spain. (And the unlucky loss of two English horses: one was killed by a stray shot as his rider was watching the battle from the shore; the second was happily eating hay in a Deal stable when a cannonball took its head off.)

All of these events Nehemiah described to Winthrop at length. He recounted how he had gone aboard a Spanish ship that took refuge from the Dutch at Plymouth and spoken to her captain. He offered his respects to Winthrop's wife, to his son, to John Cotton and John Wilson. He asked 'your remembrance to God for us'. Finally, when he couldn't put it off any longer, he added a postscript:

> Your otter you were pleased to commend to me to present to the king after we had kept her very carefully in the ships hold 3 weeks, one day while we were at duty she got up between decks and run out in to the sea through a little scuttle hole in the ships counter that I conceived she could not have gotten out of and was drowned. It much troubled me for the present but it could not be helped.[9]

The *Sparrow* stayed in England over the winter, while Nehemiah and Thomas Hawkins bought provisions and sold passages for the return voyage. In January 1640 their ship was cleared to leave for America with fifty passengers, and when she sailed that March Nehemiah, who had decided to stay on in London for the time being, used the opportunity to send another letter to Winthrop.

He was unsettled – by his absence, by the lack of progress he was making as a transatlantic merchant, by the times. His business was 'unprofitable'. Massachusetts was still the promised land, but he was conflicted about where his home really was: 'I . . . have looked many times toward that good land, and not altogether without some breathings and longings, after those precious liberties once enjoyed', he said. 'I hope this long abstinence will make me set a higher price upon New England than ever.'[10] But in the meantime, 'I thinke it behooves all the Lord's people to double their duty and improve all the interest they have in heaven for this poor land.' The country was mobilising: after eleven years of personal rule the king had summoned Parliament with the express purpose of raising money for a renewed assault on his uncooperative Scottish subjects. 'The times that are approaching threaten heavy and sad things', predicted Nehemiah.[11] At the end of February Thomas Hawkins joined the Gentlemen of the Artillery Garden, the English progenitor of Massachusetts' Military Company, whose aim was 'the better increase of the defence of this our realm'.[12] Four days later Nehemiah followed his example.

William Rainborowe senior – Captain Rainborowe, as everyone still called him – responded to the gathering storm in England by going into politics. His brief sea trial of the *Sovereign of the Sea* in the summer of 1638 had been the last time he put to sea; in the intervening two years he had moved to Billingsgate, only a few hundred yards west of his old stamping ground, and just inside the City walls between the Tower and London Bridge. He let his Wapping house to Alexander Bence, a powerful merchant and shipowner who divided his time between London and his family estates at Aldeburgh in Suffolk. And William devoted himself to his shipping ventures – he was part-owner of at least one ship on the transatlantic routes, the *Confidence*; and he may well have kept an interest in others – and to the maritime security of the nation. When trouble with Scotland was first brewing in 1639 he proposed that 10,000 pieces of ordnance should be kept in readiness to arm colliers and other small ships as fighting vessels.

Writs were issued to summon a Parliament in December 1639. Charles I was well aware of the risks he ran by providing a forum for the very men who were so unhappy at his arbitrary approach to government. But he had no choice if he was to raise funds for an army to go against the Scots for a second time, and as the Earl of Clarendon later recalled, the king and his advisers believed 'notwithstanding the murmurs of the people against some exorbitancies of the court, that sober men, and such as loved the peace and plenty they were possessed of, would be made choice of to serve in the House of Commons'.[13] They thought they could manage the dissidents, in other words. And they were wrong. 'I think men's hearts are shaken more than ever notwithstanding the Parliament', thought Nehemiah.[14]

When Parliament met in April, Captain Rainborowe was returned as MP for Aldeburgh, along with Alexander Bence's brother Squire (a forename rather than a title), a sea-captain and merchant like himself. On Monday 13 April 1640 Charles I entered the House of Lords to open the session. It was eleven years, one month and three days since he last addressed the assembled Lords and Commons. Then he had delivered a bitter speech in which he denounced the 'vipers' of the Lower House whose 'undutiful and seditious carriage' in questioning his authority had left him with no choice but to dissolve Parliament.[15] Now he was faced with no choice but to summon it.

The eleven years of personal rule had taught Charles many things, but not how to please a crowd. 'My lords and gentlemen,' he began, 'there was never a king that had a more great and weighty cause to call his people together than myself.'[16] The assembled Lords spiritual and temporal, the knights, citizens and burgesses chosen to attend this present Parliament, waited, breathless, to hear what came next.

'I will not trouble you with the particulars.'

That was it.

The speech was over almost before it had begun, and it was left to Lord Finch, the Lord Keeper, to explain at some length that the great and weighty cause was Scotland's perfidy. The Scots 'have taken up arms against the Lord's anointed, their rightful prince and undoubted sovereign'; they have turned to foreign states for help. As a result, the king has resolved 'by the means of a powerful army, to reduce them to their just and modest condition of obedience and subjection'.[17] This was going to be expensive, but there was no time to lose. The king would like both Houses to pass an Act to subsidise the army as quickly as possible. Once that was done, time could be found to address any lingering grievances.

That concluded the business. It was so simple. All Parliament had to do was to finance the war on Scotland. How could they refuse?

Within days the Commons had proposed 'a Model of Grievances'.[18] In a two-hour speech John Pym, a Devon MP who emerged as one of the leaders of the opposition to the king, argued that the king's eleven-year refusal to summon Parliament had led to all kinds of abuse, and went on to enumerate them: illegal proclamations had been published; ship money had been levied without parliamentary consent; Archbishop Laud's attempts at enforcing uniformity of worship had infringed ecclesiastical jurisdictions and (as Pym might as well have said, since so many of his fellow MPs believed it) prepared the ground for the introduction of Catholicism.

While MPs debated eleven years of arbitrary tyranny, the king was growing impatient. Eleven days after Parliament first sat, he made a speech to the Lords, complaining that instead of considering 'my weighty affairs', the Commons had spent their time discussing religion and parliamentary privilege; 'and so have put the cart before the horse'. He needed money to prosecute the war against the Scots that summer, and 'if the supply come not in time, I will not say what mischief may and must follow'.[19] The Lords took the hint, and decided to send down a message to the Commons urging them to get a move on and vote some funds for the war effort.

This had exactly the opposite effect. Years later the Earl of Clarendon recalled that the Lords' decision 'was no sooner reported in the House of Commons, than their whole temper seemed to be shaken'.[20] Annoyed at being pushed around, MPs suspended all business – including any question of subsidies for the king – while they debated whether or not the Lords had interfered with their ancient privileges in presuming to advise them.

Realising the cause was lost, Charles I called both Houses together on 5 May and dissolved Parliament. William Rainborowe's first experience of national politics had lasted a day over three weeks, and his sole contribution to the war effort was a report to the government by him and Squire Bence on the amount of time it would take to equip twenty merchant ships of 300 tons each for the king's service. The English strategy for the summer of 1640 included ambitious naval blockades of Scottish ports, an amphibious landing in the Firth of Forth and a 9,000-strong invasion fleet sailing from Ireland to attack western Scotland. The only way the Crown could possibly find enough seapower for the task was by hiring as many merchant ships as possible, and as quickly as possible. Rainborowe and Bence advised that if the navy's victualler were supplying the victuals from store, the vessels could be ready to sail in three or four weeks; if the ships' owners were to provide them, then they would need six weeks or two months to bring everything together. 'It will cost almost as much to fit a ship for one or two months as for then. This is our opinion.'[21]

The king's attempts to prosecute the war with Scotland unaided ended in humiliation that August, when a Covenanter army led by Alexander Leslie crossed the Tweed into England, routed the English forces at the Battle of Newburn and occupied Newcastle upon Tyne and Durham. Charles's plans for converging seaborne assaults on Scotland were forgotten; he couldn't even muster an army powerful enough to eject the Scots from England, let alone invade Scotland. He was forced to sue for peace. The Scottish response was to keep possession of Newcastle as security against an English change of mind, and to demand that the king pay £850 a day towards the Scottish army's maintenance while it remained on English soil. He couldn't possibly find that kind of money without recourse to taxation.

And for that he needed Parliament.

When new elections were held that autumn, William was returned again as MP for Aldeburgh. Squire Bence decided not to stand, and his seat was taken by his elder brother. Alexander Bence was a well-connected force in the City, a member of the Grocers' Company and brother-in-law to the radical London MP Samuel Vassall, who had already been committed to gaol sixteen times for his opposition to the king's policies. Of the fourteen members returned for Suffolk in November 1640 ten, including William and Alexander, leaned towards Parliament rather than the Crown.

'There was a marvellous elated countenance in many of the members of Parliament be they met together in the House', recalled Clarendon. Even men who six months earlier had been prepared to compromise 'talked now in another dialect both of things and persons; and said "that they must now be of another temper . . . that they had now an opportunity to make their country happy, by removing all grievances, and pulling up the causes of them by the roots"'.[22] When Charles I opened Parliament for what would be the last time in his life, urging both Houses to consider the distracted condition of the kingdom, he spoke, said Clarendon ruefully, 'with too little majesty'.[23]

While some of the more disaffected MPs lamented the miserable state of the nation and queued up to heap blame on the king's chief advisers, the Earl of Strafford and Archbishop Laud, William Rainborowe made up for his lack of contributions during the Short Parliament by throwing himself into Commons committee work. On 21 November he was appointed to a committee which was set up to consider how payments were to be made to the Scots, the state of the king's army, 'and what commanders, or other inferior officers, are papists'.[24] His fellow committee members included John Hampden, whose determined and very public condemnation of the ship-money levy as an illegal tax had made him one of the king's most prominent opponents; and William

Purefoy, who in 1649 would sign his name to Charles I's death warrant. A month later, on 18 December, William was appointed to a committee which sat to consider a dispute between rival traders in Virginia; Hampden and Purefoy were also members, as was John Pym, who that morning had successfully moved that the Commons formally charge Archbishop Laud with high treason.

So during those first months of the Long Parliament, William was moving in radical company. We need to be wary of drawing too many conclusions from that, of course: other members of those same committees were loyal supporters of the king. Henry Wilmot, for example, who sat with William and John Hampden on the army committee, would be one of Charles I's main cavalry commanders in the coming war. Others were uncommitted; a few were blithely unconcerned. Because *we* know that war was coming, that battle lines would be drawn, that Hampden would die in battle and Wilmot would die in exile, it is so tempting to indulge in hindsight. But in the winter of 1640–1 no MP dreamed that friends, brothers, neighbours would be killing each other, that a king would lose his head and a country would grasp at a chance to make itself anew. They were troubled; they felt the approach of the heavy and sad things that Nehemiah Bourne saw lumbering towards England like a leviathan; but nobody thought it would end the way it did. Nobody thought the world would be turned upside down.

While it is hard to understand why William should have been part of a parliamentary committee charged with considering the state of the king's army, his knowledge of the transatlantic trade and his connections in America made his involvement with the Virginia Planters' dispute more explicable. That holds even more true for a piece of legislation which was perhaps his most important contribution to the Long Parliament – an Act 'for the relief of the captives taken by Turkish Moorish and other pirates and to prevent the taking of others in time to come'.[25]

Towards the end of 1640 Parliament turned its attention to the problem of Barbary Coast piracy. However impracticable William's proposals for an expedition against Algiers had seemed in the winter of 1637–8, the need for action was shown beyond doubt in the intervening two years. Losses increased at an alarming rate: those for the nine years from 1629 to 1638 – seventy-three ships and 1,473 people – were almost equalled in the single eight-month period between May 1639 and January 1640. An English treasure ship, the *Rebecca*, was taken off Lisbon at the beginning of 1640 with more than £200,000 of silver aboard, a disaster so great it caused a slump in the pound. The Levant Company announced that it was unsafe to trade into the eastern Mediterranean without naval protection. And that summer, the problem came closer to home. Watchers on the shore at Mousehole in Cornwall were appalled to see four Barbary pirates taking nine ships and their crew in the Bay of Penzance in broad daylight. The *Elizabeth*, homeward-bound from Virginia, was attacked and boarded by pirates in the same waters; she managed to fight them off, but her master reported seeing 'many small vessels about two leagues from the shore without sails or crew', which he believed had been stripped by the same pirate fleet.[26] The mayor of Exeter in Devon pleaded with the government to take action. 'There are many Turks lying upon these coasts', he wrote, 'to the great danger of us all, if they be not prevented.'[27]

On 10 December William was appointed to a parliamentary committee set up to receive petitions on behalf of captives being held in Algiers and Tunis, to examine ways to secure their release, and 'to think of some course for the securing of navigations, and of His Majesty's subjects'.[28] The committee also included John Pym, who had no obvious involvement in maritime or commercial matters. On the other hand, it was certainly in the interest of men like Pym to demonstrate how completely the king's ship-money levy had failed to deliver one of its promised objectives, the suppression of Barbary piracy.

Shortly after the committee was formed William went to the king with Sir Henry Vane, who had returned from New England and was now treasurer of the navy. They informed him there were ten pirate ships 'upon the western coasts', and asked that two English ships 'may forthwith be sent to scour the seas, and secure the merchants' – i.e. protect their trade.[29] The pirates had gone by the time the warships reached the Cornish coast.

In January 1641 Trinity House submitted its own recommendations on solving the problem, and given their nature it is hard not to see William's influence behind them. The only way to suppress the pirates of Algiers and Tunis and secure the release of

an estimated 3,000 captives was to send a massive expeditionary
force of three squadrons, two of which would patrol inside and
outside the Strait of Gibraltar, while the third would ride in the
Bay of Algiers and blockade the harbour, as William had done at
Sallee in 1637. The Trinity House elder brethren reckoned the
cost of all this at £170,960.

The Committee for the Captives in Algiers, as it was called,
reported to the Commons on 1 March. MPs were told there
were between 4,000 and 5,000 of the king's subjects held captive
in Algiers and Tunis (a significant increase on Trinity House's
figure); and that between them these two bases would put to
sea a fleet of sixty ships that summer, half of which could be
expected off the western coasts. There was no mention of
an expedition. Instead, MPs were urged to ask the king to maintain a larger naval presence of six or seven warships near the
western ports; and shipowners were encouraged to show some
enterprise and go after the pirates themselves. When a bill finally
reached the statute books in January 1642, it bore little resem-
blance to the committee's original recommendations, although it
did represent a step forward in the battle against the pirates. Its
main clause was a 1 per cent duty on all imports and exports
which was to go towards financing a fleet 'for the enlargement
and deliverance of those poor captives in Argier and other places'.
In case the king was at all unsure as to whose fault it was that
the pirates were such a menace, the 'Act for the relief of the
captives' told him, in no uncertain terms. The ship money that
should have financed anti-piracy operations had been 'exhausted
by evil ministers and not applied to their proper uses so that
Your Highness's good subjects have been exposed to the merciless
cruelty of those pirates and barbarous infidels'.[30]

In August 1641 William was invited to consider the state of
the navy, how it might be made fit for sailing the following spring,
and to address the question of how ships might be provided 'for
transporting the ordnance and ammunition from Hull', where a
massive supply of weapons and ammunition had been stored for
the use of the English army in the Second Bishops' War of 1640.[31]
A few days later he was one of those who heard a petition by a
group of merchants who wanted to set up 'a Company for America
and Africa', trading (in slaves?) between West Africa, the Cape

Verde Islands and the New World. And the same week he had business much closer to home as one of several MPs who were asked to consider whether or not Wapping should secede from Whitechapel and become a parish of its own. (Evidently not, since Wapping didn't achieve parochial status for another fifty-three years.)

Ten days later he was one of forty-eight MPs who were entrusted with carrying on the business of the House during the six-week autumn recess. Every Tuesday and Saturday the Recess Committee gathered at nine o'clock in the morning in the Exchequer Chamber at Westminster. They monitored the reception of a declaration which Parliament had issued on the last day before the recess, ordering every parish church in the land to remove the rails from Communion tables, to prevent genuflection and to ensure that 'all crucifixes, scandalous pictures of any one or more persons of the Trinity, and all images of the Virgin Mary, shall be taken away and abolished'.[32] They continued the negotiations with the Scots, and accepted petitions from disaffected soldiery who were looking to be paid for their service in the recent Bishops' War: 'we could not refuse to accept their petitions, lest they should grow to tumults', said Pym; but something needed to be done quite quickly to get them to leave London.[33]

William Rainborowe's last bow was taken in the Commons on 22 November 1641. Violence had erupted in Ireland the previous month, as a group of disaffected Catholics led by Sir Phelim O'Neill tried to put a halt to the expansionist tactics of Protestants, largely Scottish planters, in Ulster. Parliament and the king both took steps to raise armies for Ireland, and in an atmosphere of heightened tension both turned their thoughts to securing the munitions store at Hull. That day the officers of the ordnance at the Tower of London were commanded by Parliament to estimate how many ships would be needed to transport Hull's munitions, and William was asked to find out what ships were available on the Thames, 'and to give an account of it tomorrow morning'.[34] That same night, around midnight, the Commons passed the Grand Remonstrance, a catalogue of 204 grievances and demands which set down in devastating detail exactly how the king's advisers had worked to curtail the Protestant faith, the privileges of Parliament and the liberties of the people.

William may have been present in the Commons on 4 January 1642, when Charles I breached parliamentary privilege by entering the House and attempting to arrest Pym, Hampden, Denzil Holles, Sir Arthur Hesilrige and William Strode on charges of treason. Or he may already have been ailing with the sickness which was about to kill him. On 1 February he added a codicil to his will, depriving a niece of a £50 legacy because he had already given her 'the sum of ten pounds and all her wedding clothes'.[35] He died eleven days later, and was buried at St John's Wapping on 16 February. 'The Grand Admiral and General Captain Rainsborough is this day buried', a facetious young naval officer informed Admiral Sir John Pennington; 'but with what pomp I cannot relate.'[36]

The same day, the Speaker of the House of Commons issued a writ for a by-election at Aldeburgh to fill William's seat. And the nation marched to its doom, unmindful of this small sadness.

The Rainborowes are wraiths. Sometimes – now, at this moment in their story – I reach for them and they vanish like smoke, taking their secrets with them. I follow them down the years and they're gone. I watch as the tribe spreads out across the world: Martha in the alien forests of Massachusetts, with her piety and her precious china; half-brother William, struggling to make his way in the New World while his cousin Nehemiah struggles to come to terms with the old. And Thomas, the head of the family now, buying and selling in the blue waters of the Aegean. Where are the young Rainborowes, Joan and Judith and Edward, consigned to the care of their two older half-brothers by their father? They circle the rim of history, just out of reach. Did they kneel at his bedside as he died? Did they hold his hand, kiss his cold forehead, repeat the words of Solomon beloved of Puritan preachers? 'The day of death is better indeed than the day of birth.'

William Rainborowe's life was not a long one. He was born in the year Sir Francis Drake sailed into the Bay of Cadiz and singed the King of Spain's beard, and he died on the eve of the English Civil War. The fifty-five years that intervened took him to worlds unknown to most Englishmen – into the souks and citadels of the Ottoman Empire, the desert-fortresses of Africa. They led him down the corridors of power, and gave him riches, and made him a force to be reckoned with on all matters connected with ships and the sea. When he spoke, this hard-nosed, God-fearing merchant-mariner from Wapping, the nation's leaders listened. For a time, he was important. But the times were changing.

> Alas, alas, the great city, wherein were made rich all that had ships in the sea by reason of her costliness: for in one hour is she made desolate.
>
> Revelation 18:19

10

Hard Liberty

*M*artha Coytmore's admission to Charlestown's gathered church in 1639 was important: it drew her
further into the community, raised her status in the
eyes of her neighbours, gave her an identity. But the consequences
of church membership in New England were more far-reaching
(in this world, at least) for a man than they were for a woman.
Thomas Coytmore's admission to the same church in February
1640 was also a ticket to full participation in the political life of
the colony. Unless he was a freeman, Thomas could not stand for
office or vote for officers and, as the General Court had decreed
in 1631, 'no man shall be admitted to the freedom of this body
politic, but such as are members of the some of the churches
within the limits of the same'.[1]

Having joined Charlestown church, Thomas was admitted as a
freeman of the Massachusetts Bay Colony at Boston on 13 May
1640, along with his brother-in-law Thomas Graves and 141 other
male settlers. The ceremony was brief, without any of the public
interrogations that attended membership of the church: each

applicant had to produce evidence that he *was* a member of his church, and then swore 'by the great and dreadful name of the ever-living God' to be true and faithful to the commonwealth, and 'to give my vote and suffrage as I shall judge in mine own conscience may best conduce and tend to the public weal of the body'.[2]

'None have voices in elections of governors, deputy, and assistants', noted Thomas Lechford, a lawyer who arrived in Massachusetts in 1638; 'none are to be magistrates, officers, or jurymen, grand or petite, but freemen.'[3] It was the freemen who gathered in the new meeting house on the south side of Town Hill in Charlestown to choose constables and highway surveyors, to make land grants, to punish minor offences. As the little community grew, it was the freemen who chose nine or ten of their number to act as a town council, with delegated powers; and the freemen who chose the governor of the colony, the deputy governor and the assistants, who together exercised all the functions of government, executive, legislative and judicial. If you weren't a freeman, you had no say in the running of the colony. And if you weren't an admitted member of a church, you couldn't be a freeman.

In the first years of the colony's existence, before the Coytmores' arrival, that would have been where the freemen's involvement in government ended. Although the Massachusetts Bay Company's charter stipulated that it was they, assembling at the General Court, who had the power of making laws, John Winthrop and the other senior members of the Company who made up the Court of Assistants took that power upon themselves, forestalling criticism by refusing to let anyone else see the charter. The 1630s had seen the gradual erosion of this high-handed approach, which was either a fine example of strong leadership or the worst kind of arbitrary tyranny, depending on your point of view. First of all, pressure from a group of Watertown freemen in 1632 forced the General Court to invite two delegates from each town to come to Boston to consult with the assistants on matters of taxation. Two years later, these delegates asked politely but firmly to see the charter, and as they read it, they realised they were entitled to a much greater role in government. Winthrop tried to fob them off, saying that when the charter was written no one had envisaged that there would be so many freemen:

> Now [he told them] they were grown to so great a body, as it was not possible for them to make or execute laws, but they must choose others for that purpose: and that howsoever it would be necessary hereafter to have a select company to intend that work, yet for the present they were not furnished with a sufficient number of men qualified for such a business, neither could the commonwealth bear the loss of time of so many as must intend it.[4]

This wouldn't do. At the next General Court, which took place in May 1634, Winthrop was ousted as governor, and the court decreed that it alone (i.e. the body of freemen rather than the Court of Assistants) had the power to elect officers, raise taxes and establish laws. The May 1634 General Court also ordered that the freemen of every settlement should have the right to depute two or three of their number 'to deal in their behalf, in the public affairs of the commonwealth'.[5] This was an important step: the establishment of a representative legislative assembly. If it wasn't as representative as it might have been, it was still a great deal more democratic than both the system it replaced and the system the colonists had left behind in England.

The same session saw another innovation. Until now the election of officers – governor, deputy governor and assistants – had been by show of hands. That was how elections were conducted at home in England. But, perhaps because those who were present felt uneasy about being seen to vote the powerful John Winthrop out of office, the 1634 election for governor was by paper ballot. And the practice caught on: it was used for the election of all members of the Court of Assistants, and in 1635 the General Court ordered that 'hereafter, the deputies to be chosen for the General Courts shall be elected by papers, as the governor is chosen'.[6] Democracy was a long way off. But a step had been taken.

The next General Court after Thomas Coytmore's admission as a freeman was convened in October 1640, and Thomas attended as one of Charlestown's deputies. It was a family affair: neighbour and brother-in-law Increase Nowell was one of the eight assistants; and William Tyng, who was married to Coytmore's sister Elizabeth, was treasurer to the court and a deputy for Boston.

Deputies and assistants gathered together in Boston's meeting house on 7 October. One of the General Court's first acts that day was to confirm an earlier decision making adultery a capital offence. This didn't bode well for the subject of the next piece of business. Captain John Underhill was charged with committing adultery with a cooper's wife. But Underhill had prepared the ground earlier by appearing before the Boston congregation in his scruffiest clothes and tearfully confessing his adultery — although he rather ungallantly said that once he had overcome the woman's reluctance to cheat on her husband, she was an enthusiastic participant. The court, 'being charitably and well persuaded of the truth of his repentance', suspended judgement while they waited to see if that repentance was genuine.[7]

The rest of the business was more prosaic. The exchange rate for wampum was fixed at four white beads to a penny and two blue beads to a penny. Citizens were ordered to be more zealous in preserving the hides of animals. A bounty was offered for killing wolves. Lands were granted, boundaries established, petitions heard. The town of Colchester had its name changed to Salisbury.

One item on the agenda was of particular interest to Thomas. Charlestown was outgrowing its bounds, and in the course of the session the General Court granted it an additional four square miles of land near Horn Pond, one of the sources of the Mystic river, to make a village which would soon be named Woburn. One-fifth of the grant went straight to Thomas Coytmore.

No other grantee was named, and it isn't clear why Thomas was singled out for special treatment. But what *is* clear is that Thomas was moving up the social and economic ladder. In 1638, within months of his and Martha's arrival, the Charlestown Book of Possessions showed that besides their homestead and two acres on Wapping Street, and commons for four cows, they had eleven other parcels of land within the town limits. Some were small, like the acre of meadow lying in the high field marsh, or the piece of ground, perhaps a shipyard, 'butting south-east upon the harbour, south-west upon Wapping Dock'. Others were quite substantial:

seventy acres here, thirty-five acres there, fifteen acres of woodland in Mystic field. Thomas also had a quarter-share in a project to build a new mill for Charlestown, damming a tidal pond on the shoreline south of the town.

The General Court was a legislative body: it didn't involve itself in criminal or civil cases. Those things were the province of the Court of Assistants, which met quarterly in Boston, and more frequently as the need arose. There was general agreement among commentators that law-breaking was a rare occurrence, and that drunkenness and immorality were all but unknown. 'Profane swearing, drunkenness, and beggars, are but rare in the compass of this Patent', reported Thomas Lechford, who was no friend to the colony.[8] He was backed up by other writers: 'In seven years, among thousands there dwelling,' declared Hugh Peter, looking back on his time as minister of Salem, 'I never saw any drunk, nor heard an oath, nor [saw] any begging, nor Sabbath broken.'[9] Having lived in the Bay for twelve years 'I may confidently say,' declared Nathaniel Ward in 1647, 'I never heard but one oath sworn, nor never saw one man drunk, nor ever heard of three women adulteresses.'[10]

How, then, to reconcile these remarks with the evidence of the records of the Court of Assistants, which are peppered with every imaginable vice, crime and misdemeanour? Joseph King and Henry Pitts are 'sharply reprehended' for their obscene speech and fined forty shillings each 'for distemper in drinking wine'.[11] William Perkins, also convicted of drunkenness, is ordered to stand at the next General Court for an hour in public view 'with a white sheet of paper on his breast, having a great D [for drunkard] made upon it'.[12] Sarah Hales is convicted of adultery and sent to the gallows with a rope about her neck to sit perched on the ladder for an hour, before being banished. Mary Osborne is severely whipped for dosing her husband with quicksilver. Two boys, Robert Wyar and John Garland, are whipped for raping two girls; so are the girls. An Irish servant, Teagu Ocrimi, is sentenced to stand on the gallows with a halter round his neck 'for a foul and devilish attempt to bugger a cow of Mr Makepeace's'.[13]

Clearly the city on a hill had some dark alleys. But among the hundreds of tales of drunkenness and sexual abuse and theft and violence, what strikes home is not so much the low moral standards of the colonists, or even the harshness of some of the punishments, but the court's reluctance to take life. The death penalty was imposed on only a handful of occasions during the first years. Two men were hanged at Boston for murder in 1637, and the following year poor Dorothy Talby was convicted of killing her three-year-old daughter, who was named Difficult Talby. Dorothy was mentally ill, claiming she had been 'so possessed by Satan, that he persuaded her (by his delusions, which she listened to as revelations from God) to break the neck of her own child, that she might free it from future misery'.[14] She was hanged in the square at Boston, on gallows flanked by the prison and the meeting house, twin symbols of the colony's civil and spiritual wrath. And she remained unrepentant. Winthrop, who recorded the episode in his journal, commented with sadness that 'Mr Peter, her late pastor, and Mr Wilson, went with her to the place of execution, but could do no good with her.'[15]

But time and again a court would opt for leniency. In cases of adultery, for example, the magistrates often accepted a couple's assurances that though they had been found in bed together they had not actually had intercourse; or cited the legal requirement for two direct witnesses, quite a tall order in cases of adultery; or found them guilty of the lesser offence of adulterous behaviour and let them off with a whipping.

Nevertheless, there were rumblings of disquiet at a system which allowed the magistrates so much discretion in the way they meted out justice. They were criticised for their partiality; anyone offending against a magistrate or his family was likely to be treated very severely indeed, as in the case of John Stone, who in 1633 was banished for calling one of the assistants a 'just as' rather than a 'justice'.[16] They were criticised on occasion for their general harshness: a correspondent in England warned that 'I have heard diverse complaints against the severity of your government' after the court sentenced a mentally disturbed servant who uttered 'malicious and scandalous speeches' to be whipped, have his ears cut off, be fined £40 and be 'banished out of the limits of this jurisdiction'.[17] And they were criticised for being too lenient. John Winthrop was rebuked publicly by his fellow magistrates after he postponed a banishment order on two men on the grounds that it was winter, and if they had been sent away they would have perished.

Throughout the 1630s there were calls for a codification of the law, and a corresponding stalling action by magistrates reluctant to see a curb on their discretionary powers. Winthrop argued that it was against scripture – 'I would know by what rule we may take upon us, to prescribe penalties where God prescribes none' – and, with perhaps more honesty, that it would undermine the status of the magistrate. If penalties were fixed, he said, any schoolboy might pronounce sentence on a convicted person. 'And then what need were there of any special wisdom, learning, courage, zeal or faithfulness in a judge?'[18]

At the General Court of May 1635 the then governor, John Haynes, Deputy Governor Richard Bellingham, John Winthrop and Thomas Dudley were asked 'to make a draught of such laws as they shall judge needful for the well-ordering of this plantation'.[19] They didn't, preferring to stick with a system which allowed them to exercise their judgement and discretion. In 1636 John Cotton produced a draft code, fortified with liberal references to the Old Testament and filled with dire punishments for those who strayed from the paths of righteousness. Anyone who committed blasphemy or idolatry, or profaned the Lord's Day, or 'revile[d] the religion and worship of God' should receive the death sentence, along with rebellious children who continue 'in riot or drunkenness after due correction from their parents'.[20] Cotton proposed that a total of twenty-four offences be punishable by death or banishment. Theft, on the other hand, was not, because there was no ground in Scripture for it as a capital offence. Nor was rape, nor violent assault.

Cotton's code was quietly set aside by the General Court. But a desire for a more transparent legal framework persisted, and in 1639 the Cotton Code was submitted again, along with a competing draft by Nathaniel Ward, a minister with legal experience. Winthrop noted that 'the people had long desired a body of laws, and thought their condition unsafe, while so much power rested in the discretion of magistrates . . . At length (to satisfy the people) it proceeded, and the two models were digested with divers alterations and additions, and abbreviated and sent to every town, to be considered first by the magistrates and elders, and then to be published . . . that if any man should think fit, that any thing ought to be altered, he might acquaint some of the deputies therewith against the next court.'[21] This process of consultation, compromise and revision was already well established in the colony's religious life. When a contentious issue came up – whether women should wear veils in public, whether it was right for church elders to hold senior positions in civic government – ministers and lay members of the congregations would discuss the matter publicly and look to other churches for advice and guidance. The Anne Hutchinson affair had shown all too clearly the dire consequences for society when this process of consensus broke down.

After the October 1640 session, Thomas Coytmore attended the General Court again in June 1641 as deputy for Charlestown, taking part for the first time in his life (and as it turned out, the only time) in the annual election of officers – governor, deputy governor and assistants. Although Winthrop had dominated the political life of the colony throughout the 1630s, serving as governor seven times with a break in 1634–6, he had been persuaded not to stand for the office in 1640: a group of elders had a quiet word with him and suggested it was time for a change, 'lest the long continuance of one man in the place should bring it to be for life, and, in time, hereditary'.[22] That year he was succeeded by the autocratic and irascible Thomas Dudley, although he was elected as one of the eight assistants, as was his son John Winthrop junior. (There was no year between 1630 and 1648 in which Winthrop senior did not serve as either governor, deputy governor or assistant.) In 1641 Dudley was opposed by Richard Bellingham, who had been politically active in the colony from the moment he arrived in 1634, and who had an annoying habit of supporting the views of the deputies and freemen rather than standing shoulder to shoulder with the other assistants.

The election process was a good deal more sophisticated than comparable elections to public office in England, where more than 200 years later *The Times* was still sneering at the very idea of a secret ballot, which would inevitably bring about the loss of 'those national characteristics which alone make freedom durable, or even desirable – the manly pride that scorns concealment, and the sturdy will that refuses to bend to coercion'.[23] In the more enlightened environment of the Boston meeting house (and that's a phrase one rarely sees), the freemen of the colony gathered and, at a given signal, trooped in one door, placed their votes 'in paper' down on a table and then left through another door. Those freemen who were unable to attend the election were allowed to send in their votes by proxy. 'All being delivered in', said Thomas Lechford, who witnessed the proceedings, 'the votes are counted, and according to the major part, the old governor pronounceth, that such an one is chosen governor for the year ensuing.'[24] The process was repeated for the election of the deputy governor.

Then came the assistants. Until 1639 it had been the custom for the governor to nominate suitable candidates; but in that year Winthrop, who was then the governor, upset the freemen by nominating his brother-in-law Emmanuel Downing; and from 1640 onward the freemen themselves nominated them. Again, the process was conducted by paper ballot rather than by show of hands, with each freeman handing in a paper for each man named. Lechford described how it worked: 'If a freeman give in a blank, that rejects the man named; if the freeman makes any mark with a pen upon the paper which he brings, that elects the man named.'[25]

The 1641 election was a close-run thing. Over a thousand freemen were eligible to vote, but Richard Bellingham won the governorship by just six votes. He wasn't a particularly popular man, and there were grumblings about the way the election was conducted: a number of freemen came into the meeting house late, saying they still had to vote, 'which was denied by some of the magistrates, because they had not given them in at the doors'.[26]

There were tensions outside the court, as well. It was the outgoing governor's right to choose a preacher to deliver the election sermon; but some of the freemen ignored tradition and chose Nathaniel Ward, who took the opportunity to give what a disapproving John Winthrop called 'a moral and political discourse' to the assembled crowd, which included Coytmore and the other deputies, and quite possibly Nehemiah Bourne and William Rainborowe junior: the convening of the new court was a public holiday, attended by men and women from all over the colony.

The code of laws which was circulated around the towns of the colony in transcription that summer and autumn, and which has come to be known as the Body of Liberties, was and is a remarkable achievement – in parts. The death penalty was prescribed for twelve offences, ranging from treason and murder to blasphemy and witchcraft, and taking in adultery, sodomy and bestiality along the way. All except treason were supported by scriptural references. 'If any man or woman shall lie with any beast or brute creature', for example, not only will the offender be put to death, but also 'the beast shall be slain and buried and not eaten', in accordance with Leviticus 20:15–16.[27]

But Old Testament brutality was tempered by a great deal of New England advanced thinking. The list of capital laws took up one out of ninety-eight clauses in the Body of Liberties; Ward and his collaborators devoted the remainder to setting out the rights, privileges and liberties of the individual and the limits of the state in relation to that individual. They set the tone of the code with the very first clause:

> No man's life shall be taken away, no man's honour or good name shall be stained, no man's person shall be arrested, restrained, banished, dismembered, nor any ways punished, no man shall be deprived of his wife or children, no man's goods or estate shall be taken away from him, nor any way indamaged under colour of law or countenance of authority, unless it be by virtue or equity of some express law of the country warranting the same, established by a general court and sufficiently published.[28]

Everyone within the colony's jurisdiction, 'whether inhabitant or foreigner', should enjoy the same justice and law.[29] No inhumane, barbarous or cruel punishments were allowed; nor torture, except when it was clear that a man was guilty of a capital offence and he refused to name his confederates; and even then such torture as was used must not be 'barbarous and inhumane'.[30] (The Body of Liberties didn't go into details of what might constitute a humane method of torture.) When it came to government, 'it is the constant liberty of the free men of this plantation to choose yearly at the Court of Election out of the freemen all the general officers of this jurisdiction'.[31] A General Court couldn't be dissolved or even adjourned without the consent of the majority, and no censure by a church was allowed to put a man out of office.

No one should be pressed against his will into service of any kind, something which happened regularly in England. No court cases should founder on technicalities, as they often did in England, so long as 'the person and cause be rightly understood and intended by the Court'. Husbands were forbidden to beat their wives (a right they possessed in England). Foreigners – Christian foreigners, anyway – who came to Massachusetts seeking asylum or escaping war and famine had the right to be 'entertained and succoured amongst us'.[32] Even dumb beasts had rights they didn't possess in England: the code's ninety-second law stipulated that no man should 'exercise any tyranny or cruelty' towards any domestic animal.[33]

The rights of individual churches to function independently were guaranteed, as one would expect in a community made up of people who had left their homeland because of the government's obsession with uniformity of worship. According to the Body of Liberties, every church had the freedom to elect and ordain its officers, to celebrate fastdays and days of thanksgiving, to admit and expel members and to discipline any member, even if they were magistrates or deputies.

The Body of Liberties was adopted in the autumn of 1641 at the third and last General Court that Thomas attended as one of Charlestown's deputies. The code wasn't perfect: apart from setting out the twelve capital offences, for example, it made no attempt to set penalties for crimes, and colonists who mistrusted the magistrates' discretionary powers still called for consistency in sentencing. The Body was more concerned with rights than punishments, and therein lies its importance. 'A bold avowal of the rights of man', said one nineteenth-century historian, 'and a plea for popular freedom, it contains the germ of the memorable Declaration of July 4, 1776.'[34] It seemed so advanced for its time that subsequent writers believed the ideas must have originated in England. Others noted that the drive to codify the common law in England during the 1650s derived from experiments on the other side of the Atlantic. 'The impetus . . . came largely from New England, which had been called "its regenerating influence".'[35] The truth, as usual, lies somewhere in between. Radical political thought found breeding grounds in both old England and New England, and both communities benefited from the cross-fertilisation which was taking place around 1640. Nevertheless, having gone over in search of liberty and opportunity, the three Rainborowes who were living in the Massachusetts Bay Colony at the time – Martha, Judith and William junior – and the other members of their clan, Thomas Coytmore, Nehemiah and Hannah Bourne, the Nowells and the Graves, found themselves with undreamed-of freedoms.

11

They On the Trading Flood

*A*n unforeseen consequence of the troubles in England was that both Nehemiah Bourne and Thomas Coytmore took up their old trades of shipwright and ship's captain, in the cause of their new homeland. And this was because the deteriorating political situation in Britain threw New England into crisis. While the looming threat of war might have been expected to fuel transatlantic migration, it did exactly the opposite: with the summoning of Parliament and the beginnings of a coordinated opposition to Archbishop Laud, the godly decided that the city upon a hill might be built in the more comfortable setting of Lincolnshire or Sussex or Somerset, rather than in the wilderness of Massachusetts. When the Grand Remonstrance called for Laud's impeachment, and 'our great enemy' was imprisoned in the Tower, the prospect of change 'caused all men to stay in England in expectation of a new world', as John Winthrop confided to his journal.[1]

After the boom years of 1637–8, when the Coytmores, the Bournes, the Graves – and 4,500 others – arrived, swelling the population of Massachusetts to just over 11,000, migration slackened in 1639 and slowed dramatically in 1640 and 1641. Puritans who might have turned to New England for refuge began to consider the disadvantages more carefully, now the prospect of a reformed Church of England seemed close. The decline in the number of immigrants plunged the colony into economic crisis: the new settlers had brought money with them, which was used to buy the agricultural surplus produced by farmers; and it was this steady inward flow of new cash which had paid for the goods which the merchants of London and Bristol unloaded at Boston and Charlestown. Massachusetts exported very little; having disposed of their cargos, English vessels tended to move on to Newfoundland or Maine or Virginia to take on fish or timber or tobacco before heading for home.

Some colonists went back. 'Why should a man stay until the house fall on his head?' asked Thomas Hooker in 1640.[2] William Rainborowe junior, who bought a homestead at Watertown on the Charles river in December 1640, returned to England in the spring of 1642, drawn there by his inheritance, perhaps – his father had left him £1,000, several houses in Wapping and a half-share in the care of his three youngest half-siblings, Joan, Judith and Edward. Now a man of property in old England as well in New England, that summer he married a Suffolk girl, Margary Jenney; and although he made another visit to Massachusetts in 1643 – when he was being chased for two guns he had borrowed from the colony's store, and he was in turn petitioning the General Court for £100 owed to him – England was now his home again.

Colonists had always drifted back to England, persuaded by personal circumstance or conviction that their destiny lay, after all, in the Old World rather than the New. But now the trickle became a flood. Looking back, the Boston minister Increase Mather reckoned that 'since the year 1640, more persons have removed out of New England, than have gone thither'.[3] The moment men and women realised that there was a real chance of finding their promised land in the more congenial surroundings of home, the hard life they were forging for themselves in Massachusetts lost its allure.

John Winthrop dated the beginning of the reversal precisely, to 10 December 1640. It was on that date that an English fishing vessel arrived in the Gulf of Maine bringing the news that the

Scots had invaded England, that Charles I had summoned
Parliament, and that there was now the hope of a thorough
reformation back home. From that moment on, reckoned
Winthrop, 'some among us began to think of returning back to
England. Others despairing of any more supply from thence, and
yet not knowing how to live there, if they should return, bent
their minds wholly to removal to the south parts.'[4] Land values
plummeted: a man whose holdings had been worth £1,000 at
the peak of the boom was lucky to sell for a fifth of that; the
prices of grain and cattle collapsed. The court passed a law which
laid down that 'no man shall be compelled to satisfy any debt,
legacy, fine, or any other payment in money, but satisfaction
shall be accepted in corn, cattle, fish, or other commodities'.[5]

That may have seemed like a good idea at the time, but it
served to further deter English merchants from doing business
with the colony. A merchant in London or Bristol wasn't about
to venture hundreds of pounds' worth of iron goods or tools or
cloth on a hazardous 3,000-mile voyage across the Atlantic to be
paid in fish.

The colony responded to the crisis by sending a three-man
delegation to England. William Hibbins was a prosperous Boston
merchant whose main claim to fame rests with the fact that his
wife, Anne, was hanged for witchcraft in 1656, earning herself a
role in Hawthorne's *Scarlet Letter* two centuries later. The other
two were ministers: Thomas Weld, the pastor of Roxbury; and
Hugh Peter of Salem. Peter may have had personal reasons for
wanting to leave New England for a while. He suffered periodic
bouts of depression – 'deep melancholy is getting fast upon me
again', he wrote in 1640 – and his recent and reluctant marriage
to Deliverance Sheffield, a widow who also had mental health
problems, did nothing to lift his spirits.[6] He left the woefully
misnamed Deliverance behind in Salem, along with their baby
daughter.

Peter, Weld and Hibbins were charged by Winthrop and the
other leaders of the colony with placating anxious creditors and
giving their fellow saints in England some guidance 'as it should
be required, for the settling the right form of church discipline'.[7]
Their more general role was to drum up support for the colony's
efforts to stand on its own two feet. It was obvious to merchants

and mariners that there was a viable alternative to either leaving for more prosperous parts or relying on English credit for survival. Massachusetts could begin to trade on its own account, using its own fleet of merchant ships, if it could find the right markets. Peter had been urging this for a while: and shortly before he left for England he persuaded Salem to pull together and start building a ship of 300 tons. (By way of comparison, the *Mayflower* was about 180 tons.) The venture didn't go smoothly – at least one man was killed when the rope he was using to hoist a heavy timber broke – but Salem's efforts spurred Boston to follow suit. As Winthrop recalled in 1641, 'the general fear of want of foreign commodities, now our money was gone, and that things were like to go well in England, set us to work to provide shipping of our own'.[8] Commercial contacts in London and Bristol advised that Spain and the wine islands of the eastern Atlantic – Madeira and the Canaries – were potential markets for timber and grain; and, oblivious to the irony that Catholic southern Europe was to be their saviour, the merchant-mariners of Boston swung into action. This was their business, their vocation. This was what they did.

One of the leading figures in the initiative was Nehemiah Bourne, now returned from England and living in Boston with Hannah and his baby son, also Nehemiah on a homestead by the North End shore. His business partner Thomas Hawkins lived on one side of them, but there was vacant land on the other; and in January 1641 a committee of Boston worthies declared it suitable 'for a place for building the ship, the which he [i.e. Nehemiah] desires may be given him for the same use'.[9]

He got it, but he wasn't about to bear the cost of building the ship by himself: a syndicate of merchants took shares, as was the way in England. Individual towns and the colony at large also played their part in establishing the new industry. The following month, a 'brother Wright' bought sixty acres of land from Boston for £3 10s.; he was asked to pay the money directly 'to Mr Bworne [*sic*], towards the building of the ship'.[10] Nehemiah, Thomas Coytmore, Thomas Hawkins and Increase Nowell were appointed by the General Court to set the appropriate rates of 'wharfage, porterage, & warehouse hire';[11] and because 'the country is now in hand with the building of ships, which is a business of great importance for the common good', the General Court appointed and paid for qualified surveyors after the English way, with the authority to examine work in progress and to require shipwrights to amend any substandard construction.[12]

At 200 tons, Nehemiah's new ship was no *Sovereign of the Sea*, but her construction still presented him with a formidable task. For a three-masted, square-rigged roundship like the *Trial*, as she was called, the basic process involved either digging out a dry dock or building directly on the ground and shoring up the structure with timbers. All vessels of the period were carvel-built, beginning with the laying of the keel, attaching to it the stem and sternpost and then building up a skeleton of frames or ribs, and beams. Planks were then nailed to the frames, laid flush against each other and caulked with oakum and hot pitch.[13] Many hundreds of wooden pins or trenails, less prone to deterioration in salt water than iron nails, were used to fasten the timbers together. The vessel was launched before being fitted out; it wasn't unusual to make quite radical adjustments, both at this stage and later. The most dramatic, called 'furring', involved ripping off the planking of the hull, inserting extra timbers and then reattaching the planks, to broaden a ship's beam or to make her sit higher in the water. Sir Henry Mainwaring condemned the practice from the bottom of his sailor's soul, declaring 'it an infinite loss to the owners and an utter spoiling and disgrace to all ships that are so handled'.[14] But shipbuilding was an individual and some-times idiosyncratic business, with one shipwright adopting a scientific approach and making carefully measured drawings on paper and another relying on experience and a good eye. The results varied considerably, as one exasperated seventeenth-century authority pointed out: '[I] could never see two ships builded of the like proportion by the best and most skilful shipwrights though they have many times undertaken the same . . . because they trust rather to their judgement than their art, and to their eye than their scale and compass.'[15]

The greatest problem for Nehemiah and the *Trial* wasn't an absence of skill or science; it was a scarcity of materials. Of course there was an abundance of timber in New England; but a ship needed rope for rigging, heavy cables, iron for the anchors. These all had to come from the other side of the Atlantic. So although the hull of the *Trial* was completed by the late summer of 1641, Nehemiah had to wait until the following year before his new ship was ready to put to sea.

The rigging arrived in July 1642, when two ships from England anchored in Boston Bay, bringing with them little else, only five or six passengers and a handful of other goods. The following month the *Trial* was ready to sail with a cargo of pipe staves and fish. The plan was for John Cotton to give a sermon from the deck asking God's blessing on the new ship and the 'divers godly seamen in her'.[16] But when the appointed day dawned, so many people turned up that Cotton was forced to change his plans and preach from the pulpit of the Boston meeting house instead.

The *Trial*'s first captain was Nehemiah's kinsman from Wapping, Thomas Coytmore; and the next day, 'being bound forth to sea', as he said, Thomas made his will.[17] He and Martha had a son, born earlier in the year, and while he was anxious to leave his family provided for, Thomas was concerned that 'in these uncertain times it's very difficult if not impossible to set a due valuation upon temporal estates'.[18] So rather than leave specific legacies, he adopted the practice of his kin and divided his estate into sixteen parts, as if it was a ship. Martha and their baby son got six parts each. His mother Katherine was still dependent on income from property she had left behind in London, and he stipulated that 'as times are very hazardous in Europe therefore in case things should so pass in England that my dear mother . . . be deprived of her estate', she should have the remaining four parts as an annuity during her lifetime, after which they reverted to his and Martha's child or children.[19]

And here Thomas came across a problem faced by all married mariners who set out on a long voyage: what if Martha were pregnant? 'If my wife have another child by me, then, wife have but five p[ar]ts, & son Thomas five, mother three, & youngest child three.'[20]

For the *Trial*'s first voyage, Thomas took his pipe staves and fish over to the little island of Faial in the Spanish-held Azores, a distance of 2,250 miles as the crow flies. English merchants didn't think much of the Azores: there was woad, which was in demand by dyers, and the islands were a useful supply station for fresh water and goat meat. But 'other matter of trade it affordeth not', said the great seventeenth-century authority on international trade, Lewes Roberts.[21]

Unusually, Roberts was wrong. Thomas found a market for his goods – 'an extraordinary good market', in fact.[22] He took on not woad or goat meat, but wine and sugar. The next port of call was St Christopher Island in the West Indies, where he exchanged some of the wine for cotton and tobacco. He also bought quantities of iron – in short supply in New England, despite attempts to exploit the country's rich mineral resources – which the islanders had salvaged from ships that had come to grief around its coastline.

This gave Thomas an idea. He had an audience with St Christopher's colonial governor, Sir Thomas Warner, and struck a deal whereby he and his crew were given permission to dive at wreck sites on the understanding that Warner received 50 per cent of the value of whatever they managed to raise. And they raised a lot. Using a makeshift diving bell, probably little more than an upturned wooden tub, they managed to bring up anchors, cables and no fewer than fifty guns. Thomas also traded for some gold and silver which had already been salvaged from the clear blue waters of the Caribbean.

And then they headed for home. The *Trial* sailed into Boston Bay at the end of March, after a round trip of well over 7,250 miles lasting some six months. 'And so, through the Lord's blessing', wrote John Winthrop at their homecoming, 'they made a good voyage, which did much encourage the merchants, and made wine and sugar and cotton very plentiful, and cheap, in the country.'[23] A pair of ketches came back safe from the West Indies with a cargo of cotton not long after; and three more ships from Madeira and the Strait soon after that, confirming divine approval of the new venture and the colony's approval of these profitable new markets.

The *Trial* was sent out again in June, this time with Coytmore's brother-in-law Thomas Graves as captain: he took a cargo of fish to Bilbao in northern Spain, freighting round to Malaga on Spain's Mediterranean coast and returning the following March laden with wine, fruit, oil, iron and wool. By now Nehemiah Bourne's shipyard at North End was no longer on its own, but part of a burgeoning industry. Shipwrights and merchants prospered; so did the farmers who had new and lucrative outlets for their wheat and cattle, the coopers who made the barrels to hold the exported goods, the dockers and porters who carried them, the shopkeepers and market traders who sold the imported goods to the rest of Massachusetts and beyond, the innkeepers who gave food and drink to those who came to a town which had become the commercial hub of the promised land. The London trade slowly picked up again, with the difference that the settlers could now take the initiative. Thomas Hawkins started to build a 400-ton vessel, bigger than anything New England had yet seen; Nehemiah gave up shipbuilding and returned to the transatlantic trade, leaving Hannah and their children – there was now a little Hannah as well as a little Nehemiah – behind in Boston.

A few surviving manifests from the *Trial* give us a hint of the kind of goods that were pouring into Boston. On his return voyage from London in 1645 Thomas Graves brought over six tons of rope, twelve winches of cable yarn, thirty-six barrels of tar and eight pigs of lead. He brought 148 iron pots and kettles, four hogsheads of nails, 221 lb of black and brown thread. He brought all kinds of cloth, from heavy Leiden duffel to linen and lace; gunpowder and shot, pins and needles, 'one pack cont[aining] 50 bibles, 30 unbound. 200 bibles in 12 sheets. 200 pasteboard. one small pack cont[aining] 20 bibles with notes'. He brought red wine and brandy wine and wine vinegar; seventy dozen shoes, forty pairs of boots, 'seventy-four doz. men's woollen stockings'. And one dozen felt hats.[24]

It was as if the boom times of the 1630s had returned. As if nothing had changed.

But things *had* changed. There was a war.

12

The Brandished Sword of God

Within weeks of William Rainborowe senior's death in February 1642, his two eldest sons were embarking on a new venture. It was the colonisation of Ireland. And it did not go well.

The Irish rising of October 1641 caused panic in England. Irish Catholic forces captured Newry, Charlemont and Dungannon and laid siege to Drogheda. Over the winter the rebellion spread; and refugees began to pour into Dublin and other garrisons which still held out for the king, and then into Bristol, Falmouth and London, bringing stories of appalling atrocities. That November 160 Protestant civilians had been driven into the river Blackwater at Portadown and shot at or forced back into the icy water until they drowned. Two weeks later the rebels burned a church at Blackwatertown in Co. Armagh with a crowd of Protestants inside: their 'cries being exceeding loud and fearful, the rebels used to delight much in a scornful manner to imitate them, and brag of their acts'.[1] The following February, news began to filter through to England of a massacre at Shrule, on the border of Co. Mayo and Co. Galway. A convoy of English and Scottish Protestants from Mayo were being led to the Royalist stronghold of Galway town under a safe conduct given by the Catholic Archbishop of Tuam, when their escort turned on them. A hundred men, women and children were butchered.

The Irish Rebellion spawned a literary genre of its own, with a flood of pamphlets appearing over the winter of 1641–2, each trying to outdo the others in blood and horror. *A Bloody Battell* told how seven soldiers 'of the Papists faction' had burst into the house of a Mr Atkins outside Kilkenny, murdered him and 'ripped up his wife's womb being great with child, and afteward burnt her and her child in most lamentable manner'.[2] A tract promising 'bloody news from Ireland' described how the rebels, 'set upon nothing but mischief, and bloody villainy', tied a a good Protestant man to his own table and dismembered him with a hatchet in front of his wife.[3] By the autumn of 1642, English Protestants were claiming – and believing – that one million of their co-religionists had been murdered in Ireland.

The important thing about this literature of horror was not that it was true – most of it wasn't – but that it was believed, enraging Protestant opinion in England and leading to repeated calls for vengeance against the barbarous Irish papists. While the Scots reacted swiftly to assaults on their own settlers by sending a 10,000-strong army to Ulster (and asking the English government to pay for it), Parliament's response was more complicated. There were rumours in London that the rising was supported by Charles I's Catholic queen Henrietta Maria, even by the king himself; and those rumours were fuelled by the fact that the rebel leaders were declaring to all and sundry that they possessed a royal warrant authorising them to take control of Ireland. It was a forgery, but it helped to convince Parliament that it wouldn't be wise to raise an army and hand over command to Charles I.

But the cries of suffering Protestants would not be silenced. 'Oh! we sigh and grieve for the English forces', wrote one to a cousin in London.[4] On 11 February a group of London merchants approached Parliament with an enterprising solution: they would raise an expeditionary force to defeat the insurgents, provided that they could choose their own officers, that the state would supply the arms and ammunition, and that 'they may have such satisfaction out of the rebels' estates, (the war being ended) as shall be thought reasonable'.[5] After a little tweaking, the Adventure for Irish Lands received royal assent on 19 March. Thomas and William Rainborowe invested £200 in the scheme. If the venture proved successful, the brothers' investment would entitle them to a share in 2.5 million acres of confiscated Irish land. Their £200 could buy 1,000 acres of Ulster, rather less in Connacht, Munster and prosperous Leinster.

The Adventure was a holy war, offering that combination of profit and piety which appealed so strongly to Puritan businessmen. The Rainborowe brothers could expect to reap their reward both on earth and in heaven, having a share in the confiscated Irish estates and also, declared Parliament, 'a share in that most glorious work of propagating the Gospel of Jesus Christ, and demolishing the kingdom of Antichrist', securing the kingdom of Ireland for the future by replanting it with Protestants.[6] The Adventure wasn't simply a privately financed punitive expedition. It was jihad.

Around 1,200 men and women – merchants and ministers, clerks and cooks and farmers – were sufficiently attracted by the prospect to contribute to the scheme. The mayor, bailiffs and commonalty of Exeter stumped up an enormous £9,890 10s.; a Yorkshire widow handed over her mite of £5. The Rainborowes' friend, Alexander Bence, invested £600; the MP for Cambridge, Oliver Cromwell, put in £300. Altogether the Adventure for Irish Lands raised over £300,000 – short of the £1 million that the framers of the scheme had hoped for, but still a substantial sum.

But not enough to move the Adventure forward. By May, while the money was still trickling in and the king and Parliament were locked in an acrimonious quarrel over who exactly should approve the expedition's officers, and who should have ultimate control of the forces that were levied, a group of fifteen London merchants and mariners, all bar one of whom were radical Protestants, came up with a second plan – a smaller private fleet which would sail almost immediately with reinforcements for the beleaguered Protestant garrisons in the south of Ireland. Again, both Thomas and William Rainborowe were involved in the scheme. In fact Thomas was one of the syndicate of fifteen who proposed it.

The Rainborowe brothers were moving in advanced circles now. All the members of this new syndicate were London merchants, or men with trading connections to the City; between them they had already invested £4,400 in the Adventure for Irish Lands, and now they put up a further £8,550. There was only one Royalist among them: Sir Nicholas Crisp, a militant supporter of Charles I who within the year would be hunted by Parliament, accused of spying for the king and playing a central role in a Royalist plot to take over London. Everyone else was for Parliament and godly Protestantism: and not in a lukewarm way, either, if their subsequent histories are anything to go by. Gregory Clement, a New England merchant with a big house by London Bridge, was one of the signatories to Charles I's death warrant in 1649. Richard Shute was a militant spokesman for liberty and Puritanism, one of those who in 1643 would condemn attempts at reconciliation with the king and proclaim that 'the safety of the people is the supreme law'.[7] The powerful Thompson brothers were merchants with interests in just about every colonial enterprise you could imagine, from the East Indies and the Levant to West African slavery and North American furs; Maurice, the eldest, was godly enough for John Winthrop to hope he 'would, ere long, come settle with us'.[8] William Willoughby and William Pennoyer would later join the hard-line Tower Hamlets militia in East London; Samuel Moyer expected the imminent arrival of Christ on earth and the coming of the Last Days. Many of these men would serve in the Parliamentarian army and involve themselves in the more radical reaches of Protestantism during the 1640s and 1650s.

They were also astute entrepreneurs, something reflected in the deal they struck with Parliament. The syndicate was to equip and provide twelve ships and six pinnaces, and raise a force of 1,000 horse and 2,000 foot soldiers, with a view to reducing 'the rebels in the said realm of Ireland to their due obedience . . . and like-wise, by all possible ways and means, to assist and help His Majesty's good subjects there, and to infest, spoil, and waste the said rebels by land and sea'.[9] In return, Parliament authorised the original Irish Adventure to reimburse their expenses at the usual rate for the hire and victualling of ships up to a maximum of £40,000 in Irish land. They could sail under English colours. They could board any ships they came across and search them for rebels or supplies that might be destined for the rebels, using force if necessary. And 'for the better encouragement of the said Adventurers', they were to have all ships, goods, moneys, plate, pillage and spoil which they captured, 'without any account whatsoever thereof to be made', except that the Admiralty wanted documentary evidence that any ships taken were actively involved in the rebellion.[10]

It was a privateering raid, in other words; and Thomas Rainborowe and his fellows had pulled off the rather clever feat of having Parliament underwrite the entire cost without asking for a penny of the prize money.

At the same time, principle and profit went hand in hand. The venturers saw themselves as instruments through whom God would smite the papists and rescue his suffering people. Laud and his bishops had failed Ireland. 'The unfaithfulness of most of our ministers,' explained the expedition's chaplain, 'the scurillity and monstrous ignorance of our English, have administered oil to their flame in abundance, and brought down wrath from heaven.' The church had become so corrupt that it was hard to tell Catholic from Protestant with all the 'holy days, fasts, hallowed places, images, vestures, gestures, &c.' Now it was time for the godly to act, 'quenching that flame broke out . . . in that miserable kingdom', said the chaplain.[11]

That chaplain was Salem's Hugh Peter, who had been diverted from his mission to reassure old England of New England's credit-worthiness. His half-brother Benjamin Peter, another London merchant, was admiral of the armada, which was a little smaller than originally planned, consisting of fifteen ships and pinnaces and about a thousand soldiers under the command of Alexander Lord Forbes. There were other New England connections. William Rainborowe sailed with the expedition; and the rear admiral of the fleet was Robert Thompson, another of the Thompson brothers and a Massachusetts merchant who had been living in Boston, a neighbour of Nehemiah Bourne. The vice admiral of the fleet was Thomas Rainborowe. He was named in the official account as 'Captaine *Thomas Rainsborough Zant*-man', an acknowledgement of his reputation as a Levant merchant – Zante was the island of Zakynthos in the Ionian Sea, famed in the seventeenth century for its currants, which were imported into England by the shipload.[12]

Once Parliament had passed an 'Ordinance for the Sea Adventure to Ireland' on 17 June, events gathered momentum with astonishing speed. Twelve days later, ships and men had been hired, supplies and munitions had been taken on board and, after a day of fasting and prayer, the fleet was gathered off Dover. They set sail that day, immediately running into foul weather which sank two of the ten barges they were towing 'for landing men, and rowing into rivers'.[13] While Thomas Rainborowe and two of the pinnaces went for the Isle of Wight to take on a company of soldiers and two of the other captains headed for Falmouth and Weymouth for the same purpose, the remainder of the fleet headed west to Mount's Bay in Cornwall, and then struck a course past the Scilly Isles and out into the Atlantic. They were scattered in more heavy seas and stormy weather, and when the fleet's flagship carrying Forbes and Hugh Peter (whose published journal is our chief source for the expedition) made Kinsale, Co. Cork on a foggy, wet Monday 11 July, ten of the fifteen ships were missing. Four turned up over the next couple of days, but there was still no sign of the other six, including Thomas Rainborowe's, when the little army marched off to relieve the garrison at Rathbarry, some thirty miles away across difficult and hostile terrain. Lord Forbes heard that there were rebels in the area from some locals, 'whom before their death we examined', says Hugh Peter with chilling matter-of-factness; but he was unable to find the enemy, although he did attract a grisly band of about a hundred 'pillagers', who supported no side but followed in their wake and killed women and children, 'stripped the slain, [and] made havoc of all'.[14]

Forbes wasn't the best military commander. He was impetuous, hungry for plunder and woefully ignorant of the nuanced complexities of Irish society, in which the Old English, whose families had come to Ireland with the expeditionary forces of Henry II and King John in the Middle Ages, and who were mostly Catholic, were wavering between the native Irish Catholic rebels and the New English Protestants who remained loyal to the Crown. He attacked Timoleague Castle, even though its owner, Sir Roger O'Shaughnessy, was a Royalist, burned the local abbey and tortured local people. 'We could get nothing out of them,' wrote one of the English officers, 'so our men mangled them to pieces.'[15]

Returning rather swiftly to Kinsale, the expedition re-embarked
and headed westward around the Cork coast, raiding enthusiasti-
cally as they went. They blew up a rebel fort at Castlehaven and
burned another in Baltimore, set fire to houses, destroyed crops,
'captured' livestock, and all without making a great deal of difference to the counter-insurgency's strategic objectives.

On Saturday 29 July, while Forbes and the fleet were anchored
near Baltimore and their boats were out stealing livestock, Thomas
Rainborowe caught up with the expedition. The next day was
spent in prayer; but on the Monday Thomas, who was raring to
go, mustered the men and the commanders held a council of war.

They had three courses open to them: to move against Limerick,
which was in the hands of the rebels; to relieve Duncannon Fort
in Wexford, which guarded two important river approaches; or to
sail on to Galway, where the townspeople hovered between the
rebels and the governor, the Earl of Clanricarde, who was managing
with some difficulty to preserve the place for the Crown. Forbes
decided on Galway; and a couple of days later the fleet arrived in
Galway Bay. When a contrary wind prevented them from gaining
the harbour, wrote Hugh Peter, 'our vice admiral's boat went ashore,
and took some cattle, burnt some houses, and killed some rebels'.[16]

Forbes fired off a threatening letter to the mayor, demanding
that the town should lay down its arms and open its gates to the
Adventurers. Whether the plan was to occupy Galway or ransack
it isn't clear; but the mayor wisely refused his ultimatum and
appealed instead to Clanricarde, who was twenty miles inland at
Loughrea and who immediately complained to his superiors. The
expedition's arrival in Galway Bay, he wrote, 'doth much disquiet
and disturb my thoughts in many respects, apprehending, by several
circumstances, that they come without any particular commission,
or direction for this government, or any relation or respect to
me'.[17] He was related to Sir Roger O'Shaughnessy, the loyalist
whose home the Adventurers had attacked at Timoleague, and he
was still bristling over that. Worse, he'd heard that Forbes was
pillaging the estates of Daniel and Turlough O'Brien, 'the only
two that remained in firm obedience there, and preserved and
relieved the English to the best of their power, and sent their long
boats to me for the relief of the fort [at Galway] when it was
besieged'.[18] It may have been the lands of the O'Briens that Hugh

Peter referred to when he wrote blithely that while the Adventurers waited for the mayor to reply, 'our soldiers went out for fresh meat, and brought home some, and burnt a whole town'.[19]

Clanricarde sent letters that he was on his way to Galway, and the Adventurers settled in, occupying a nearby abbey and building gun positions in preparation for an assault on the town. They passed the time by raiding into the interior, coming back with 'about 100 cattle and as many sheep having burnt four Irish towns and corn as they went by the way'[20] – and oblivious to the fact that these cattle, sheep, cornfields and villages belonged to Clanricarde's tenants.

By the end of the week Clanricarde had arrived, as had the Lord President of Connacht, Lord Ranelagh, who came rushing over from Athlone to try to repair the damage that the Adventurers were doing to the loyalist cause. Ranelagh found Lord Forbes under the influence of Hugh Peter, whom he dismissed as a 'pragmatic chaplain from London', and who was urging Forbes to launch a direct assault on Galway town. Now 'the lieutenant-general of the additional forces by sea and land, sent by His Majesty', as Forbes now styled himself, proposed another plan: that Ranelagh should organise an army to march out of Dublin, joining up with the Scottish army in Ulster and the Adventurers in Munster. Together, Forbes thought, 'we shall make a considerable body to march forth, and daunt the rebels in any part of this kingdom'.[21]

Ranelagh and Clanricarde burst out laughing. It was hard enough to send *letters* into the more remote parts of Ireland, the rebels were so strong and so united. The thought of marching through hostile terrain (and leaving English-held towns defenceless in the process) was absurd. And with a sideswipe at Thomas, Clanricarde noted with heavy sarcasm that the plan was 'approved of by the well-experienced commanders of the city of London, who attended my Lord Forbes'.[22]

Thomas, Forbes and the rest of the Adventurers were finally persuaded to leave Galway at the beginning of September. Their intention was to relieve Tralee, which was under siege by the rebels; but they couldn't resist a detour to the Aran Islands where, inevitably, they 'took 300 head of cattle, destroyed many with very good houses, burnt their corn and towns, and slew and hung many of the rebels'.[23] While they pillaged the Arans, Tralee fell to the rebels.

Time was pressing now. Not for Tralee – it was too late for Tralee – but for the Adventurers. They had only hired their ships for three months, and at Michaelmas, 29 September, they had to give them back. Sailing into the Shannon they captured 'roaring Meg', a big gun with which the rebels had been bombarding Royalist strongholds; and they pondered over the practicalities of using it to destroy Sir Daniel O'Brien's house at Clare Castle, even though O'Brien was not a rebel. Instead, they stormed Glin Castle on the banks of the Shannon, after the Knight of Glin had produced a letter of introduction from Clanricarde which assured them of his loyalty. 'The plate and silver was gone for Limerick', remarked Hugh Peter ruefully.[24] With that, the Sea Adventure for Ireland came to an inglorious end.

The venturers had taken five ships worth £20,000, Peter boasted. They had burned corn worth at least that amount, killed hundreds of the enemy, 'fired many Irish towns, relieved many English in forts and castles, took and spoiled thousands of cattle, burnt and spoiled many castles, houses of note, and mills of the enemy [and] guarded the coast from Kinsale almost to Londonderry'.[25] They had blockaded Limerick and Galway and, he claimed, diverted the rebels from their other designs.

What they had actually done was to alienate large sections of the community in Munster and Connacht, confirming the rebels in their belief that they had nothing to lose since the English would show them no mercy; confirming the waverers in the righteousness of the rebels' cause; and confirming the gentry who had stayed loyal to the Crown in their suspicion that England had no idea of the complexities of Irish realpolitik. Clanricarde, whose patience was stretched to breaking point by the Adventurers' antics in Connacht, wrote a formal complaint to the government in which he listed Forbes's errors of judgement and ended with a cold promise: 'I shall never willingly entertain any forces into this government, except in case of great necessity, if they be not properly assigned to my command.'[26]

The Rainborowe brothers' first experience of war had not been a success.

13

War Then, War

*N*ews from home was a long time coming to New
England in the autumn and winter of 1642–3. When
it did come, aboard two fishing vessels that arrived
early in February, the colonists' fears were confirmed. There was
war.

The wars with Scotland, the Irish rebellion – with each succes-
sive conflict New England had watched old England sliding towards
its own day of judgement, watched as friends and relations groaned
under the twin burdens of God's wrath and Man's intransigence.
The colonists had heard their preachers lament 'the dividing of a
king from his subjects' and nodded wisely as those same preachers
warned that the consequences, 'even the gloomy and dark consequences thereof, are killing and slaying, and sacking and burning,
and robbing and rifling, cursing and blaspheming'.[1] They had felt
a self-righteous glow at the news that Strafford was impeached and
Archbishop Laud had been consigned to the Tower of London.
'Lord prelates, deans, prebends are fallen', exulted William Hooke
from his pulpit in Taunton, Massachusetts. But now war had come,
the colony's leaders didn't quite know what to do.[2]

From a twenty-first-century vantage point, it seems obvious. Parliament, or a significant section of it, was sympathetic towards Puritanism and the goals of the godly. The king was not. That's all there was to it.

But it wasn't that simple. With no native manufacturing industries to speak of, Massachusetts and the other New England colonies were still dependent on supplies from home. If they declared for Parliament, and the king's party won, where would that leave them? The Massachusetts Bay Company enjoyed special privileges over and above those granted to freeborn Englishmen at home, including (in the eyes of the colony's leaders, at least) absolute power of government. But those privileges were in the gift of Charles I, and if he saw fit to recall their charter, as he had already attempted to do in the 1630s, the colony would be in a difficult position indeed.

In fact it was already in a difficult position. Trade with England was falling off because of the war, and as the ships stopped coming, so did news from home, increasing the settlers' anxieties. And the ships that did make the crossing were liable to search and seizure by king and by Parliament. At different times during the war William Rainborowe and Nehemiah Bourne both armed ships for transatlantic voyages with cannon borrowed from the colony.

Massachusetts, Connecticut and New Haven formed a mutual support group in May 1643, with Plymouth joining them in September, and one of the reasons cited for their confederation of united colonies was the trouble back home. They felt the need for 'a firm and perpetual league, offensive and defensive', they declared, because they feared natives and other European settlers would seek to take advantage of their isolation.[3] Having heard of 'those sad distractions in England', enemies and commercial rivals in the region would know 'we are hindered from that humble way of seeking advice, or reaping those comfortable fruits of protection which at other times we might well expect'.[4]

A policy of cautious neutrality seemed best. It enabled New England to reinvent itself as a different kind of safe haven – not from prelates and papists, but from the horrors of war. And it allowed business as usual. The efforts of Hugh Peter and Thomas Weld to further Massachusetts' cause in England looked to be paying off when a ship arrived in June carrying twenty children 'sent by money given one fast day in London', and £300-worth of goods bought with donations from friends in England. Even more welcome was the news that Parliament had issued an order exempting all imports to and exports from the New England colonies from customs duties and tax.

Those who were already in England, or who were passing back and forth, responded in different ways. Weld and Peter were expected back in Massachusetts with each ship that dropped anchor in Boston Bay. And yet somehow, something – politics or providence, financial difficulties or ill health – always seemed to prevent them. They and their wives, who had joined them in England, were ready to return in the late summer of 1643; their sailing was delayed and they decided they dared not venture 'our own & our wives' healths & lives in a winter voyage'.[5] Weld dithered for years, before accepting a living in the north of England at St Mary's, Gateshead. He never went home.

Nor did Hugh Peter. Instead, he threw himself into the struggle against the king. At the end of 1642, he put his name to a petition urging Parliament to stand fast against those who wanted peace at any price, and declaring himself prepared 'with life and fortune to assist the Parliament, till the king be brought to his Parliament, and matters concerning religion, laws, and liberty be settled'.[6] By this time he had made enough of a name for himself to be satirised in the Royalist press, which laughed at his efforts to send over to Massachusetts 'many babes borne out of the estate & covenant of grace (though by this malignant called bastards)'; and sneered at Peter himself, 'whose zealous doctrine we have stayed so long to hear on a fast day, that we have even bepissed ourselves'.[7]

And war or no war, the men with interests on both banks of Jordan – merchants and traders and sea-captains like Nehemiah Bourne, Thomas Hawkins, Thomas Graves – continued to make the crossing. William Rainborowe was owed money in Massachusetts, and after the Irish expedition he was in need of it: he was back in Boston in 1643, before going to England once again and joining the Parliamentarian army as a captain of a troop of horse.

Two of John Winthrop's sons were also in England during the early years of the war. The eldest, John junior, who was

married to Hugh Peter's stepdaughter, went over in 1641 with
samples of ore from Braintree in an attempt to attract inves-
tors to an ironworks project. His father, always mindful that
England might lure settlers away from his city on a hill, wrote
to remind him of what a blessed sanctuary New England was
in troubled times: it was 'a land where we enjoy outward
peace and liberty . . . Many thousands there are who would
give great estates to enjoy our condition.'[8]

Governor Winthrop's second son, Stephen, had made his first
Atlantic crossing with his father on the *Arbella* when he was
eleven years old. Eight years later, in 1639, he was back in England
on business for his parents. ('I have brought your things . . . and
put them in a chest', he wrote anxiously to his mother in Boston.
'Your feather bed is left behind. I know not the reason.'[9]) And
he had scarcely had time to catch his breath on his return to
Boston before he was off on a trading venture to Bermuda.

Stephen was an earnest young man. When he was only fourteen
he suffered a period of profound religious disturbance in which
he was plagued by wicked thoughts, 'whereby Satan buffeted
him, so as he went mourning and languishing daily'.[10] The
twenty-first-century cynic might think this a pretty fair description of adolescence. Puritan Boston, inclined to see the Devil at
work in all things, even teenage angst, took such episodes more
seriously; and when Stephen managed to overcome temptation
through prayer and good counsel, he was welcomed into Boston's
church as a full member eight days short of his fifteenth birthday.
By the time he was twenty he was trading as a merchant on his
own account and in partnership with William Goose, master of
the *Sparrow* and 'an honest godly man of our church', according
to Hugh Peter.[11] That same year the General Court noted
succinctly that 'Mr Stephen Winthrop was chosen to record
things':[12] his role as recorder of all legal transactions in Massachusetts
earned him a fee of sixpence a time, and a place at his father's
side in the administration of the colony.

It seems safe to assume that Stephen was on good terms with
William Rainborowe during the latter's first stay in New England,
and also with Martha and Thomas Coytmore. Safe, because at the
end of 1642 Stephen went over to England again; and when he
came back to Boston nearly a year later, he brought with him

a wife – Judith Rainborowe, the nineteen-year-old sister of William, Martha and Thomas. Judith gave birth to their first child at Boston in November 1644. The boy, named for his father, was baptised at the First Church three days later.

By the end of 1643, then, two Rainborowes had settled in New England: Martha, married to a successful sea-captain; and Judith, daughter-in-law to one of the most powerful men in Massachusetts. William, unsettled and unsure, was drifting from one side of the Atlantic to the other in search of a cause. And their eldest brother Thomas had found one.

Thomas Rainborowe was in financial difficulties, not only because, like William, he had lost his investment in the Irish Adventure, but also because as one of its commanders he had personally commissioned supplies for the troops. In June 1643 he was pleading with Parliament to enforce payment by the Committee for the Irish Expedition, claiming that 'divers bills for provisions, and others, are returned and protested against him'.[13] His plea bought him a temporary respite from his creditors: the Commons ordered that no one should bring an action for non-payment 'till the said Captain Rainborow shall return from the public service of the kingdom'.[14]

That public service was in the Parliamentarian navy. After the outbreak of war Parliament purged its gentlemen captains (those who hadn't already deserted to the king), replacing them with a new type of naval commander drawn from the London merchant-mariner community. Thomas, experienced at sea, committed to the reformation of religion, hostile towards the Crown and the son of one of the most influential figures in English maritime affairs, was exactly the kind of man the reinvented navy was looking for; and by the spring of 1643 he was given the command of the 478-ton *Swallow*, in a fleet of twenty-two warships led by the Earl of Warwick.

Within weeks he moved to take command of the 620-ton *Lion*, sailing under Admiral Richard Swanley as part of the Irish Guard. His duties consisted of patrolling for Irish privateers and Royalists bringing over supplies and munitions, and in June he intercepted a ship carrying 170 Irish and thirty Scots who claimed they were en route to Dieppe. Since they were off the north-east coast of Scotland with only two days of victuals aboard,

Thomas suspected they were bound for Newcastle upon Tyne
and the king's army in the north, and arrested them. The editor
of one London newsbook speculated that the 'Irish' may in fact
have been Highland Scots, who 'in former times went naked, &
were called Picts, in regard they painted themselves with some
fearful kind of creatures upon their bodies'[15] – a notion which
led the writer to muse on how sensible the Romans had been
to build Hadrian's Wall.

Thomas brought his captives into Yarmouth on the Norfolk
coast, locked them up and went down to Westminster to report to
Parliament in person. The newsbooks reported that an order had
gone to the Earl of Warwick as Lord High Admiral, 'to try [them]
and execute them'.[16] This was half true: the matter was referred to
the parliamentary Committee of the Navy, for whom the prisoners'
nationality was a matter of importance. Although no one in England
would bat an eye if Irish rebels were hanged, with the Privy Council
of Scotland currently considering an alliance with the English
Parliament, it would not do to hang Scots without at least considering the consequences. Warwick was asked to try 'the Irish pirates'
under martial law. What their fate was, we don't know. They could
at least count themselves lucky that they were not taken by Thomas's
fellow officer Richard Swanley, who when he captured a number
of Irish soldiers at Caernarfon in May 1644, bound them back to
back and tossed them into the sea.

The war was going badly for Thomas's side in the summer of
1643. A crushing defeat for a Parliamentarian army under Sir
William Waller at the Battle of Roundway Down in July was
followed by the fall of Bristol, the kingdom's second city, two
weeks later. There was a Royalist rising in Kent. Most of Cornwall,
Devon and Dorset was controlled by the king's forces. In the
north, a Royalist army commanded by William Cavendish, Earl
of Newcastle, was pushing down towards London and Westminster,
where a sizeable number of MPs were calling loudly for an end
to the war and a negotiated peace with the king. Almost the only
part of the country where the Parliamentarian cause seemed
secure was the east – the rich agricultural counties of Essex,
Hertfordshire, Norfolk, Suffolk and Cambridgeshire which were
under the control of the Eastern Association, commanded (from
August 1643 onwards) by the Earl of Manchester, assisted by a

middle-aged MP and landowner with no military experience at all, Oliver Cromwell.

Cromwell's cousin John Hampden, one of the most able leaders of the war party in Parliament, was wounded in a skirmish at Chalgrove in June, and died six days later. For his comrade at Westminster John Pym, who was already suffering from the bowel cancer which would kill him before the year was out, an alliance with the Scots seemed the only way of avoiding defeat. He despatched Sir Henry Vane, now an influential member of the war party in England, to Edinburgh, and on 25 September both Houses of Parliament and the Scots ratified the Solemn League and Covenant. The Covenant, a remarkable diplomatic coup for Vane, provided that both countries would work 'to bring the Churches of God in the three kingdoms to the nearest conjunction and uniformity in religion', getting rid of the bishops and stamping out popery, 'that the Lord may be one, and His name one in the three kingdoms'.[17] The Scots took this to mean the adoption of their own brand of Presbyterianism, while Vane held that the wording managed to 'keep a door open in England to Independency', that is, to congregationalists and separatists.[18] And both nations agreed to a mutual defence policy, paving the way for a massive Scottish army to cross the border early the following year.

In New England, one of John Winthrop's friends wrote exultantly to tell him the news: 'It is the high way of God for their deliverance. I hope it is now the day of Antichrist's great overthrow at Armageddon.'[19]

At the beginning of October Thomas Rainborowe and the *Lion* were ordered north to support the beleaguered town of Hull, where a Parliamentarian army commanded by Lord Ferdinando Fairfax was under siege from the Earl of Newcastle and a force of 15,000 men. Fairfax, a Calvinist landowner whose battle standard carried the Spanish motto *Viva el rey y muerra el mal govierno* ('Long live the king and death to bad government') was the leader of Yorkshire's Parliamentarians; his eldest son, Sir Thomas Fairfax, served as his general of horse. Since the beginning of the year their troops had been in retreat, forced back by Newcastle, who now controlled the whole of Yorkshire – except for Hull.

The town was well placed to withstand an attack from the land: it was walled on all sides, and bounded on the south by the Humber and on the east by the river Hull. In Henry VIII's time the defences were strengthened by the construction of two blockhouses, and between them Henry built a strong castle, placed so that the three forts could cover one another in the event of an enemy attack. They were linked with an equally strong wall of cemented brick and stone, twenty-four feet high and fifteen feet wide.

Just as effective as the Tudor defences was an expanse of low-lying meadow to the west. Sluices kept out the water at flood tide, and by opening them and cutting the banks of the Humber and the Hull it was possible to flood the meadows for miles around, confining attackers to high-built lanes and islands of high ground, and making a direct assault impossible.

Without mounting a blockade at the mouth of the Humber to prevent the town from being resupplied by sea – something which was well beyond the Royalists' means – there was little hope of taking Hull. Newcastle should have bypassed the town and continued his advance southward, pursuing the Royalists' grand strategy of a convergence on London from the north and the west. But he was unhappy at the thought of leaving an enemy stronghold at his rear to disrupt his lines of communication.

On Saturday 2 September the Royalist army arrived within sight of the walls and began constructing a series of earthworks overlooking the town. They possessed two great brass demy-cannon brought over from Holland by Queen Henrietta Maria, 'the queen's pocket-pistols': these guns, which weighed two and a half tons each, fired 36 lb shot which Newcastle's gunners heated up in a furnace and sent into the town in an attempt to burn the defenders out. Lord Fairfax responded by ordering tubs of water to be set outside every house, with fire-guards at the end of every street; powder and combustible materials were stowed away in the deepest cellars. There were in fact few casualties among the defenders: one of the most serious losses of life came about two weeks into the siege when a gunner went into the north blockhouse, which was being used as a munitions store, to fetch cartridges. Like all soldiers on service he was carrying a length of lighted match for his musket, and in retrospect he would have been well advised to leave it outside. The explosion killed him and four others and blew out a wall of the blockhouse.

Lord Fairfax flooded the western meadows on 14 September, forcing Newcastle's men back to higher ground. On 5 October Thomas Rainborowe and the *Lion* arrived, together with a merchant ship, the *Employment*. They were carrying supplies and reinforcements commanded by a Scottish professional soldier, Sir John Meldrum. After an attack by Royalists on the quay was repulsed, Lord Fairfax resolved to launch a counter-attack. The plan was for a thousand musketeers escorted by troops of horse to march out in two battalions and storm the enemies' trenches. Meldrum was in overall charge of the operation, and one of the battalions of infantry was led by one of Lord Fairfax's officers, John Lambert. The other was given to Thomas Rainborowe.

For a serving naval officer to be handed the command of an infantry battalion in this way wasn't as unusual as it might seem. Two of the three eyewitness accounts of the fight that day describe Thomas specifically as a ship's captain; the third, by Meldrum, calls him 'Colonel Rainsborough', suggesting it was Meldrum who gave him his commission.[20] He was also referred to as a colonel by Parliament from this point on. No one commented on his switch, but then lines of demarcation between land and sea fighting were not particularly well defined – Thomas had already experienced a land campaign of sorts as vice admiral during the ill-fated Irish Adventure.

At seven on the morning of Wednesday 11 October the defenders gathered inside the western gate, almost 1,500 in all. Since before dawn the sentries on the town walls had been reporting glimmers of light all over the enemy camp as the Royalist musketeers and gunners lit their matches in readiness – Newcastle was expecting trouble. To persuade him that it was coming from another quarter, Fairfax gave orders that the guards on the north side of the town were 'to flash powder, as if they were lighting many hundred matches', so that the enemy would think the attack would come through the north gate.[21]

At nine o'clock the west gates swung open and men poured out, overrunning the Royalists' lines and pushing them back and back again, 'the enemy abandoning one work after another, till we had made ourselves masters of their ordinance', Meldrum reported to Parliament a couple of days later.[22]

Not for long. A hundred Royalist pikemen launched a counter-attack so furious that it turned the triumphant advance into a headlong retreat. Ignoring their officers' orders the soldiers, seamen and townspeople who made up the ragtag raiders fled back into Hull. Thomas Rainborowe wasn't among them. No one knew exactly where he was. Meldrum wrote that he was 'either taken prisoner, or killed dead, and so fallen into some ditch, for he could not be found, but his man's dead body was found'.[23]

Fairfax ordered the gates shut as he and Meldrum rallied their frightened forces. The Lord General urged them to think of their honour, of their experience of God's assistance in the past, of 'the cause of God, and the kingdom, for which they now fought'.[24] And he promised them money.

That did the trick. The army regrouped and charged the Royalist siege-works, and once again they overran them, this time manning the enemies' guns so that when Newcastle tried to march the main body of his army down to the fight from their camp a quarter of a mile away, he found himself facing his own artillery. 'Thereupon', wrote Meldrum, 'they were all instantly forced to a most wretched retreat', and left to watch as their adversaries dragged nine pieces of heavy ordnance into the town, including one of the queen's pocket-pistols.[25]

When the defenders looked out the next morning they saw to their surprise that Newcastle's army had gone, pulling up bridges and opening sluices behind them 'to fill the ways with water, to prevent our sallying out'.[26]

It wasn't until the Saturday that anything was heard about Thomas. Sir John Meldrum was sitting in his lodgings at Hull and writing to inform Parliament of his success. He had already broken the news that Thomas was missing, and he was in the middle of composing a stirring conclusion to his report – 'we may perceive, that God is certainly upon the stage, and that Dagon must down' – when he broke off to say that since he began writing he had heard 'that Colonel Rainsborough is safe'.[27] Safe – but embarrassed and a long way from Hull. In the confusion of the first retreat, when his men ran from the Royalist pikes, he had ridden over to join a troop of Fairfax's cavalry – only to find that they weren't Fairfax's cavalry at all, but Newcastle's. The Royalists promptly took him prisoner and when Newcastle abandoned the siege and retired to York, Thomas went too.

He was in no danger. Out of the heat of battle both sides treated officer prisoners well, looking to exchange them for their own or for ransom. But Fairfax and Parliament made strenuous efforts to secure the release of 'that valiant and worthy commander Captain Rainsborow'.[28] Newcastle's opening demand was four of the *Lion*'s best guns; Fairfax replied by offering two knights, or any of the Royalist captains he was holding. That was refused, and Thomas's wife Margaret petitioned Parliament to arrange an exchange for Thomas Kettleby, a Royalist officer taken the previous year. The exchange was approved at the beginning of November, but it turned out to be unnecessary. Browne Bushell, a Whitby naval officer who had recently gone over to the king's party, begged the Earl of Newcastle to give Thomas to him, and then sent him back to Hull in return for a promise of £500. The deal didn't please Hull's citizens, who were expected to stump up the cash; but Lord Fairfax decided Parliament could sort it out and sent Thomas back to London.[29]

Thomas wasn't the first to confuse friend with foe. At this stage in the war combatants didn't wear distinguishing uniforms, relying instead on the use of passwords and field tokens. At Newbury in September, when the main army under the Earl of Essex clashed with Charles I's army, the Parliamentarian soldiers wore sprigs of broom in their hats and identified themselves by the password 'Religion'. In other set-piece battles, the two sides wore coloured scarves: when Sir Faithfull Fortescue's regiment switched sides on the field at Edgehill and came over to the king en masse, seventeen or eighteen were killed by their new allies because they weren't quick enough in removing the orange scarves which marked them out as the enemy. So Thomas's blunder wasn't as stupid as it might seem, and its consequences weren't unpleasant enough to deter him from military service. He left the navy after Hull and joined

Meldrum's army, serving as a reformado, an officer without a command of his own.

By the summer internecine feuds were fracturing the Parliamentarian cause. Lords and Commons fought over their roles, over whether peers and MPs who had gone over to the king and then changed their minds should be allowed to sit in Parliament, over funding for the army. Supporters of Manchester and the Earl of Essex squabbled over which of them was in charge of the military. A party headed by Sir Henry Vane prosecuted the war and resisted attempts by Essex to reach an accommodation with the king. In religion, Independents who favoured separating congregationalism, a more extreme variety of the system of gathered churches which was prospering in New England, fell out with their Calvinist brethren in the Presbyterian church who with their Scottish allies wanted to impose uniformity and strict regulation by assemblies of lay elders.

Confusing though that picture is, it still doesn't come close to the complexities of the Parliamentarian position in the summer of 1644. Some MPs – most, in fact – formed a middle group which wavered between war and peace. Others argued for the retention of bishops and the continued existence of the Church of England in a modified form. Radicals challenged the traditional social order while conservatives expressed concern that 'men of estate' were pushed aside in favour of 'common men, poor and of mean parentage', or that promotion in the army went to 'those that call themselves the godly; some of them profess they have seen visions and had revelations'.[30]

Independents were particularly prominent in the Eastern Association, where four colonels of foot were condemned by suspicious comrades as 'professed Independents'.[31] One was Thomas, who raised his own infantry regiment for the Association that June.

Wherever possible, Manchester preferred his colonels to recruit in the county where a regiment was raised, arguing that this 'made the soldiers more united among themselves'.[32] In practice recruitment was beset with problems: village constables charged with conscripting soldiers succumbed to the temptation to get rid of local paupers or vagrants who were a charge on the parish.

They used impressment to work out personal grudges against hated neighbours; or sometimes simply crumbled in the face of intimidation and violence from their peers. Men rushed to join the trained bands, knowing that this gave them exemption from the press. They opted for imprisonment and fines rather than go to war, or deserted at the first opportunity. On one occasion, when Thomas's new regiment was at Grantham in Lincolnshire, he was forced to ask the town bailiffs to apprehend any of his soldiers they found; 'near 200 [had] run within a month'.[33]

But while some men ran from the fight, others ran towards it. They sailed across the wide ocean to make a new city upon a hill, a new England in the fields and towns and villages of the old.

When Thomas Rainborowe raised his regiment, the saints came to join him.

14

And Get Themselves a Name

*O*ne of the dozens of Massachusetts merchants who made trips to England during the early years of the war was Israel Stoughton of Dorchester, a veteran of the Pequot War of 1637. For years Stoughton had been an advocate of action to curb arbitrary authority in Massachusetts, arguing against magisterial power and for elected deputies. Back in 1635, after he circulated a paper challenging the authority of the magistrates, an exasperated John Winthrop condemned him as 'a worm . . . and an underminer of the state'.[1] The General Court ordered that the paper 'which hath occasioned much trouble & offence' be burned; and Stoughton was barred from holding any public office in the colony for three years.[2] However, the ban was lifted two years later, and on the same day he was made a magistrate, the court having decided it was safer to have him inside their judicial tent.

Stoughton's role as one of the expedition commanders in the Pequot War completed his rehabilitation, and this 'underminer of the state' transformed himself into a distinguished member of the Massachusetts establishment, standing as assistant every year from

1637 to 1644, serving on various committees and meting out justice to the colony's delinquents. He also maintained his interest in military affairs: he belonged to the Honourable Artillery Company, and served as captain for Dorchester and as sergeant major to John Winthrop's colonel in the amalgamation of town militias which became known as the South Regiment.

In 1643 Stoughton went to England on business, and returned with a girl. A kinsman in the Parliamentarian army who was 'approaching his end', according to a contemporary, asked Stoughton to take his teenage daughter back with him to New England 'out of the perils of the civil war then raging in England'.[3] He also returned with a determination to be part of the struggle playing out on the other side of the Atlantic, a conviction that it wasn't enough to turn your back and stay safe as the godly fought a life-and-death battle against arbitrary tyranny and the abuse of power. So, resigning his place as sergeant major in Winthrop's militia regiment in October, he gathered together a number of the colony's best men and took them to England that winter to join the Parliamentarian army. They included Nehemiah Bourne, who left his trading ventures and his Boston shipyard, his wife Hannah and his two little children; John Leverett, the twenty-eight-year-old son of a ruling elder in Boston church; William Hudson, whose father was a Boston baker; and Francis Lyle, one of Boston's barber-surgeons. At least a dozen colonists, all active members of the Military Company, went over to fight for Parliament; there were probably many more. John Winthrop, who would have much preferred them to stay put, nevertheless noted with pride that they all 'did good service, and were well approved'.[4]

This band of brothers is next heard of in the summer of 1644. Stoughton was in London, where because, he said, he was 'now likely to run some part of the hazard of war', he decided to put his affairs in order.[5] He left behind a wife and six children – seven, in fact, since Elizabeth Stoughton had been expecting another baby when he came away; and he devised a complicated formula to ensure that his firstborn son should receive a slightly higher proportion of his estate than the others – 'unless he prove himself unworthily', in which case it went to the next, or the next, and so on. 'Provided the difference in matter of grace and virtue appear not very evident, or the eldest his vice not very evident, then let the double portion remain his absolute due.'[6]

He also left a collection of books in Dorchester, and he bequeathed 'to son Israel one fourth part of my small library, & unto John another fourth p[ar]t, & unto Wm the other half, for his encouragement to apply himself to studies, especially to the holy Scriptures'.[7] He expected rather less of his three daughters: they were to pick one book each, not so that they could apply themselves to *their* studies, but simply so they 'may have something they may call their father's'. In a touching aside he urged his wife 'not to weep for me, as one of those without hope. If I now die, what love she owed unto me, [I wish] that it may be bestowed (after me) upon our poor dear children for my sake'.[8]

And with that he took a commission as a lieutenant colonel in the army of the Eastern Association.

Israel Stoughton didn't join just any regiment. He enlisted in the new regiment of foot being raised by Thomas Rainborowe. So did Nehemiah Bourne, who became Thomas's major; and John Leverett, who captained a company under him; and William Hudson, who served as Leverett's ensign. Francis Lyle didn't stray too far from them, either: he put his medical skills to use as a field surgeon to the Earl of Manchester.

Why did these men leave wives and children, farms, businesses? None of them applied to their churches for dismission, so it's safe to assume they intended to return to Massachusetts. All were active in the colony's Honourable Artillery Company, serving alongside Thomas Rainborowe's brother William; and this, together with Nehemiah's family connections with the Rainborowes, helps to explain their choice of regiment. But parading around on Boston Common in scarlet plumes was one thing; fighting in a real war was another. The New Englanders' arrival in England is proof that not everyone in Massachusetts shared John Winthrop's determination to stay out of the fight. As John Cotton admitted, plenty felt unease at the accusation that they had 'fled from England like mice from a crumbling house, anticipating its ruin, prudently looking to their own safety, and treacherously giving up the defence of the common cause of the Reformation'.[9]

Their decision throws into high relief the pendulum-swing of allegiance in a community in transition. With family and friends on both sides of the Atlantic, settlers seldom forgot their origins and their identity: if they did, there were preachers in pulpits all over Massachusetts reminding them that 'there is no land that claims our name, but England . . . there is no nation that calls us country-men, but the English'.[10] Divines quoted from Jeremiah 46:16, 'Arise, and let us go again to our own people, and to the land of our nativity, from the oppressing sword.' Relatives wrote about every-thing from the uncertainty of the times to the experience of having their homes plundered by the enemy and the death of loved ones in battle. The wonder is not that these New Englanders – and dozens, perhaps hundreds more whose names are lost – went over to fight. The wonder is that more did not go with them.

The new recruits joined Thomas Rainborowe in the summer of 1644, at a time when the high command of the Eastern Association was pulling itself to pieces in the aftermath of its greatest victory.

The Earl of Manchester's troops stormed and captured Lincoln that May, securing the county and allowing the main Association army, which had previously concentrated on protecting its home territory, to head north to support Scottish Covenanters under the Earl of Leven and Lord Fairfax's Northern Association army who were besieging the city of York. Rainborowe's regiment stayed behind on garrison duty in Lincolnshire; unlike the other regiments of the Eastern Association, it was funded directly by the committee for that county, which suggests it was raised specifi-cally for the defence of Lincolnshire.

As a result, neither Thomas nor his New England officers took part in the biggest battle ever fought on British soil, involving five armies and 46,000 men. On the evening of 2 July, Leven, Manchester and Fairfax scored a dramatic victory over the Earl of Newcastle and a relieving force commanded by Charles I's nephew Prince Rupert of the Rhine at Marston Moor, seven miles west of York. In a fight lasting little more than two hours the Royalists lost around 4,000 men, with all their artillery, ammu-nition and thousands of weapons. Another 1,500 surrendered. Newcastle was so humiliated that he fled into exile on the Continent and took no further part in the war, declaring he could not 'endure the laughter of the Court'.[11] The three victo-rious generals declared a day of public thanksgiving throughout their armies. The Royalist garrison at York surrendered two weeks later.

The Earl of Manchester's forces returned to Lincoln at the beginning of August, trailing dissent and anxiety rather than clouds of glory. The earl had always seen the Eastern Association as a coalition of saints, a godly alliance united in common purpose against the papists, the bishops and the wicked men who surrounded the king and forced their advice on him. But it was never his intention to topple Charles I. He had hoped for a negotiated settlement, believing 'it might be disadvantageous to bring the king too low', and that 'it would not be well for the kingdom if [the war] were ended by the sword'.[12] Marston Moor showed him there was a real possibility that the war *could* be ended by the sword, and he didn't like it. Nor did he like the bloodshed, the horror. 'That sweet, meek man', as one of the Scots Presbyterians called him, was appalled at what he witnessed on the field, at the sufferings of soldiers and civilians.[13] His experiences at Marston Moor, where the screams of the dying deafened men's ears, strengthened his determination to bring the war to an end as swiftly as possible.

He reckoned without his lieutenant general. Marston Moor confirmed Oliver Cromwell's conviction that Parliament had God on its side. He saw it as a victory obtained by the Lord's blessing on the godly party; it would be contrary to God's will not to prosecute the war as vigorously as possible. Cromwell was also exasperated with the Presbyterians in the Eastern Association, and in particular with Manchester's major general of foot, the Scottish Presbyterian Lawrence Crawford. They in turn were vehemently opposed to the toleration of Independents within the army, and appalled at the way in which junior officers and common soldiers abused the ministers of the Church of England. Some sectaries had even 'gone up into the pulpits . . . and preached to the whole parish'.[14] In a very public spat over Crawford's attempt to cashier one of his own senior officers who was an Anabaptist, Cromwell told him in no uncertain terms that 'the state, in choosing men to serve it, takes no notice of their opinons . . . Take heed of being sharp, or too easily sharpened by others, against those to whom you can object little but that they square not with you in every opinion concerning matters of religion.'[15]

Stoughton, Bourne and the others were exactly the sectaries that the Presbyterians condemned and Cromwell supported. 'When any New English man or some new upstart Independent did appear', complained one of Cromwell's opponents in the Eastern Association, 'there must be a way made for them.'[16] There were other complaints about the subversive effect which the New England way was having on old England's Puritans: the great seventeenth-century divine Richard Baxter, writing years after the war, remembered how New Englanders had disturbed the Parliamentarian garrison at Coventry: 'One or two that came among us out of New England . . . had almost troubled all the garrison, by infecting the honest soldiers with their opinions.'[17] The Royalists heaped scorn on their 'new gospel, which teacheth us . . . to rebel and resist the king' and laid the blame squarely on 'the ministers that brought it over from New-England, the Land of Canaan'.[18]

It was a 'pamphlet-glutted age', said Hugh Peter, by this time the most prominent of the politically active New Englanders; and pamphlets associating Independency with the New England way poured off the London presses. The Independent minister John Goodwin published with approval a letter from John Winthrop to Peter, which described a recent assembly of elders at which 'the way of our churches was approved, and the presbytery disallowed'.[19] From New Haven, the minister John Davenport dismissed Presbyterianism as holding back the cause of reformation in England, saying the members of a presbytery 'were but thirteen bishops for one'.[20] The other side countered by publishing a letter from Thomas Parker, minister at Newbury, Massachusetts, insisting that his own experience of the New England way led him to believe that 'the ordinary exercise of government must be so in the presbyters, as not to depend upon the express votes and suffrages of the people'.[21] Manchester's chaplain, Simeon Ash, reissued correspondence from seven years earlier in which a group of English clerics interrogated the New England churches on a range of issues, including whether or not they believed a set liturgy to be unlawful, and how much power they allowed to a congregation rather than its pastor. The reason for airing these differences now, wrote Ash, was to counter those who 'cry up the church way in New England, as the only way of God'.[22]

Bickering about the finer points of church governance might seem a rash thing to do in the middle of a war. Discussion of issues such as whether a minister could perform ministerial acts to another congregation than his own, or whether members of a congregation should be allowed to leave without the consent of their fellows, had their place, but that place wasn't on the battlefield.

But the English Civil War was a war of religion. And this was especially true for the Eastern Association, whose officers and men were drawn from the Puritan heartlands of East Anglia. Like their friends and relatives who emigrated to New England from Boston and Braintree and Cambridge, taking with them to Canaan so much more than place names, they were convinced that God involved Himself directly in the workings of humankind on a daily basis, conferring favours on the just and punishing the evil-doer. When Cromwell said of the victory at Marston Moor that it had been 'obtained by the Lord's blessing upon the godly party' he wasn't using a figure of speech.[23] Nor was Thomas Rainborowe, when a few years later he expressed the hope that decisions made by the army high command were 'sent from God'; or Nehemiah Bourne, when he ascribed the defeat of his enemies to the 'whirl-wind of the Lord'.[24] All three men meant this quite literally, just as John Winthrop meant it when he ascribed the rescue of a child from drowning or the killing of Anne Hutchinson by Algonquins to the direct working of Providence.

It followed that if God was a real and enabling presence in the lives of many of the Eastern Association commanders – and in the lives of the rank and file who, if anything, were even more devout and more radical than their officers – the freedom to worship Him in the way He wanted was fundamental to their cause. They were not prepared to fight and die to topple one regime which imposed uniformity of worship, Laud's Church of England, only for another to take its place. Presbyterians wanted to bring the king to heel and do away with priests and prelates; but they certainly didn't want the anarchy which separatist congreg-ationalism seemed to promise, a non-system of church government in which mechanics and artisans could set themselves up above ordained ministers. They saw the New England churches as hotbeds of heresy, while their Independent opponents pointed to New

England as a shining example of what could be achieved if the godly were allowed liberty of conscience instead of the religious repression practised by the Church of England – and now advocated by the Presbyterians. 'Some rivers have been noted to differ in the colours of the water, yet running in the same Channel', wrote Hugh Peter. 'Let Jesus Christ be lifted up by us all; let us love him whilst we dispute about him.'[25]

Except that liberty of conscience was not something most leading New Englanders cherished. Still scarred by the Hutchinson crisis, John Winthrop and the other leaders of the colony remained determined not to tolerate the slightest deviation from their own particular brand of Protestantism. In 1644, for example, Anabaptists were singled out in Massachusetts for punishment as 'incendiaries of common wealths, and the infectors of persons in main matters of religion, and the troublers of churches'.[26] The General Court ordered that anyone within the jurisdiction of the Massachusetts Bay Colony who opposed the practice of infant baptism was to be banished. The more libertarian elements in Protestantism threatened to 'bring us to a mere democracy', warned John Winthrop.[27]

In August 1644 Winthrop's account of the Hutchinson controversy, *A short story of the rise, reign, and ruin of the Antinomians*, was published in London by Thomas Weld. It described at length how colonists, having escaped 'the cruel hands of persecuting prelates', were infected with the plague of antinomianism, and how the authorities in Massachusetts had banished Anne Hutchinson and her disciples to a life of misery on a remote island (actually Rhode Island, which wasn't all that remote), where the heretics spent their time 'hatching and multiplying new opinions, and cannot agree, but are miserably divided into sundry sects and factions';[28] with the exception of Anne herself, of course – 'this American Jezebel', 'this great imposter, an instrument of Satan', who had suffered the vengeance of God through His instruments, the members of the Algonquin war party which slaughtered her and her family and burned their Westchester homestead.[29]

Weld meant well in making Winthrop's *Short Story* available to the English public. But he had made a massive miscalculation: his vision of the gathered churches had not moved on from the divisions of the 1630s, and he remained intent on countering old criticisms that New England fostered heresies. *A Short Story* played

straight into the hands of the English opponents of congregationalism, who seized the opportunity to portray New Englanders
as oppressive bigots. 'In New-England', crowed the Presbyterian
polemicist Thomas Edwards, 'they will not suffer Brownists,
Anabaptists, Antinomians. Mr Cotton the greatest divine in
New-England, and a precious man, is against tolerations.'[30] It was
precisely because of this lack of toleration in America, Edwards
argued, that sectarian extremism had come to infect England:

> How many cast out of New England for their Antinomianism,
> Anabaptism, &c. have come over, and here printed books for their
> errors, and preach up and down freely; so that poor England must
> lick up such persons, who like vomit have been cast out of the
> mouth of other churches, and is become the common shore and
> sink to receive in the filth of heresies, and errors from all places.[31]

The attack was joined from New England itself. In 1643 the great
dissenter Roger Williams came over to England to lobby Parliament
for a patent which would protect the colony he had founded at
Rhode Island from its more authoritarian neighbours, Massachusetts,
Connecticut and New Haven. Williams had experienced the
intolerance and repression of the New England way at first hand,
having been hounded out of Massachusetts and Plymouth
Plantation for his views on the separation of church and civil
authority and the need for toleration, among other things. In July
1644, shortly before he went back to Providence with his patent,
he published *The Bloudy Tenent of Persecution*, in which he set out
his stall in uncompromising terms:

> God requireth not an uniformity of religion to be enacted and
> enforced in any civil state; which enforced uniformity (sooner
> or later) is the greatest occasion of civil war, ravishing of
> conscience, persecution of Christ Jesus in his servants, and of the
> hypocrisy and destruction of millions of souls.[32]

He also reported that the New England way with dissidents was
finding little favour with Parliament. One MP, he said, asked in
the course of a speech to the Commons, 'What, Christ persecute
Christ in New England?'[33] This distaste was confirmed by Stephen

Winthrop, who arrived in London on a trading venture at the beginning of 1645. 'Here is great complaint against us for our severity against Anabaptist[s]', he wrote to his brother in Boston. 'It doth discourage any people from coming to us for fear they should be banished if they dissent from us in opinion.'[34]

In Boston, John Cotton was moved to write against *The Bloudy Tenent*; but transatlantic communications being what they were, it was a long time before he saw it and three years before his reply, *The Bloudy Tenent, Washed, and Made White in the Bloud of the Lambe*, appeared in England. The timing was not good: Cotton held that monarchy and aristocracy were ordained by scripture. As for democracy, he condemned it as not being fit for church or state – 'If the people be governors who shall be governed?'[35] Such opinions weren't likely to endear him to the Commons in 1647, when the book was published. Nor did he make any attempt at conciliation with those who held different religious views. After his uncomfortable brush with Anne Hutchinson and antinomianism he went out of his way in *The Bloudy Tenent, Washed* to justify the persecution of erroneous opinions.

The Hutchinson controversy had left its scars on other ministers, who had seen at first hand the harm that could be done by charismatic dissidents. As the New England position came under fire from Independents in old England, Thomas Shepard wrote from Cambridge, Massachusetts, to defend it to his old colleague Hugh Peter:

> You have had experience of the gangrene in New-England & how soon it spread in a little time, & how God hath borne witness against that generation . . . I know there may be some connivance for a time while 'tis tumultous & while the wars call all spirits thither, but Toleration of all upon pretence of Conscience I think God my soul abhors it.[36]

This was at least more honest than another of Shepard's claims, that in New England 'we never banished any for their consciences, but for sinning against conscience'.[37]

15

They Fierce Were Coming

*T*homas Rainborowe and his New England officers were in the eye of this storm. I'd give a lot to hear their talk, to see their faces as they walked in the Minster Yard at Lincoln, or sat round a table in one of the city's inns and imagined the shape of victory. There are no likenesses of Nehemiah Bourne or Israel Stoughton or Ensign William Hudson. John Leverett's portrait, painted in London around this time, shows a sharp-faced, gimlet-eyed young man, unsmiling in a buffcoat and pale leather gauntlets – slightly stiff, self-conscious in a conventional pose with his right hand resting on his helmet and his left clenched against his hip. It is a picture to hang on a father's wall, a remembrance of a young man who, in Stoughton's phrase, was 'now likely to run some part of the hazard of war'.

Thomas Rainborowe's portrait, also painted around this time, shows a different character altogether. The colonel is big, barrel-chested and balding, but with flowing locks falling long, well below his broad shoulders. He is clean-shaven except for a slight moustache, and his face is dominated by a long nose and quiz-zical, heavily hooded eyes. He smiles slightly, appraising the viewer, with a kindness and an openness that give no hint that before the war was over this man would be famous, notorious, as a champion of the common people, a ruthless ideologue who smote the enemies of God and liberty with a flaming sword. But then what should a champion of liberty look like?

It was Sir Charles Firth and Godfrey Davies in their 1940 classic, *The Regimental History of Cromwell's Army*, who first suggested that Thomas's connection with the New Englanders influenced his political views. Stoughton and Bourne, as the second- and third-in-command of the regiment, must have shared their experiences and enthusiasms for building Canaan with a commanding officer who was already sympathetic, who had shared connections and a shared outlook, and who in Bourne's case was a kinsman and an ex-neighbour. He knew plenty about the covenanted churches of New England from them, from brother William (who was now also fighting for Parliament, as captain of a troop of horse in the army of the Earl of Essex), perhaps even from Hugh Peter and the Coytmores. And the three officers were well placed to discuss the advantages of a godly government which had evolved at arm's length to the king; and which, while hardly democratic, managed to exist without intervention from bishops or nobles.

The learning process, the process of radicalisation – if that is what it was – could work both ways. For Bourne and Stoughton and the junior officers, contact with the Independents in the Eastern Association army offered a new model for New England to consider; one in which the godly could admit their differences and still, as Hugh Peter hoped, love Jesus Christ even while they disputed about Him.

For months it seemed as though disputing was as close as Rainborowe's new regiment was going to get to the war. While the army was resting in Lincoln in August, Cromwell made a concerted attempt to purge its higher ranks of Presbyterians, telling the Earl of Manchester that 'he desired to have none in my army but such as were of the Independent judgement'.[1] The reason he gave Manchester, incidentally – that if there were moves towards a negotiated peace on unfavourable terms, 'this army might prevent such a mischief' – showed Cromwell's brilliance as a strategic thinker, prefiguring as it did the mighty struggle that would later take place between army and Parliament over just this question.[2]

That September, in an effort to force the two sides to patch up their differences, an exasperated Earl of Manchester brought Cromwell and Crawford like naughty children before the Committee of Both Kingdoms, a joint council of lords, MPs and Scottish commissioners convened earlier in the year to oversee the conduct of the war. The committee pointed out that there was a war on and ordered the earl to sort out the problem himself, or at least to keep his officers under control until they reached their winter quarters at the end of the year's campaigning. In the meantime Manchester was ordered to take his army south to guard the approaches to London.

At first he refused to go, convinced by now that 'it would be better for the kingdom if [the war] were ended by an accommodation'.[3] When he did move, it was at a snail's pace: by the middle of October he had crept as far as Reading, having ignored sixteen directives from the Committee of Both Kingdoms and three orders from the Commons. Rainborowe's regiment remained behind on garrison duty in Lincolnshire, holding the line against occasional Royalist raiding parties from Newark and Belvoir – which meant they missed the Association's disastrous part in the second Battle of Newbury on 27 October, when Manchester's determination to ignore the advice of Cromwell and his reluctance to engage the enemy allowed the king's army to escape. He then failed to storm the Royalist stronghold of Donnington Castle, allowing the king to relieve it; and didn't turn up at the siege of Basing House a few weeks later, leading to the abandonment of the siege.

Cromwell reacted by going to the Commons and launching a savage attack on Manchester's leadership. The earl, he said, 'by constant backwardness to action and unwillingness to engage with the enemy has lost many advantages and opportunities against the enemy'. He had repeatedly ignored or expressed contempt for the orders of Parliament and the Committee of Both Kingdoms. And, Cromwell charged, 'there is good reason to conceive that this backwardness and neglect in His Lordship to take advantages of the enemy was out of a design or desire not to prosecute the war to a full victory'.[4] He demanded nothing less than Manchester's removal as commander-in-chief of the Association.

Officer after officer, many but not all Independents, gave evidence of the earl's reluctance to prosecute the war, of his repeated statement that it would never be ended by fighting and, more seriously, that he didn't *want* it ended by the sword. He fought back, both in the Lords and by letter, asserting that he and his senior officers had to share joint responsibility for the Association's recent tactical failures, and trying to deflect attention by attacking Cromwell's radicalism. His lieutenant general was implacably prejudiced against the Scots, he said, in spite of the Solemn League and Covenant which joined the two nations together. Cromwell had often criticised the Westminster Assembly, the Presbyterian-dominated gathering of divines charged by Parliament with reforming church government and preparing a form of worship to replace the Anglican Book of Common Prayer. According to Manchester, Cromwell condemned members of the assembly, saying they 'persecuted honester men than themselves'. And most dangerous of all, he accused Cromwell of challenging the established social order: 'for his expressions were sometimes against the nobility; that he hoped to live to see never a nobleman in England, and he loved such better than others because they did not love lords'.[5]

By the beginning of December it was obvious to everyone that there wasn't room in the Association for Manchester and Cromwell. One of them would have to go.

While their senior officers were tearing at each other's throats in London, Thomas Rainborowe and the New Englanders earned themselves an honourable mention in the history of the war. When the bulk of the Association army began its slow march into Berkshire in September, Royalists in Nottinghamshire and Leicestershire seized their chance and renewed their attacks on the Association's frontier. One of their targets was Crowland, an isolated town with a ruined Norman abbey in the heart of the fens. In spite of its remote situation Crowland was strategically important – the key to the Association, it was said, and a vital link in a chain of defences from the Wash down to Peterborough and beyond. It had already been fought over in 1643, when it was taken for the king by a Captain Welby, 'a most pernicious and desperate malignant', according to Parliament's propagandists, 'and a most mischievous mover of rebellion and sedition in those parts'.[6] Cromwell managed to capture it that April, but only after a particularly nasty assault in which the defenders positioned local Puritans on top of their earthworks to deter the attackers – to the disgust of the Parliamentarian troops, who raged against 'the horrible villainy & more than Turkish cruelty of our ordinary atheistical and ignorant Protestants at large'.[7] It changed hands again – twice – in the spring of 1644. Now, with the Association's army gone, Royalists from Newark and Belvoir broke out in a series of raids across south Lincolnshire throughout September and early October. Crowland fell to them once again in a surprise attack.

Manchester ordered Rainborowe's regiment to retake the town, 'a most *malignant town,* but a place of very great consequence', probably in early November.[8] It was a hard nut to crack. Although the Royalist garrison was small – fewer than 250 men with a couple of light field pieces – the troubles of the past two years had resulted in the creation of a formidable system of earthworks. The newsbooks acknowledged that 'a few men have employed many hundreds by land, and by water to keep them in, and yet received checks and affronts many times, by sallies out of the town'.[9] Even more formidable than the fortifications was the obstacle posed by the surrounding countryside: heavy autumn rains had flooded the fens, turning them into a vast shallow lake. It was impossible for Thomas to bring any guns within range of the enemy's positions.

Or so the defenders thought. They reckoned without the naval experience of Thomas and his Massachusetts militiamen. Early one morning the sentries on the Royalist positions were surprised by a small fleet of longboats scudding across the fields towards them, bristling with soldiers and ordnance. According to one contemporary account, the attackers had batteries mounted on the boats. Thomas and his men launched a sudden and successful waterborne assault on Crowland's outer defences. He manoeuvred his boats to take control of the enemy's outworks, and his gunners proceeded to bombard the defenders with their field pieces.

They used the same fleet of longboats to blockade the town. By the first week in December the London press was reporting that 'Crowland is driven into that great distress for want of victual that they cannot long hold out'.[10] The rumours flew. The defenders had plenty of ammunition left; it was almost gone. They still had food; 'they suffer many pale extremities for want of bread'.[11] They had been battered into submission; they still held out in the hope of relief. One source announced Thomas had offered terms, but they had been refused, and he had warned 'they should never again have the like conditions whilst he was able to lie before it'.[12] However, the same news-book, *Perfect Occurrences of Parliament*, called him Colonel Gainsborough and gave the wrong dateline (November instead of December), which suggests accuracy wasn't its strong point.*

With a landing place secured, Thomas prepared to storm Crowland; but like any siege commander, he preferred to achieve his objective by negotiation, and terms were agreed at a parley with the Royalist leaders over the weekend of 7–8 December. The defenders would be allowed to march out unmolested, the officers with their swords and pistols. The common soldiers had to leave their arms behind, and all the ammunition and the two field pieces were to be left for the use of Parliament. Thomas's men occupied Crowland that same weekend. It stayed in Parliament's hands for the rest of the war.

Crowland made a hero out of 'the valiant and virtuous Colonel Rainsborough'.[13] The audacious amphibious assault was celebrated in the Parliamentarian press (and ignored by the Royalist news-books); Crowland itself was likened to a pirates' nest manned by malignants whose nuisance value was out of all proportion to their numbers, raiders who would have continued to harass the coun-tryside all around if Thomas and his men hadn't taken such daring action to bring them to heel.

Crowland was the first and last major battle for the New Englanders and for Rainborowe's regiment in the Eastern Association. That same month, December 1644, Israel Stoughton fell sick at

---

* In its favour, the same issue of *Perfect Occurrences* (6–13 December 1644) offered its readers the most succinct account of the difference between Presbyterians and Independents. The Presbyterians would have their ministers chosen by the assemby of elders; the Independents would have them chosen by the congregation. 'And this is all the difference.'

Lincoln and died; and of the others, only Francis Lyle elected to stay in England for good. By the beginning of March Nehemiah Bourne, John Leverett and William Hudson had embarked for Massachusetts. According to John Winthrop, they were briefly back again in old England later in the year, but they had all returned to Boston once more by the end of 1645. Leverett, who kept the buffcoat in which he was painted – it still exists today, patched and battered, in the collections of the Massachusetts Historical Society in Boston – used the connections he made in England to set up a transatlantic trading venture, buying shares in at least three ships and importing everything from fine linens to pots and pans while he divided his time between Boston and London. Nehemiah settled back into the life of the colony. Having put some money into a venture of his own before he left, he sailed from London with Thomas Graves in the *Trial* in March 1645, and returned to Hannah and his shipbuilding yard in Boston.

Poor young William Hudson had a nasty surprise waiting at home. He had entrusted his business and his wife Anne to a servant, Henry Dawson, who while he was away grew over-familiar with his mistress. So over-familiar that the pair were found together in her bed, brought before the magistrates and charged with adultery. They admitted being in bed together, but denied they had had sex; and wanting to believe the best, the jury brought in a verdict of guilty to the lesser charge of adulterous behaviour, to the annoyance of magistrates and church elders. That meant they escaped with their lives, but their sentence was still harsh and shaming: they had to stand on the gallows with ropes around their necks for an hour, and then submit to a flogging. William, 'although he condemned his wife's immodest behaviour', was so convinced she was telling the truth that he took her back. 'And they lived lovingly together', commented John Winthrop.[14] Given the moral climate in Boston and the vigour with which sexual transgression was condemned, that was quite an achievement.

Why did the New Englanders leave the field of battle so suddenly? Israel Stoughton's death played a part. If, as Winthrop suggested, it was Stoughton who organised the expedition to England in the first place, it was natural for the others to lose their motivation along with their leader. But a much more pressing reason for their going was the discontent and confusion that was developing within the Eastern Association that winter. At the very moment that Parliamentarian newsbooks were reporting the victory at Crowland, those same newsbooks were also talking excitedly of moves for 'new moulding the army', and discussing the Commons' conviction that the army 'will run more swift on new wheels, and with more success', if the command structure was streamlined.[15]

This drive for reform was a by-product of the continuing battle between Manchester and Cromwell. Rather than single out individuals for dismissal or demotion, Parliament hit on a simple and apparently impartial plan: that no member of either the Lords or the Commons 'during the time of this war, shall have or execute any office or command military or civil'.[16]

The Self-Denying Ordinance, as it was known. would have meant the removal from the army of twenty-four senior commanders, including moderates like Manchester, Essex and Fairfax. It would have meant the Earl of Warwick stepping down as Lord High Admiral. And it would have meant that Cromwell had to choose between giving up his command and giving up his seat in the Commons. The fact that he supported the Ordinance and was thus prepared to sacrifice one or the other speaks volumes for the strength of his feeling about Manchester's inadequacy.

Rather to everyone's surprise, the Self-Denying Ordinance passed through the Commons on 19 December. But the Lords, who didn't have the option of resigning from the Upper House if they wanted to continue in the army or the navy, were less enthusiastic, perceiving the move as a way of strengthening the war party's hand in the army. The Ordinance was finally passed in a modified form in April: Manchester resigned his command, as did Essex and Warwick; the Commons judged Cromwell to be so important to the war effort that he was kept as lieutenant general without having to resign his parliamentary seat. In the meantime, the leaders of the war party, including Cromwell and Sir Henry Vane, began to organise a new army, drawing on the officers and men of the existing armies of Manchester, Essex and Waller. On 11 January 1645 the Commons authorised the formation of 'the new Model', to consist of ten regiments of horse, a thousand dragoons and twelve regiments of foot. Thomas Fairfax, son of Lord Ferdinando Fairfax, was named commander-in-chief; and when a list of officers was read on the floor of the Commons at the end of February, it included Thomas Rainborowe as colonel of one of the new infantry regiments. None of the New Englanders were named as officers in that or any other regiment.

So with their regiment disbanded, Bourne, Leverett and Hudson may have felt it was best to go home. They could have stayed with Thomas. They could have tried to enlist, to obtain new commissions. Instead, they chose New England. Home for them, for now, lay on the other side of the Atlantic.

They left behind them a legacy of advanced political thinking. Thomas Rainborowe had acquired a reputation for radicalism by the spring of 1645, so much so that when the army lists went up to the House of Lords his commission was rejected by peers determined to purge the New Model Army of its militant tendency. His brother William, who had served briefly with the Earl of Essex in 1644 and who had been recommended for a captaincy in one of the new regiments of horse, was rejected for the same reason. Both men harboured dangerous ideas.

MPs ignored the Lords and confirmed both men's commissions.

16

This Avenging Sword

Thomas Rainborowe's first experience of a great set-piece battle, a clash of armies, took place on a breezy Saturday morning in June 1645, in a field in Northamptonshire.

Thomas had spent the spring of 1645 in Abingdon, training and drilling and moulding his new regiment, which contained officers and men from three other regiments in Manchester's army. He brought none of his old officers with him, and there was no sign of a New England contingent – although there are a couple of tantalising hints. His new major, John Done, and one of his captains, George Drury, both bore the names of men who enrolled as passengers for Massachusetts in 1635. Other members of the clan were serving in the New Model Army that spring: Hugh Peter was chaplain to the artillery train, and Thomas's brother William was now a captain in Sheffield's regiment of horse.

On 8 May Thomas received orders to take his regiment and join Cromwell, who was operating around Oxford and attempting to prevent Charles I from gathering his army together. (The king had in fact marched his army out of Oxford the previous day.)

The regiment was well below its theoretical strength of 1,200 men: the New Model as a whole was finding it hard to recruit new soldiers, and those who did take Parliament's shilling were not always the best. Poor-quality recruits and a propensity to desert were continuing problems. Most counties, moaned one of Thomas's fellow colonels, 'press the scum of all their inhabitants, the king's soldiers, men taken out of prison, tinkers, pedlars, and vagrants that have no dwelling . . . It is no marvel if such run away.'[1] But whatever state they were in, Thomas marched his men towards Oxford, equipped with muskets and pikes and dressed in the red coats with blue facings that were the new uniform of the New Model. Sir Thomas Fairfax, having been ordered by the Committee of Both Kingdoms to head for the south-west, where another Royalist army under Lord Goring was besieging Taunton, was now told to come to Oxford. He arrived two weeks later and began to lay siege to the city in earnest, believing its governor could be persuaded to deliver it up without too much trouble.

Thomas's men had their first taste of action as a regiment at the end of May, when they were ordered to take a Royalist garrison ten miles west of Oxford. Gaunt House was a heavily fortified and moated manor house which controlled the crossing over the river Windrush near Standlake. After battering it for a day – the sound of his guns could be heard in the centre of Oxford – Thomas invited the garrison to surrender. Initially the governor refused. But the next day, after watching from a window as Thomas brought up carts and ladders and prepared to storm the place, the governor had second thoughts and gave in.

Oxford was not quite as ready to yield. In any case, Fairfax's siege was overtaken by events. While Thomas was laying siege to Gaunt House, ninety miles to the north the king's army under Prince Rupert was laying waste to the town of Leicester and its inhabitants with a brutal enthusiasm learned in Europe during the Thirty Years War. The news appalled the Committee of Both Kingdoms, which to Fairfax's frustration had insisted on retaining ultimate control over the New Model. Believing the king's men were about to sweep into East Anglia, the committee now ordered Fairfax to leave off his siege and intercept them. Then on 9 June, belatedly realising that military operations could not be conducted from Westminster, it gave him authority to direct the campaign himself. Cromwell was appointed his second-in-command and lieutenant general of horse the following day.

The king was not about to sweep into East Anglia. In fact he wasn't sure quite what to do. Should he march north into Lancashire and Cheshire, as Prince Rupert suggested, to clear out rebel resistance and establish control in the north-west before moving to confront the New Model? Or should he consolidate his forces in the East Midlands? Or go to the aid of Oxford? As Fairfax came closer, Charles I and his commanders dithered over whether to move south to relieve Oxford, not yet knowing the siege had been lifted. When they heard that it had, they decided to head north into Lancashire and Cheshire.

It was too late. On the evening of 12 June forward scouts from the Royalist camp near Daventry in Northamptonshire encountered an advance party from the New Model only four miles from the deer park where the king and his retinue were hunting. The alarm was raised and the next day his army retreated north to Market Harborough; but it became obvious that with Fairfax intent on battle, the Royalists weren't going to be able to keep a safe distance between them and the New Model without putting their supply train of some 200 or 300 wagons at risk. The king decided to stand and fight. Before dawn on 14 June he moved his troops, around 9,000 of them, out of Market Harborough to positions on a ridge outside the little village of Naseby. Fairfax's much larger force of 14,000 faced them across a boggy valley. A distance of about a thousand yards separated the two armies, Charles I's to the north and Fairfax's to the south. Local villagers gathered on the hillside to watch the show.

Which is how Thomas Rainborowe found himself standing in a field with his regiment that Saturday afternoon, with well over 20,000 soldiers spread out in battle array all around him. Both armies adopted the same traditional formation, with cavalry on each flank and the infantry drawn up in the centre of a battle line that was, in this case, more than a mile long. Cromwell commanded Parliament's cavalry on the right flank, and Henry Ireton, a long-time supporter of Cromwell, commanded the left. Philip Skippon, one of the few experienced professional soldiers in the New Model, led the infantry. Thomas and his men were deployed as a reserve just behind the main line.

The preparations for a battle on this scale were slow, stately, ritualistic. As everyone moved into position, Fairfax gave out the password for the day, 'God Our Strength'. Hugh Peter delivered a rousing pre-battle sermon and then prepared himself: when the fighting started he was in the thick of it, Bible in one hand and pistol in the other, riding from company to company and urging the men on. Some of the infantry were wearing white pieces of paper or linen in their hats as field signs; the cavalry all wore scarves of their general's colours 'as a good and visible mark in time of battle to know one another by'.[2] Sheffield's horse were on the right wing with Cromwell, and Thomas would have been able to see his brother William only a few yards away. His own musketeers and pikemen were drawn up in formation, company colours flying. Smoke drifted across from the lengths of smouldering match held by every musketeer. Some companies were praying aloud. Others sang psalms. Skippon told his soldiers to 'remember the cause is for God. Come my brave boys! Let us pray heartily, and fight heartily, and God will bless us.'[3] Cromwell, riding along to order his troopers, 'could not . . . but smile out to God in praises in assurance of victory', he recalled afterwards.[4] On the other side of the valley, the Royalists paraded a wooden doll which they called 'the God of the Roundheads'.[5]

Soon after ten o'clock the trumpets sounded, the drums beat, and both sides let out great shouts and began to move forward. On the Royalists' right wing Prince Rupert's cavalry advanced fast, probably because Rupert saw dragoons from the New Model taking up positions on the other side of a long north–south hedge on his right flank, from where they would soon be able to fire on his cavalry as they passed. He clashed with Ireton's five regiments of horse, charging with incredible courage and fury, forcing two from the field and chasing them back towards where the New Model's supply train lay three miles away at Naseby village. Ireton's own regiment did rather better, advancing so far in their own charge that they were able to turn and help Skippon's infantry, some of whom were getting the worst of it as they encountered veteran Royalist units led by Sir Jacob Astley. But in the melee Ireton had his horse shot from under him; he was run through the thigh with a pike, and stabbed in the face with a halbert before being taken prisoner. Skippon took a musket ball in his side, fired accidentally by one of his own men; he refused to leave the field, telling Fairfax 'he would not go so long as a man would stand'.[6] Only on Parliament's right wing was Cromwell's cavalry unequivocally successful, overwhelming the Royalist horse of Sir Marmaduke Langdale. 'Langdale's brigade ran away basely' was the terse comment of Fairfax's secretary John Rushworth, who was present at the battle; and Royalists agreed. 'Had our left wing but at this time done half so well as either the foot or right wing,' said one, 'we had got in few minutes a glorious victory.'[7]

It was at this point, as the New Model's infantry were driven so far back by Astley's men that they began to run, that Thomas and the other commanders of the reserve signalled their drummers to beat the 'Battle', at the sound of which each man was 'undauntedly to move forward, boldly stepping in good order into the place of his fellow soldier that shall happen to fall down dead before him'.[8] Their advance was orderly, methodical. One or two ranks of musketeers came forward ten or twenty paces from the rest, fired at the enemy and then wheeled off to the rear to reload, while their place was taken by the next rank or ranks. When they were too close to Astley's men to continue this tactic safely, their pikemen would come up and lower their pikes at the enemy, while the musketeers remained behind them, still firing, wheeling off and reloading. If the two sides closed 'at push of pike', the musketeers would use their muskets as clubs in hand-to-hand combat.

The reserves repelled the enemy, forcing them to a disorderly retreat. In the lists of wounded that were published after the battle, Thomas's regiment suffered only ten casualties; this, and the fact that recent archaeology at Naseby has unearthed a large number of musket balls around the hill where this part of the battle took place, suggest that disciplined fire from the reserves was enough to halt Astley's advance. The outcome of the battle turned upon it. Indeed, one modern historian calls it '*the* decisive moment of the English Civil War'.[9] If Thomas and the reserves had broken, the New Model would have lost the most important battle of the war.

They didn't break. When Prince Rupert and his men returned to the field after unsuccessfully trying to take Fairfax's supply

train, they found Langdale's cavalry running back to Leicester and
Astley's infantry unable to withstand the firepower of Thomas
and the reserves. Cromwell was attacking Astley's flank, and the
main body of Skippon's New Model infantry had regrouped and
rejoined the attack. What had seemed only an hour before to
have the makings of a great victory for the Royalists was turning
into a disaster.

Desperate to rally his men Charles I tried to ride down into
the field. In one of the battle's most famous episodes, the king
was on the point of charging the enemy when, according to
Clarendon:

> the Earl of Carnwath, who rode next to him . . . on a sudden
> laid his hand on the bridle of the king's horse, and swearing
> two or three full-mouthed Scots' oaths (for of that nation he
> was) said, 'Will you go upon your death in an instant?' and,
> before His Majesty understood what he would have, turned
> his horse round.[10]

Carnwath's action inadvertently made matters worse. Troops in
the field interpreted the king's turn as a signal to march away
from the battle; and although some came back for a last stand,
others didn't. What might have been an orderly retreat became a
rout; and by one o'clock there was not a horse or man of the
king's army to be seen, apart from prisoners. The New Model's
foot busied themselves pillaging the dead, while the cavalry went
in hot pursuit of the flying enemy. All that afternoon and evening
men were cut down in the fields as they ran. Irish camp-followers
found by the Royalist baggage-train were savagely treated, 'about
100 slain of them, and most of the rest of the whores that attended
that wicked Army are marked in the face or nose, with a slash
or cut'.[11] The baggage-train itself was taken, along with munitions,
cannon, 9,000 firearms – even the king's own papers, including
his private correspondence with his generals and with Henrietta
Maria, showing that she was busy trying to drum up reinforcements on the Continent. The letters were immediately published
under the title of *The King's cabinet opened*, bolstering suspicions
that Charles was prepared to bring 10,000 French and 6,000 Irish
troops into the fight, and hardening hearts against him.

Naseby was a catastrophe for the king. Fairfax and the New Model killed around 400 soldiers and took prisoner more than 4,000, including hundreds of senior officers. They destroyed the Royalists' main field army. And by noon two days later the entire New Model was standing before Leicester, and bringing up guns captured from the Royalists at Naseby to play on the defences. The next night, Leicester's governor asked for a parley and Fairfax sent Thomas Rainborowe and Colonel John Pickering to negotiate. At midnight they agreed terms for the surrender of the town: it had been held for just eighteen days.

While the prisoners from Naseby were paraded through London with their captured colours, like the vanquished opponents of some Roman general, Fairfax turned his attention to the west of England, where a Royalist force under Lord Goring was still besieging Taunton. The army marched through Warwickshire, Gloucestershire and into Wiltshire; when it reached the town of Marlborough on 28 June it had covered 113 miles in a single week.

In three years of fighting, Thomas Rainborowe had never experienced war on this scale or at this level of organisation. Nor had most of his brothers-in-arms. The New Model Army was powerful, efficient, well equipped. Parliament hired merchant ships to pick up supplies in London and take them round the coast to Plymouth and Weymouth, where carters were also hired to have them ready for the troops when they arrived in the West Country. Discipline was strict: deserters and thieves were hanged; blasphemers had their tongues bored with hot irons; officers who falsified their musters were cashiered; soldiers who were found guilty of sexual misconduct were whipped. 'A general reformation is passed through the soldiery', declared one commentator that summer; 'no oaths, nor cursing, no drunkenness, nor quarrelling, but love, unanimity is amongst them'.[12] There was no room for sinners in God's own army: no room for transgression among His instruments. These were fighting men who sang psalms as they marched into battle. 'What say you now, who scorned this raw army', asked the Parliamentarian press, exultant. 'What think you of that saying, *The army that shall destroy Antichrist root and branch, shall be faithful and chosen?*'[13] At the army's next big battle, even the chaplain Richard Baxter was surprised when the officer next to

him, Major Thomas Harrison, 'with a loud voice [broke] forth
into the praises of God with fluent expressions, as if he had been
in a rapture'.[14]

Thomas continued his progress towards the West Country as
the New Model marched across Salisbury Plain and down into
Dorset in pursuit of Lord Goring's Royalists. (As they passed
Stonehenge, Hugh Peter urged Fairfax to pause long enough to
demolish 'the monuments of heathenism'; luckily for the English
tourist industry, the general decided he had more pressing matters
to attend to.[15]) Worried that he was going to be cut off from
Royalist strongholds at the ports of Bridgwater and Bristol, Goring
lifted the siege of Taunton and took up a position near the little
village of Langport, to cover the withdrawal of his supply train
to the relative safety of Bridgwater. He chose the place for his
stand well: his men occupied a steep western hillside scattered
with hedged enclosures that provided good cover for his musketeers. There was a stream running past at the bottom. Fairfax's
army took up positions on the opposite, eastern bank. Their only
access to Goring was across a deep ford and up a narrow lane,
flanked by hedges.

This time Thomas wasn't in the reserve. After another rousing
pre-battle sermon from Hugh Peter, the New Model's artillery
silenced Goring's guns and forced his cavalry to withdraw a little,
while Thomas led his musketeers down to the ford. His mission
was to flush out the enemy from the cover of the hedges. Once
that was achieved, Christopher Bethell led an astonishing charge
up the hill 'with as much gallantry as ever I saw men in my life',
said fellow officer John Lilburne, 'forcing them with the sword
to give ground'.[16]

It was at this point, as Goring's men turned and ran, that Harrison
broke out in his spontaneous religious rapture. No doubt he wasn't
alone.

It is hard to track the role of Thomas's brother William in the
West Country campaign of 1645. His regiment served with Fairfax
throughout the summer, so he was presumably at Langport in
July and the actions which followed. But after Langport the nature
of the war changed. As they waited for the king, who was trying
to drum up new recruits to his battered army in Wales, Royalists

in the west retreated to a series of fortified garrisons. For the rest of the summer the war in the west consisted mainly of sieges, in which the cavalry played a minor part and in which William's name did not figure at all. Thomas, on the other hand, was in the thick of it. Over the next eleven weeks he took a leading role in no fewer than five major sieges.

As that timescale suggests, the New Model didn't favour drawn-out operations. Officers took their cue from Fairfax, who 'was still for action in field or fortification, esteeming nothing unfeasible for God, and for man to do in God's strength, if they would be up and doing', said his chaplain, Joshua Sprigge. 'Thus his success hath run through a line cross to that of old soldiery, of long sieges and slow approaches; and he hath done all so soon, because he was ever doing.'[17] It was rare for the army to indulge in the kind of time-consuming siege-works that were normal on the Continent, in which encircling trenches were dug outside the range of the defenders' guns, and then a further network of zigzag trenches taken closer and closer until they reached the walls, so that engineers could mine underneath and place explosive charges.

This was partly because of inexperience. Until the war broke out there had been no call for the English to engage in siege warfare for well over a century. As a result, they weren't very good at it – nowhere near as expert as their European contemporaries, who had learned the craft in Germany and the Low Countries during the Thirty Years War.

But it also had a lot to do with the New Model's zeal, its conviction that God was overseeing operations, its impatience to get on with the job. Much better to intimidate a defender, who knew that if he refused terms of surrender he and his garrison might expect no mercy. Much better to sing a psalm and storm a town than to wait. The New Model's God helped those who helped themselves.

The arguments for and against a protracted siege were rehearsed at Bridgwater, to which Goring's army retreated after Langport. Bridgwater, which stands on both banks of the river Parrett, was heavily fortified and surrounded by a deep thirty-foot-wide ditch which filled with water at every tide. Fairfax called Thomas and the other regimental commanders to a council of war to review the options, while without even being given orders the rank and file began making bundles of sticks, or faggots, to throw into the ditch as a makeshift bridge, until Thomas Hammond, the lieutenant general of the ordnance, put them to work making eight portable bridges, long enough to span the ditch. Everyone was agreed that they had to take the town, and quickly. 'To sit down before it . . . leaving the enemy at liberty to rally his broken forces, seemed very hazardous', remembered Joshua Sprigge. Someone suggested blockading it by putting up forts on either side of the river. Someone else proposed cutting trenches. 'But it was considered, that if we should have gone that way, it would have proved very tedious.'[18]

17

By Battery, Scale, and Mine

airfax decided to storm Bridgwater before dawn on Monday 21 July. The forward planning was meticulous. Lots were drawn to decide who was to take part in the assault, who would form the reserve, and who would distract the defenders. On the Sunday morning Hugh Peter preached 'a preparation sermon, to encourage the soldiers to go on'; and towards the end of the afternoon he appeared again to exhort them to do their duty 'with undaunted courage and resolution'.[1]

Just after two o'clock on Monday morning, three heavy guns sounded in quick succession. This was the signal for the assault to begin on the eastern half of the town, while troops on the western side made all the noise they could to convince the defenders that this was the direction from which the attack was coming. Hammond's bridges were brought up and thrown over the ditch. The forlorn hope, as the advance party was called from the Dutch *verloren hoop* or 'lost troop', scrambled over the enemy's earthworks, turned their own ordnance on them and lowered the drawbridge into the eastern town, admitting the New Model cavalry, who began clearing the streets of the enemy. Some 600 of the defenders immediately surrendered. The remainder drew up a second draw-bridge that connected the two parts of the town and barricaded themselves in.

Fairfax hoped this would be enough to persuade Bridgwater's governor, Edmund Windham, to surrender. When Windham refused to treat, the general sent word that he would allow women and children to leave the town – a humanitarian gesture in keeping with the New Model's high moral tone, but one also calculated to leave Windham in no doubt of his intentions. 'They were no sooner come forth', wrote Sprigge, 'but our cannon played fiercely into the town, grenadoes were shot, and slugs of hot iron in abundance, whereby several houses in the town were fired, and the wind being high increased the flame.'[2] That was enough, and Windham sent out a messenger to ask for Fairfax's terms.

On Wednesday 23 July, twelve days after the New Model arrived at Bridgwater, they took control of it, along with around a thousand officers and men, 1,500 weapons, forty-four cannon, forty-four barrels of gunpowder and a quantity of goods which were sold off, and five shillings a man raised on the sale 'to be bestowed as a reward upon the common soldiers for their good service in the storming of the place'.[3] There were few casualties on Parliament's side – yet another sign, as Sprigge reported, that 'God was the bridge by which our army got over.'[4]

Thomas's next two sieges, at Sherborne and Nunney, were different in scale and tactics. After Bridgwater, the army moved into central Somerset. Fairfax set up his headquarters at Wells, detaching two regiments towards Bath, which gave in without much of a struggle after dragoons, exhilarated with victory, crept up to the city gates on their stomachs, grabbed hold of the barrels of the sentries' muskets poking through the grate and shouted at them. The sentries were so shocked they dropped their weapons and ran, whereupon the dragoons blew up the gate and the garrison surrendered.

Thomas and the rest of the army were sent to take Sherborne Castle, twenty miles south of Wells and just across the county border with Dorset. Sherborne was the headquarters of the Royalist courtier-diplomat Sir Lewis Dyve, whose strong local connections made it a powerful rallying point for opposition in the county. The medieval castle, actually a fortified palace built for the Bishops of Salisbury back in the twelfth century, was a formidable obstacle to the New Model's progress. Standing on a raised platform of ground at the edge of the town and surrounded by earthworks and a deep ditch, its curtain wall was twelve feet thick and thirty feet high, and punctuated with towers in which Dyve stationed his 'keepers of parks' armed with birding-pieces, which were more accurate and more deadly than the ordinary musket. It would be costly to storm the castle, and Fairfax decided on more orthodox tactics: soldiers were set to work digging trenches (and paid an extra twelvepence a day for the hot and hazardous work); and miners were sent for from the Mendips.

While they waited for cannon and miners to arrive, Thomas and his men were tasked with guarding the troops working on the approaches, which left them exposed to enemy fire, and they suffered hard as a result. The snipers took aim with their long fowling pieces through the loop holes in the wall and targeted Thomas's officers. A captain lieutenant was shot dead one day, and one of his best captains the next. They were buried with military honours in Sherborne Abbey. The regimental major, John Done, and two more of the regiment's captains, Thomas Crosse and Thomas Creamer, were all shot and injured as they fought to push the Royalists back from a new battery they were making. They were, Fairfax's secretary John Rushworth reported to Parliament, 'most valiant men as any in the army'.[5] Done and Crosse died of their wounds.

By Monday 11 August, ten days after the siege began, heavy ordnance and Mendip miners had arrived; and although it took a while to bring the guns into position, on Thursday about eleven in the morning they began to bombard the walls. By six they had beaten down one of Sherborne's towers and made a breach in the castle wall wide enough for ten men at a time to pass through. By this point the trenches were so close to the walls that the defenders couldn't use their muskets, and they were reduced to dropping stones on the besieging soldiers. Another tower was taken, forcing the Royalists back into an inner courtyard, and it was with evident satisfaction that Sprigge reported that 'our musketeers playing into the castle, recompensed with a fatal shot one of the enemies' chief marksmen, that had so often shot out of the tower with the birding piece, and killed our men'.[6]

As the miners prepared to spring their mine, and the infantry prepared to storm, Sir Lewis Dyve sent Fairfax a polite note, acknowledging 'the advantage you have of me, by being master of my walls'. If they could come to honourable terms, he went on, he was prepared to surrender the castle; 'otherwise I shall esteem it a far greater happiness to bury my bones in it, and the same resolution have all those that are with me'.[7] Fairfax's reply was typical, terse and intentionally intimidating: no terms but quarter, and unless Dyve surrendered immediately, he was not to expect even that.

While the governor considered his response, events – in the form of an enthusiastic group of New Model soldiers – overtook him. These troops, waiting to storm the breach, 'some of them before their time appointed leaping over the works . . . so daunted the enemy, that they fled out of one work into another, and so into the castle'.[8] The rest of the infantry swarmed into the court-yard after them, and before Dyve could offer to surrender his men had raised a white flag and thrown down their weapons. The besiegers spent the rest of the day ransacking the castle and plundering its occupants (although without harming them, 'inclining rather to booty than revenge', noted Sprigge).[9] The next day, Saturday 16 August, was market day in Sherborne town; and the troops held a grand sale for the people of the surrounding area, who poured into town to buy the plundered goods.

Invincible, inexorable, the army marched on towards Bristol, the kingdom's second city and the only important port still held for the king. It had been taken by Prince Rupert in the summer of 1643, and after Naseby Rupert was in residence again, with a force of around 3,500 regular troops.

There was some opposition to Fairfax's decision to besiege Bristol, particularly in Parliament, where there were mutterings that the New Model was wasting time and allowing the Royalists to regroup instead of pursuing Goring's shattered army into Cornwall. Fairfax and his pamphleteers countered by pointing out that if Bristol wasn't taken, there was a real danger that Goring could move up from the west and the king could move down from Wales to join him. If Goring, Rupert and Charles were allowed to rendezvous the Royalists would have a much stronger force.

It was also argued, both in Parliament and in the army, that because there was plague in the city and the surrounding villages, it would be better for Fairfax to keep his distance, rather than risk having his regiments infected. He thought otherwise. 'Let us trust God with the army,' he declared, 'who will be as ready to protect us, in the siege, from infection, as in the field, from the bullet.'[10]

As the New Model and its miles of supply wagons and carts lumbered north, Thomas was despatched with two cannon and two regiments of foot to reduce a Royalist garrison in the little Somerset village of Nunney, a few miles east of the army's route to Bristol. The castle there, a tall, beautiful and strangely romantic structure with round corner-towers crowned by conical roofs, was held for the king by a recusant named Richard Prater and a force of about eighty soldiers, also mainly Catholics. Fairfax rode over to survey the place, which rather unusually, was surrounded by a curtain wall and within the curtain, by a narrow moat. The general pronounced it to be 'a very strong piece' and left Thomas to deal with it.[11]

He did, with ruthless efficiency. The curtain was breached, Prater surrendered and two days later Thomas was on his way to rejoin the main army.

'The city of Bristol stands in a hole', said Sir Bernard de Gomme, the Royalists' chief military engineer; and the fact that it was overlooked vastly increased the problems of the defenders.[12] They needed to hold an outer perimeter nearly four miles round which encompassed the strategically important hills to the north-west and south. A line of five forts commanded the summits of these hills, linked by double ditches, covered ways and parapeted walls over twenty feet high, presenting a formidable challenge to the besiegers. To the east, the defences were weaker, and the walls lower; but the entire perimeter was bristling with cannon – 140 pieces distributed around the line, on redoubts and bastions and half-moons as well as on the fortresses themselves. The strongest of these was the Great or Royal Fort on the west, a massive five-sided citadel designed by de Gomme; but the most strategically important was its neighbour, Prior's Hill Fort, which commanded the northern heights above the city.

By 23 August, only eight days after the fall of Sherborne Castle, the army was positioned in a great girdle around Bristol. Fairfax was undecided as to whether to storm the city or not; a Parliamentarian fleet was blockading the mouth of the Avon, and he spent several days weighing the pros and cons of starving Rupert out or starting conventional trenchworks and mines. Half a dozen times over the next week Rupert's men tried unsuccessfully to break out through Fairfax's lines, encouraged by unseasonably wet and misty weather. Two sallies from Prior's Hill Fort were pushed back by Thomas's men, who had taken up positions below it and killed several senior Royalist officers. Another sally by 1,600 men from the Royal Fort was also repulsed, although when they retreated back inside the walls the party took a valuable prisoner with them: John Okey, colonel of the New Model's dragoons, who had lost his way in the mist and ridden into the enemy's ranks by mistake.

Fairfax was in a hurry, as always. There was a chance that Royalist reinforcements might arrive. In any case, the foul weather was making life miserable for the troops in the field. When they were brought together to see how they would take the idea of storming the city, they gave a great shout of approval: 'more courage, joy, and resolution could not appear in men', noted an approving John Rushworth.[13]

In the meantime Fairfax and Rupert engaged in the customary polite exchanges. Fairfax's opening invitation to the prince to surrender is of particular interest because it rehearses the arguments, then still accepted by most of the military, as to why they were fighting – not to topple the king, but to remove his wicked advisers:

> The king in supreme acts concerning the whole state, is not to be advised by men of whom the law takes no notice, but by his Parliament, the great council of the kingdom, in whom as much as man is capable of, he hears all his people, as it were at once advising him, and in which multitude of counsellors lies his safety, and his people's interest . . . To set him right in this, hath been the constant and faithful endeavour of the Parliament, and to bring these wicked instruments of justice, that have misled him, is a principal ground of our fighting.[14]

Rupert wasn't about to swap ideological justifications with the general. Instead he played for time. He asked for permission to send a messenger to get the king's consent to handing over the city. He offered an impossible set of terms, including one that the cathedral clergy in Bristol 'shall quietly enjoy their houses and revenues belonging to their places' and another that no minister should be turned out of his living.[15] He claimed he couldn't quite understand the crystal-clear terms that Fairfax offered. Eventually he resorted to the simple ruse of holding on to the Parliamentarian trumpeter who brought the messages for hours, sometimes even a day or more, before sending him back through the lines.

Fairfax was having none of it. A day was set aside for the army to seek God through prayer and fasting, 'to direct them in what they were to undertake'; and Hugh Peter preached a sermon to the men, and another, on horseback to a vast gathering of local Somerset men, around 3,000 of whom were persuaded to join in the siege.[16]

God directed an assault, and planning for it was meticulous. On the south a brigade of four regiments commanded by Colonel Ralph Weldon was to attack at three points. Each assault was to be led by a forlorn hope of 200 men with twenty ladders; each musketeer following the ladders was to carry a faggot and be ready to throw it down into the ditch to make a crossing. They were to be followed by twelve files of six men each, 'with fire, arms, and pikes, to follow the ladders to each place, where the storm is to be'.[17] Parties of pioneers brought up the rear; their job was to flatten the line so that the horse could come in after them, while gunners were tasked with taking the enemy's guns and turning them on the city.

A second brigade commanded by Colonel Edward Montague had similar objectives in the east; and a third, commanded by Thomas Rainborowe and consisting of his own regiment and four more, had orders to attack the line from the north and to storm Prior's Hill Fort 'as the main business'.[18]

At midnight on Tuesday 9 September everyone took up their positions in the darkness. The storm was to start when the attackers saw a flaming pile of straw and heard four of the great guns firing in succession. There were two words for the night: 'David' as the assault began; and 'The Lord of Hosts', once the soldiers were inside the perimeter. At two o'clock the straw was lit, the cannon were fired and with a great shout of joy the men went in.

Montague's brigade broke through the eastern defences, bridging the ditches and letting in the cavalry. They took batteries and redoubts and came right up to the gate of the city with hardly any losses. Weldon was less fortunate. His men threw up their scaling ladders against the Royalists' works, to find the ditch was deeper than they had realised and the ladders were too short. 'So they only alarum'd the enemy.'[19]

The most savage fighting of the night took place around Prior's Hill, where Rainborowe's regiment was struggling to storm the fort. Oliver Cromwell recalled a few days later that Thomas 'had the hardest task of all'. His men were under constant fire from the fort, the scaling ladders barely reached the parapet, and yet for nearly three hours he led his men in assault after assault. 'His resolution was such, that notwithstanding the inaccessibleness and difficulty, he would not give it over.'[20] One of his officers, Captain Sterne, was killed. Others were at push of pike on the edge of the parapet for two hours; soldiers repeatedly clambered up the ladders only to be beaten back down again.

Just before dawn Hammond's regiment blew one of the gates further along the line and Christopher Bethell, who had led the charge at Sherborne, proved just as daring now, leading his cavalry against the royalist horse who were waiting for them. Bethell was shot and fatally wounded, but his men pushed the enemy back far enough for Hammond to move up inside the defences, joining with Lieutenant Colonel Pride's men, who had also fought their way across the line, and breaking into Prior's Hill Fort from the rear. Pride's soldiers put up their ladders on this inner side and launched a surprise attack which was enough to shock the defenders into running for shelter into the rooms of the fort. Thomas Rainborowe's soldiers swarmed in after and killed them.

The storming of Prior's Hill gave Bristol to the New Model. It was 'a piece of service . . . as bravely performed, as ever thing was done by man', announced one of the official despatches. A few hours later Rupert asked for a parley. Thomas was delegated to negotiate terms; and on Thursday 11 September at two o'clock the Royalists marched out, bound for their last big stronghold at Oxford. Referring to the religious differences which were simmering both in the ranks and in Parliament, Cromwell wrote exultantly that Presbyterians and Independents had worked together in the same spirit of faith and prayer to fight for a remarkable victory for the instruments of God. The fall of such an important city was 'none other than the work of God. He must be a very atheist that doth not acknowledge it.'[21]

In other times, Thomas's contribution to the storming of Bristol might have earned him a rest. Fairfax had one: he took himself off to Bath for a few days, 'having been wearied out, and spent with that great business'. But before he went he handed out orders for the coming week. 'The face of God now shining again upon Bristol,' wrote Joshua Sprigge, 'on Saturday, September 13 a council of war was called, to advise what was fit next to be done.'[22] Instead of marching down into the far west, Fairfax decided it would make more sense to clear out pockets of Royalist resistance which endangered Bristol's communications with Gloucester and London. Cromwell was despatched to take the castle at Devizes, which commanded the main route between the west and London. Thomas took a brigade up to Berkeley Castle, where a garrison commanded by Sir Charles Lucas, a professional soldier and a veteran of Edgehill and Marston Moor, threatened the route between Bristol and the Parliamentarian stronghold of Gloucester.

Berkeley presented quite a challenge. It was enormously strong, well victualled and manned by more than 500 horse and foot, and Lucas replied to Thomas's summons to surrender with one of those rhetorical flourishes which the king's side did so much better than the Parliamentarians. Rather than yield the castle, he said, he would eat horse flesh; when that ran out, he would eat human flesh. His lieutenant colonel seconded him, declaring that 'God damn him he would go quick into hell, rather than yield the castle to the Roundheads.'[23]

So Thomas got down to business with the determined and brutal efficiency he had shown all summer. Bringing up their scaling ladders, his men stormed Berkeley's outworks and took the nearby church, whose tower overlooked the castle walls. They put forty of the defenders to the sword, and took ninety more prisoner, with little loss to their own side, although one of Thomas's comrades was shot through the hat as he led his soldiers into action.

Once in possession of Lucas's outworks, Thomas brought up his heavy ordnance and began to pound the castle walls. 'This was such a terror and discouragement unto the enemy within the castle,' wrote Sprigge, 'to see the resolution of our soldiers, and the execution done upon theirs in the church and out-works', that Lucas began to reconsider his position.[24] Realising the likely outcome if he continued to hold out against Thomas's troops, he sued for terms.

After Berkeley, Thomas returned to Fairfax and the main body of the army, which was waiting for him at Warminster in Wiltshire. His movements for the rest of the year are sketchy. He may have fought with Fairfax at Tiverton in Devon towards the end of October, where God and good fortune attended the New Model yet again: a lucky shot broke the chains holding up the drawbridge; it dropped down; and a party of besiegers were able to rush across and take the place. In December he was at the siege of Corfe Castle in Dorset, but before it fell his regiment was ordered up to Abingdon to take part in another blockade of Oxford, where Charles I, increasingly out of touch with the reality of his situation, was trying to negotiate a treaty with Parliament while treating separately and often clandestinely with the Scots, the Irish, various foreign powers – even the Pope, who was offered concessions for Catholics in return for military aid. While he dreamed of victory his forces were in tatters. Goring had fled to France. The remains of his army in the north had been defeated. In Wales, resistance to Parliament was crumbling.

As Sir Charles Lucas was leaving Berkeley Castle, a defeated Royalist spoke to one of Thomas's officers. The king's cause was doing so badly, he said ruefully, it was as though God had turned Roundhead.

Thomas would have disagreed. God had always been a Roundhead.

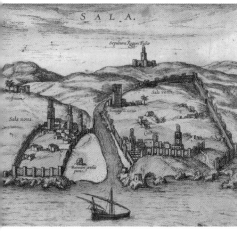

St Katharine by the Tower and Wapping, seen from the south bank of the Thames. 'Here for almost two miles we saw an infinite number of ships on the river', wrote a German visitor in 1609.

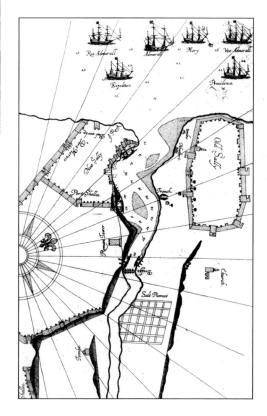

An early view of Sallee from the west. The artist has reversed the two parts of the town. Sala nova, New Sallee, was on the south bank of the Bou Regreg, and Sala vetus, or Old Sallee, was on the north bank.

William Rainborowe senior's fleet stationed at the mouth of the Bou Regreg, positioned to blockade the pirate stronghold of New Sallee.

William Rainborowe
senior's last command:
the *Sovereign of the Seas*.

Travel between England
and Massachusetts
took anything between
five weeks and five
months. It required
a strong stomach
and a cool head.

Several dozen Puritan settlements sprang up around Boston Harbour
in the middle decades of the seventeenth century.

John Winthrop, the authoritarian governor of Massachusetts and the second husband of Martha Rainborowe.

The Irish rising of 1641 spawned a new genre of hate literature. This example is from *The Teares of Ireland*, which purported to show the 'unheard-of cruelties' carried out by Catholic rebels against Protestants.

Driuinge Men Women & children by hund: reds vpon Briges & casting them into Riuers, who drowned not were killed with poles & shot with muskets.

G

M.ʳ Blandry Minister hanged after pulled his flesh from his bones in his wiffes sight

H

4

Stephen Winthrop, husband of Judith Rainborowe and 'a great man for soul liberty'.

Thomas Rainborowe: 'a joy to the best, and a terror to the worst of men'.

(*Below*) Thomas Rainborowe's signature.

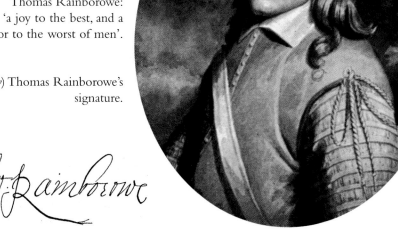

Laying siege to a town. Thomas Rainborowe was one of the New Model Army's most experienced siege-commanders.

Hugh Peter, one-time minister of Salem and the Puritan that English royalists loved to hate. This piece of propaganda depicts him spouting blasphemy, rebellion and heresy from the pulpit.

Sir Thomas Fairfax chairs a meeting of the Army Council, 1647.

The deaths by firing squad of Sir Charles Lucas and Sir George Lisle after the fall of Colchester in August 1648. Royalists never forgave Thomas Rainborowe for the decision to execute the two men.

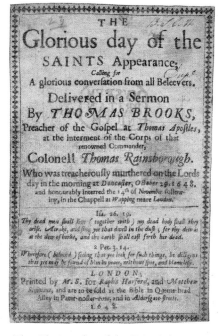

The Glorious day of the Saints' Appearance, the sermon preached at Thomas Rainborowe's funeral by his old chaplain, Thomas Brooks. 'What though this worthy's body be mangled here and there by bloody butchers, yet this body shall appear glorious at the last.'

Major William Rainborowe's battle standard, depicting the severed head of Charles I. The Latin motto translates as 'Let the good of the people be the supreme law'.

The 'damnable and diabolical opinions, their detestable lives and actions' of the Ranters fascinated Commonwealth England and proved the ruin of Major Rainborowe.

18

The Wasteful Deep

There were lights out there in the darkness.

They made everyone uneasy. Above the steady roar of the passing waves, the sounds of straining sails and creaking timbers, the men on deck called to each other in the night, straining to see. How many were there? Were they moving? Were they changing course to follow?

The waters around the Strait of Gibraltar were some of the most dangerous in the world. This was where the pirates of Barbary hunted: Moroccan carvels full of hate-driven Moriscos from the Atlantic coast ports of Sallee and Safi; the warships of the Algerian *tá'ifat al-ra'ís*, the guild of corsairs, with their shaven-headed slaves and their decks packed with fearsome janissaries; Tunisian mujahideen on a sea-jihad against Christendom; and worst of all, the wild European renegades, English and Dutch and French and Spanish, whose lust for riches had led them to abandon God.

It was three years since Thomas Coytmore had taken Nehemiah Bourne's *Trial* on her maiden voyage to the Azores, and in that time he had slipped easily back into the familiar life of the sea-captain. He and Martha still lived in Charlestown, when he wasn't at sea;

and they still had just the one child, Thomas junior. Martha had given birth to another baby in February 1644, a boy called William for his Rainborowe grandfather. He lived for only twelve days.

Thomas was no longer a deputy. In fact he played little part in the civil life of Charlestown or Massachusetts any more. There had been a point when he might have been persuaded, when the General Court had pressed him to accept a post as captain of the harbour defences. But there were opportunities in the Atlantic trade which he would hardly be in a position to take if he were in command of a fortress in the middle of Boston Bay.

Which was how he came to be nearing the Strait of Gibraltar on the night of 26 December 1645 – St Stephen's Night, although Thomas was hardly likely to think of it as such: the New England colonies didn't recognise Christmas Day, and the only saints the gathered churches recognised were still in this world. (Thomas's friends even made a point of calling St Christopher Island in the West Indies 'Christopher Island', so as not to condone papist superstition.) He was on board the pride and joy of Boston's shipbuilding community, Thomas Hawkins's 400-ton *Seafort*, recently launched, heavily armed and beautifully decorated with paintings and carvings, like a smaller version of the *Sovereign of the Seas*. She was bound for Malaga with a cargo of cotton and tobacco, and then for London with a group of families who had decided to go home. They included Coytmore's old Charlestown neighbour, the barber-surgeon Abraham Pratt, and his wife Jane. After fifteen years in Massachusetts Pratt had made the decision to leave, unhappy at the money he was making in the colony and lured by prospects in England since, as John Winthrop noted, 'surgeons were then in great request there by occasion of the wars'.[1]

It was prudent not to pass through the Strait alone. The *Seafort* was in the company of a New Haven merchantman whose master, Captain Carman, had good reason to fear the coast of Barbary: a couple of years earlier he had been taking a cargo of clapboards to the Canaries when he was boarded by Barbary pirates off the island of Palma. He escaped, badly injured and with his ship shot through, only after three hours of hand-to-hand fighting.

The two vessels had managed to keep together since they left Boston five weeks earlier – no mean feat in the stormy Atlantic winter. In fact it was quite adventurous to be making the crossing at all at this time of year. Although a third vessel had left around the same time and made straight for England, most of the passengers had chosen to go the long way round in the *Seafort* – they felt safer in a bigger, stronger ship.

Around dusk some of the company thought they sighted land, but the ships sailed on, with a fair wind in their sails. Now, in the early hours of the morning, there were lights far off. In the darkness the two captains signalled to each other as their crews prepared for a fight, handing out small arms, manning the guns, dragging bolts of cotton on to the decks to use as cover. And believing attack was the best form of defence, they both changed course and made directly for the enemy.

Except that there was no enemy. The lights were on the Spanish coast, near Cadiz. Three hours before dawn on Saturday 27 December the *Seafort* and her companion ran aground.

The sound of a ship's timbers scraping, breaking against rock is terrifying. The *Seafort* was tiny in comparison with a modern ocean-going liner: she displaced less than 1 per cent of the *Titanic*'s 52,000 tons; and when she foundered, there was no gentle judder deep in her bowels. The entire vessel would have shaken, hard enough to break bones and crush skulls. And there was no half-remembered safety drill, no hunting for life jackets. No lifeboats. No light. Barefoot, bewildered, half-naked, the passengers who could still stand ran out on deck in the pitch darkness. But as the heavy seas pushed the *Seafort* off the rocks and towards the coast they were powerless to do anything but gather their valuables together and pray.

She broke up before she reached the shore. Men, women and children were pitched into the sea and left clinging to the wreckage. Those broken timbers and spars are what saved them – those, and the initiative of one of the seamen, who swam to the shore with one end of a rope and helped them to the safety of the beach where, as the sun rose over a scene of exhaustion, misery and loss, the local people came down – and stole anything of value they could find.

Nineteen people drowned in the wreck. Captain Carman was one. Abraham Pratt was another, and his wife Jane. And perhaps the greatest loss to the colony was Thomas Coytmore.

An English ship was at anchor in Cadiz Road and her captain brought the survivors aboard and took care of them. Hawkins, who was among them, struck a deal with the local governor whereby he received £500 for the wreck of the *Seafort*, and he and the others were in England a few weeks later.

Still it was months before Martha learned that Thomas wasn't coming home. His estate, valued at £1,266 9s. 7d., was divided between her and their son, with provision being made for mother-in-law Katherine Coytmore. Martha was left a wealthy woman: she had effective control over their fine house and garden, the 500 acres of land granted to Thomas at Woburn, a further 215 acres scattered around Charlestown, and half-shares in two mills. She had her striped silk curtains, her silk red and green quilt, her china plates and saucers.

But she didn't have a husband.

Puritan attitudes to widowhood were ambiguous on both sides of the Atlantic. On the one hand there was general agreement that, as one conduct manual put it, a widow was 'tossed at all adventures, as a ship, lacking a master, and is carried without discretion and consideration, as a child when his overseer is out of the way'.[2] She was 'affrighted and amazed with a dismal prospect of difficulties which appear insuperable', declared Cotton Mather, and obviously in need of a husband to take care of her affairs.[3] On the other hand, widows – especially women of property like Martha – were advised to remain single as a safeguard against predatory men who, in Mather's memorable phrase, 'may count hers more than her'.[4] Better for her to devote her remaining years to Christ and her children, and to savour the autonomy and independence which widows enjoyed.

In practice, the likely number of those remaining years was a crucial factor in determining whether a widow remarried or not. Puritan preachers quoted St Paul's advice to Timothy, that while widows over sixty should stay single, younger women, and especially those of childbearing age, were better off marrying again; otherwise they would begin to 'wax wanton', and turn into 'prattlers and busybodies, speaking things which are not comely'.[5]

Martha was only twenty-eight. There was no immediate need to remarry: she had enough property to assure her and Thomas junior of a good standard of living, and just as importantly, she had a strong and well-connected support network in Charlestown, consisting of her matriarchal mother-in-law and a brace of sisters- and brothers-in-law: Increase and Parnell Nowell, and Thomas and Katherine Graves. A third Coytmore sister-in-law was living in Boston with her husband William Tyng. Martha's own sister Judith was there. So were Nehemiah and Hannah Bourne. She had freedom – for the first time in her life – and she had friends and family around her, people who formed an influential elite within the colony, people with whom she could share memories of her dead husband, people who would help her to keep that dismal prospect of insuperable difficulties at bay.

But all of this came at a price. Effective support networks and the empowering consequences of widowhood are the stuff of sociology. They didn't compensate Martha for an empty bed, for prayers said alone, for the silence in the night and the absence of familiar laughter. They didn't make up for the loneliness.

Nehemiah Bourne – Major Bourne, as he would style himself for the rest of his life – was doing his best to settle back into Boston life after his experiences in the war. He had a new project – the *Merchant*, a vessel 'of burden 250 ton or thereabouts', which he was currently building.[6] But his experience in Thomas Rainborowe's regiment had changed him, and now he was reluctant to accept the autocratic New England way with dissenters. In October 1645 he joined with three other merchants in petitioning the General Court for the repeal of two repressive pieces of legislation. The first was a law passed in the aftermath of the Hutchinson contro- versy, requiring strangers to obtain prior permission from magistrates before settling in the colony. The second was a more recent law banishing anabaptists from the colony. Nehemiah argued that both caused offence to the godly in England, and that they had led to churches on the other side of the Atlantic refusing Communion to New Englanders.

It was no good. Bowing to pressure from church elders, who expressed concern at the spread of anabaptism in the colonies and pointed to the poor example set by England, 'where they had gathered divers churches and taught openly', the court rejected the petition;[7] and when a counter-petition was presented a few months later from concerned citizens of Dorchester and Roxbury, pleading for the continuance 'of such orders, without abrogation or weakening, as are in force against anabaptists, and other erroneous persons', it was granted without qualification.[8]

If Nehemiah needed further proof that Massachusetts was not prepared to move on the subject of toleration, he got it that autumn. A Parliamentarian named Partridge arrived in Boston with his wife and children, intending to settle there. During the voyage over he had been heard to express religious opinions which seemed tainted with antinomianism, and he was accordingly hauled before the magistrates. He refused to answer their charges, although John Cotton, who examined him, reckoned that given time he could be persuaded to see the error of his ways. That wasn't enough for the magistrates: disregarding the onset of the savage New England winter, they banished Partridge and his family, who eventually found sanctuary in that haven of dissent, Roger Williams's Rhode Island. Even the normally intransigent John Winthrop was shocked at his colleagues' severity. 'Sure the rule of hospitality to strangers, and of seeking to pluck out of the fire such as there may be hope of to be reduced out of error and the snare of the devil', he wrote with real humanity, 'do seem to require more moderation and indulgence of human infirmity.'[9]

Any kind of dissent unsettled the magistrates not only because it posed a challenge to orthodoxy, but because it reminded New Englanders that their leaders were exercising precisely the kind of arbitrary tyranny which so many of them had fled from in the first place. For independently minded colonists, the opportunity to advance God's work away from the confines of the New England way was sometimes enough to outweigh any loyalty to the idea of building that city upon a hill in America. There were plenty of other reasons to go home: family ties, business ties, the chance to be at the heart of things rather than struggling to make a life in a colonial outpost in the back of beyond. But a powerful incentive was the kind of soul liberty which was now within their grasp in the old world, and which seemed a distant dream amidst the repressive orthodoxies of the new.

One of these returnees was Judith Winthrop's husband, Stephen. With one interruption, Stephen's career had continued its transatlantic path through the early years of the war as he traded between London and Boston, sailing westward with mixed cargos of cottons and silks and pewter and, on one occasion, two chests of window glass; and making the return voyage to the Canaries and on to London laden with grain, pipe staves, tobacco and fish. The one interruption was brief, but unwelcome: early in 1645, Stephen arrived in London and was arrested.

Bizarrely enough, Stephen had fallen foul of a long-running dispute between two French outposts in Acadia, a colony of New France which stretched rather vaguely from northern Maine through eastern Quebec and up to Nova Scotia, New Brunswick and Prince Edward Island. In September 1644 an English ship commanded by a Captain Bailey arrived in Massachusetts Bay carrying Françoise-Marie de la Tour, the formidable wife of one of the protagonists in the struggle for supremacy in Acadia, Charles de Saint-Etienne de la Tour. Madame de la Tour had chartered Bailey's ship in London to bring supplies to her husband, whose settlement at the mouth of the Saint John river in New Brunswick was being blockaded by his rival, Charles de Menou D'Aulnay. Unfortunately Bailey didn't share Madame de la Tour's sense of urgency, and stopped off the Newfoundland Banks to fish for several months before bringing her not to the Saint John, but to Boston. Before he could leave again, she sued him for breaking the terms of his charter, and the General Court awarded her £2,000. She took the settlement in kind – £1,100 of it, at least – by impounding all of Bailey's cargo, and secured a judgement against the ship's owners for the rest.

With the money she had, Madame de la Tour hired three ships that happened to be in Boston harbour and set off for the Saint John and her husband, while on 26 December an irate Captain Bailey returned to England in company with a Massachusetts ship carrying seventy passengers, one of whom was Stephen Winthrop. Bailey reached London first, and went straight to the merchant who had lost out by de la Tour's action, a powerful City alderman named William Berkeley.

New Englanders were particularly unpopular in London just then. Stories were flying round the capital about their harsh treatment of dissenters, and it didn't help that in seeking to justify themselves in print New England polemicists were rather too eager to dwell on where their co-religionists in old England were going wrong. 'To contend . . . with novelties, and every new device of unstable minded men,' declared Thomas Shepard in his undiplomatically titled *New Englands lamentation for old Englands present errours*, 'while the common enemy is in the field, and the sword of the Lord stands at every man's door almost, this argues deep distempers, close hypocrisies, and such unreasonable wanton-ness and abuse of liberty, that the Lord Christ will not pass by without darkening the sun, and turning the moon into blood.'[10]

Not the kind of rhetoric likely to endear oneself to old friends. The French were also unpopular in London circles because they were aiding the Royalist war effort; because they were Roman Catholics; and – well, because they were French. The Massachusetts General Court's actions in siding with Madame de la Tour against a prominent merchant seemed likely to provoke strong and nega-tive reactions.

There was another strand to the story, one that Stephen may have known nothing about. Alderman Berkeley had a long-standing grudge against the French in North America. Back in 1629, when England and France were at war, he had backed a daring expedition to capture Quebec and move in on the Saint John river fur trade. The expedition was successful but badly timed; the war was over when the raiders reached French North America, and Berkeley and his partners were made to give Quebec back and pay heavy damages to the French. Berkeley never accepted the justice of that, launching a series of counterclaims over the years (he was a litigious man), petitioning the English ambassador in Paris, the Secretary of State, and even the king himself in his battle to secure restitution for what he considered to be wrongs committed in Canada. He also applied for letters of marque which would have allowed him to prey on French shipping as a way of recouping his losses. And he kept up his efforts to move in on the French fur trade until the early 1640s, when he was forced out by de la Tour. Sir William Berkeley did not like the French in Acadia, and he did not like de la Tour.

He first impounded the Boston ship in which Stephen came over. Persuaded to release her, he had Stephen arrested on the grounds that he had been the recorder when Bailey and Madame de la Tour appeared before the court, which made him party to the dispute. Another passenger, Joseph Weld, who had sat on the jury that tried the case in Boston, was also taken; and both men had to find sureties for the colossal amount of £4,000 against their appearance to answer Berkeley's charges in the High Court of Admiralty. The two men wrote for help to the General Court back home, but the only answer they got (and that when it was far too late) was that the court 'know no way to help the petitioners, but to certify the truth of the proceedings of the Court between Madam Lator, Bayley & Barkly'.[11]

Fortunately, New England still had friends in the circles of power. In a lull between campaigning for Independents to fill vacant parliamentary seats and taking up a new post as chaplain to the train in the New Model Army, Hugh Peter mobilised support for Stephen. It came from an unlikely quarter – the leader of the war party in Parliament, Sir Henry Vane, whose flirtation with Anne Hutchinson and antinomianism as governor of Massachusetts had ended in disaster eight years earlier. Vane's refusal to bear a grudge now earned him the admiration of Stephen's father, who declared that when he 'might have taken occasion against us . . . he showed himself a true friend to New England, and a man of a noble and generous mind'.[12] Vane used his position as treasurer of the navy to have Berkeley's suit in the Admiralty dropped.

The aggrieved merchant wouldn't give in. He applied for a court order barring Stephen from leaving the country; and when that failed, he petitioned the House of Lords for letters of reprisal 'pretending great injuries, which he was not able to prove'. The letters weren't granted, and Stephen was back in Boston that September aboard the *Dolphin* of London with a mixed cargo of ironware, fabrics, '60 doz. hats [and] 20 doz. shoes'.[13]

Stephen's next Atlantic crossing turned out to be his last. Towards the end of 1645 he shipped a quantity of grain and fish aboard the *Dolphin* and set off for the Canaries. The voyage was long and stormy, and when he arrived in Tenerife he was faced with a market so glutted with goods that prices were the lowest in living memory. The setback hit him hard. 'Things tend continually to my observation to bring me to a low condition', he told his father, before breaking the news that he had offloaded not only his cargo, but also his teenage brother Samuel on to an English merchant in Tenerife. 'Resolving not to trust to his study for his future maintainance', Samuel 'did think it his best course to settle to some settled calling'. He wanted to go into trade; and since the merchant in question didn't ask for any money to take on the boy (the going rate was anything up to £500, with a further bond for £1,000 as security against theft) Stephen decided to let him have his way.[14]

Depressed by the poor returns in Tenerife, Stephen travelled on to London, where he found Captain John Leverett on the point of leaving for Boston, and Alderman Berkeley continuing to hound him over the de la Tour affair, 'which adds very much to my other troubles', he wrote mournfully to his brother John, before telling him that merchants were refusing to honour their bills. He ended by asking John to 'persuade my wife to be cheerful'.[15] That may have been difficult: with 3,000 miles of ocean between her and her husband, Judith was seven months pregnant. She gave birth in Boston to their second child, John, on 24 May.

19

My Sect Thou Seest

he king's Western Army had surrendered just as
Stephen arrived in England, giving Fairfax control
of Devon and Cornwall; and the last Royalist army
under Sir Jacob Astley followed suit at Stow-on-the-Wold nine
days later, on 21 March. The Prince of Wales fled to the Scilly
Isles and the king, a virtual prisoner at his court in Oxford, was
retreating into a fantasy in which he would return to Westminster
– something he suggested to Parliament two days after Stow,
provoking a polite but firm refusal – or make allies of his enemies
the Scots. He 'hath no forces left considerable', noted Stephen,
'but stands out [and] demands great things'.[1]

The Winthrops' kinsman, Hugh Peter, was riding high in
Parliament's estimation now. Having delivered to Parliament the
news of the collapse of the Royalist army in the west, he was
rewarded with a grant of lands worth £200 a year. And on 2
April, a week after Stephen's letter home, the ex-minister of Salem
was asked to preach to a congregation which included both
Houses of Parliament, the Assembly of Divines and the lord mayor
and aldermen of London. He gave a masterly performance, just

the right blend of triumphalism and caution. Having reminded his listeners that the war was not of their making, he exhorted them to 'tell your little ones this night the story of '45: the towns taken, the fields fought . . . let them know it was for the liberty of the English subjects you fought, charge them to preserve the liberties that cost so dear, but especially the liberties purchased by the blood of Christ. And above all, let them know that the God of heaven is the God of England.'[2]

If they wanted instances of God's favour to their cause 'since the breaking out of these distempers', he could give them – and almost as an aside, he did, forty-two of them. This was not a short sermon.

Then Peter went on the attack, determined that with the war all but won, it was time to fight for the right kind of peace. 'You may think it looks now like the afternoon of the day to you,' he told his distinguished congregation, 'and as if your work were towards an end.'[3] It wasn't – there was still a way to travel before they came 'to their enjoyments of Canaan's milk and honey'.[4] He pleaded for toleration, for harmony amongst saints. He begged those in authority to hold firm and not to be seduced by empty promises from the king, but to 'remember what we all fought for, prayed for, adventured all for, let not all be lost in the kiss of a royal hand'.[5]

Peter's words didn't go down well with his audience. Some actually laughed at him. When he said that everyone who supported a closer union between City and Parliament should raise their hands, very few did. They mistrusted 'the Vicar General and Metropolitan of the Independents, both in New and old England', as the Presbyterians called Hugh Peter.[6] Too many wanted a return to order and hierarchy. They wanted a king who would rule in conjunction with Parliament, a disciplined church rather than the anarchy which a nation of schismatics seemed to promise. An army that would do their bidding and then disappear. There were some among the Lords and Commons, divines and City dignitaries who sat down to their celebratory dinner at Grocers' Hall after the service, who worried at the implications of one of the most significant passages in Peter's sermon. 'You have the army you wished for', he told them.[7] Some thought uneasily that they should have been more careful in what they wished for.

Stephen had no such qualms. Hugh Peter was a shining example of how God favoured those who worked for a thorough reformation of society. So was brother-in-law Thomas Rainborowe, still busy in the service of Parliament. While Hugh Peter was berating Parliament and Stephen was lamenting his losses in business, Thomas was mopping up Royalist outposts in the Midlands, coming closer and closer to Oxford and the king. By mid-April his regiment was laying siege to Woodstock Manor, just eight miles north of the city. On 17 April, eager to finish the business, Thomas tried to storm the house, but his men were pushed back. So he decided to wait: the roads between Woodstock and Oxford were blocked, and the defenders had no hope of relief. Eight days later he received a deputation from Oxford: they had come, they said, to negotiate for Woodstock's surrender.

It was quite a group, including John Ashburnham, treasurer of the king's army, the Earl of Southampton and the Earl of Lindsey, both known for their desire to bring the war to a peaceful end. What they proposed was more than giving up Woodstock. They said that if Thomas and the other senior officers present would undertake that the king 'may be defended from violence, and continue king; then the king would come into our quarters, there to remain' and do whatever they wanted.[8]

Thomas sent a messenger to Parliament to ask for orders. 'We beseech you give us your commands touching the premises.'[9] The next day, while he was still waiting for a reply, Charles I slipped out of Oxford with Ashburnham in one of the displays of duplicity which would eventually be the death of him. Having told his supporters that he was heading for London, he made straight for the Scottish camp at Kelham in Nottinghamshire and on 5 May he surrendered to the Scots.

The war was effectively over. On 10 June Charles issued a warrant to all his supporters who were still holding out against Parliament, authorising them 'upon honourable terms to quit those towns, castles, and forts entrusted to you by us, and to disband all the forces under your several commands'.[10] While Thomas camped outside the walls of Oxford, Edward Whalley's regiment of horse took Banbury and then rode into Worcestershire, where there were still pockets of Royalist resistance.

Most of these pockets gave in easily. Rather too easily, according to their comrades. It was later claimed that the governors of Dudley, Hartlebury, Madresfield and Ludlow (which lies just across the border in Shropshire) 'delivered up traitorously, cowardly, and basely four such strongholds, the weakest whereof could withstand an army, as themselves asserted, for a quarter of a year'.[11] It is difficult to see what they were meant to do: their side no longer had an army in the field, and their king had left them. On the other hand, some of the deals did look rather murky: the governor of Dudley made a private and secret arrangement to protect his family estates, and the governor of Madresfield surrendered after Whalley agreed to pay him £200 in ready money.

Worcester was a different matter. While the townspeople were keen to give in, its governor, Henry Washington, was not. Whalley offered terms and, at the end of June, Royalist commanders and citizens held a meeting to discuss them. It didn't go well. A prominent Royalist, Fitzwilliam Conyngsby, argued that it was the garrison's duty to stand firm until they heard anything to the contrary from their king. (Charles I's warrant hadn't yet reached them.) Washington asked 'if they would live or die with him upon the walls, and fight it out to the last man?' Conyngsby said they would; and that any who wouldn't should be tossed over the city walls, a suggestion which didn't appeal to the mayor and the townsfolk. While the defenders bickered among themselves, Whalley grew more and more impatient. 'The kingdom is at great layings out after you and the city,' he told them severely, 'and much increased by the addition of forces.'[12] This was costing money.

Then on 9 July Whalley was replaced by Thomas Rainborowe, and everything changed.

There are two explanations for Thomas's arrival. The strategic one is that Whalley wasn't making much headway; and after Oxford surrendered (on 25 June), Thomas's siege-veterans were better occupied at Worcester. That is the line put forward by Joshua Sprigge: 'there was a great want of foot for a regular and close siege' at Worcester, he said; 'and that garrison [at Oxford] surrendered, was instantly supplied, Colonel Rainsborough being sent with a brigade thither'.[13]

No doubt this was part of it. But Whalley's friend and chaplain Richard Baxter had another interpretation. He claimed the real reason for Whalley being replaced was because he 'grew odious among the sectarian commanders at the headquarters . . . and he was called a Presbyterian'.[14] (He wasn't a Presbyterian, but he did favour a more structured approach to church matters than some of his fellow officers.) So Thomas was brought in, said Baxter, 'to head and gratify the sectaries, and settle the city and country in their way'.[15]

Thomas brought his efficiency – and more importantly, his reputation for ruthlessness – to the siege of Worcester. After setting up his headquarters to the east of the city, he established new batteries (one of which hit a fortified tower in the centre of Worcester from a mile away) and tightened the blockade. On 18 July, nine days after his arrival, he sent in his terms, making it clear that they were non-negotiable. Washington stalled for time, saying he didn't understand the detail and asking if he could send out a representative to get a clearer sense of them. Thomas replied within two hours, and with icy politeness:

Sir

Although I am not sensible of the least obscurity in the articles, yet, that I may not be wanting in anything which is civility, I have sent a pass for Mr Goodwin according to your desire, and remain

Your humble servant

T. Rainborowe[16]

As Mr Goodwin discovered, and as Washington already knew, the terms were clear enough. At ten o'clock on 22 July, Worcester was to surrender. Twenty-four hours later all officers and soldiers were to present themselves at a rendezvous outside the city, and to 'engage themselves by promise never to bear arms against the Parliament of England'. They would then be given passes to go home, or to go abroad. Thomas promised to preserve the city and its inhabitants from 'all plunder or violence of the soldiers'.[17] When Goodwin protested that these terms weren't as generous as those obtained by Oxford a couple of weeks earlier, Thomas countered that Worcester should have surrendered then. He wouldn't alter a single article, and he wanted an answer within two days. He wouldn't extend that deadline.

The defenders debated among themselves, but not for long. There was hardly any powder left within the walls, and only two weeks' worth of provisions. Many of the garrison's troops had deserted during a temporary ceasefire agreed with Whalley back in June; and with no hope of relief, a citizenry disinclined to make heroic gestures, and the awful prospect of being stormed with no quarter by Rainborowe's regiment, Washington gave up. He agreed to the surrender, asking if he might send a messenger to Fairfax to try to obtain better conditions. Thomas said 'No.'

At 6 a.m. on Thursday 23 July the garrison's officers and gentlemen assembled in the cathedral where the Royalist Bishop of Worcester, John Prideaux, led them in divine service. It was the last time many of them would hear the Anglican liturgy, and the last time for fourteen years that a bishop would preach in the cathedral: Parliament abolished the episcopacy ten weeks later. After the service Washington led his men out to their rendezvous with Thomas on a little hill three-quarters of a mile away. And there their war ended, as Hugh Peter, whom the Royalists hated with the bitterest hatred, and who had arrived to witness the surrender, handed out their passes and heard their promise never to take up arms against Parliament again. At five in the afternoon Thomas entered the city. Peter preached 'at our coming in', the minister wrote afterwards, 'and did observe a door open to the Gospel'. He also singled out his kinsman for special praise. 'Truly I wish Colonel Rainborow a suitable employment by sea or land', he reported to Parliament. 'Foreign states would be proud of such a servant.'[18]

Peter's determination to promote Thomas's interests didn't end with the fall of Worcester. It was probably due to his influence that his kinsman by marriage was appointed governor of the city, although it was Fairfax who on 1 August formally requested permission from the Speaker of the Commons to make the appointment, saying 'I need not give you any arguments to move you to it, seeing you have found him very faithful, valiant, and successful in many undertakings since you put him under my command.'[19] Thomas had already taken to the role of governor with gusto: within twenty-four hours of entering Worcester he ordered the citizens to bring in all their arms on pain of death, and issued a degree forbidding Royalists from wearing swords within the city walls.

It must also have been because of Peter that at the end of the year, while Thomas was still governor, he was returned to Parliament as member for Droitwich, seven miles to the north. He had already tried to get into the Commons once that year, at King's Lynn in Norfolk; then he had lost to a local man. In November, after the two Royalist MPs for Droitwich had been disabled 'by judgement of this House, to serve any longer as a member thereof', Thomas was one of those elected to replace them, at a time when Peter was, according to his enemies at least, working very hard to ensure that vacant seats were filled by Independents.[20] Whenever radical candidates were standing, claimed one, Peter appeared to campaign 'for the army's instruments'.[21] As both a family connection and one of the army's most committed instruments, Thomas was a perfect fit.

Stephen Winthrop saw how Thomas and Hugh Peter were coming ever closer to the heart of things, and he saw it at close quarters. By August 1646, still lamenting his business failures – 'I have not yet mad[e] one penny of all the adventure I had to Spain' – he was staying at Worcester with Thomas, and while he was there he reached a decision.[22] He was going to remain in England, for the time being at least; and he was going to join the army. Between them Thomas and Hugh found him a commission, and that summer Stephen Winthrop the failed New England merchant became Captain Stephen Winthrop, an officer in the New Model Army.

Just as Stephen joined the New Model, Nehemiah Bourne was making up his mind to give up on Boston and search for Canaan in more tolerant surroundings. The ostensible reason for what was, he insisted, a temporary move, was that his mother-in-law had recently returned to England with the Bournes' two small children; and that he and Hannah wanted to go back to visit them. There was no intention, he said, 'to pluck up my stakes or to disjoint myself' from the church at Boston.[23]

Perhaps. But over the autumn of 1646 he borrowed six small cannon from the colony to arm a ship for the voyage, rented out his house on the North End shore and sold the workshop next door, 'together with all things belonging thereunto, as bellows anvil & other tools', recorded the town's notary.[24] His ship was ready by the end of November and the Bournes sailed for London on 19 December 1646.

At their leaving there happened a slight, sad episode; one of those things which, having no great significance beyond itself, refuses to be pushed aside even when the death of kings and the fall of empires clamour for attention. John Winthrop told the story of how the Bournes left behind them a twenty-two-year-old servant girl, Mary Martin, whose father had also gone back to England. Mary had been living in Casco Bay on the southern coast of present-day Maine before she came to work for them, and while she was there she had an affair with a married man. Once in Boston she found that she was pregnant and, too ashamed to admit it to anyone, she concealed the fact – not as hard as one might expect in an age when women wore loose-fitting clothes and tended to bear rather smaller babies than today. Mary behaved herself so modestly that when people came to Hannah Bourne and told her their suspicions about her maid, she 'would not give ear to any such report, but blamed such as told her of it'.[25]

The girl gave birth by herself in secret, in the night, in a back room of the Bournes' house. Hard to imagine. But there was more. As the newborn baby started to cry Mary placed it on the floor and knelt on its head until she was sure it was dead. Then she laid it beside her.

It was strong. Stronger than she thought. And after a time it started to cry again. So she battered it to death, and put it in her trunk, and cleaned the room, and got up the next morning as though nothing had happened.

Six days later Nehemiah and Hannah boarded their ship for England, and Mary Martin went to another place in Boston, taking her trunk and its dreadful contents with her. Without Hannah's protection, she was powerless when a local midwife who had been convinced of her pregnancy confronted her and 'found she had been delivered of a child'.[26] She confessed, but maintained the baby had been stillborn and said she had thrown its body on the fire. Then her accusers opened her trunk. She was brought before a jury who, making use of an old superstition that if a murderer touched the head of his or her victim, their guilt would be revealed, produced the baby's body and forced her to touch its face – 'whereupon the blood came fresh into it'.[27] A surgeon found that the child had a fractured skull; Mary confessed to killing it and was sentenced to hang on the gallows in the square at Boston.

The last act in this sad little tale of panic and retribution is the worst. John Winthrop tells it. 'After she was turned off and had hung a space, she spake, and asked what they did mean to do. Then some stepped up, and turned the knot of the rope backward, and then she soon died.'[28]

There are all kinds of ways in which the story of Mary Martin illuminates our understanding of the past. We can treat it as an example of sexual exploitation (where was the baby's father in all this?); as an instance of peer pressure in Puritan communities, or of the role of folk customs in the judicial process. We can shake our liberal heads at the brute horror of capital punishment, and thank God that the past is another country.

But sometimes, I think it's no country for old men like me. 'She spake, and asked what they did mean to do.' That poor girl.

In the spring of 1647 John Winthrop's wife Margaret fell ill. Their twenty-nine-year marriage had been a good one, loving and mutually supportive. Margaret, the daughter of a prominent Chancery judge, was a kind woman, well read, pious and sensitive: 'We do not prize our happiness here', she wrote when news of the outbreak of war in England reached Boston. 'I wish we were more sensible of the calamities of others that we might cry the more mightily to God for them.'[29]

Margaret's relationship with her husband was consistently warm and affectionate. She referred to herself in their letters as 'her that loveth you with an unfeigned heart', and wrote how 'your love to me doth daily give me cause of comfort, and doth much increase my love to you'.[30] John's conventional portrayal of her in his journal as 'a woman of singular virtue, prudence, modesty, and piety', and his habit of sending her sermons rather than love letters – 'the ground and pattern of our love is no other but that between Christ and his spouse . . . The prime fruit of the spirit is love. Galatians 5:22' – belies the strength of his feelings for her.[31] She was 'my sweet love', 'sweet heart', and he ended his letters to her with 'the sweetest kisses' from him 'that prizeth thee above all things in the world'.[32]

In May of 1647 Margaret recovered a little from her illness. Then she worsened, and on 14 June she died, leaving John at fifty-nine a widower for the third time in his life. Messages of sympathy, tempered with the expressions of faith in God's mysterious working, poured in from all over America and England. 'Your conjugal loss I cannot but deeply condole', wrote one correspondent; 'but you that are a comforter to all, God will not be wanting to guide you with his goodness in all things.'[33] A kinsman in England mourned 'the loss of your dear yoke fellow'.[34] Son Stephen, to whom John sent Margaret's Bible and ring, was stoical: although he felt the loss as much 'as any son's could be in a mother', yet 'I know God calls me to submission.'[35] A distraught Samuel Winthrop, in contrast, wrote from St Christopher's to mourn the death of 'a dearest mother, to whom I may go but to me she ne'er can come'. He tried to say more, but 'grief cuts me off that I cannot write either what nor as I would'.[36]

John also fell ill that year. But neither grief nor sickness kept him long from looking for a new wife; and he proved so successful in the task that barely ten months after Margaret's death, a planter friend in Barbados was writing to congratulate him on the fact that 'the Lord hath graciously recompensed your incomparable loss with another most virtuous and loving wife, many and happy be your days together.'[37]

John's new bride was Martha Coytmore.

The shape of Martha's life between Thomas Coytmore's death at sea and her marriage to John Winthrop is a complete blank. She knew John well enough, through Judith's marriage to Stephen Winthrop. Both sisters were rearing young children without their husbands – Thomas was dead, and Stephen was living in England – and there were plenty of opportunities for socialising in both Boston and Charlestown.

The courtship began with what seemed like indecent haste to later generations, accustomed to the tyranny of mourning. By

December 1647, a mere six months after Margaret's death, Martha had agreed to marry John and with the help of Increase Nowell was busy thrashing out the financial arrangements of the union. The usual custom, whereby the wife (or her family) stumped up a dowry in return for the husband's agreement to settle on her either a fixed annual sum or a proportion of his estate in the event of his predeceasing her, couldn't be applied in this case. John was not well off – his affairs had never properly recovered from a financial setback years before when his steward had contracted huge debts on his behalf and without his knowledge – and 'having disposed of his estate among his children & such p[er]sons as he was engaged unto . . . he hath not to endow ye said Martha'.[38] He was twice Martha's age, making it likely that she would be widowed again. To protect Thomas junior's interests, his share of the Coytmore estate was put into trust until his twenty-first birthday, with Martha having all the income from it until then 'for my own use & benefit, & for education of my said child'.[39]

This wasn't particularly unusual; but Martha went further. To ensure that her own half of the Coytmore property wasn't swallowed up by John's debts, leaving her dependent on the time-limited income from her son's share if John died, she also entered into a covenant – with John's agreement – ensuring that while the couple would receive all rents, profits and benefits from the property, it would remain hers rather than theirs, with the same trustees who administered her son's estate – Increase Nowell, William Tyng and two Charlestown merchants – overseeing the arrangements. A rare seventeenth-century example of a prenuptial agreement, if you like.

Martha signed the indentures setting out these arrangements on 20 December. Later that day, before a magistrate rather than a minister, since marriage in New England was a civil contract rather than a religious ceremony, she became the fourth Mrs Winthrop.

20

Of Rebel Angels

*I*n England the war was over, and the peace was already
threatening to turn into a bloody battlefield. 'I fear
more hurt by peace than war as yet to come', one
returned colonist wrote anxiously to his friends in Boston.[1]

In December 1646 the Scots accepted an offer from Parliament
of £400,000 to withdraw their forces from the north of England
and leave Charles I behind; and on 30 January 1647 the English
moved into Newcastle, handed over half the money and took
charge of the king who, in spite of his requests to be moved to
London, was brought down to Holdenby, a vast mansion in
Northamptonshire acquired by his father James I forty years
earlier.

With Charles in custody and the Scots, as Hugh Peter's brother
Thomas rather quaintly put it, having begun 'to revade into
Scotland', Parliament was faced with the task of working out a
settlement with the king.[2] At the same time MPs needed to
decide what to do with the victorious and increasingly restless
New Model Army, which threatened to interfere with efforts to
return the country to pre-war normality.

Parliament's answer, worked out in a series of debates over February and March, was to disband the New Model. Some 8,400 troops, drawn mainly from regional forces rather than the New Model, would be placed on garrison duty in case of a Royalist insurgency; scattered in forts and towns across the country, they could pose little danger to the stability of the nation. A further 12,600 troops were to be sent to fight the rebels in Ireland, where they would pose even less of a threat to the kingdom. Some cavalry regiments would be kept on as a kind of mobile reserve, but the rest, along with 'all the foot throughout the Kingdom of England, and Dominion of Wales, except such as are to be kept in the garrisons, and are to be employed in the service of Ireland, [would] be forthwith disbanded'.[3]

At the beginning of April 1647 the *Moderate Intelligencer* reported that Colonel Thomas Sheffield's regiment of horse, in which William Rainborowe was still serving as captain, was to be disbanded. A week later Colonel Sheffield offered to take his regiment to Ireland.

But many officers and most of the common soldiers were less enthusiastic about the idea. They were owed large arrears of pay, and Parliament wasn't prepared to give them more than a small portion of the arrears, with vague promises of the rest at some later date. And although they had been promised indemnity against prosecution in the civilian courts for acts committed during the war, the Act of Indemnity was reckoned to be inadequate – as indeed it was.

When the soldiers presented a petition outlining their grievances in the spring of 1647, a nervy Parliament condemned them. Led by the irascible MP Denzil Holles, 'the frankest amongst them in owning his animosity and indignation against all the Independent party' and one of the chief organisers in Parliament of the movement for a negotiated peace with the king, both Houses declared their 'high dislike of that petition' and censured the petitioners as 'enemies to the State, and disturbers of the public peace'.[4] Under no circumstances was the petition to be promoted in the army. And to press home the point Parliament resolved to proceed at once with disbanding those elements of the New Model who wouldn't go for Ireland.

The Declaration of Dislike, as it became known, infuriated the army. Was this what they had fought for, to have their rights ignored and their honour impugned? Fairfax, unsure of what to do next, decamped to London on the pretext of needing to see his doctor. Major General Philip Skippon, who had been appointed to lead the Irish expedition, arrived in London from the north in the last week of April to be handed a letter signed by representatives from the eight horse regiments. All were below the rank of captain. *The Apologie of the Common Souldiers* expressed their concern at being asked to go to Ireland. 'Can this Irish expedition be anything else but a design to ruin, and break this army in pieces?' it asked. And what about the promised Act of Indemnity? 'Where shall we be secured, when the mere envy of a malicious person is sufficient to destroy us?'[5] An anonymous pamphlet claimed disbandment was a plot to destroy the army and 'enslave all the freeborn of England'.[6]

The sixteen representatives of the cavalry regiments who put their names to the first *Apologie* called themselves 'commissioners' and then 'adjutators' or 'agitators' – words that at this time meant simply 'agents'. The idea of the rank and file having their own agents to present their views spread to the foot regiments, and it quickly became the norm for each troop or company to choose representatives.

In Saffron Walden at the beginning of May, Skippon did his best to sell the Irish expedition. He gave an eloquent and measured speech to a gathering of 180 of his officers and sent them back to their regiments to consult with their men.

They returned to Walden the following week. The meetings which took place in the huge parish church of St Mary the Virgin over the weekend of 15–16 May involved 200 officers and an unknown number of private soldiers; around forty officers and troopers contributed to the debate that followed. There was no one from Thomas Rainborowe's regiment, but Captain William Rainborowe was there with his commanding officer, Thomas Sheffield.

Skippon opened the proceedings with a short speech outlining his expectations. He was, he told his audience, hoping to hear how they had done their best to reassure their men of Parliament's best intentions, and to receive their reports as to 'how you find the temper of your several regiments'.

Cromwell, who sat at Skippon's right hand, chimed in with a word of support: what the major general said was 'the sense of them all'.[7]

It was not going to be that simple. An unnamed soldier piped up to say there were other grievances to be considered. A major in Nathaniel Rich's regiment, John Alford, announced that some officers had taken down the grievances of their men in writing, and wanted to present these written reports. This infuriated Colonel Sheffield: 'I know nothing of it', he snapped; 'and I conceive I, being colonel of a regiment, may know of it, as well as a trooper or an inferior officer.' His major, Richard Fincher, supported him. William Rainborowe did not, telling the meeting that he had been present at his regiment's rendezvous, and that the men had given him their ideas in writing 'that there may be no mistake at all in the tender of their just grievances'.[8] His meaning couldn't be plainer. The men did not trust their own colonel.

Skippon tried to calm tempers. He read out a letter announcing that the Commons had granted a fortnight's pay to those soldiers whose regiments were being disbanded, and a further fortnight's advance of pay to those who agreed to go to Ireland; and had also passed the longed-for Act of Indemnity.

A lieutenant from the Life Guards spoke up immediately to say he wanted to deliver a report. Then an unidentified trooper said that he had a written report from *his* regiment, and he wanted it read out. 'This is a meeting for officers', protested Colonel Sheffield. If troopers were allowed to speak for their regiments, then what was the point?

Sheffield was testy not only because he felt his authority was being undermined (which it was) but also because he was well aware of differences amongst his men, and was doing his best to prevent them being aired in public. After the acrimonious exchanges had continued for a time, Skippon eventually insisted on adjourning the meeting. 'Tomorrow at five of the clock in the afternoon', he said, 'we shall be here again.' He was prepared to hear the reports of commanding officers, and to receive 'any papers from any other that they shall think fit to deliver in to us. And I think that may give satisfaction to all.'[9]

The next day he posed the question again: how did the regiments feel about serving in Ireland? He had scarcely finished urging everyone to behave 'discreetly, fairly and orderly', without interrupting each other, when squabbling broke out among rival factions, each claiming to be the true voice of the army. When things calmed down again – 'Gentlemen,' exclaimed an exasperated Skippon, 'I do desire it again and again, and I think it is all our desires, that you will hear one another with sobriety' – the field officers rose in turn to give an account of their own regiments.[10] Most chose their words carefully, insisting their men were quiet, not inclined to mutiny, but still not prepared to go to Ireland until their demands had been met.

Unlike the other colonels present, Sheffield made no attempt to offer a verbal report on his own regiment's grievances, preferring to snipe at others. Eventually William could bear it no longer. He addressed Skippon directly:

> May it please your Honour, not having heard any thing fully spoken as to my colonel's regiment, though superior officers are here, I hope I shall not be mistaken in that which I am now to speak.[11]

He went on to explain he had gathered his troop together by themselves, explained the situation to them and advised them 'not to do anything too rashly'. They had appointed representatives to bring their grievances, and at no time had they done anything but that which 'did become them as soldiers'. William's only concern was that the ranks might not understand some of the issues. 'Many of them cried out "Indemnity," "Indemnity," and afterwards asked me what it was.'[12]

A lieutenant from the regiment spoke up to support William, earning himself a rebuke from Colonel Sheffield – 'I wish that gentleman would keep to his duty' – and giving as good as he got by pointedly telling Sheffield that not *all* officers present were motivated by self-interest.

The meeting finished with most of the officers asking Skippon and the other three officer-MPs present, Cromwell, Ireton and Colonel Charles Fleetwood, to represent their grievances to the Commons. The next day, Monday 17 May, Sheffield and the pro-Ireland faction produced what was, in effect, a minority report. They wrote to the four officer-MPs to defend themselves against the charge that they hadn't represented their soldier's grievances, and stated their conviction that Parliament would deal fairly with the army regarding the arrears, so that soldiers 'may return with cheerfulness to their abodes and dwellings, or be encouraged to a farther engagement'.[13]

Thomas wasn't with his brother at Saffron Walden. He was busy preparing a seaborne assault on the last Royalist stronghold of all.

Jersey had been a problem for Parliament since November 1643, when a small force of Royalists led by Captain George Carteret (the same George Carteret who had sailed against the Sallee rovers with William Rainborowe senior in 1637) ousted the man who had been put in to govern the island, a Major Lydcot. Carteret overhauled the defences and built new forts around the coast; and since then he had ruled Jersey from his stronghold of Elizabeth Castle, a forbidding fortress on a rocky islet in St Aubin's Bay. As the war drew to an end, Royalist fugitives had found refuge on the island – the Prince of Wales was entertained there for several months in the spring of 1646 – and Carteret encouraged the activities of privateers who used Jersey as a base from which to harass English shipping and even raid English ports, where they stole vessels from under the noses of the harbour authorities.

Early in 1647 news reached Parliament that a merchant ship on its way to Ireland with £15,000-worth of munitions, food and clothing for the troops had been taken by a chaplain-turned-privateer with the apt name of Captain Cannon and brought into Jersey, where they were used to re-equip the garrison at Elizabeth Castle – and to line Carteret's pockets. The Committee of Both Kingdoms was asked to consult with Major Lydcot, who had a proposal to retake the island. But when the committee reported back to the Commons on 23 April, they brought in two proposals. One was Lydcot's; the other was from Thomas Rainborowe.

The Jersey expedition had an obvious appeal for Thomas. It involved exactly the kind of strategic and tactical challenges he relished: an amphibious assault, a difficult siege of a heavily fortified garrison. And since his entire regiment of nearly 1,200 men was to go, it postponed indefinitely the moment when he and his officers would have to decide about disbandment or engaging for Ireland.

As for the Commons, there was no contest. Although Lydcot had first-hand knowledge of the Channel Islands, it had been acquired during a brief period before Carteret's arrival in 1643 had forced his ignominious retreat; not much of a track record compared to Thomas's. Lydcot needed to raise a relief force; Thomas already had one, and it was filled with battle-hardened veterans with plenty of experience in siege warfare. MPs immediately resolved that 'this House doth allow and approve of the propositions made by Colonel *Rainsborough*, for taking in and reducing the Isle of *Jersey*'.[14] They voted two months' arrears to the regiment and a further one month's advance of pay for victuals; and ordered the Committee of the Navy to provide Thomas with all the guns, ammunition and equipment he required; and to organise a fleet at Portsmouth to transport the invasion force to the Channel Islands. Lastly, the Commons ordered 'that Colonel Rainsborough do forthwith advance, with his men, to the seaside'.[15]

By the beginning of May arrangements were in hand to raise £6,700 for Thomas's use, and to provide him with an array of mortars, pikes and bandoliers, coats and knapsacks, and basic siege equipment: pickaxes, shovels and spades, wheelbarrows and ladders. Fairfax was asked to send a troop of horse, to be placed under Thomas's command. At some point in late April his regiment left their quarters at Worcester and marched 130 miles south to Portsmouth, where they waited for the order to embark.

There were the usual Chinese whispers. Venetian agents in Paris heard that Thomas was being paid £8,000 for his trouble. In Boston, John Winthrop had news that Thomas had gone for Ireland rather than Jersey, and was worried that Stephen Winthrop had gone with him. In Jersey, Carteret rushed to review his defences and reorganise the militia after he received word that an expeditionary force of 12,000 was preparing to leave England, its ranks being swelled daily by volunteers tempted by the prospect of plunder.

Carteret drilled his militia. The Committee of the Navy ordered the victualler at Portsmouth to provide biscuit, cheese and beer for the soldiers during their voyage. Parliament reassured the restive people of Hampshire that Rainborowe's regiment would be out of their lives any day now. But the invasion force didn't sail. Nothing happened.

The sticking point was Thomas's politics. After the Commons passed the ordinance on 23 April ordering him to command the forces going to Jersey it was sent up to the Lords for their approval. But they did not approve. Thomas was not to the taste of the Presbyterian grandees.

On 12 May an exasperated Commons sent up a reminder, telling the Lords that 'the passing or not passing of this vote will be the saving or losing of that isle' of Jersey.[16] Still the Lords refused to move, and another reminder the following day produced no more than a promise to think about it. On 18 May the Lords sent down an alternative proposal, suggesting a less radical commander for the expedition. The Commons ignored them and sent a third reminder, on 25 May, complaining that they were still waiting for the Lords to approve Thomas.

Three days later, incensed by news that Parliament was beginning the immediate disbandment of the New Model, Thomas's regiment mutinied. They left their quarters in Hampshire and marched for Oxford, determined to secure the artillery train and magazine which had been kept there since the city surrendered in 1646.

Thomas was in London at the time, standing witness in the Temple Church at the marriage of his fellow officer Richard Deane. The Commons ordered him to set off in search of his men as quickly as he could. 'And that he do take course to stay his regiment in the place he shall find it.'[17]

This was on Friday 28 May. He found the regiment, which had marched towards Oxford and was quartered in the villages around Abingdon, on the Sunday morning. The locals were up in arms at the way the soldiers were extorting money from them for food. The regiment's officers were hiding, and there had been fighting. The major sergeant was almost killed by his own soldiers; so was one of the ensigns, who gave as good as he got, hurting two of his attackers so severely that they looked likely to die of their injuries.

Thomas decided at once that the best way to restore order was to call his men together and 'persuade them [to] yield obedience'.

Not one man dared to raise an objection 'whereupon', he reported to the Speaker of the Commons, 'I peremptorily commanded them to repair together no more, unless by special order; but to keep their several quarters . . . on pain of the highest and most severe punishment'.[18]

21

War In Heaven and Battle Proud

*T*homas's swift action calmed his men – for the time being. But events were tumbling, one upon another. In May and June fifty-seven senior regimental officers left the army, either because they felt their allegiance lay with Parliament, or because they were forced out by their own men for their lack of solidarity. Rank-and-file soldiers petitioned Fairfax to cashier 'such officers as have under specious pretences gone about to divide the army'.[1]

Eight colonels were replaced out of twenty-four, along with two lieutenant colonels and seven majors. The losses included William Rainborowe's colonel, Thomas Sheffield, and his major, Richard Fincher. His three fellow captains went as well. Major Thomas Harrison – the same Harrison who had burst out in a religious rapture at the Battle of Langport – was given Sheffield's regiment, and William was promoted to major.

As with several of the other reorganised regiments, the effect was to strengthen the hand of the radicals. Among Harrison's new

captains was Stephen Winthrop, whose commission was no doubt
due to his brother-in-law's influence. Stephen had always been
clear where he stood when it came to taking up arms against
the king: the previous year, after the fall of Bristol, he announced
to his father that he had 'good news from England. The Parliament
still prevaileth. The king hath been once more beaten.'[2] Contact
with William and Harrison politicised him further. Having assured
his father in Boston that he had joined the army because it offered
the only prospect of decent employment, now he could hardly
conceal his excitement at the path events were taking:

> The Kingdom is now upon a great turn. God is doing some
> great work, for when the adversaries were with all violence
> setting up injustice and persecution of the saints it pleased God
> by the army to put them to a stand and quite turned the bias
> of their proceedings, so far as that they daily unvote what
> formerly they did vote and are contented to have the house
> purged, the heads of that faction impeached and suspend[ed]
> and suddenly will come to trial . . . I thank God I am free in
> my spirit to engage in what the army hath propounded.[3]

The events to which Stephen referred with such evident joy, the
triumph of the saints over their Presbyterian adversaries, unfolded
with high drama during June and July. Fairfax ordered a general
rendezvous of the army at Newmarket for the first week of June:
before it could take place his own regiment of foot mutinied at
Chelmsford when parliamentary commissioners arrived to disband
it. The soldiers greeted the commissioners with cries of 'There
comes our enemies!', ransacked their munitions wagons and set
off for Newmarket. That same day, 31 May, Parliament ordered
the artillery train and magazine at Oxford to be brought down
to London, for 'safe-keeping'. Seeking to forestall them and secure
it for the army, a junior officer in Cromwell's regiment, Cornet
George Joyce, led a contingent of 500 horse to Oxford. They
arrived on 1 June, found that the garrison had no intention of
handing the train over to Parliament, and moved on in search
of bigger game.

   On the morning of Thursday 3 June Joyce and his troops
arrived at Holdenby House, where the king was held. They

occupied it and sent away the king's guards. That night Joyce went to see Charles, who was in bed, and told him he and his comrades had decided 'to secure [him] in another place from such persons as could cunningly or desperately take him away'.[4] The next morning Joyce and his troopers left for Newmarket. They took Charles I with them.

The general rendezvous of the army began at Newmarket that same day; and Fairfax moved his men from there to Cambridge, to Royston, to St Albans, each move a step closer to London. A frightened Parliament rescinded the hated Declaration of Dislike, ordering it to be 'razed and expunged out of the books of the said Houses, and wholly taken away, and made void'.[5] This was what Stephen had meant when he said the House 'daily unvote what formerly they did vote'. But it was too late.

The army rendezvous produced two new manifestos. The first, *A Solemn Engagement of the Army*, provided for the establishment of a General Council, including two officer-agitators and two soldier-agitators from each regiment; and registered the army's determination not to disband or divide until its demands had been satisfied. On 10 June Thomas Rainborowe, along with other senior officers, set his name to a placatory letter to the lord mayor of London, reassuring him that while they would have religious toleration, they did not seek to interrupt 'the settling of the Presbyterian government'; nor do they want 'to open a way to licentious liberty, under the pretence of obtaining ease for tender consciences'.[6] This was followed within days by a second manifesto that went far beyond a demand for the settling of grievances. *A Declaration, or Representation from . . . Sir Thomas Fairfax, and of the Army under his Command* called for a purging of Parliament and fixed-term parliaments for the future. The House of Commons mobilised the trained bands and ordered that 'halberds, halspikes, and other arms, be brought into the outer room [of the chamber] forthwith'.[7]

It was a summer of declarations and counter-declarations and hardening of hearts. The army issued a remonstrance on 21 June, demanding, among other things, that Parliament suspend eleven leading Presbyterian members and expel from London the refor-madoes, ex-soldiers who were hanging around Westminster behaving belligerently. The citizens of London published a

remonstrance asking for the return of the king and the establishment of Presbyterian government, and pleading with Parliament
to 'restrain the fury of frenzied minds, who are too violent'.[8] The
apprentices published a remonstrance. So did the reformadoes;
and the eleven Presbyterian members; and the 'Shee-Citizens of
London', who pleaded on behalf of the freeborn women of
England for free trade and 'the king's speedy coming to London'.[9]
Londoners responded to the *Solemn Engagement of the Army* with
their own *Solemn Engagement of the Citizens of London*, also
demanding the king's return to Westminster.

And tension escalated, with London mobilising its defences
against attack and Fairfax playing an expert game of intimidation.
By the end of June his headquarters were at Uxbridge, twenty
miles from the city, with infantry regiments deploying at forward
positions even closer to Westminster. Thomas and his men were
sent to Windsor, where they occupied the castle. Reinforcements
were ordered down from Lincolnshire, and the king was kept at
a safe distance from London, in spite of repeated requests from
Parliament that he be brought closer. That would only bring him
into danger from enemies of the kingdom, said Fairfax.

The Presbyterians in Parliament were rattled, so much so that
the eleven members were persuaded to withdraw from the House,
and propitiatory noises were made about arrears of pay. As a result
Fairfax withdrew his headquarters to Reading, bringing the king
with him and convening a meeting of the new General Council,
which heard a petition from the agitators calling for the impeachment of the eleven members, for a declaration against inviting any
foreign troops into England, and for a march on London to enforce
the army's will. Committees were set up, counter-arguments were
made; and in the end Thomas, never happy to talk when he could
act, expressed his frustration with the whole proceedings. 'For my
part, I shall be weary of the meeting.'[10]

A week later Thomas was still talking, only now it was with
the king himself. He and three other senior army officers spent
three hours trying to persuade Charles to accept a series of outline
propositions offered as a basis for peace by the army, independent
of Parliament. The main points were toleration; controls over the
powers of the bishops; fixed-term biennial parliaments; a fairer
reorganisation of parliamentary constituencies; parliamentary

control over government and army appointments for the next ten years; and the exclusion of Royalists from office for the same period (later reduced to five years). Compared with what was to come, the *Heads of the Proposals offered by the Army*, as they were called, were quite modest; nevertheless, Charles rejected them and turned in secret to the Scots for support.

But the summer wasn't all talk. On 24 July, under pressure from the army, both Houses of Parliament denounced the *Solemn Engagement of the Citizens*. Two days later a crowd stormed Westminster, bullied the Lords into retracting their denunciation; and then burst into the Commons chamber, where they demanded that MPs follow the example of the peers. When the Commons gave in – after six hours, and after sending repeatedly for help from the lord mayor and aldermen to disperse the mob – Speaker Lenthall was held down in his chair and the House was ordered to vote for a resolution inviting the king to London.

That was enough for the Independents in Parliament. Frightened by stories that a huge crowd of apprentices and reformadoes was planning to gather at the door when the Commons met again, Lenthall sought refuge with the army. So did the Earl of Manchester, Speaker of the Lords, and fifty-six Independent peers and MPs. Those who remained in Parliament recalled the eleven members and ordered Fairfax to keep the army at least thirty miles from London. The trained bands manned the city's defences, and all the reformadoes and other soldiers were ordered to assemble in St James's Fields with horses and arms. Fairfax wrote to Parliament to tell them how upset he was to hear how they had been treated by the crowd. 'And however others have neglected their duty towards them for their security and defence', he went on, 'yet as God shall enable me, it shall be my great business to improve all that is in my hand for the preserving of them.'[11]

And the army marched on London.

Or more accurately, it marched to Hounslow Heath, twelve miles from Westminster, where 20,000 troops massed on Tuesday 3 August. Members of the Common Council, whose nerve had failed in the face of Fairfax's implacable determination – and the threat of anarchy in the City, where Independent petitioners for peace at the Guildhall had been attacked and killed by militia, and where rumours were circulating that far from defending

London, the undisciplined reformadoes were preparing to plunder it – sent a deputation to Hounslow asking for peace, only to be told that Fairfax intended to enter the City and expected the eleven members to be taken into custody and handed over.

That night, citizens south of the Thames in Southwark disassociated themselves from the City's stand and called on Fairfax for help. At two o'clock on Wednesday morning a brigade of infantry commanded by Thomas Rainborowe occupied Southwark with a small artillery train and two cavalry regiments in support, taking the fortifications around the southern end of London Bridge without a shot being fired. 'Their civil deportment', reported one contemporary, 'hath gained the general appliance and affection of the people, even to admiration.'[12] That's no surprise. Thomas was raised a stone's throw from Southwark. The people sleeping in their beds as he and his men marched along the Borough on their way to London Bridge, the militia on sentry duty at the riverside blockhouses – these were his neighbours, people he had grown up with.

As the only permanent river crossing for miles, the bridge itself was heavily fortified. Thomas found the gates at the Southwark end shut tight, and the portcullis lowered. Content to bide his time, he set two cannon against the gate, posted sentries – and waited.

Later that day the City surrendered. They handed over to the army all the defences to the west of London, and told Fairfax they were giving orders 'for quitting such forts on Southwark-side, as are not as yet in possession of your forces'.[13] In an impressive and theatrical display, Fairfax entered Westminster and rode on into the City. A few days later the army marched through the streets of London on their way to new headquarters in Croydon, leaving behind a couple of thousand men to prevent fresh outbreaks of unrest in the streets. At the Tower of London, Fairfax demanded to see Magna Carta. When it was brought out, he declared, 'This is that which we have fought for, and by God's help we must maintain.'[14]

There was still a Presbyterian majority in the Commons to contend with, and its leaders were determined to assert the supremacy of Parliament and to reach a negotiated settlement with Charles I. But then so were Fairfax, Cromwell and most of the officers and men under their command. As long as the army's grievances were heard and addressed – the arrears paid, the reassurances about indemnity given – as long as their role in the victory was acknowledged and their honour was not impugned, most were happy for the king to return in some reduced capacity, and for a free Parliament to work out the details. Fairfax told the City that the army wanted nothing more than 'the quiet and happy settlement of a firm and lasting peace'.[15]

Thomas, however, was developing a different attitude – more assertive, more determined to see the army play a role in making the peace. While he was discussing the *Heads of the Proposals* with the king at Woburn, others noticed that he was not inclined to negotiate. 'Of all the army', said one of the king's advisers, Thomas 'seemed the least to wish the accord'.[16]

The same adviser, John Berkeley, accused Thomas of presenting a distorted view of the negotiations to the army, and stirring up hostility towards the king 'with all the artificial malice he had'.[17] That may be true: Thomas's republicanism was developing quickly over the summer of 1647. He was just as determined that a Presybterian-controlled Parliament must be taught to do the army's bidding. When, during a meeting with senior commanders, Berkeley looked for guarantees that Parliament would accept the *Heads of the Proposals* if the king did, Thomas spoke out: 'If they will not agree, we will make them.'[18]

On the night of 16 August an English frigate, the *Nicodemus*, intercepted a small ketch on its way to Holland. She was found to be carrying five of the eleven members. They were brought back to the Downs where William Batten, vice admiral of the fleet and commander at sea, went aboard and examined their passes. Everything seemed in order and Batten let them continue on their journey the next morning. Four days later another of the eleven, Denzil Holles, turned up with a pass from the Speaker of the Commons and an order from the Committee of the Admiralty for a ship to take him to France. Batten assigned the *Leopard* (William Rainborowe senior's old ship) to take him over to Saint-Malo.

Technically, the vice admiral was within his rights. The six members' papers were in order, and there was nothing known

against them. But the fact that Batten didn't even try to detain
them, coupled with his known Presbyterian sympathies, told
against him. Within days of the incident a hostile pamphlet
appeared, claiming that although Batten knew full well that the
MPs were on their way to Henrietta Maria's court at Saint-
Germain-en-Laye to betray Parliament, he entertained them to
dinner and issued them with passes himself. And by the end of
the month the Independents had decided he had to go.

Thomas was the obvious man to replace him. He was the only
senior army commander with naval experience. And his popularity
was so great by now – even his enemies in the Royalist camp
acknowledged that his 'credit with the common soldiers is not
inferior to any officer of the army' – that Fairfax may well have
thought it politic to keep him in the Downs than at Westminster.[19]
The other members of the Independent coalition had different
plans.

Sir Lewis Dyve, imprisoned in the Tower of London after his
defeat at Sherborne, was receiving intelligence from sources in
the army and passing it on to the king. Dyve was told that a
faction including Cromwell and Sir Henry Vane was anxious that
Thomas already had too much power, and was convinced it
wouldn't be able to control him if he was given more. 'Knowing
him to be a man of such a temper as would rather act according
to his own than other men's principles, [they] conceived it might
be dangerous to trust him with a place of so great a command
at sea.'[20] Far better to give Batten's place to someone less popular
with the rank and file, and more biddable.

But by now Thomas was too powerful to alienate completely.
So his 'friends' in Parliament hatched a peculiarly Machiavellian
plan. They would persuade the Earl of Northumberland, who was
riding high in the army's estimation after siding with them against
the Presbyterians, to propose someone else for the vice admiralcy.
Cromwell would publicly push for Thomas, but would then, to
break the engineered deadlock, suggest his own compromise candidate – Richard Deane, at whose wedding in May Thomas had
stood as a witness, but who was politically much closer to Cromwell.

It was a clever scheme. Only Thomas found out about it.

On 9 September he was one of five Independent MPs drafted
on to the Committee of the Navy; and a week later, while the

moderate Independents were in conference together at army headquarters in Putney, he walked in on them and slammed the door behind him. He found Cromwell and Sir Henry Vane with some others; and, according to junior officers who were in the next room, there was quiet for a time. Then they heard voices raised, in anger or exasperation; first Cromwell's, then Thomas's. Even through the closed door there was no mistaking the sound of Thomas bringing his fist down on the table with a crash and shouting that the lieutenant general was no friend to him and that 'he would have the place or make him repent it'.[21]

The quarrel over the vice admiralcy was a way for the two men to express much deeper differences. Cromwell was pushing a negotiated settlement with the king, albeit one hedged about with safeguards. He wanted the senior command to agree to a process whereby Parliament would draw up plans 'for securing the rights and liberties of the people; and the just privileges of a free Parliament'. Once Charles had given these bills the royal assent, he would be allowed to return to London, 'and sit with his Parliament, for the settling, and securing the rights, liberties, peace, and safety of the kingdom'.[22] Thomas, convinced that the king couldn't be trusted, was vehemently opposed to this strategy.

The others intervened and calmed him down. But not for long. Within moments he was on his feet again, shouting that he didn't deserve this treatment from Cromwell and 'it should cost one of them their lives but that he would have the place' of vice admiral.[23] The two men squared up for a fight, and again the others had to step in to keep them apart. Thomas couldn't get his way over breaking off negotiations with the king, but to placate him Cromwell did agree to his vice admiralcy. The following afternoon Batten appeared before the Committee of the Navy, whose members included Thomas and Vane, and reluctantly handed in his resignation. 'Why . . . I was displaced by a committee at the headquarters at Putney with the advice of their adjutators, I could never understand', he wrote later. It was because of the affair of the six members, 'this, and because I was not of the temper of the army'.[24]

For the moment, the list of commanders for the next winter fleet had a blank space where the vice admiral's name should be; but by the beginning of October Parliament had agreed that

Thomas's name should fill that blank, and that he should receive £1,000 towards payment of his arrears. The decision fuelled Batten's bitterness. 'Another (such another) [was] thrust in to be my successor as till then I never imagin'd would be vice admiral of a navy,' he wrote; although quite why he thought Thomas such an unlikely candidate is hard to understand – both men shared the same background as merchant mariners and sons of mariners.[25]

The unlikely friendships and political manoeuvrings which took place that summer made the alignments and realignments of the past decade seem positively straightforward. There were rumours that Fairfax's wife was passing information about the deliberations of the Army Council to the king. Even Parliament's £1,000 grant to Thomas was seen by some as a plot to reduce his standing with the army rank and file, who 'look upon all the acts of the House as tending to their ruin and the enslaving of the subject'.[26] Sir Lewis Dyve, still in the Tower, received his information about Thomas's quarrel with Cromwell from Thomas Creamer, who had been in the next room at the time: Creamer was a serving captain in Thomas's own regiment, which says something for the nature of the Royalists' intelligence networks, as does the fact that Dyve was able to send regular reports from the Tower to the king, now being held outside London at Hampton Court. One of Dyve's fellow prisoners was John Lilburne, sent to the Tower by the House of Lords for, among other things, suggesting that the House of Commons was the 'supreme power of England' and that the Earl of Manchester was so involved with the king's interests that his head 'hath stood too long upon his shoulders'.[27] Working to reduce the radicals' power in both the Commons and the army, Cromwell went to the Tower on the pretext of surveying the munitions store, in reality to urge Lilburne's help in moderating radical demands.

And through it all Charles I played his own game, asking politely that he should be allowed to enter into personal negotiations with Parliament over his future role, doing his best to exploit the divisions in the army, conducting secret negotiations with the Scots and hinting that he might accept Presbyterianism in England.

The issues remained. What was to be done with the king? What was to be done with the kingdom? And crucially, who should decide? By the end of September the Independent movement in Parliament and the army was breaking in two. Cromwell, Ireton and Sir Henry Vane still argued for a personal treaty with the king along the lines of the *Heads of the Proposals*. Thomas aligned himself with an emerging group of Levellers, men who wanted fundamental change, freedom of conscience, safeguards for individual liberties and rule by Parliament rather than monarchy. A list of names and ciphers produced around this time and belonging to the radical MP Henry Marten included Thomas and linked him not only with Marten – an outspoken advocate of the abolition of the monarchy – but also with John Wildman and Maximilian Petty, both of whom were currently helping the agitators in the army to articulate their grievances and produce a manifesto for political change. Thomas was also seeing John Lilburne, who from his prison quarters had just condemned Presbyterian MPs in print as 'traitors and enemies to their country', and vented his anger at the 'turncoat, Machiavell practices and underhand dealings' of Cromwell, Ireton 'and the rest of their hocus-pocus faction'.[28]

The Levellers had no coherent political programme (they weren't yet even 'Levellers' – the term wasn't in use until the late autumn); but the company Thomas was keeping suggests a radicalisation had taken place during the summer. He had shifted from his earlier stance, that the army could and should enforce its will on Parliament, to dwell on the possibilities. The army had established that it could be an instrument for change; now it was time to consider what that change might be.

The pamphleteers flourished. Nathaniel Ward, the same Nathaniel Ward who had formulated Massachusetts' Body of Liberties, was back in England and launching a series of attacks on the army. 'Mr Ward hath made himself odious and ridiculous here by books and sermons', Stephen Winthrop reported to his father.[29] Ward lambasted senior officers for setting themselves up as the 'supreme law of the realm', for overriding the will of Parliament, for championing liberty of religion.[30] The army's response, *A word for the Armie. And two words to the Kingdome* was one of Hugh Peter's finest pieces of polemic. He began by poking fun at those who blamed the army for all the kingdom's ills – 'the word *Army* must answer all the doubtful mischievous deadly questions in the world'.[31] But nobody, he went on, called the army a bad thing when it was fighting at Naseby, or working to secure a sound Parliament, or delivering up a free kingdom 'to an ungrateful inhabitant'.[32] The army's failing wasn't its refusal to disband; it was its reluctance to complete its task, its 'not designing a government from first to last'.[33] And having cleared the soldiery of all charges, he set out a programme of reform which covered everything from defining prerogative, privilege and liberty to toleration and a modified form of the New England way in which public officials at all levels had to be 'godly men' and church members.[34]

Elements in the army were growing ever more impatient with the way Parliament was sidestepping their grievances and looking for a compromise with the king. And they were moving from a consideration of how those grievances should be addressed to the formulation of a plan for the government of the kingdom. Around the beginning of October five regiments replaced their agitators; and on 18 October the new agents presented Fairfax with *The Case of the armie truly stated*, a manifesto of discontent. The *Case* set out the army's complaints yet again – the disrespect offered by the Declaration of Dislike, the failure to provide for maimed soldiers and widows and orphans, the continued efforts to disband regiments and send others to Ireland. Added to these were the promises broken, the repeated failures to act.

But they wanted more. Lamenting that 'the rights of the people in their Parliaments, concerning the nature and extent of that power, are not cleared and declared', the *Case* insisted on far-reaching reforms established by 'law paramount' which couldn't be altered or repealed by future Parliaments.[35] They wanted biennial elections, a written constitution. The Parliament thus formed should have the supreme right to make or repeal laws (depriving the Crown and the Lords of those rights by implication), because 'all power is originally and essentially in the whole body of the people of this nation, and ... their free choice or consent by their representors is the only original or foundation of all just government'.[36]

Fairfax responded to the demands of the agents of the five regiments by inviting them to a conference at army headquarters in Putney, where they could debate the questions which were dominating men's thinking in the autumn of 1647. What did the future hold for the soldiers of the New Model Army? What did the future hold for the new England?

22

The Great Consult Began

'*I* shall crave your pardon if I may speak something freely', Thomas Rainborowe announced to the soldiers gathered in the little church of St Mary, Putney. 'I think it will be the last time I shall speak here.'[1]

Thomas hadn't planned to attend the General Council of the army which convened at Putney on 28 October 1647. It wasn't at all clear that he had any *right* to attend, since he was now technically in the navy and Parliament had ordered him to sea weeks before. Nor is it clear why he hadn't gone. The reason for his presence at army headquarters, he said, was that he had received information that his regiment had been given to Cromwell's crony Richard Deane, with immediate effect and without consulting him; and he didn't like it. He had thought, rather optimistically, that he could hang on to his military command while serving as vice admiral. 'Rather than I will lose this regiment of mine,' he complained, 'the Parliament shall exclude me the House, or imprison me.' It was this which had brought him to Putney, and not *The Case of the armie truly stated*, he said. 'But now I shall speak something of it.'[2]

Thomas had chosen a very public forum for airing his grievance. The meeting was chaired by Cromwell. (Fairfax, who was uncomfortable with politics and increasingly bewildered by the ideological struggle taking place in his army, had absented himself on health grounds.) Cromwell was supported by Henry Ireton, who was not only his son-in-law but also commissary general of the army. The lieutenant general of the ordnance, Thomas Hammond, was there along with at least eight regimental commanders and several other senior staff officers; a dozen or so officer-agitators; half a dozen or so trooper-agitators; two civilians, brought along by the representatives of the five regiments to help them argue their case; and an unknown number of clerks and clergy.

Mindful of Thomas's short temper, Cromwell replied smoothly that he was pleased to see him here, and not sorry for the occasion that had brought him, since 'it argues we shall enjoy his company longer than I thought we should have done—'

'If I should not be kicked out', interrupted Thomas with a snort.[3]

The meeting was marked from the beginning by hostility and suspicion. One of the first to speak, Edward Sexby, began by telling Cromwell and Ireton to their faces that 'your credits and reputation have been much blasted' by their attempts to treat with the king. Parliament consisted of 'a company of rotten members'; the king would never be content 'except we go about to cut all our throats'.[4] Cromwell in turn vehemently denied rumours that in the Commons he had claimed army support for a renewed attempt to negotiate with the king.

As the grandees reminded everyone of the purpose of the meeting – to discuss *The Case of the armie truly stated* – representatives of the five regiments caused confusion and consternation by presenting the General Council with a new manifesto. *An agreement of the people for a firm and present peace upon grounds of common right and freedom* was actually an admirably simple development of a few of the ideas set out in *The Case of the armie*. It contained just four proposals: that parliamentary constituencies should be reorganised 'according to the number of the inhabitants'; that the present Parliament should be dissolved at the end of September 1648; that Parliaments should be elected every other year, on the first Thursday of March, and sit from the first Thursday in April until the end of September; and that this biennially elected House should be the supreme power in the land, although it would be constitutionally prohibited from imposing religious uniformity, impressing men into the army, passing unjust or unequal laws or prosecuting anyone for their actions in the war.

It was as clear a political programme as one could imagine. And the fact that it *was* a political programme unnerved Cromwell, who was expecting to do battle over soldiers' back pay and defence cuts. How were these constitutional reforms to be established? By force? 'It is not enough for us to insist on good things', he told the council.[5] In any case, the army had made promises to Parliament and the country, and those 'engagements' might not be compatible with the agents' manifesto.

Ireton supported him. 'There are things really good in it', he said of the *Agreement*. 'There are those things that I do with my heart desire.'[6] But the council must adjourn, and appoint a committee to compare the *Agreement* with past declarations, 'that we may either resolve to make them good if we can in honest ways, or at least not make it our work to break them'.[7]

Thomas waded in with a different and passionate view. Of course it would be difficult to implement the *Agreement*. But 'if ever we [had] looked upon difficulties, I do not know that ever we should have looked an enemy in the face'.[8] His speech, scribbled down in shorthand by army stenographers, shows a rhetorical gift beyond what one might expect from a taciturn Wapping merchant-mariner:

> Let the difficulties be round about you – have you death before you, the sea each side of you and behind you – [and] are you convinced that the thing is just, I think you are bound in conscience to carry it on; and I think at the Last Day it can never be answered to God, that you did not do it.[9]

He appealed to history, arguing that the laws of England had always been the product of conflict. 'There have been many scufflings between the honest men of England and those that have tyrannised over them.'[10] All freedoms that were now accepted as the rights of the many had once been seen as encroachments on the privileges of the few. But having raised the issue of precedent, he discarded it, insisting that there was only one test that mattered – 'the justness of the thing'.[11] Did the *Agreement* promise people a way of life which was an improvement on the government under which they currently lived?

They were a long way from consensus. Cromwell and Ireton wanted a committee to consider potential clashes between the reforms and their previous 'engagements'. The new agitators urged speed. 'If we tarry long,' said one, 'if we stay but three days before you satisfy one another, the king will come and say who will be hanged first.'[12] Lieutenant General William Goffe, who even in a church filled with godly men stood out as more godly than most, urged the assembly to use the adjournment to seek God, who having thrown down the king and the City of London, would throw down the army if they did not humble themselves before Him. 'I hope our strayings from God are not so great but that a conversion and true humiliation may recover us again,' he said, 'and I desire that we may be serious in this.'[13] The following day should be set aside for prayer.

After hours of argument the council broke up, having agreed that a committee of twelve officers and six agitators would meet the following afternoon to confer with those agents of the five regiments who could get to Putney and their civilian advisers about the *Agreement* and the army's own 'declarations and engagements'. The officers represented a fair cross-section of opinion, from the conservative – Cromwell, Ireton, Deane – to the radical, including Thomas and colonels Tichborne, Overton and Okey. Sexby was one of the agitators. Cromwell urged them all to come with open minds. Ireton urged that 'the main thing is for every one to wait upon God, for the errors, deceits, and weaknesses of his own heart'.[14] And taking up Goffe's suggestion, they agreed to spend the morning doing just that – not in St Mary's church, ironically enough, since that would smack too much of institutional religion, but in the Quartermaster General's lodgings in the town.

Twice during the first day of the Putney debates Thomas emphasised this would be the last time he attended a meeting of the General Council, daring anyone to challenge his right to be there. When he spoke in support of one of the new agitators, he was at pains to say he had never seen the man until now. He had only seen the *Agreement* by chance.

All of which leaves open the question as to whether he was working in collaboration with other Levellers in and out of the army. (And they can now have their name, since days after the Putney debates began, a Royalist newsletter announced that they had 'given themselves a new name viz. Levellers, for they intend to set all things straight, and raise a parity and community in the kingdom'.[15]) When he was attending the army headquarters he usually stayed with his brother William, who had a house just across the river in Fulham; but this time, when the day's business was done, he headed straight back into London – possibly to talk to Harry Marten, or to visit Lilburne in the Tower, or to confer in private with John Wildman and Maximilian Petty, the two civilian advisers to the five regiments. He was late back to Putney the next afternoon, apologising that 'the ill disposition of my body caused me to go to London last night'.[16] Perhaps.

When representatives of the agents of the five regiments arrived at the Quartermaster General's lodgings on Friday afternoon the committee was still seeking God, who was proving annoyingly hard to find. Deane moved that the committee should reconvene on Monday morning to resume the search. Goffe referred everyone to the Book of Revelations, and suggested helpfully that the Last Days were at hand. Robert Everard, a trooper in Cromwell's regiment and a signatory to both *The Case of the armie* and the *Agreement of the people*, used Goffe's speech to plead for a swift decision and an end to talking. 'This message God hath sent me to you', he told the committee, 'that there is great expectation of sudden destruction – and I would be loath to fill that up with words.'[17]

If anyone had expected a quiet discussion behind closed doors, they were disappointed. The chamber was crowded with officer-agitators, staff officers, clerical staff. Major William Rainborowe had come in his capacity as officer-agitator for Harrison's regiment. As Cromwell's chaplain, Hugh Peter had led the morning's prayers, and he stayed on to watch the proceedings. Altogether there were forty men or more crammed into the Quartermaster General's lodgings.

Cromwell didn't like it. The prayers had gone on for so long that he didn't feel prepared to discuss the *Agreement*, and the idea of carrying on what he called 'a general loose debate' in this quasi-public forum worried him. Things might not go his way. So he argued for a private session with the agents for the rest of the afternoon. 'All this company might meet about nine or ten o'clock' to hear the results of their deliberations.[18]

No, said Thomas. Whatever they had to say should be said in the open. 'I think it an advantage that it should be as public [as possible]', he declared, 'and as many as may, be present at it.'[19] Cromwell responded by producing a copy of the recently printed *Declaration of the Engagements, Remonstrances, Representations, Proposals, Desires and Resolutions . . . of the Army* and waving the fat little volume about, insisting that their task was still to decide how its 163 pages fitted with the agents' *Agreement*.

Again Thomas disagreed. He was here to discuss the *Agreement*. There was some urgency in the matter – 'I could give you reasons for it, which this day I have from very good hands', he said mysteriously, 'which I think is not prudent to declare so publicly' – and they might spend the next ten days 'going over that book' and still not get anywhere.[20] There was a paper on the table; it should be read and debated; and the committee should decide 'whether it be a way to deliver us yet or no'.[21]

Others weighed in on both sides, as the previous day's arguments were picked over once again. Was the *Agreement* compatible with the army's published promises, and if not, did that matter? William Rainborowe urged the committee to remember its priorities: 'that which is the engagement of all, which is the rights and freedoms of the people'.[22] Eventually Henry Ireton, who was chairing the day's proceedings, gave in. The *Agreement* was read out in its entirety – it is a very short document – and then the first of its four articles, the one asking for a more equitable arrangement of parliamentary constituencies proportioned 'according to the number of the inhabitants', was read out again.

There were 507 seats in the Commons. Ninety belonged to knights of the shire from the counties, elected by freeholders owning property worth at least forty shillings a year. The rest were occupied – in less troubled times, at least – by men returned by the parliamentary boroughs, which varied in size from large cities to tiny villages, and whose electorates varied just as dramatically. In some, voting was confined to public officials, the mayor and a dozen or so aldermen; in others to a handful of freemen or property holders. Some were controlled by major landowners, and few were entirely free from their interference. Ireton took the word 'inhabitant' in the first article to imply a seismic shift in suffrage: a demand that every man was to be equally considered, and to have an equal voice in the election of MPs. 'If that be the meaning,' he said, 'then I have something to say against it.'[23]

Extending the franchise wasn't explicitly mentioned in the *Agreement* or *The Case for the Armie*, although four months earlier John Lilburne had offered up a package of parliamentary reforms which included a more equal distribution of seats and a system whereby every free man could vote for their representative, 'it being a maxim in nature, that no man justly can be bound without his own consent'.[24] A better tactician than Ireton might have been inclined to steer the debate away from the topic, rather than asking, as he now did, if such a dramatic extension was *really* what the signatories to the *Agreement* intended. Thomas's response has a place in the history of parliamentary democracy:

> I think that the poorest he that is in England hath a life to live, as the greatest he; and therefore truly, sir, I think it's clear, that every man that is to live under a government ought first by his own consent to put himself under that government; and I do think that the poorest man in England is not at all bound in a strict sense to that government that he hath not had a voice to put himself under; and I am confident that, when I have heard the reasons against it, something will be said to answer those reasons, insomuch that I should doubt whether he was an Englishman or no, that should doubt of these things.[25]

There it was. Every man should have a say in choosing the government.

This was a startling thing to say. No nation on earth had universal male suffrage in 1647. It would be another 145 years before Revolutionary France took the first halting steps towards abolishing property qualifications. Britain didn't achieve universal male suffrage until 1918, and the United States had to wait until the Voting Rights Act of 1965. It was such a remarkable proposal, in fact, that historians have argued either that Thomas was an eccentric figure whose views had no support among the other Levellers, a notion which assumes mistakenly that there *was* a consistent Leveller ideology at this point; or that he didn't really mean what he said. In this view of events, he was carried away with his own rhetorical flourishes; or he was taking it for granted that servants, apprentices and paupers would be excluded from the franchise.

Ireton certainly thought he meant it. He immediately launched into a long and impassioned defence of the property qualification, while Thomas, who was sitting next to him, scribbled notes. ('My memory is bad', he explained.[26]) No person 'that hath not a permanent fixed interest in this kingdom' had a right to choose those who framed the laws and ran the kingdom, Ireton said, using an argument that would be repeated by the opponents of reform for the next 250 years. Why should those with no stake in the land have a say in disposing it? One might as well give foreigners the vote. In fact if Thomas had his way, 'we shall plainly go to take away all property and interest that any man hath either in land by inheritance, or in estate by possession, or anything else'.[27]

The exchange grew heated, with Ireton continuing to insist that by removing the requirement for an elector to have a 'permanent and local interest' in their constituency, Thomas would undercut the basis of property ownership; and Thomas getting angrier by the minute. Of course there was no threat to property, he replied: God's commandment, Thou shalt not steal, ensured that. 'And for my part', he concluded irritably, 'I wish you would not make the world believe that we are for anarchy.'[28]

No one was suggesting that Thomas *wanted* anarchy, intervened Cromwell; just that anarchy would be an unlooked-for consequence of extending the franchise to include all men. 'We should not be so hot one with another.' Ireton also tried to calm Thomas, although he succeeded only in being patronising. 'Truly, for that gentleman [i.e. Thomas] that did take so much offence, I do not know why he should take it so. We speak to the paper – not to persons.'[29]

With an effort, Thomas agreed to address 'the thing itself'. If the property qualification was itself a property, then the law that made it so was a bad law, 'the most tyrannical law under heaven'.[30]

Worse, it meant the people of England had been, and would continue to be, enslaved by a law which they played no part in framing. And he brought the question back, as he always did, to the war. 'I would fain know what we have fought for.'[31]

The arguments went on for hours, with Petty, Wildman and some of the officer-agitators pressing for an extended franchise and Ireton setting his face against it, with occasional support from Cromwell. Hugh Peter, keen to keep the peace, suggested a subcommittee to consider the question. Thomas returned like a terrier to his theme. 'I say still, what shall become of those many that have laid out themselves for the Parliament of England in this present war, that have ruined themselves by fighting, by hazarding all they had?'[32] And again, 'I would fain know what the soldier hath fought for all this while? He hath fought to enslave himself, to give power to men of riches, men of estates, to make him a perpetual slave.'[33] This wasn't just about the people of England for Thomas. It was about the rank and file. About his regiment. Even Peter, normally quite a moderate in political matters, was convinced that at least soldiers who had fought should have the vote. Ireton's answer, that men had fought to prevent the king from overruling their representatives in Parliament, was accurate but unpalatable to the radicals.

The inequalities, the distinctions of degree that were bothering Thomas, showed among them there in the Quartermaster General's lodgings before the evening was out. An earnest discussion on whether property sprang from the law of God or the law of nature or civil authority was interrupted by an outburst from Edward Sexby. 'There are many thousands of us soldiers that have ventured our lives; we have had little propriety in the kingdom as to our estates, yet we have had a birthright', he told the room. 'But it seems now, except a man hath a fixed estate in this kingdom, he hath no right in this kingdom. I wonder we were so much deceived.'[34] And he went on to announce that whatever was said, he was not going to give his birthright away. And now could they all stop talking and reach some decision on the matter?

He was met with a mild reproof from Ireton, who pointed out that they were there to discuss, and not simply to declare their positions. Then came a hard verbal slap from Cromwell: 'I confess I was most dissatisfied with that I heard Mr Sexby speak, of any

man here, because it did savour so much of will.'[35] Thomas leapt
to the agitator's defence: how was it that when a junior officer
expressed an opinion it was wilfulness, and when a senior officer
did the same it was reason? Sexby also sought to defend himself.
He was there to represent the views of his regiment. 'There are
many that have not estates that in honesty have as much right
in the freedom of their choice as any that have great estates.'[36]
And he threw at Ireton and Cromwell the familiar question. 'Do
you not think it were a sad and miserable condition, that we
have fought all this time for nothing?'[37]

The evening was drawing on, and the onlookers were exasperated with the personal sideswipes and bored with the circularity
of the arguments. 'We should speak with moderation', broke in
one.[38] 'I would humbly move that we should put a speedy end
to this business', said another.[39] We'll be here until next March,
said a third.

It did no good. Cromwell insisted that he couldn't go against
his conscience and then, with a cheery lack of irony, repeated his
criticism of Sexby for being wilful. Ireton announced that he
really shouldn't speak again, and then did. At great length. Both
moved for a subcommittee to consider the franchise and for
maintaining the status quo in the meantime, at which Thomas
hit back by pointing out that this course would benefit them
alone. 'If a man hath all he doth desire, [he may wish to sit still];
but [if] I think I have nothing at all of what I fought for, I do
not think the argument holds.'[40]

Ireton and Wildman argued over the need for unity in the
army. Thomas suggested ominously 'that the army might be called
to a rendezvous, and things settled'.[41] Soon afterwards the stenographers gave up. No transcripts were made when the committee
reconvened on Saturday, either, but the scraps of notes that were
taken show a consensus of sorts was finally achieved. The recommendations were for the present parliament to end on
1 September 1648; for a biennial parliament, which could appoint
committees and a Council of State, on whose advice the king
could summon extra parliaments; and for the Commons to
establish a framework for a more equitable distribution of seats.
When it came to the franchise, compromise triumphed. It was
left to the Commons to give 'as much enlargement to common

freedom as may be, with a due regard had to the equity and end of the present constitution'; but with two important provisos. All soldiers who had served against the king up to and including 14 June 1645 (the date of the Battle of Naseby) were given the vote, even if they weren't otherwise qualified; and anyone who had fought against Parliament was barred from voting or standing for office 'until the second biennial parliament be past'.[42] If Thomas didn't quite get the broad franchise he wanted, at least he now had a clearer answer to his question as to what his soldiers had been fighting for.

23

Disobedience

On Sunday Thomas was back in London. He went straight to the Tower, where he spent two hours discussing Putney with John Lilburne.

The source for this meeting was again Sir Lewis Dyve, who told Charles I that Thomas was 'the likeliest man to become head of this faction out of the hatred he bears to Cromwell and the general good esteem is of him in the army'.[1] According to Dyve, Thomas confided that he was opposed to those who called for the king's removal, adding that the greatest part of the army wouldn't countenance it and that they knew their own safety 'depended upon Your Majesty's preservation'.[2]

Dyve didn't always get things right, either because Lilburne deliberately misled him or because in his letters to Charles he was trying too hard to see a silver lining in every cloud; but he insisted that while he hadn't been present at the meeting, 'there were several persons besides Lilburne that heard him, who told me of it not without some admiration, supposing no man to be more averse in his inclination towards Your Majesty than himself'.[3] If he was right, it shows that at this point even a senior commander as republican as Thomas was still undecided as to how to treat the king. Other Royalist intelligence sources were more circumspect, and Charles soon replied to Dyve with a warning to treat Thomas with caution.

The next day, Monday 1 November, Thomas was back at Putney in time for the General Council, which kept up the *Sturm und Drang* of Friday's committee meeting. When staff officers, agitators and agents reconvened in the afternoon after another session spent seeking God, the divisions among the officers showed themselves at once, as Cromwell – now back in the chair – went round the table inviting everyone to tell 'what God had given in answer to their prayers'.[4] Several of the officer-agitators declared He had told them He supported the idea of removing both the king and the Lords from power, until Cromwell, still convinced it was possible to reach a settlement which didn't completely exclude either – and still, incidentally, trying to preserve Parliament, rather than the army, as the nation's instrument of government – was driven to remark that clearly they were mistaken, and this was not the mind of God speaking to them at all. That earned him a mild reproof from Goffe – 'I could wish we might be wary of such expressions' – and a series of exchanges in which biblical texts were hurled back and forth between Cromwell and some of the agitators.[5] George Bishop, one of the officer-agitators (and later a prominent Quaker) spoke up against preserving the king, calling him 'that Man of Blood' – a phrase which conjured an image of Charles I as King David, cursed by Shimei: 'The Lord hath returned upon thee all the blood of the house of Saul, in whose stead thou hast reigned; and the Lord hath delivered the kingdom into the hand of Absalom thy son: and, behold, thou art taken in thy mischief, because thou art a bloody man.'[*]

This was the last fully reported day of the debates, and the arguments revolved around the question of what powers should be allowed the king and the House of Lords. Maximilian Petty had already made the Levellers' position clear when he declared that 'it hath pleased God to raise a company of men that do stand up for the power of the House of Commons, which is the

---

[*] 2 Samuel 16:8. The 1560 Geneva Bible, preferred by many Puritans over the King James version, translated 'bloody man' as 'murtherer'.

representative of the people, and deny the negative voice of king and Lords' (by which was meant the right of both to veto laws made by the Commons).[6] John Wildman emphasised that position – 'It will never satisfy the godly people in the kingdom unless that all government be in the Commons, and freely' – while Ireton and Cromwell pressed, as they had from the beginning, for a more moderate path.[7]

Cromwell did his best to emphasise areas of agreement. All things being equal, he said, no one present would want to set up the king or the Lords to have any controlling interest in the government of the people. But all things weren't equal: they already had that role. Nor would anyone want to preserve either if it was clear that they presented 'a visible danger and destruction to the people and the public interest'.[8] So the only point at issue was whether allowing king and Lords to continue was compatible with the safety of the kingdom. His tone was conciliatory, urging his opponents to 'avoid the bringing of a scandal to the name of God' by doing something dishonourable in His name; and at the same time conceding that if these commitments really did seem to be leading to things inconsistent with 'the liberty and safety and public interest of this nation', then it would be everybody's duty to break with them.[9] The committee would later resolve, without explicitly denying the negative voice to the king or the Lords, that the Commons should be able to enact, alter or repeal laws 'without further appeal'.[10]

Thomas played a smaller part in Monday's debate than he had on previous days. He made no long speeches, and his contributions were largely confined to sniping at Ireton. At one point, for example, he launched into the middle of an obscure spat between the commissary general and one of the officer-agitators over the inequity of the Norman prerogative (a favourite theme with Levellers, who held that the English Commons had lost their ancient rights at the Conquest). Criticising Ireton for squabbling over historical precedent, he told him to consider 'the equality and reasonableness of the thing [the rights of the Commons], and not to stand upon constitution, which we have broken again and again'.[11] Then, not to be outdone when it came to displaying a knowledge of England's history, he cited the fate of Richard II, deposed for his refusal to agree when 'wholesome laws' were offered him by the Commons for the people's safety. If they *were* looking for a precedent, he said, there it was. Ireton was forced to agree.

Thomas was tiring of asking for support from Cromwell and Ireton, and the disagreement over a future constitution was turning into something more dangerous – a dispute over who controlled the army, its senior commanders or the dissidents. Cromwell was well aware of the danger: at Monday's meeting of the General Council he had responded firmly to Thomas's call for a rendezvous of the troops, pointing out that 'it is not in the power of any particular men to call a rendezvous of a troop or regiment, or in [the] least to disoblige the army from those commands of the general'.[12]

A few days after the General Council adjourned – having resolved wearily to meet again in the morning, 'and so from day to day till the proposals be all debated' – Thomas took advantage of an occasion when Fairfax was for once in the chair and Cromwell was absent in Westminster, to push through a letter to the Commons claiming the army didn't want them to make any further advances to the king. Ireton stormed out in protest, and they were forced to retract the letter as 'utterly a mistake of our intention and meaning'.[13] Fairfax agreed to a rendezvous of the army; but the grandees were rattled. On Monday 8 November the agitators turned up at the General Council expecting a free debate on the question 'whether it were safe, either for the army, or the people, to suffer any power to be given to the king'.[14]

Instead, Cromwell gave them a good telling off, repeated his conviction that the widening of the franchise 'did tend very much to anarchy' and threatened to withdraw his agreement to it.[15] Officers and agitators were sent back to their regiments until Fairfax saw fit to summon them to Putney again (he never did); and the council was adjourned.

Then everything changed.

On the evening of 11 November 1647 Edward Whalley, whose regiment was responsible for guarding Charles I while he was being held at Hampton Court, entered the king's bedchamber. It was empty, except for a cloak and a letter thanking him for his hospitality. There had been a rumour that Thomas Rainborowe might be appointed to guard the king – 'the double of guards troubles me not', wrote one of his sympathisers, 'but the employing of such devils doth'[16] – and fearing an assassination attempt, Charles had slipped out of his lodgings and down to the Thames, where a boat took him across the river to where three gentleman servants, William Legge, Sir John Berkeley and Jack Ashburnham, were waiting with horses. They discussed riding straight into London and appealing to the people for support, or sailing for Jersey or France. In the end the king was taken to the Isle of Wight, where the governor, Colonel Robert Hammond, was keeping his head down and hoping that the troubles between king and Parliament, Parliament and the army, would pass him by.

Ashburnham misread Hammond's reluctance to become embroiled in events as evidence of Royalist sympathies. In fact the governor was appalled at the sight of his royal visitor. 'Oh gentlemen, you have undone me by bringing the king into the island', he wailed. 'Between my duty to His Majesty, and my gratitude for this fresh obligation on the one hand, and my observing my trust to the army on the other, I shall be confounded.'[17] Charles was held in Carisbrooke Castle.

In the meantime, Fairfax was having second thoughts about calling a general rendezvous of the army. The advisability of bringing so many men together in one place was playing into the hands of Thomas and the other dissidents who were pressing not only for the army to prevent Charles I from resuming any position of power, but also for the abolition of the monarchy itself. On the day the king escaped from Hampton Court William Rainborowe's colonel, Thomas Harrison, arrived in Putney and told a committee of officers which included Fairfax, Cromwell and both Rainborowes that the king 'was a Man of Blood' – that phrase again – that any previous engagement with him was nullified, and that they must prosecute him.[18]

Fairfax decided on three separate rendezvous, 'to draw off the army from joining together to settle those clear foundations of freedom propounded to you', claimed the agitators in a letter to their regiments.[19] The high command prepared a remonstrance of its own, condemning the agitators for dividing the soldiery and threatening 'the greatest forfeiture of the faith and honour of the army, that ever it incurred' by their insistence on its breaking its engagements.[20] Fairfax, still enormously popular with the troops, announced he was not prepared to continue as the head of the army unless they agreed to his terms. As far as they related to the army itself, those terms were familiar and unexceptionable: arrears, indemnity, freedom from impressment, provision for maimed veterans and widows and orphans. His plans for the kingdom were less precise: to have an end to the present parliament (although when that might be wasn't stated); to determine fixed lengths for subsequent parliaments (the period wasn't mentioned); and 'to render the House of Commons as near as may be an equal representative of the people that are to elect'.[21] Everything else must be left to Parliament.

Thomas was in London and attending the Commons on Friday 12 November, and he may have taken part in one of several large meetings convened in and around the City that weekend by agitators and their civilian sympathisers, along with fellow MP Henry Marten. There was a story in Royalist circles that Marten and Thomas spent the Saturday night together working on a plan to impeach Cromwell and Ireton for treason.

By the morning of Monday 15 November Thomas had ridden north to Corkbush Field in Hertfordshire, twenty-five miles from London. And he was there to present the Levellers' case to Fairfax in person.

Four regiments of horse and three of foot gathered together at Corkbush Field that day for the first of the three scheduled rendezvous – between 6,000–7,000 men massed in the field, with standards flying in the cold November air. The atmosphere was tense. As the troops waited for Fairfax to arrive and address them, several officers, including a New England returnee named William Eyres and the MP Major Thomas Scot, rode among them urging them to subscribe to the *Agreement of the people*. Agents were handing out copies of the *Agreement* to anyone who would take them. Worryingly for Fairfax and the other grandees, Harrison's regiment had also shown up, though they were not invited; and some of Harrison's troopers were wearing copies of the *Agreement* in their hats, printed in huge letters on the cover with the motto 'England's Freedom, Soldiers' Rights'. Even more worrying was news which arrived just as Fairfax prepared to begin his review: companies from Robert Lilburne's regiment of foot, sent north to join their colonel at Newcastle, had disobeyed orders and turned on their officers. Two soldiers had been killed and a lieutenant had lost his hand. And the mutinous soldiers were at that moment marching to join their comrades at Corkbush Field.

So as Fairfax took the field, with Cromwell at his side, he faced a crisis. He also faced Thomas, who rode up at the head of a small delegation and presented him with the *Agreement*, and a petition complaining that redress for the army's grievances was no closer, and declaring that the signatories, 'many officers and soldiers under [Fairfax's] command', were bound 'in conscience from the sense of our duty to our native country, and in mercy to our selves, to keep together with our swords in our hands, to maintain these our freedoms'.[22]

This was bold. Thomas had no right to be there at all: he was no longer an officer in the New Model, nor was his old regiment, the one now commanded by Richard Deane, present at the rendezvous. He could hardly claim to be there in his capacity as an MP, since by showing his support for the *Agreement* he was in effect calling on the army to overrule Parliament. Was he trying to foment dissent among the men, as his fellow MP Major Scot was doing, 'not only testifying his own discontent', as Fairfax later said, 'but stirring up others also to the same'?[23] Or was he making a bid for power, relying on his popularity in the ranks? Did he want to start a mutiny?

Some of the civilian Levellers expected great things from Corkbush Field. John Lilburne, out on bail from the Tower, had ridden up to the nearby town of Ware in readiness. So had Richard Overton, a prominent Leveller and Baptist, and one of the first radicals to call publicly for the execution of Charles I. Papers were posted up in churches and on the City gates, inciting the population of London to rise up 'and free themselves from the tyranny of their taskmasters at Westminster'.[24]

It seems as if Thomas was indeed making a play for power, convinced that he and his cause had the support of the rank and file; and that confronted by 7,000 men calling for England's freedom and soldiers' rights, Fairfax and the other grandees would throw in their lot with the revolution. And it would be a great mistake to underestimate Thomas's idealism. In the Machiavellian world of army politics, where there were many sides and every side was prepared to court king or Commons or Lords or Scots to gain the upper hand, he was trying to do the right thing. He believed in the *Agreement*. He believed in a radical extension of the franchise, in the supremacy of an elected House, in freedom of worship and equality under the law. In common rights and liberties. In justice.

But if that simple act of handing the *Agreement* to Fairfax was meant to start the revolution, the result was a humiliating anticlimax. Fairfax was having none of it. Thomas was ordered to leave the field; and he did. Before the day was out the general had despatched a complaint to Parliament about his behaviour, 'for being too forward in promoting some petitions'.[25] Major Scot was packed off back to Westminster in the custody of an officer. Other less well-connected officers were arrested at once, along with several civilian agents. Then Fairfax reprimanded the soldiers from Harrison's regiment and told them their wrongheaded actions were the result of their being misled by their agitators. Faced with an angry and authoritative general, and with no sign of their comrades in other regiments joining them, their revolutionary fervour evaporated. Or as Fairfax would have it, 'they were no sooner informed of their error, but, with a great deal of readiness and cheerfulness, they submitted to me'.[26]

So did the rest of the troops. When the review finally began, Fairfax rode from regiment to regiment, pausing at the head of each to have his *Remonstrance* read out. The general's reiterated commitment to the troops' immediate demands was enough, and they were happy to subscribe, both to the terms and to Fairfax's own demand for the reimposition of strict military discipline in the ranks. His secretary William Clarke reported to the Commons that 'they generally by many acclamations declared their affections and resolutions to adhere to the general'; while the fact that the ranks signified their approval by shouting 'For the king and Sir Thomas!' was an indication to those who were hoping for a different result of just how wide was the gap between Leveller aspirations and those of the ordinary soldier.[27] The revolution was postponed indefinitely.

But the excitement wasn't quite over. Late that afternoon, companies of mutineers from Robert Lilburne's regiment began straggling on to the field wearing the *Agreement* in their hats, 'as if they had been going to engage with an enemy', wrote a pamphleteer.[28] The only one of their officers in sight was a lone captain lieutenant, William Bray; and it wasn't at all clear whether Bray was there to restrain them or to urge them on. He was immediately arrested, but that did nothing to calm his men. A major rode up and urged them to submit to military discipline, only for some in the ranks to pelt him with stones. Fairfax came up with his staff and ordered them to remove the *Agreement* from their hats. They refused, and officers went in among them and began snatching away the papers. According to a Royalist account, Cromwell himself waded in, sword drawn. The rest began to submit.

By this time more officers from Lilburne's regiment were arriving on the scene, and Fairfax asked them to identify the ringleaders. Eight or nine were picked out as examples to the rest. A court martial was convened on the spot, in full view of the regiment; and three were tried, found guilty and sentenced to death. Fairfax then announced that only one would have his sentence carried out. The three drew lots; and the unlucky loser, private Richard Arnold, was shot to death by his two reprieved comrades at the head of his regiment. His officers rejoiced that the just hand of God had ensured that the lot went to one of those who most deserved punishment; and the survivors blamed their officers for leading them astray and promised to behave themselves in future. As well they might, having had the consequences of misbehaviour demonstrated so swiftly and so brutally.

The consequences for Thomas were almost as swift, if rather less brutal. Parliament received Fairfax's report on the rendezvous the next day, Tuesday 16 November. The Commons summoned Thomas to attend the House and give an explanation of his actions, while the Lords moved that 'Colonel Raynsborow, who is named in the general's letter to have been active with others at this rendezvous, may not be suffered to go to sea, till this business be fully examined.'[29] 'Colonel *Rainborough* is like to come to a *sea* of troubles', reported the Royalist press with glee.[30]

Thomas had lost his regiment in the New Model, his place on the General Council. He had played for and lost the leadership of the Levellers. He had fought for and lost the command of the fleet, and the Lords in particular weren't minded to forgive him. Now Cromwell told anyone who would listen that he wanted him out of the Commons – in fact Thomas's insistence on extending the franchise to men without property had been instrumental in convincing the lieutenant general that the 'drive to levelling and parity' must be stopped at all costs.[31]

What could Thomas do to retrieve his career and his reputation?

24

In Mutiny

On Tuesday 21 December the Army Council gathered at their new headquarters in Windsor Castle for a bout of truth and reconciliation; and for three days of prayer, fasting and forgiveness 'for offences that had, through weakness, come from brethren'. John Rushworth, who compiled an account of the meeting, noted the 'exhortations to unity and affinity', the expressions of 'sweet harmony' from one officer to another, the parade of contrite comrades who were there to admit the error of their ways.[1] Most of the following day was given over to prayers and fasting. For ten hours, from nine in the morning until seven at night, Cromwell, Ireton and the ubiquitous Hugh Peter led them in seeking God.

When the prayers were over, Thomas appeared before them to make his peace.

He was contrite. Fairfax reported that he 'expressed to myself and divers principal officers such a deep sense of the late distempers and miscarriages in those things whereunto he had appeared too inclinable, and such resolutions to decline the like for the future, as gave us large satisfaction concerning him'.[2] The council agreed unanimously that on account of his recantation and his service record he should, after all, be made vice admiral. Even Cromwell seems to have been convinced. Asked how he could ever trust a man who was capable of such a dramatic volte-face, and one moreover whom he had so recently schemed to remove from office, he answered that the assurances given him by Thomas were 'as great as could be given by man' that he would be directed by himself and Ireton when it came to managing 'the whole business at sea'.[3]

Parliament, however, remained unconvinced, and Thomas remained in limbo, a colonel without a regiment, a vice admiral without a fleet, a rebel without a cause. Although the Lords had ordered that he 'may not be suffered to go to sea', no steps had been taken to appoint anyone else to the vice admiralcy.[4] The Commons confirmed the Lords' resolution, voting on 10 December – by the narrow margin of sixty-one to fifty-eight – against a motion that he 'be ordered forthwith to go to sea'.[5]

But he was needed. And once he had reconsidered his enthusiasm for the *Agreement of the people*, an impatient Fairfax urged Parliament to get a move on and order him to the fleet. 'There is some want of good guards at sea about the Isle of Wight, though there be now more than ordinary need thereof thereabouts', he wrote in exasperation to Speaker Lenthall; 'and indeed the whole business of your sea service seems to be elsewhere in too loose a posture, considering the condition of affairs.'[6] So would they please send the new vice admiral down to his fleet?

This did the trick with the Commons, who approved Thomas's appointment. Not so the Lords, in spite of another letter from Fairfax. On 28 December they confirmed that 'their Lordships hold it not fit that he should be put into a place of so great concernment', and asked the Commons to support their decision, without success.[7] So when rumours reached Westminster on New Year's Day of a mutiny on the Isle of Wight, MPs decided to ignore the Lords and resolved, with the tacit approval of Fairfax and the army high command at Windsor, 'that Colonel Rainsborough the vice admiral be required forthwith to repair to the Isle of Wight with such ships as he shall think necessary for that service'.[8]

Three things combined to give Thomas the post he had wanted so much for so long. Firstly, his move to distance himself from the *Agreement of the people*, humiliating though it was, reassured his superior officers about his suitability for the job. Secondly, the urgency of the situation played out in his favour: neither the Commons nor the army high command could bear the prospect of a rudderless fleet in the Downs at a moment when the king seemed to provide an obvious focus for insurgents on the Isle of Wight, when Irish privateers were attacking English merchantmen with impunity, and when the loyalty of sections of the navy was suspect.

And thirdly, in the weeks after Charles I's escape from Hampton Court, Fairfax and Cromwell moved towards Thomas's own position on the futility of negotiating with the king, whose duplicity as he hunted for alliances was impossible to ignore. On top of the escape itself, by which Charles broke his word, there was evidence that he was trying to negotiate with the Scots at the expense of the army. He also sent a peace proposal to Parliament, accepting Presbyterianism for a three-year period during which divines would be asked to come up with a church settlement to be agreed by himself and both Houses. And he despatched Sir John Berkeley off to Windsor with a proposal that the Army Council should support him against Parliament. Fairfax rejected the plan out of hand; Berkeley recalled in his *Memoirs* that when he nodded to Cromwell, Ireton, and other members of the Army Council whom he knew, they 'saluted me very coldly'.[9] Was he surprised?

So in some respects the army high command was moving towards Thomas's position, just as he was swallowing his principles and trying to accommodate theirs. The Committee of the Admiralty's instructions to 'Col. Rainsborough, vice admiral and commander-in-chief of the fleet' were clear and ambitious. He was to blockade the rebels in Ireland, gather intelligence on the coasts of France and Holland, guard the south coast and patrol the western seas off Cornwall and 'resist, take, scatter and destroy' any invasion force.[10] He had thirty-nine ships under his command: his flagship was the 742-ton *Constant Reformation*, a ship built in James I's time, equipped with forty guns and a crew of 250. He was also directed to find out if any of the fleet's officers had Royalist sympathies and to replace them if he was in any doubt.

His predecessor William Batten had been well liked in the navy, and Thomas wasn't a popular choice among the seamen. His Leveller sympathies were not shared by most in the fleet, and in spite of his naval experience, his appointment was regarded as an attempt by the army to take control of the navy and, not quite the same thing, as a move by radical Independents to extend their influence. 'That they might establish their Government both by sea and land', wrote one Royalist commentator, 'Rainsborough, the bellwether of the republicans, is set over the fleet.'[11] When on 8 February the Commons resolved to call the fleet 'the Parliament's ships' rather than the king's navy, the seamen's disquiet increased.

At first, the loyalty of his officers concerned Thomas less than the state of their ships. The fleet was nowhere near ready to sail, and as soon as he reached the Downs he fired off a letter to the Commons, asking them to speed up its fitting and supply. Irish rebels, he said, were everywhere, 'to the great hazard of the trade of England'; they had already taken a number of merchantmen and they were threatening shipping off the Isle of Wight.[12] He renewed his appeal in a letter sent to Speaker Lenthall on 18 February: 'I should not discharge my duty if I did not let you know that it very much concerns you to speed forth the ships, appointed for the Summer Guard, for the Irish men-of-war do not lessen but increase.'[13] An Irish ship had just taken four English vesssels off Plymouth, he said, and he had intelligence that there were eleven Irish raiders cruising between the Isle of Wight and Torbay. It was vital to put two squadrons into the Channel as soon as possible, one patrolling as far east as Dover and the other as far west as Land's End. 'And this is impossible to be put in execution till the fleet be come forth.'[14]

Thomas was also worried about the activities of Samuel Kem, a soldier-parson with a living at Deal in Kent who was a long-standing ally of William Batten and a noisy advocate of a negotiated settlement with the king. Thomas suspected Kem of stirring up some of the seamen against Parliament, and he asked several times for the cleric to be moved inland to a parish where he could do less harm.

It wasn't just Kem. Tension was rising everywhere, as Royalists played on a wave of popular support for the king. In the Midlands, they formulated a plan to seize Warwick Castle. In Scotland, a bitter struggle between hard-line Presbyterians, who remained opposed to any agreement with Charles, and a party led by the Duke of Hamilton which favoured an alliance with the king, ended in victory for Hamilton and preparations for war. Lancashire and Cheshire were said to be ready to rise up the moment the Scots crossed the border.

On 24 March, armed resistance to Parliament and the Army Council surfaced in Wales, where officers refused an order from Fairfax to disband their troops and surrender Pembroke Castle. Three days later, on the anniversary of the king's accession, bonfires were lit all over London, and demonstrators on the streets forced passers-by to drink the king's health. And on Sunday 9 April a minor scuffle in Moorfields exploded into a full-scale riot, in which a mob 3,000–4,000 strong marched on Whitehall shouting 'Now for King Charles!' Although the march was dispersed by Cromwell's regiment, which happened to be in the Mews at Whitehall at the time, trouble erupted again that night when the lord mayor's house was fired on by rioters and the mayor was forced to seek refuge in the Tower.

There was a violent demonstration in Norwich. Royalists took the castles of Berwick and Carlisle, and prepared to welcome the Scottish army when it arrived. Cromwell was despatched to put down the insurgency in Wales. In the middle of May a petition to Parliament was circulated in Kent, asking that the king 'may with all speed be admitted in safety and honour, to treat with his two Houses of Parliament'; and that the army be disbanded as soon as possible.[15] There were 20,000 names supporting it, and half as many were arming themselves and preparing for a mass rendezvous at Rochester on the Prince of Wales's birthday, 29 May. Thomas boarded a ship lying off the Kent coast after hearing reports that its master intended to aid the king's escape; he couldn't find any reason to impound the ship, but he was urged to look again by the Derby House Committee (the exclusively English council which had replaced the Committee of Both Kingdoms in January, after the alliance with the Scots broke down, and which was named for its meeting place in Westminster). 'The design continues still', they told him. 'The escape will be about Thursday or Friday night next.'[16]

On 20 May there was startling news. The Prince of Wales had just been put ashore near Sandwich, only five miles from Thomas's headquarters at Deal. Although he was dressed very shabbily, he had settled himself in the Bell Inn and was receiving his followers and their offers of drink. 'Many people flock thither to kiss his hand', a worried Thomas reported to Lenthall.[17] One of those who flocked to see the prince, by now being showered with gifts and decked out in a suit of crimson satin, was the Royalist courtier Sir Thomas Dishington, who knew him personally. When Dishington arrived in Sandwich he took one look at the young man, declared he was an impostor, 'and desired leave of the mayor to kick him'.[18] Instead, Dishington himself was thrown into prison, which was perhaps as well. 'The women, and mariners, would have stoned me in the streets', he said later.[19]

Thomas would have been even more worried if he had read a cyphered message from an unidentified Royalist agent about the state of the fleet. Confiding that Batten was prepared to go over to the king's side, the spy wrote that he could bring the fleet with him. 'Many of the seamen have promised to bring many of the ships whenever C.[aptain] B.[atten] desires it, neither will the commanders in any of the ships dare to dispute against him when the seamen shall hear C. B. to be engaged.'[20] There was mutiny in the wind.

The Derby House Committee asked for a description of the so-called prince, and the mayor of Sandwich gave an account of a short blond man. Prince Charles was tall and dark with black hair. On 23 May they ordered Thomas to go to Sandwich and arrest the pretender, taking a party of musketeers from the fleet, and securing the town against the Royalist insurgents who had gathered there, 'and so preserve that place in the obedience and service of the Parliament'.[21]

But things were getting out of hand. It seemed as though the whole of Kent was mobilising and the rebels, who declared that they held Sandwich for the king, wouldn't allow Thomas to set foot in the town. The fleet was caught up in the same mood of rebellion. The seamen had just been paid; some of them found their way into Sandwich in search of the things that sailors on shore leave always seek, and were won over by the prince's claims. They were buying him drinks in a tavern while their own vice admiral was being turned away at the town gate. (Their prince turned out to be an adventurer named Cornelius Evans; he was handed over to Parliament and thrown into Newgate Gaol when his true identity was discovered a few days later.)

On 24 May Thomas wrote an anxious letter to the Committee of the Admiralty lamenting that 'the present distemper of the county is such, as hath put as sad a face on things as ever England saw'.[22] Garrisons all over Kent were in danger of falling to the Royalists, who had seized Sandwich, Rochester, Sittingbourne and Faversham in the king's name, and the dockyard at Chatham, from where they were busy removing barrels of gunpowder for their own use. The Commons voted 169 to 36 in favour of opening negotiations with Charles I.

Orders streamed from Derby House. Thomas was to guard against 'any danger that might come to this kingdom from foreign parts'.[23] He was to force disaffected persons out of Sandwich. He was to dispatch two ships 'under such commanders as you can confide in' to ride at the mouth of the Medway, intercepting all vessels and preventing the Royalists from building fortifications on either bank.

And in the middle of this, his relations came to visit.

After a separation lasting more than two years, Stephen Winthrop finally brought Judith and their two boys over to England early in 1648. Having accepted a captain's commission in William Rainborowe's regiment the previous summer, he felt eager to settle down and do God's work. 'I am not born for myself,' he wrote, 'and if I may be serviceable and found in a way of advancing God's kingdom it is all I desire.' Once that decision was made, he reasoned that 'it is my duty to send for my wife and wait what God in his providence may sort out for me'.[24] The eldest boy, also Stephen, was three. John was not yet two: he had never set eyes on his father until he arrived in England, and the reunion lasted a matter of weeks before Stephen left for Wales with Cromwell to put down the insurgency there.

All of which is some explanation, perhaps, for the fact that while Thomas Rainborowe was grappling with a rapidly deteriorating security situation in Kent, his wife Margaret, his half-sister Judith, his sister-in-law Margery (Major William Rainborowe's wife) and an assortment of children came to stay with him in the captain's lodgings at Deal Castle.

If Thomas thought of moving the women and children to a place of safety at any point, he was hard put to find one. Fairfax, who had been poised to march north to meet the threat of invasion from Scotland, was ordered instead to Kent. There was fighting at Westminster, and London was expected to declare for the king. Surrey and Essex both presented petitions to Parliament calling for a negotiated settlement with the king. There was nowhere to go.

Thomas's immediate concern was to secure the three forts that guarded the anchorage in the Downs – Deal, Walmer and Sandown, which lay within walking distance of each other. Eight or nine miles to the south, Dover Castle was also threatened. On Friday 26 May he held a council of war aboard his flagship with his captains, all of whom gave him assurances that they and their crews would stay loyal to Parliament. He had already separated out two ships whose commanders he doubted, the *Convertine* and the *Providence*, and sent them off to the north. Two others were on convoy duty. That left six in his squadron: his own *Constant Reformation*, the *Swallow*, the *Satisfaction*, the *Hind*, the *Roebuck* and the *Pelican*. Together, they carried more than 140 guns and around 600 men.

Two hours after the council of war, Thomas took a party of seamen ashore, intending to leave them to reinforce the garrisons at Walmer and Sandown. He was on the roof at Deal Castle, waving his sword angrily at a party of Royalists who were riding past, when he heard a great shout coming across the water from the ships riding at anchor in the Downs. Going to investigate in a small pinnace, he discovered to his horror that his own crew wouldn't allow him aboard. They had gone over to the king.

His own lieutenant turned on him; his own boatswain declared himself the new vice admiral. And worst of all, virtually the entire squadron followed them. Unknown to Thomas, Samuel Kem, the Deal parson whom he had suspected of stirring up discontent, had been doing just that, secretly visiting every ship. The majority of officers and men were won over, declaring for the king and the liberty of the kingdom.

Thomas's exchanges with the mutineers were understandably fraught, with 'many threats and uncivil passages', according to one witness.[25] As it dawned on him that his men couldn't be moved, he began to appreciate the awkwardness of his own position. The mutineers didn't show any signs of wanting to capture him or harm him. Far from it, he was free to take his belongings and go. He had, they told him, 'been a loving, and courteous colonel to them; and in that respect should have no injury offered unto him, nor should he suffer any the least damage in person or goods'.[26] But where should he go? Were the sailors he had just put ashore to guard Walmer and Sandown castles party to the conspiracy? And how safe was Deal Castle? His wife and child, Judith and Margery and their children were there.

How safe were they?

He demanded one of the pinnaces to take him and his family to London. His coxswain called across from the deck of the *Reformation*: 'Sir, we cannot spare you any the least vessel in the Downs, they are engaged for better service. But there is a Dutch fly-boat at shore, and for sixpence you may have a passage in her.'[27]

That's what he did. Collecting Margaret and Judith and Margery and the children, he commandeered the fly-boat and ordered her to sail for Harwich forty miles away on the Essex coast, in the hope that he could persuade the *Tiger*, which was anchored there, to remain loyal. He found the *Providence* also there, and managed to extract promises from the officers and crew to remain true to Parliament.

Thomas made his base at Landguard Fort at the entrance to Harwich harbour, and it was from there on Saturday afternoon that he wrote to tell Speaker Lenthall what had happened. 'My last was sad,' his letter began, 'this most sad. As I told you my fear, it is now come to pass that my ship, the *Swallow*, the *Satisfaction*, the *Hind*, the *Roebuck*, the *Pelican*, are all declared for the king.' It was vital that messengers be sent to the garrisons in the north and west, 'that if any of the fleet come within their command they stop them, and take heed least they be betrayed by them, for there is good reason to believe, those gone several ways will be in the same posture, so soon as they hear this'.[28]

Within days, triumphant Royalist propagandists were at work. The newsbook *Mercurius bellicus* crowed:

That sea hog Rainsborow, is kicked out of his commission, by the valiant, and ever to be renowned blades of Kent, who had once intended to have sent him on embassage for them to the court of Neptune, but the monster made such moan unto them and so earnestly besought them that they would not send him the way of all fish, that they altered their decree, and licensed him to ride upon ten toes up to London.[29]

Another Royalist newsbook claimed he would have been hanged 'but for the tears and entreaty of his wife'.[30] The mutineers issued a declaration of their own the day after the revolt, spelling out their support for the Kent petition and explaining why they turned out their commander. 'We conceive him to be a man not well-affected to the king, Parliament and kingdom.'[31] Three weeks later their declaration was reissued with more explanations. There were three reasons for their actions, said the seamen. They resented the fact that Parliament gave out commissions in its own name rather than the name of the king. They resented that soldiers had been made naval officers. And they resented 'the insufferable pride, ignorance, and insolency of Colonel Rainsborough, the late vice admiral, [who had] alienated the hearts of the seamen.'[32] Any memory of Thomas having been a loving and courteous colonel to them was forgotten.

He arrived in London on Monday 29 May. That same day his unhappy letter describing the revolt in the Downs was read to the Commons, while in the Lords the Earl of Warwick read another he had received from the mutineers, asking him to lead them. That afternoon Parliament passed an ordinance appointing Warwick to his old job of Lord High Admiral, and urged him to get to the Downs immediately. He sailed from Tilbury the next day, and on Wednesday attempted to board the *Constant Reformation*, to find the seamen wouldn't have him unless he signed up to the Kentish petition. He held a council of war with his own officers and decided that 'considering the high distempers of the seamen' it might be politic to return to London and report to Parliament.[33] The City petitioned for Batten to be given back his old place.

Warwick's failure made no difference to Thomas. His naval career was over. And in a bizarre twist, on the day that Parliament heard of the revolt and despatched Warwick to try and repair the damage, the Lords also heard a statement from Cornelius Evans claiming he had pretended to be the Prince of Wales at Thomas's request. Apparently the vice admiral had noticed him at Deal and sent members of his crew to urge him to the impersonation, saying it wouldn't be long before the real prince landed and that he would be well rewarded for it.

The idea that Thomas Rainborowe was a closet Royalist was too much for anyone to swallow. The question remained – and still remains – as to what went wrong in the Downs. Was the mutiny Thomas's fault?

Taking their cue from the mutineers' later assertion that they couldn't stomach his 'insufferable pride, ignorance, and insolency', historians have tended to blame his arrogance for the revolt. He was 'dreaded and disliked, and accused of being rough and over-bearing', said Samuel Rawson Gardiner in 1891, contrasting his desertion of the navy for land service with Batten's good seaman-ship and popularity with his men.[34] Seventy years later J. R. Powell and E. K. Timings wrote that 'he had the maddening self-righteousness of the convinced social reformer'.[35]

Such views don't sit easily with the fact that Thomas was loved by the army rank and file. True, he believed with a passion in the righteousness of his cause, in a way that others, Batten and Warwick included, did not. Pragmatism and compromise didn't come natu-rally; and when he was forced to trim, as he was after Corkbush Field, it only hardened him. But it was the cause and not the man which led to the mutiny in the Downs. Ironically enough Batten, who fled to Holland in July after Parliament finally discov-ered the extent of his double-dealing, explained it best when he declared the mutineers had acted from a mistrust of Thomas's politics, 'it being most reasonable that that man should hold no command who openly professed himself to be a Leveller'.[36]

This was confirmed by the mutineers themselves. On 8 July the crews of the ships that had been 'lately rescued for His Majesty's service', as they put it, issued another declaration, calling on the rest of the fleet to join them.[37] Whoever wrote it was well educated and politically sophisticated, able to articulate the anxieties of a section of the navy which thought it had been fighting to preserve the rights and liberties of Parliament, not to remove the king and replace him with a republic. Such men thought things had gone too far, that the Independents, instead of seeking to reconcile differences, were out to turn the world upside down. 'The powers and affairs of the navy', claimed the declaration, 'were put into such hands as were not only enemies to the king and kingdom, but even to the monarchy itself.' The prayer book had been discarded. There was no settled form of divine worship, and the only preaching on board ship was conducted not by ordained ministers but 'by illiterate and mechanic persons'.[38]

The mutineers regarded Thomas Rainborowe as the embodiment of this dangerous egalitarian radicalism. He was, they said, 'a man of most destructive principles both in religion and policy, and a known enemy to the peace and ancient government of this kingdom'.[39] And they were quite right. He wanted a new world and an end to old hierarchies. That was why they turned him out. He wanted to pull down the past and build the promised land. That was why they hated him.

25

The Rebel King

*A*t seven o'clock on the evening of 1 June 1648 Fairfax and seven regiments of the New Model Army arrived at Maidstone in Kent, where several thousand Royalists were waiting for them behind barricades and earthworks. Fairfax intended to wait until morning to storm the town, but some of his forward units clashed with the insurgents, and as more and more men were sucked into the fighting he decided on a general assault. Soon after midnight, after some vicious street-fighting, his men secured the centre of the town.

The bulk of the Royalist army hadn't taken part in the battle, gathering instead just outside the town. Commanded by the Earl of Norwich, they made their escape northwards, hoping to enter London. But Fairfax had anticipated the move, and the Kentish men found London Bridge fortified and boats removed from the south bank of the Thames. Some deserted. Others retreated into Surrey. Others still crossed the Thames downriver from the capital, commandeering small boats and swimming their horses with them. They were desperate to reach Essex, where another group of Royalists had just revolted. A combined force might move up into Suffolk and Norfolk, gathering support as it went, and eventually join up with the Scottish army, which was expected to cross the border any day.

Having sent troops to secure the coastal forts at Dover, Deal, Walmer and Sandown, Fairfax came in pursuit. The Earl of Norwich managed to join with the Essex Royalists led by Lord Arthur Capel and Sir Charles Lucas, increasing his strength to around 5,000 men, and opted to head for the walled town of Colchester. This was Lucas's power base: his family had been prominent in the town's affairs for 300 years, and he argued that by staying there for a night or two the insurgents could hope to recruit more supporters to their cause. His assessment was optimistic: the townspeople refused to let the Royalists in, and it was only after a skirmish in which one of the defenders was shot that they reluctantly opened the gates. Colchester 'was not glad of their company', wrote Clarendon.[1]

Fairfax was only hours behind them. At noon on Tuesday 13 June, the day after they occupied the town, the Royalists received intelligence that his army was approaching: in fact, the advance guard was already engaging with some of their sentries in the suburbs.

Fairfax's plan was to storm the town immediately, as he had at Maidstone. But Lucas proved too quick for him, and too good a soldier. He drew up his men in formation across the London Road, just outside the western wall of the town, and held the line as an infantry brigade launched three furious assaults. Eventually, outflanked by the Parliamentarian cavalry, Lucas and Sir Arthur Capel ordered their men back into the town, but even now they had the better of their adversaries, who followed them through the open gates and into a trap, coming under crossfire from soldiers waiting in the side streets. The Parliamentarians were forced to retreat, Lord Arthur Capel personally charging at them with a pike and pushing them back through the gate, which he then barred with his cane.

Taking stock, Fairfax realised there was no prospect of a quick victory. The next morning he ordered his men to set up checkpoints and barricades on all roads into Colchester. That night they started the difficult task of digging trenches and throwing up redoubts and forts to encircle the town.

For all his extremism and his recent humiliation in the Downs, Thomas was still one of the best siege commanders the New Model Army possessed; and he had encountered Lucas before, when he forced the Royalist to surrender Berkeley Castle in 1645. But he doesn't seem to have been involved in the siege's early days, although it is hard to be sure: apart from the fact that he went to Harwich and then London after the naval revolt, his movements are a mystery. Judith Winthrop with her two boys and, presumably, the other Rainborowe women and children, had gone from Harwich to Ipswich and then, frightened by the Royalists' advance into Essex, to London, where the fates conspired to heap more misery on Judith's homecoming when both of her young sons caught smallpox and died. She and Stephen 'sit down meekly under the Lord's correction', observed John Winthrop, with characteristic faith in the providential working of God.[2] Meanwhile a passing reference in a letter from Nehemiah Bourne persuaded John, quite wrongly, that having seen the women safe at Harwich, Thomas had gone straight back to Kent to lay siege to Deal Castle, where he 'was gotten within the moat, so as, it was conceived, the castle could not hold out many days'.[3]

A Royalist newsletter claimed in the days after the mutiny that Thomas 'is come up to town most outrageously mad & will in all haste raise a regim[en]t at least'.[4] He didn't, and his old regiment was with Cromwell at Pembroke, under the command of Richard Deane. But his chance to see active service against the enemy came six weeks later, and by a roundabout route. One of the regiments at Colchester was the Tower Guards, formed in 1647 to garrison the Tower of London and officered in the main by Independents. Their colonel was shot and mortally wounded in the first battle before the town, and his successor took a fatal bullet – a poison bullet, according to some, which led to a series of brutal reprisals against Royalist prisoners – early in July during an attempt to halt one of the garrison's periodic forays in search of supplies. On 14 July the command of the Tower Guards passed to Thomas Rainborowe.

Fairfax's strategy at Colchester was hard and simple: to cut off the garrison's communications with the outside world by enclosing the town within a ring of siege-works; and to prevent any civilians from leaving, thus putting the maximum pressure on already scarce provisions and turning the townspeople against the defenders, while meeting with open arms any Royalist soldiers who wanted to surrender. He refused absolutely to have anything to do with Lucas, whom he believed to have betrayed his trust once already, having given his word not to take up arms against Parliament after Berkeley.

It was a wet, miserable summer, punctuated by skirmishes and raids and random acts of savagery. After two troops of cavalry broke out one night and escaped by crossing the river Colne at the Middle Mill on the north side of the town, Thomas led his Tower Guards in a night-time assault, surprising the guards and setting fire to the mill before being forced back across the river. The garrison was rattled, believing the raid to be the prelude to an all-out assault; but they still managed to save the mill by using their hats to scoop up water and hurl it at the flames. The Royalist press claimed that Fairfax's snipers were targeting poor towns-people gleaning corn in the fields: 'such is the cruelty of the saints, that they . . . make nothing to shoot poor old women, and other feeble persons'.[5] The besiegers were also accused of ransacking the Lucas mansion, breaking open the family vault and the lead coffins it held and rifling through the ancient corpses. The pro-Parliament *Moderate* in turn accused Lucas and his men of rape, torture, extortion, and using pregnant women and children as human shields.

Colchester's defences were too strong for a direct assault. 'It must be famine that must get us the town', predicted the press.[6] That would take time: and when after much dithering the Duke of Hamilton finally brought his Scottish army over the border on 8 July, it seemed that time was running out. But the remnants of the insurgency in Wales surrendered to Cromwell three days later, and he set off to confront Hamilton, taking some of the pressure from Fairfax to end the siege and go north himself. Nevertheless, morale among the besiegers was flagging by the end of July. The correspondent for the *Moderate Intelligencer*, normally so positive about the army's prospects, allowed himself an uncharacteristic burst of frustration. 'We see no way of gaining this place but by starving,' he wrote, 'and when that we know not. Some say they are in great want, and eat horseflesh, others that they have corn, sack, haberdine [salt cod], oil, and fruits of Spain for six months.'[7]

Within the walls, salt cod and sack were the stuff of dreams. Daily rations of bread fell to ten ounces; then to seven. The water supply had been cut off. A council of war decided to slaughter one in every three cavalry mounts; within a week or so 'the greatest part of our horse had changed stables for slaughterhouses and their riders took up with foot arms'.[8] By the middle of August the defenders were eating cats and dogs. The Parliament press reported a pathetic incident in which one of the army's horses was shot and killed before the walls: defenders made a sally to try and drag it into the town, only to be fired on and beaten back. The next day they tried again, risking their lives to hack pieces from the creature's corpse.

The mayor and aldermen sent out a petition to Fairfax begging 'that they might have liberty to leave the town and disperse themselves into the county'.[9] He refused, knowing that the presence of so many starving civilians within the walls could only make matters worse for the defenders. Anyone who tried to leave would be shot, he said.

This was hard. 'Unchristianlike, though politic' was the realistic verdict of the defenders.[10] And it fell to Thomas to put his general's unchristianlike order into practice. A few days after it was issued, the gate in the north wall flew open and a crowd of women and children poured out and began walking towards the Tower Guards' position a few hundred yards away. Thomas gave the order to fire a cannon, to scare them without hurting them. They kept coming. Then he told some of his men to load their muskets with powder only and discharge them at the women. Still they came on. Finally, he sent out soldiers with orders to strip the women, 'which made them run, but none of them were stripped'.[11] The Royalists had closed the gates behind them, and now they wouldn't let them back in, leaving them trapped in the no-man's-land between Rainborowe's line and the town wall. They took refuge in a mill, while furious messages went to and fro between Fairfax and Lucas, culminating in the army firing papers wrapped around arrows over the walls, warning the Royalists that 'if they exposed the wives and children of the inhabitants to such

extremities they would put them all to the sword'.[12] The civilians were allowed back inside.

On 22 August a message was smuggled in to the defenders
announcing that Hamilton and the Scots had scored a great victory
over Cromwell's army, raising hopes of relief. Their celebrations
were short-lived: two days later the besiegers flew a paper kite
over the town, one of the Royalists inside the walls recalled.
'Hovering a good while over, that the soldiers might take notice
of it, at last they let drop in the midst of it, with many papers
fixt to it.'[13] The kite carried news from the north: on 17 August
Cromwell and John Lambert had routed Hamilton's invasion force
at Preston. The Scottish army was in tatters, with thousands dead
or captured. Just at the moment when the desolate defenders
were reading the printed accounts of the battle, Hamilton was
trying to negotiate his own surrender with the governor of
Stafford, only for Hugh Peter to whisk him away, declaring
jubilantly that the defeat had shown beyond doubt that 'we are
for God, they work against God'.[14] ('My brother Peter took the
Duke of Hamilton prisoner', John Winthrop proudly told his
eldest son when the news reached New England.[15]) William
Rainborowe and Stephen Winthrop both came through the
fighting unscathed.

There was no help now for Colchester. With hardly any ammunition, and food for only another forty-eight hours, the Royalist
leaders decided to gather all their men together with whatever
powder and shot they could find, and storm the army lines under
cover of darkness. 'This I confess would have been a desperate
enterprise', recalled one of the survivors of the siege, 'but as noble,
and had it proceeded to action, it might (for ought I know) to
as honourable success, by a glorious victory.'[16]

It didn't proceed to action. When they heard of the plan, the
rank-and-file soldiers in the town immediately suspected that it
was a ploy to let their leaders escape and leave them to face
Fairfax's fury. They mutinied, and announced that if Norwich,
Lucas and the other commanders wouldn't make terms with the
besiegers, they would throw their officers over the walls and make
terms for themselves. Norwich had no choice but to open negotiations for a surrender. The terms offered by Thomas Rainborowe,
Henry Ireton and the other army negotiators were harsh. At ten

o'clock on Monday 28 August the surrender of all soldiers and officers under the rank of captain was to be taken in a yard by the east gate, where 'they shall have fair quarter'. One hour later the 'lords and all captains and superior officers and gentlemen of distinction shall be drawn together to the King's Head and there submit themselves to the mercy of the Lord General'.[17] When the Royalists queried the difference between 'fair quarter' and 'mercy', they were told the rank and file would be fed and clothed and not ill-treated in any way. But when the senior officers rendered themselves up to mercy, 'the Lord General may be free to put some immediately to the sword (if he see cause)'.[18] The fate of men hung on these words.

Rainborowe and his Tower Guards were the first to enter the town that morning. They found a sad sight: 'so many fair houses burnt, and so many inhabitants sick and weak, with living upon horses and dogs'.[19] The tower of the church of St Mary's at the Walls, an observation post and hence a target for the army's guns, had been destroyed. So had the medieval Gatehouse, part of Sir Charles Lucas's family home; it had held a large store of powder until soldiers lobbed in grenades during a bout of close quarters fighting and blew it to bits. The skeletal timbers of burned-out houses punctuated rubble-strewn streets. Around 2,000 of the garrison had died or deserted; no one knew how many civilians were lost, victims to sniper fire or cannon shot or dysentry or malnutrition. Thomas had marched into vanquished towns before – Bristol, Worcester, Oxford. London. None of them had looked like this.

There was worse to come.

The senior Royalists gathered together at the King's Head, according to the terms of the treaty. After a wait of several hours Colonel Isaac Ewer, a hardliner who would later put his name to Charles I's death warrant, arrived, saluted Norwich and Lord Arthur Capel, and announced that Fairfax would like to speak with Sir Charles Lucas and three others: Sir George Lisle, a ring-leader of the Kent Rising; Sir Bernard Gascoigne, a soldier of fortune; and a Colonel Farre. Farre was nowhere to be found, having slipped away during the confusion of the surrender. The other three followed Ewer across to the Town Hall, where they found a council of war including Thomas and Edward Whalley and presided over by Henry Ireton, who calmly told them they had been condemned for taking up arms against Parliament, and that they should prepare themselves for death. Sentence would be carried out later that day.

At seven o'clock the three men were brought into the castle yard, where a six-man firing party was waiting for them, with Thomas, Ireton and Whalley as witnesses. After a few moments in which Lucas, Lisle and Gascoigne embraced, affirmed their loyalty to the king and said their farewells, Lucas turned to the three officers and asked them outright by whom he was condemned – Fairfax alone, or a council of senior officers?

'Know, yourself as all others that engage a second time against the Parliament are traitors and rebels,' replied Ireton, 'and they do employ us as soldiers by authority from them to suppress and destroy. Would you know our commission, it's that.'[20]

Lucas and the others had surrendered without promise of quarter, he said, and they knew exactly what was meant by rendering themselves at mercy, because Thomas and the other negotiators had told them. The decision to execute them had been made by Fairfax himself on the advice of his council of war.

Lucas wouldn't accept this. He was fighting for his life. 'Sir,' he replied, 'this is a very nice point to take away a man's life, when there is a law in the kingdom.'[21] Sir George Lisle chipped in. Addressing Thomas and the other colonels directly, he said: 'Gentlemen, lay your hands seriously upon your breasts, you that were of the council of war, and consider what it is to take away a man's life in this kind.'[22]

Ireton dismissed this: civil law did not apply in time of war. 'Had you not by arms stopped the laws of the land, you and other men might have had the justice of the laws of the land.'

With six soldiers standing by, firelocks at the ready, Lucas was frantic. He tried another tack: 'It was never known that men were kill'd in cold blood, before.'[23]

Now Whalley spoke, reminding everyone of an incident in 1644 when a Parliamentarian garrison in Wiltshire had surrended and submitted to mercy, only for fourteen of them to be hanged by their Royalist captors. An ensign tried to bring up another example, but Lucas spoke over him, begging that Fairfax might 'excuse me with my life'. Two more soldiers broke in angrily, claiming that after the taking of Stinchcombe in Gloucestersire in 1645, Lucas himself had refused quarter to his prisoners. On that occasion twenty were put to death in cold blood. 'I have given many hundred men quarter', said Lisle desperately.

It was no good. Thomas, Whalley and Treton were implacable. Their men were angry and unforgiving. Lucas embraced Lisle and Gascoigne once more, then said to his executioners, without much conviction, 'I pray God forgive you all, I pray God forgive you, gentlemen. Farewell, I pray God vengeance may not fall on you for it.'[24] His cap was pulled down over his face, and the squad fired.

Lisle bent down to kiss his body, then stood and faced his judges. The squad fired again.

Gascoigne was reprieved at the last moment, Fairfax having discovered he was Bernardo Guasconi, a Florentine with links to the Tuscan court: the general didn't want to take responsibility for an international incident. As men of quality, Norwich and Lord Arthur Capel were sent up to London for trial: both were condemned to death, although Norwich was later pardoned.

The execution of Sir Charles Lucas and Sir George Lisle was perhaps the single most controversial episode in the Second Civil War, and historians have been arguing over its legitimacy ever since. Fairfax had no doubts. The day after the killings he wrote to Parliament, informing them of what had happened:

> For some satisfaction to military justice, and in part [to] avenge for the innocent blood they have caused to be spilt, and the trouble, damage, and mischief they have brought upon the town, this country, and the kingdom, I have with the advice of a Council of War of the chief officers both of the country forces and the army, caused two of them who were rendered at mercy to be shot to death before any of them had quarter assured them. The persons pitched upon for this example were, Sir

Charles Lucas, and Sir George Lisle, in whose military execution I hope your lordships will not find cause to think your
honour or justice prejudiced.[25]

For the Royalists, staggering under the impact of their defeats in
Kent, Preston and Wales, Lucas and Lisle were martyrs. Charles I
burst into tears when he heard the news of their deaths. Elegies
and diatribes poured from the presses. The dead men were
'incomparable and noble warriors', who had suffered for righteousness' sake.[26] They were paragons, 'matchless twins of valour',
noble and honourable and everything that their murderers were
not.[27] They came from good families, unlike 'they, whose ruder
tongues can cry, Advance mechanics, down with majesty'.[28] They
were Saul and Jonathan, 'lovely and pleasant in their lives, and
in their death they were not divided'.[29]

Fairfax and Ireton, on the other hand, were 'brethren in ini-
quity', leading 'a merciless pack of . . . cruel bloodthirsty tyrants'.[30]
The execution of Lucas and Lisle, like the siege of Colchester
itself, was emblematic of a harder, more doctrinaire approach by
the army to its opponents, an anger and a sense of frustration.
The rank-and-file soldiery wanted their deaths; it is significant
that the army's nominal masters in Parliament weren't given a say
in the matter.

And Thomas? As one of the army's negotiators, he knew the
terms of the surrender well enough, and as an experienced soldier,
he knew what they meant. (And so, of course, did Lucas and
Lisle, no matter what they claimed.) He was a member of the
council of war that urged Fairfax to have the matchless twins of
valour shot; he watched as they died.

And it was Thomas who was singled out for most blame,
warned in the press to expect God's judgement for his part in
the execution. 'Divine Justice may sleep, but cannot slip.'
Monsters like him were 'seldom known to die natural deaths'.[31]
A street ballad claimed that it was he who had pushed for the
death sentence, making him say that 'I would not give the
General rest, till he unto their deaths had sealed', and struggling
with the guilty knowledge that 'by my means those worthies
fell'.[32] The council of war's deliberations haven't survived, so
it is impossible to say how much of this is true, and how much

the result of Thomas's role as a favourite bête noire of the Royalists for his levelling tendencies and his uncompromising attitude toward compromise.

At the end of September he was on the road from London to army headquarters at St Albans with one of his captains when they were attacked by three Royalists. There was 'a little bickering', according to one account; and then, according to another, 'the Cavaliers seeing their gallantry and resolution, put spurs to their horses and rode for it'.[33] That same week a captain and a major were assassinated in London in separate incidents; Fairfax, who was in St Albans, was told two Royalists were planning to kill him there; and an MP stood up in the Commons and announced that Royalists had made a list of eighty members who opposed a treaty with the king, and planned to massacre them all.

26

The Dire Event

*A*t the beginning of October Thomas and his Tower Guards were ordered north. Their destination was the Yorkshire town of Pontefract, and their mission was to capture its castle, described by Cromwell as 'one of the strongest inland garrisons in the kingdom'.[1] Earlier that year a group of insurgents led by a young Royalist, John Morrice, had taken the castle by disguising themselves as country folk bringing supplies, and overpowering the garrison soldiers before they knew what was happening. Within days the news of the fall of Pontefract had spread all over the northern counties. 'There came speedily to us, in small parties,' said Lieutenant Thomas Paulden, one of the Royalist defenders, 'so many of our old fellow soldiers that our garrison at last was increased to 500 men.'[2] The authorities at York did their best to mobilise a counter-attack, but Pontefract Castle's situation perched on a rocky outcrop made the idea of mining or breaching the walls impossible without more resources.

The besieging force was led by a local Yorkshire MP, Sir Henry Cholmley, whose approach to siege-work was rather relaxed. There were stories that he was taking a half-share in the cattle the Royalists stole from the surrounding countryside, and that his men kept a market by the castle so they could sell provisions to the defenders. By October, locals were complaining that the enemy moved through Cholmley's battle lines at will. At the end of June a party had broken out and crossed the Trent, moving so quickly that they occupied Lincoln before its militia could organise a defence; they plundered the city, broke open the prison and continued south, gathering dissident Royalists along the way, until they were met and defeated by a small army of gentry and county militia at Willoughby Field, on the border of Nottinghamshire and Leicestershire, a good seventy-five miles south of Pontefract.

In September several veteran regiments of horse stationed at Pontefract were ordered north to help in mopping up the remains of Hamilton's Scottish army. To take their place, and to bring up soldiers who were experienced in siege warfare, Fairfax ordered Thomas to Pontefract. 'It being like to prove a tedious siege,' said Thomas Paulden, 'General Rainsborough was sent from London by the Parliament, to put a speedy end to it. He was esteemed a person of great courage and conduct, exceeding zealous and fierce in their cause.'[3]

Afterwards, the Levellers insisted that Thomas's deployment was a deliberate ruse to get him and his men away from London and Parliament. But that was later.

During the early part of October Thomas's soldiers – about 1,200 foot and two regiments of horse – began to arrive in the town of Doncaster, which lies seventeen miles south of Pontefract. By the middle of the month it was reported that although the Royalists were still sallying out, 'when Col. Rainsborough's regiment is come up to us, they shall keep them up closer'.[4] The neighbourhood was relatively quiet, although pockets of Royalist sympathisers were known to be active here and there. Sensitive to complaints about the difficulties of providing for so many men in the town, and keen to deter dissident gentry from joining the defenders at the castle, Thomas opted to maintain a visible military presence in the country, and deployed most of his soldiers to the surrounding villages. Only two companies were kept in Doncaster itself.

He arrived in Yorkshire in mid-October and went straight to York to meet with the local committee which had appointed Cholmley to lead the siege. Thomas presented his commission from Fairfax and broke the news that he had been appointed commander-in-chief of the forces at Pontefract. 'And that', as the unhappy committee informed Parliament three days later, 'did occasion a dispute, and started the consideration of many inconveniences that were feared would arise, both amongst officers and soldiers in some questions of honour.'[5]

By 'officers and soldiers' they meant Sir Henry Cholmley. Cholmley was the older man, his colonelcy had seniority and, most importantly, he would lose face in front of the neighbours and tenants who made up his regiment if he relinquished his command. So he refused to give way to Thomas until nightfall, when the two men finally agreed on a compromise. They would send to London for clarification, and while they waited 'till the pleasure of the Parliament were further known', they would command their own forces at their own posts and each would keep the other informed of developments.[6]

It wasn't perfect, but it was a solution of sorts, and that was how things were left when the meeting broke up on Tuesday night. But the next morning Thomas was back at the committee's chambers. He had had second thoughts overnight, and now he told them 'he cannot conform to his last night's resolution, nor go any whit lower than according to his commission to command in chief'.[7]

Cholmley would not back down. While the York committee wrote to tell the Speaker of the Commons about the impasse, he persuaded them to send to Cromwell, who was quartered at Durham, and ask him to come down to Pontefract 'to take care of reducing that place'.[8] And he wrote a furious letter of his own to Speaker Lenthall, begging the Commons to intercede with Fairfax and wailing about how hard it was that 'we should now have one put over us, that is but a bare colonel of foot in the army, and a younger colonel than any of us. Sir . . . we are unwilling that another should reap the reward of our labours, and with double the force that we have had, come now and gain the prize for which we ventured our dearest blood.'[9]

Squabbles over precedence and slights, both real and imagined, weren't uncommon. Six years earlier at Edgehill, the king's army came close to disaster when, as they were actually facing the Earl of Essex's soldiers in the field, the king overruled his Lord General, the Earl of Lindsey, on a question of tactics and Lindsey resigned on the spot and stormed off. Parliament knew better than to treat Cholmley's concerns lightly. Instead, they sent his letter to Fairfax, who was at St Albans, and asked him to settle the business 'so as it may be for preservation of the honour, and clearing the fidelity of Sir Henry Cholmley'.[10] Fairfax replied straight away, promising 'that he would be very tender of [Cholmley's] honour'. Exactly what he meant by that wasn't clear.

Thomas, meanwhile, had gone back to Doncaster to await developments. His lodgings were at an inn overlooking the market-place. When the landlord asked him at the end of the week if he would be dining there the next day, he said he expected orders, and so he couldn't say for sure.

That was on Saturday 28 October. Early on Sunday morning, he was asleep in his bedchamber when his lieutenant William Raisine came to the door and said there were men below with letters from Cromwell. Two of the messengers were brought into the room; they confirmed that they had orders from the lieutenant general and handed over a packet.

Thomas opened it, to find nothing but a blank sheet of paper. He looked up in surprise at his visitors, as they produced weapons and announced that he was their prisoner.

The kidnap was the idea of Captain William Paulden, who commanded the cavalry at Pontefract Castle. The Royalists' own Sir Marmaduke Langdale, commander of their forces in the northern counties, had been taken after Preston and was being held prisoner in Nottingham Castle and, with memories of the executions at Colchester still fresh in their minds, the defenders were worried by stories that the Roundheads intended to parade Langdale in sight of the castle and threaten to kill him if they didn't surrender. Captain Paulden's plan was to capture Thomas and exchange him for Langdale.

In the early hours of Saturday morning Captain Paulden led a handpicked group of twenty-two men out of the castle, past

Cholmley's guards – 'whom', recalled his brother Thomas Paulden, who was with him on the raid, 'by the favour of the night, we passed undiscovered' – and rode the twelve miles to Doncaster.[11] They rested in nearby fields during the afternoon and sent a man into the town to see if there was any word of them being out.

There wasn't; and Captain Paulden contacted a sympathiser who agreed to meet them in the fields at dawn and let them know if the streets were still quiet. 'The sign he was to bring with him, to be known by, was a Bible in his hand.'[12] He came as arranged at sunrise, and Captain Paulden set out into the town from the south-west, which was, he had been told, lightly guarded. He split his men into four groups. According to his brother's account – very detailed, but published half a century later and not exactly impartial – half a dozen riders led by a Major Saltonstall surprised the guard at the bridge over the Don to the north and threw their weapons into the river, securing their retreat. Half a dozen more burst into the room where the main guard were, 'and getting between them and their arms, bid them shift for the[ir] lives'.[13] Four men, Alan Austwick, Robert Blackburn, Marmaduke Greenfield and Charles Dallison, went into the inn to fetch their victim, while Captain Paulden and the remaining six soldiers kept watch in the quiet Sunday street outside. Dallison and Austwick stayed in the hall, while Blackburn and Greenfield climbed the stairs to their victim's bedchamber.

When Thomas stood facing his kidnappers in that upstairs chamber, he had no notion of any of this. The two men didn't identify themselves. They simply disarmed Lieutenant Raisine and grabbed Thomas's sword and pistol, both of which were close by him. Then they told the colonel that 'not a hair of his head should be touched, if he would go quietly with them'.[14] They allowed him to dress and bundled both men downstairs into the hall. It was empty, except for a maidservant.

At this point Thomas broke free and confronted them. He had no way of knowing if they were a band of Royalist sympathisers from one of the outlying villages; or if Cholmley's rage had pushed him over the edge and turned him to mutiny. 'Now gentlemen,' he asked, 'what is your business?' But they grabbed hold of him again and pulled him out into the street.

The other raiders had a horse waiting, and Thomas was ordered into the saddle. He got as far as putting his foot into the stirrup and then, seeing that there were just a handful against him, and Raisine and a sentry – whom the Royalists hadn't disarmed, for some reason – with him, he pulled his foot out and started shouting at the top of his voice, 'Arms! Arms!'

And the street exploded into violence. One of the kidnappers panicked. He dropped his pistol and flung himself on Thomas, so that the two men fell down in the street grappling with each other. Raisine grabbed up the fallen pistol and tried to cock it; but he wasn't quick enough, and another of the Royalists jumped from his horse and ran him through with his sword. Greenfield stabbed Thomas in the neck as he wrestled in the mud with his assailant, but Thomas managed to stagger to his feet, yelling at the sentry to help him. The man just stood there, paralysed with fear, saying he had no match for his musket. And no one came.

Bleeding from the wound in his neck, Thomas managed to wrest a weapon from the man on the ground. According to one report he took it from his own stomach: Austwick stabbed him in the belly and he pulled out the sword himself with both hands on the blade, 'bending the point back almost to the hilt' and forcing it out of Austwick's grasp. Someone shouted 'Pistol the rogue!' and aimed their gun at him. It failed to go off, and they threw it at his head, making him stagger and drop his guard. He was stabbed again and fell, at which his attackers left him for dead and made to ride off.

But there was still life in Thomas. He struggled to his feet again and came after his attackers. He hadn't gone more than twelve yards when he collapsed. The riders turned back and ran him through again eight times as he lay dying in the street. According to the anonymous author of 'A Letter from Doncaster', a vehemently anti-Royalist account of the episode which appeared within days of Thomas's death:

The last words the maid of the house heard him say before he fell, was, that he was betrayed, oh he was betrayed; in all this time not any appearing in the street, either for his rescue or to revenge him on them, not so much as a musket shot off, or an alarm by a drum, though his struggling with them was above a quarter of an hour.[15]

The conspiracy theories started to circulate before Thomas was cold in the ground. Captain Paulden's raiders, who had galloped out of town shouting 'Farewell Rainborowe! Fare well Cavaliers!' were back at Pontefract Castle by two o'clock that afternoon. They passed without hindrance through Cholmley's lines, riding in plain sight of 200–300 of his horse guards, who let them through without firing a shot. As soon as Morrice heard what had happened he sent a letter to Cholmley, informing his adversary that he had taken it upon himself to decide the controversy over the command, and his men had left his rival dead in the street at Doncaster. 'At the reading of which, the base, treacherous perfidious Cholmley very much laughed and rejoiced for a long time together', wrote the well-informed author of 'A Letter from Doncaster', 'so that it is more than probable that Sir Henry was an absolute complotter in the murder.'[16]

There were certainly some difficult questions to answer. Was it a coincidence that Captain Paulden's men pretended to carry letters from Cromwell just on the day when Thomas was expecting fresh orders from his superiors? If not, then who had told them? And why didn't any of the guards come to his aid while he was fighting for his life in the marketplace?

Attention focused at first on John Smith, the captain of the guard at Doncaster. Instead of being at his post Smith was accused of spending the night with a whore. He didn't help his case by fleeing to Amsterdam, from where in the second week of November he published *The Innocent cleared*, a plaintive and unconvincing explanation of his movements. He had, he claimed, inspected the guard as normal at ten o'clock on the Saturday night. But he was feeling under the weather, and eventually three of his men persuaded him to get off the street. The four of them went to warm themselves in the Hinde Inn, where he had drunk a few times before; but after an hour he felt so terrible that he sent a message to the sergeant on duty telling him he was on his own that night. Then he went to bed.

He rose the next morning fully intending to go and inspect the guard, he said. But as he was coming downstairs there was a commotion in the street. A group of riders galloped past and Smith guessed – by the way they were shouting 'For the king! For the king!' – that they might be the enemy. So he went back inside the Hinde Inn and called for help. It was some time before he heard what had happened to his colonel, at which time he 'caused all my company to stand to their arms . . . and had marched a whiles about the town in a posture of defence'.[17] The words 'stable door', 'horse', and 'bolted' spring to mind.

At this point Smith's saga of self-justification grew so absurd it might just have been true. He deserted his post after the murder, he said, because he felt he had to go to St Albans to explain the situation to Fairfax in person. Only, his money ran out before he got there, so he decided to go home to his wife in London instead, even though this meant him passing right by St Albans and extending his journey by another day's ride. All the time, he insisted, he was still 'fully resolving to go to the headquarters to acquaint the general of the carriage of the business' as soon as he could.[18] The thing that prevented him was the fact that he was arrested a couple of days later on suspicion of complicity in his colonel's killing before he had the chance to set off; he was shut up with his wife in a chamber at the Bell Savage Inn on Ludgate Hill. (Pocahontas stayed in the same inn more than thirty years before.) On the morning of 8 November a friend sent word that Parliament had considered his case, found him guilty and sentenced him to be shot (none of which was true); so after praying for guidance for half an hour, he did a bunk, 'and am now far enough from the reach of their tyranny, who thirsted after my life'.[19] With that, and a reiterated claim that he hadn't known the Hinde Inn was a brothel, Captain John Smith disappeared from history.

Thomas was killed on a Sunday. Three days later MPs were debating the king's latest message from Carisbrooke when a letter arrived from Doncaster announcing the bare facts: that a party of Cavaliers had sallied out of Pontefract early on Sunday morning; that several of them had gone up to the colonel's chamber saying they carried a letter from Cromwell; and that they had pulled him down, stabbed him in the neck and heart and escaped.

There was outrage. Thomas Rainborowe was more than a senior officer in the army, albeit a rather awkward one; he was a Member of Parliament. Over Thursday and Friday the Commons ordered Cromwell to hunt down the murderers, and 'to take special care and make strict examination concerning the said massacre, and to certify it with all speed to the House'.[20] On the Saturday, it struck them that perhaps the murder might have been the first step in a wave of assassinations, and ignobly concluding that *they* might be in danger, they forgot Thomas and ordered an immediate review of security at Westminster.

That same day further news arrived from the north: the country was up in arms at Cholmley's mismanagement of the siege of Pontefract and the way he was allowing the Royalists to come and go as they pleased, 'and more particularly, the horrid murther of Col. Rainsborough, and to return back again at noon-time of the day' without a shot being fired at them.[21] Cholmley's own officers were said to be preparing letters of complaint against him, while their status-conscious commander had refused to accept orders from Fairfax, saying 'he hath no more to do with them than with the great Turk's orders'.[22] The old accusations that he was in league with the defenders were repeated.

Cromwell arrived at Pontefract on Friday 3 November, five days after the killing. His priority, however, was not to hold an inquest into the murder, but to organise the besieging forces so that the Royalists were confined to their castle. This he did over the coming days. Then he sent a businesslike note to their leader, John Morrice, suggesting he might consider surrendering:

> Sir, Being come hither for the reduction of this place, I thought fit to summon you to deliver your garrrison to me, for the use of the Parliament. Those gentlemen and soldiers with you may have better terms than if you should hold it to extremity. I expect your answer this day.[23]

Morrice's reply was not helpful. He insisted the lieutenant general had no authority in Yorkshire and said he would only parley with Cholmley who, if he had any sense at all, must have been feeling rather uncomfortable by now.

In the week following Thomas's murder, three radical regiments presented a petition to Fairfax asking 'that inquisition be made for the blood of Colonel Rainsborough'; and presenting a series of demands for the future government of the country which were broadly in line with the *Agreement of the people* which Thomas and William had supported at Putney.[24] That same week, as pressure to abandon negotiations with Charles I mounted in the army and representatives of the Levellers and leading Independents met in London to discuss how they might reach an agreement, Fairfax summoned a General Council at St Albans to discuss the soldiers' grievances.

There were more petitions over the coming weeks demanding that the king be brought to justice, including one from the regiments of Richard Deane and Thomas Pride, calling for Parliament to proceed against Charles I 'as an enemy to the kingdom'; and another from Sir Hardress Waller's regiment in the west, demanding to know which members of either House 'have played the traitors'.[25] Several repeated the demand for justice for Thomas, although not, oddly enough, his own regiment, now back in St Albans. The framers of their petition presumably thought it might look rather awkward to call for inquisition to be made for the blood of their colonel, when half the world believed their own incompetence had been to blame for its shedding in the first place. They admitted as much in their opening lines, acknowledging that 'the unhappy loss of our highly esteemed colonel, may cause us to bear low in our reputation, and sink us into a slowness to such high actings, as the vigour of his noble spirit might have enabled us to'.[26] They went on to voice concerns in line with those of the other radical regiments, which boiled down to a single thought: 'that we fear we are deluded into the hopes of a safe peace, by the expectation of an unsafe treaty'.[27] Parliament responded by voting that 'the Tower Regiment late under the command of Col. Rainsborough should be forthwith disbanded'.[28]

The Royalists, meanwhile, were making every effort to present Thomas's murder in the best light. Dragging an unarmed man from his bed and stabbing him to death was hardly an honourable act, and in the days that followed the killing the Royalist press did its best to legitimise it by insisting Thomas had given his word to his captors to stay silent as they led him down to the street, and then broken it by crying out to be rescued. They also invoked the memory of Colchester and the deaths of Lucas and Lisle: 'no doubt the same hand of vengeance may chance to reach the rest that had a hand in that un-soldierlike and inhumane execution'.[29] The pro-Parliament newsbooks flatly contradicted Royalist accounts, claiming one of the intruders had stabbed him the moment they entered his chamber.

And the truth? Judging from the two most authoritative accounts of the killing – by Lieutenant Thomas Paulden for the Royalists and the anonymous author of 'A Letter from Doncaster' for Thomas's own side – it was more of a cock-up than a planned assassination. There is no reason to disbelieve Lieutenant Paulden's insistence that the raiders meant to kidnap Thomas; nor is there anything inconsistent with that in the 'Letter from Doncaster'. The fact that no one came to his aid is odd, but suggests the incompetence of common soldiers taken off-guard rather than a willingness to see their commanding officer captured or cut down in the street. As for Cholmley, while he came out of the business without credit or honour, one has the impression he was a venal, pompous man, but not a treacherous one. Perhaps he did indeed laugh at the news that his rival had died; but if he really thought that Thomas Rainborowe's murder solved his problems with the high command of the New Model Army, he was a fool.

Thomas's followers cried for vengeance. The 'Letter from Doncaster', which was reprinted in the Leveller newsletter *The Moderate*, ended its description of Thomas's death with a call to arms:

> And can the soldiery of this kingdom be silent, and not revenge this barbarous murder of this incomparable commander, the like for sea and land service never came out of the bowels of this nation. The Lord stir up your hearts to be avenged of these bloody enemies.[30]

And in the midst of all this rhetoric there were funeral arrangements to be made, transport to be hired, announcements to be published, personal grief to be balanced against public honour – all the prosaic practicalities which accompany the death of a prominent figure. They fell to Thomas's brother William, who had been camped only ten miles away from Doncaster on the night of the murder and who rode into the town barely half an hour after the culprits made their getaway. He arranged for Thomas's body to be brought home to Wapping for burial beside their father at St John's, and then went down to London to await its arrival. The *Moderate* announced in its 7 November issue that 'the corpse of this never to be forgotten, English champion, is to be brought to London on Tuesday next, the 14 instant, to be there interred'.[31] It was to be met by Major Rainborowe and other members of the family at ten in the morning at Tottenham High Cross, north of the City, and conducted in procession to Wapping. 'All the well affected in London, and parts adjacent are desired to accompany them.'[32]

Puritan attitudes towards the burial of the dead were complicated. On the one hand, traditional practices such as kneeling and praying by the corpse before the removal were condemned as superstitious. And since praying, reading and singing on the way to the burial and at the grave could make no difference to the dead, and encouraged error in the living, they should also be dispensed with. The Parliament-approved *Directory for The Publique Worship of God*, which replaced the Anglican Book of Common Prayer in 1645, stipulated instead that the deceased's friends should 'apply themselves to meditations and conferences suitable to the occasion', and that the minister should preach a sermon which reminded them of their duty towards God.[33]

But even Puritans couldn't bring themselves to disregard the niceties of class, and the authors of the *Directory* took pains to point out that they weren't prohibiting 'any civil respects or deferences at the burial, suitable to the rank and condition of the party deceased'.[34] There were in any case scriptural precedents for both funeral processions and for the solemnity of the funeral service. Puritan thinkers cited Genesis 50:13 on the burial of Jacob, 'For his sons carried him into the land of Canaan'; and Ecclesiastes 7:2, 'It is better to go to the house of mourning, than to go to the house of feasting: for that is the end of all men; and the living will lay it to his heart.'

The call for Thomas's friends to join William in accompanying the coffin from Tottenham to Wapping met with an astonishing response. The *Kingdomes weekly intelligencer* reported that the corpse was attended by about forty coaches, 'and many hundreds of horse'. *Mercurius militaris* said there were fifty or sixty coaches and nearly 3,000 gentlemen and citizens on horseback. Even the hostile Royalist press acknowledged the massive turnout: 'thousands of the Levelling faction went out to meet their dead champion', said one newsbook.[35] Another sneered at 'the carcass of Rainsborough' being attended through the streets by 'all the tag-rags of the faction [i.e. the Levellers] that were able to hire horses'.[36] A third, *Mercurius elencticus*, gave a nasty description of the company who gathered to escort 'the sacred corpse' of 'that unimitable pattern of independency, Col. Rainsborough'. The coffin was

> met and attended on by a great number of the well affected of all professions, Will the Weaver, Tom the Tapster, Kit the Cobler, Dick the Door sweeper, and many more eminent apron-youths of the City, who trudged very devoutly both before and behind this glorious saint, with about 100 of the she-votresses crowded up in coaches, and some 500 more of the better sort of brethren mounted.[37]

With all the solemnity of a state funeral, the cortège moved through the open countryside below Tottenham, past the mansions and farms of Islington and through Smithfield ('there they should have burnt it', jibed *Mercurius elencticus* in a vicious reference to the Marian martyrs who died there a century before), until it reached the City proper at Pye Corner, some seven miles from Tottenham High Cross.[38]

Senior figures in the army kept away. The chief mourners were William Rainborowe, Thomas's widow Margaret and at least one unidentified 'kinsman' – perhaps Stephen Winthrop. Another prominent mourner was the distinguished physician and one-time doctor to Charles I Peter Chamberlen, an Independent and a strong supporter of the army.

London ground to a halt as the cavalcade of several thousand, many wearing rosemary for remembrance in their hats and the sea-green ribbons of Thomas's old regiment, wound its way along

Old Bailey and up Ludgate Hill, past the battered Gothic form of St Paul's Cathedral and the maze of shops and stalls that surrounded it and eastward, right through the heart of the City, along Cheapside and Cornhill until it finally came to rest at St John's, Wapping. The guns at the Tower of London fired out a salute to mark Thomas's passing; his 'fellow swabbers and skippers', as the Royalists contemptuously called the mariners of East London, were there to meet him.[39] 'I have not observed', commented Thomas Brooks, who preached the funeral sermon, 'that the hearts of the people of God, have been so general and eminently affected with the loss of any worthy, as with the loss of this worthy . . . a joy to the best, and a terror to the worst of men.'[40]

Brooks, who had been asked to preach at the funeral at a few hours' notice, was a good choice: he knew Thomas well, having served as his chaplain on land and at sea. He was a radical and an Independent, with views which struck a chord with his audience. And like that audience, he was angry. The message he gave to the mourners was not one of forgiveness or reconciliation. Taking as his text the apparently innocuous Colossians 3:4, 'When Christ, who is our life, shall appear, then shall ye also appear with him in glory', he launched into a sermon studded with bitter references to Thomas's murder, and the sure and certain hope of retribution that was bound to follow.

He began magnificently, by explaining to his listeners Paul's pledge that the people of God, the saints, shall at the last day appear glorious: because God has promised them a crown of glory; because their glory will make much for the honour and glory of the Lord Jesus; and not least,

for the terror, and the horror of all ungodly wretches, that have opposed, persecuted, and murdered them. They shall appear glorious for the greater torment of such ungodly souls. O there is nothing that will make sinners in that great day, more to tear their hair, to beat their breasts, to wring their hands, and to gnaw their own hearts, than this, when they shall behold those advanced, and those appearing in their glory, whom they have slighted, and despised, and most treacherously murdered here below.[41]

Warming to his theme, he raged at the ungodly wretches who murdered the righteous. The day was coming, he promised, when Christ would pass sentence on 'all treacherous, and bloody murderers'. When everyone who had applauded Thomas's death, and especially 'all those treacherous wretches that had a hand in this unparallelled butchery' would stand at the bar of God's tribunal to answer for their actions. And Thomas would be among the saints who would appear glorious to condemn them, 'to pass a righteous sentence upon such unrighteous, bloody wretches'.[42]

Treachery and murder loomed large in Brooks's theology that day. Assured of glory in heaven, the saints should strive to do gloriously on earth, because 'God hath delivered you from the designs and plots of treacherous, murderous wretches gloriously and frequently.'[43] And whatever befell them, they were secure in the knowledge that the day of glory was coming. 'What though this worthy's body be mangled here and there by bloody butchers, yet this body shall appear glorious at the last.'[44]

But Thomas Brooks offered more than easy reassurance that God would smite His enemies and avenge the death of a saint. Sure of his audience's sympathies, he pressed for equality before the law, one of the demands of the Levellers: 'men do gloriously', he declared, 'when they do justice impartially, upon high and low, honourable, and base'.[45] He criticised elements in Parliament for being too worldly, and for refusing to commit themselves to God's cause. 'They wish the saints well, but they dare not, they will not side with them.'[46] Faint-hearted politicians who were prepared to throw down their weapons when the struggle was almost won, were traitors to the kingdom. 'Honoured commanders and worthy members of the House of Commons, for you to do gloriously, is to hold out against discouragements, and to serve your generation.'[47] That was the way to honour Thomas's name. He was, said Brook in his closing remarks,

one of whom this sinful nation was not worthy; he was one of whom this declining Parliament was not worthy; he was one of whom these divided formal, carnal gospellers was not worthy. He served his generation faithfully, though he died by the hands of treachery, I am fully satisfied, with many more, that he is now triumphing in glory, and it will be but as a day before he shall see his enemies stand at the bar.[48]

27

Loud Lament and Furious Rage

$\mathcal{T}$homas's assassination provoked a flurry of activity
from broadside poets. Several quoted the epitaph on
his gravestone, long since destroyed:

> He that made King, Lords, Commons, Judges shake,
>   Cities and Committees quake;
> He that sought nought but His dear Country's good,
>   And seal'd their Right with His last blood;
> Rainsbrough, The Just, the Valiant, and True,
> Here bids the Noble Levellers Adieu.

Without naming names, 'An Elegie upon the Death of that
Renowned Heroe Coll. Rainsborrow' blamed treason, noted that
both 'the languished land' and 'Neptune's court' lamented his
passing, and mourned that 'a great Man's fallen, in Israel'.[1] In a
series of colourful metaphors, 'A New Elegie' railed against the
'horse-leeches that drew his blood' and prophesied that Cerberus,
the three-headed dog of mythology, would tear at their guilty
consciences, 'fiends incarnate, great odds, three to one, And he

in's shirt, unweaponed, all alone'.[2] Another broadside, published on the day of the funeral, called on all brave souls to 'avenge his blood', and ended with a warning:

> Now Cholmley laugh, and ye Malignants grin:
> Yet know, from hence your Reckoning must begin.[3]

To the Royalists, Thomas's death was cause for celebration, and the extent of that celebration shows just how much they loathed him and everything he stood for:

> Of Rainsborough, this we record;
> Hated he liv'd, and dy'd abhorr'd.[4]

Instead of having such a stately funeral, the anonymous author of this couplet went on, 'it had been fitter that his rotten carcass had been drawn in a sledge to Tyburn, and there burnt by the common hangman, and his ashes scattered upon some dunghill'. The Royalists despised Thomas's Leveller politics, but more than that even, they hated him for Colchester. The newsbook *Mercurius melancholicus* published a savage epitaph 'to the immortal memory of the Leveller Rainsborough', holding him responsible for the deaths of Lucas and Lisle, and predicting a Dantesque fate in which molten lead would be poured on his head, while snake-haired furies roasted him 'on a fiery hearth' and he was forced to drink bowls of sulphur.[5] 'Colonell Rainsborowes Ghost', a piece of Royalist doggerel illustrated by a picture of a phantom Thomas draped in a white sheet, claimed that the assassins had been motivated by revenge for the execution of Lucas and Lisle. 'The death of them revenged hath been/on me, by those that loved them well', laments the phantom. 'Sweet Jesus Christ forgive my sin,/for by my means those worthies fell.'[6]

The following year Thomas was one of the main characters in a play, *The famous tragedie of King Charles I.* This entertaining version of events in the Second Civil War (in which Charles I features not at all, although Hugh Peter does, as a pander who arranges for Cromwell to slip into bed with Lambert's wife), repeats the charge that Fairfax was reluctant to execute Lucas and Lisle after the fall of Colchester – 'The law of arms will not allow

of that, they yield themselves on quarter'[7] – and that it was
Thomas who insisted on their death:

> It glads my soul, and is the only good
> That I delight in, for to spill their blood.[8]

One of the soldiers in the firing squad is so disgusted with himself
and his commander that he deserts, vowing to expiate his crime.
Some time later Thomas is lost in the dark on the road to
Pontefract when, Macbeth-like, he thinks he sees 'the ghosts of
Lucas and of Lisle, all full of wounds staring just now upon me,
there, there, dost thou see nothing?'[9] At this point the deserter
and three friends come on the scene. They fight, and Thomas
falls, handicapped by his shame – 'Oh my guilt hangs heavy on
my arm! and impedes the violence of my blows'[10] – while the
soldier goes off declaring that 'Beyond the seas, for safety I will
fly,/Till England once more be a monarchy'.[11]

   The most thoughtful of the pro-Rainborowe elegies is a piece
by 'J.T.' which appeared on 13 November, the day before the
funeral. It portrays Sir Henry Cholmley as Judas and Thomas
Rainborowe as a Christ-like sacrificial figure, 'through Cholmley's
pride and cowardice betrayed'.[12] And it asks if perhaps Thomas's
death was necessary to ensure the army held out against parliamentary pressure to reach a compromise with the king:

> What if Heaven purposed Rainsbrough's fall to be
> A prop for England's dying Liberty?
> And did in Love thus suffer one to fall
> That Charles by Treaty might not ruin all?[13]

The day after Thomas's funeral, the Commons voted that when
the treaty with the king was agreed, Charles would be allowed
to come to London 'with freedom, safety, and honour', and that
all his lands and revenues would be made good to him.[14] Three
days later the Army Council at St Albans adopted the Army
Remonstrance, an uncompromising manifesto drafted chiefly by
Henry Ireton which signalled the army's insistence 'that that
capital and grand author of our troubles, the person of the king
may be speedily brought to justice, for the treason, blood, and

mischief he's therein guilty of'.[15] And after the moderates in Parliament refused to consider the Remonstrance and continued their efforts to reach a peace with the king, the army marched into London on Saturday 2 December.

Early on the following Wednesday Pride's regiment of foot and Rich's regiment of horse took up positions in Palace Yard, while the regiments of Sir Hardress Waller and John Hewson patrolled the neighbouring streets. Thomas Pride stood on the steps with Waller and Lord Grey of Groby, an MP who shared the radicals' views on prosecuting King Charles. Pride had with him a list of about 180 MPs whose interests did not coincide with those of the army; and as they arrived, Grey identified them and they were turned back. Of those who tried to enter the Palace of Westminster, forty-one were arrested. Hugh Peter, wearing a sword 'like a boisterous soldier', according to one witness, arrived in the afternoon to make a list of their names; when they asked by whose authority they were imprisoned, Peter said simply 'by the power of the sword'.[16]

Peter, who until late October had shown little interest in punishing the king or abolishing the monarchy, now took a leading role, both arguing in council and preaching in public that 'this army must root up monarchy . . . This army is that cornerstone cut out of the mountain, which must dash the powers of the earth to pieces.'[17] The king was moved up to Windsor on 23 December and at a meeting in Whitehall on Christmas Day, Peter pressed hard for the necessity of bringing him to trial. When the Rump hesitated to pass the ordinance which would create the necessary High Court of Justice, he gave a rousing sermon in St Margaret's, Westminster, haranguing MPs for nearly three hours. The Commons, he stormed, must not prefer 'the great Barabbas, murderer, tyrant, and traitor, before these poor hearts' – and here he pointed at a group of soldiers sitting on the steps of the pulpit – 'who are our saviours'.[18]

The ardent rhetoric was needed because the Rump was by no means convinced that trying Charles I was either legal or justifiable. The idea was unpopular with the nation in general, and even within the army, where most of the enthusiasm for prosecuting the king lay, elements led by Cromwell were still looking for some sort of compromise. But in the last days of 1648 Cromwell finally came round to the conviction, held by Peter and by Pride, Harrison and half a dozen other senior army officers, and by Henry Marten and other hardliners in the Rump, that Charles I's survival was incompatible with peace.

Still, of the 135 men named as the king's judges, only half turned up for the first day of the trial, which began in Westminster Hall on 20 January. When the roll call reached Fairfax's name a masked woman rumoured to be his wife cried out from the public gallery, 'He has more wit than to be here.' John Bradshaw, who presided over the court, wore a hat lined with iron because he was so concerned that someone in the hall might take a potshot at him. Soldiers with loaded weapons kept order in the galleries and at the lower end of the hall, where among the general public there were shouts of 'God save the king!'

Charles was superb throughout the eight days of his trial – courageous, dignified, unwavering in his conviction that he and only he was right. Informed that he was impeached 'as a tyrant, traitor, murderer, and a public and implacable enemy of the Commonwealth of England', he repeatedly asked by what authority he was brought to the bar, and refused to accept the answer, that it was by the authority of the Commons in Parliament and the people of England.[19] The court was illegal, he insisted: 'Do you pretend what you will, I stand more for [the people of England's] liberties; for, if power without law may make laws, may alter the fundamental laws of the kingdom, I do not know what subject he is in England that can be sure of his life, or anything that he calls his own.'[20] And this struck right at the heart of the arguments of Thomas Rainborowe and his comrades: their desire for a more tolerant and democratic society could only be achieved by ignoring the law and imposing their will by force. Like every revolution, their brand of peace could only be achieved by the sword.

Sentence was pronounced on Saturday 27 January. For his treasons and crimes, 'this Court doth adjudge that he, the said Charles Stuart, as a tyrant, traitor, murderer, and public enemy to the good people of this nation, shall be put to death by the severing of his head from his body'.[21] His request to appeal to the Lords and Commons was turned down – 'I am not suffered to speak', he muttered as he was led away; 'Expect what justice other people will have!' The next day Hugh Peter preached a last sermon of denunciation from Isaiah 14:18–20, a passage in which the prophet condemns the King of Babylon and foretells that 'Thou shalt not be joined with [the kings of the nations] in burial, because thou hast destroyed thy land, and slain thy people.' Fairfax urged the Army Council to intervene; the Assembly of Divines pleaded for mercy. From exile in The Hague the Prince of Wales sent a blank sheet of paper, signed and sealed by himself, with a message that Parliament could write out any terms it liked if only it would save his father.

Charles stepped out on to the scaffold in front of a horrified crowd on 30 January, still convinced he was right. In his final speech he showed no hint of doubt, no hint of concession towards a world which had changed fundamentally since the outbreak of war back in 1642:

> For the people, truly I desire their liberty and freedom as much as anybody whatsoever; but I must tell you that their liberty and freedom consists in having government . . . It is not their having a share in the government; that is nothing appertaining unto them. A subject and a sovereign are clean different things.[22]

Place those words beside Thomas Rainborowe's speech at Putney in which he declared that 'the poorest man in England is not at all bound in a strict sense to that government that he hath not had a voice to put himself under'. The gulf that separates them killed them both.

In early December, while the Commons and the Army Council were still debating the king's fate, Major Saltonstall, who had been at Doncaster, was arrested in London with another Royalist after boasting that they were in the raiding party that murdered Thomas. If they were ever brought to trial, no record of it survives. Sir Henry Cholmley, having lost his parliamentary seat in Pride's Purge, lost his command a few weeks later when Lambert, who was left in charge of the siege of Pontefract by Cromwell, disbanded his regiment. Cholmley played no further part in the siege, retiring to his Yorkshire estates and becoming an active Royalist just in time for the restoration of Charles II in 1660.

The garrison inside the castle held on to the hope that the Scots might come to their rescue, but by the beginning of March, Colonel Morrice offered to begin talks about a surrender. Lambert was willing to allow the garrison to leave with honour: but he was adamant that six men would be exempted from any agreement. They were a Major Ashby, Ensign Smyth and Sergeant Floyd, members of the original Parliamentarian garrison who had betrayed the castle to the Royalists the previous summer; Morrice himself; and Lieutenant Alan Austwick and Cornet Robert Blackburn, two of the leading players in the murder of Thomas Rainborowe. William Paulden would also have been exempted, but he had died of a fever several weeks earlier. There was no mention of Dallison or Greenfield. Perhaps they were dead, too.

The talks stalled because the Royalist negotiators believed, quite rightly, that they would be signing the death warrants of the six if they accepted. 'It will be murder, they say, in them, and the first precedent of that kind in England', wrote a member of Lambert's team; 'but I believe the thought of self-preservation will make them deny their honour, forget their conscience, and put them upon some way of satisfying us'.[23] Chipping away at the flagging morale within the castle, Lambert's troops wrapped papers explaining the terms around stones and lobbed them over the castle walls, so that Morrice wouldn't be able to hide things from his men.

On 16 March the Royalists gave in and agreed to the terms. The next night, the six exempted men broke out and tried to fight their way through the besiegers' cordon. Morrice and Blackburn charged through and escaped; Smyth was killed; Austwick and the others were beaten back into the castle, where they hid themselves while the garrison surrendered and then slipped away. They were never caught.

Heavily disguised, Morrice and Blackburn rode north-west into Lancashire, hoping to reach the coast and get a passage on a ship 'to pass beyond sea'. On the wild Furness Fells they were recognised, arrested and imprisoned in Lancaster Castle. At York Assize that August they were both indicted on a statute dating back to the time of Edward III, and charged with levying war against the king in his realm. Morrice argued hard against this, and against the right of a criminal court to try a military man; then he challenged so many jurors that the judge, Lord Puleston, lost his temper and told him 'Sir, keep within your compass, or I will give you such a blow as will strike off your head.'[24] Undeterred, Morrice insisted that his commission was legal, and that it should be read to the court. 'It will do you no good', said Lord Puleston, who was not prepared to argue points of law with a defendant; 'you may as well show a commission from the Pope, all is one'.[25]

Morrice and Blackburn were both found guilty of treason. Thomas Rainborowe's murder wasn't even mentioned. Efforts to obtain a reprieve had been blocked in the Army Council by Thomas Pride, who said 'it would not stand with the justice of the army, nor the safety of the commonwealth, to let such enemies live'.[26] They were hanged at York.

William Rainborowe still looked for justice for his brother's death, without help or encouragement from the Council of State. Rumours were rife about the reasons behind the assassination, whether it was part of a concerted plot by dissident Royalists, or by the Army Council. 'Many here question the truth of the reports about Colonel R.', Emmanuel Downing reported to John Winthrop.[27] 'Colonel Rainsborough was slain treacherously', Edward Hopkins of Hartford, Connecticut, told John Winthrop junior; 'the plot (it seems) was to cut off all the chief of the army in such a way'.[28] John Lilburne hinted darkly at the complicity of the army high command:

> The ruling officers finding him as inflexible to their ends as formerly, they put him upon that dangerous and unhappy service before Pomfret (notwithstanding a commander had been appointed thereunto by the Committee of York) whether he went with much reluctancy and discontent, as wondering at the cause of his being design'd thither.[29]

Unforgivably, absurdly, for a man of property who followed such a dangerous occupation, Thomas made no will. His wife Margaret was left to cope with the consequences: financial confusion and debt on top of loss and bereavement. 'I hear his wife is now in London', reported a correspondent from Yorkshire. 'I pray God give her strength to take it patiently.'[30] Their son was in his early teens, if that. Margaret administered to her husband's effects on

24 November, but in the meantime, probably with help from William Rainborowe, she moved quickly to petition for help.

Parliament and the New Model Army were both good at looking after their own when the mood took them. As soon as the Commons heard the news of Thomas's murder, they asked the Committee of the Army to pay his arrears to Margaret, and voted £1,000, with interest at 8 per cent to be paid out every six months for the use of her child. The trustees of this fund were Major William Rainborowe, Captain Peter Peck (perhaps the Peter Peck who held land in Dorchester, Massachusetts, in the mid-1630s) and the MP Cornelius Holland, a well-known supporter of Levellers and dissenters. The money was certainly helpful, but Margaret also approached Fairfax directly. When MPs ordered the payment of her husband's arrears, and the setting up of a pension to help her son, they hadn't been told the extent of Thomas's debts, she said. And the money her husband had laid out on the Adventure for Irish Lands seven years before still rankled. Fairfax wrote straight away to the Commons, enclosing her petition. Mindful of 'the gallantry and faithfulness of that gentleman [i.e. Thomas]', he said, 'I have thought myself engaged at the instance of Mistress Rainborrow to tender her petition unto you'.[31]

Fairfax's letter was read to the purged Commons on 19 December 1648, seven weeks after the murder; and a committee was asked to consider Margaret's petition. It reported back a week later, and the upshot was that MPs declined the opportunity to settle Thomas's long-standing Irish debt, referring it instead to the Adventurers. They did, however, order that Margaret should be allowed £2,000, in addition to the £1,000 granted in November, 'towards payment of the debts of the said Colonel Rainborow; and towards the provision of maintenance for his wife and children'.[32]

This was good news. But Margaret was still a long way from seeing the money. The Commons intended that the £2,000 should come from concealed delinquents' estates; and in January she took the initiative by providing the House with the names of two suitable delinquents, both Welsh Royalists. Nothing happened. In February the Commons asked the Committee of the Army to make sure the arrears and the original £1,000 was paid. At the beginning of June they ordered that confiscated church lands should be settled on Margaret and her son in payment 'for the debt due to Colonel Raynsborow'. At the end of June the Commons framed an Act settling Dean and Chapter lands worth £3,000 – the sum of both the first and the second grant – on Major William Rainborowe and Captain Stephen Winthrop, who were appointed as trustees for Margaret and her son. According to the *Commons Journal*, it was passed with one amendment. But clearly it wasn't, because three weeks later the House was ordering that the 'Three thousand pounds due to Mrs Rainbrow' should be charged against the estate of the notorious Royalist Sir Francis Doddington, currently in hiding in France. That didn't work out either, and a year later the widow and her son were awarded £100 for their maintenance and a pension of £50 a quarter 'until an Act shall be passed, in Parliament, for settling lands' on the pair.[33]

At last, in September 1653 and July 1654, estates in Lancashire and Somerset were bought on behalf of Margaret and her son, to provide their long-delayed pension. The man who acted for her in both transactions was John Wildman, the Leveller who had stood shoulder to shoulder with Thomas in the Putney debates.

28

My Other Self

*N*ews was slow to cross the Atlantic in the late 1640s – slower than ten years earlier, when the Great Migration was at its peak and ships had dropped anchor in Boston harbour almost every week. Now the ships were fewer, the absences longer.

Correspondents usually included a quick rundown of recent events in their letters, or at least a glancing reference, but their attention to detail varied wildly. Sometimes they couldn't be bothered at all: 'For news I must refer you to the passengers', was all Stephen Winthrop had to say to his brother John when he wrote to him from England in March 1648, when the Scots were threatening war, the army was occupying Whitehall and the Commons had just decided to break off all negotiations with the king.[1] He was more respectful to his father, although hardly more informative. In a letter which went over in the same ship, he told John Winthrop senior that 'this kingdom is in a very unsettled condition and it is wonder, all falls not in pieces in one day. But at present I cannot give you so particular account of it as I would, because some occasion hinders me from being at London this six weeks: and the ship I understand is going.'[2]

Fortunately for John Winthrop, not all his correspondents were as offhand with the news. The Baptist minister Henry Jessey also wrote that week, enclosing a sheaf of printed newsletters describing 'what great alterations have been in the army, Parliament, and kingdom, since the beginning of the 4 month [i.e. June] of the last year'.[3] At the same time John's nephew George Downing, who was serving as a chaplain in the New Model Army (and whose preaching was so eloquent he was called a young Hugh Peter), wrote to offer a perceptive analysis on the state of the nation.[4] While the war was on, the king's opponents found common cause, he said. Now it was over and Charles was in custody, everyone was starting to ask not what had they been fighting *against*, but what had they been fighting *for*?

New England was at least two months behind with the news, and often much longer, especially when happenings coincided with the annual winter lull in transatlantic crossings. The same was true for old England, of course: by the time Stephen received his dead mother's ring and Bible as mourning tokens, his sister-in-law Martha had already become the new Mrs Winthrop, and hence his stepmother. John and Martha didn't hear about the events of the summer – the mutiny in the Downs, the siege of Colchester – until October, when Thomas Graves came over and Nehemiah Bourne sent a letter from Newfoundland, where he had put in aboard the *Merchant*. John passed the news on to John Winthrop junior: 'Deal Castle was surprised, and the vice adml. put from his ship, and his wife, and the major's wife, and my poor daughter Steph[en] and all their children were turned out of doors, so as the vice adml. was forced to put them aboard a small boat of 20 tons, and run over to Harwich with them.'[5] In February 1649 John was writing again to John junior with news of Cromwell's victory over the Scots at Preston; he'd had this from Stephen, who was there, and who for once managed to send his father a full account of the action. 'I have lent it forth,' said John senior, 'so I can't now send it to you.'[6] In the same letter he told his son that Pontefract Castle 'is now besieged by Col. Raynborowe'. By that time Thomas Rainborowe was dead.

The king was dead, too. But that news would arrive too late for John Winthrop.

★　　★　　★

In December 1648, less than a year after her marriage to John Winthrop, Martha went into labour. She was thirty-one and this would be her fourth child, although only six-year-old Thomas Coytmore had survived to welcome the new sibling. John was sixty. He had fathered sixteen children by his previous three wives, and buried ten of them.

Maternal mortality rates in Massachusetts were between a third and a fifth lower than in England, for reasons which are still unclear; and one might have expected the decreased risk to result in lower levels of anxiety about childbirth. This and the social nature of the experience, with a midwife in attendance and women-friends and neighbours gathered at the bedside to provide help and comfort before, during and after the delivery, have led historians to characterise childbirth in colonial America as an act of serene and sisterly solidarity, with lots of hugging and bonding.

It was anything but serene. Martha knew what to expect, so she wouldn't have experienced the fear of the unknown which gripped a first-time mother. But she knew women who had died in childbirth; and John had lost his first two wives to post-partum complications. More potently, Puritan thinking encouraged Martha to approach her time with dread and repentance. In a widely circulated sermon on motherhood written towards the end of the century, for example, Cotton Mather, the grandson of John Cotton, exhorted mothers-to-be to prepare for the worst:

> For ought you know, your death has entered into you, and you may have conceived that which determines but about nine months at the most, for you to live in the world. Preparation for death is that most reasonable and most seasonable thing, to which you must now apply yourself.[7]

Not much joy there. And the rare descriptions of childbirth in colonial America don't paint a bright picture, talking instead of confusion and distraction, of women in normal labour being ill or unwell. An eighteenth-century Chesapeake planter wrote of one of his wife's confinements, 'I found everybody around her in a great fright and she almost in despair.'[8]

Women delivered in whatever position was most comfortable to them; sometimes in bed, sometimes seated on a birthing stool with a cut-out seat which the midwife brought with her, designed to help support the labouring woman's back and to give the midwife access to the birthing canal. Published manuals provided advice, some good – midwives should cut their fingernails – some less good, such as using goose fat to grease the vagina, or shoving snuff up a woman's nose to make her sneeze and hence dislodge a baby who was reluctant to enter the world.

On 12 December Martha was safely delivered of a boy. Emmanuel Downing, who was in the Winthrops' Boston house at the time, reported to his wife in Salem that everything had gone well. Sack and claret were drunk, 'and much rejoicing there was'.[9] Martha and John initially planned to call their son William; but when John presented the baby for baptism in the First Church about five days later, he had become Joshua, named perhaps for an Irish cousin of John, although the resonances with Joshua who led the Israelites across the Jordan into Canaan would not have been lost on the couple or the congregation.

Martha's place in John Winthrop's life – and hence in the history of New England – has been minimised, ignored, erased from the narrative of colonial America. Cotton Mather, who wrote John's first biography for his magisterial 1702 history of New England, *Magnalia Christi Americana*, said that the governor buried three wives and named them, without ever indicating that there was a fourth. Later biographers would give Martha a few lines, often misunderstanding the seventeenth-century practice of calling relations 'sister' and 'brother' and describing her as a sister of Increase Nowell, and occasionally adopting a disapproving tone at John Winthrop's eagerness to remarry so soon after the death of Margaret, as though this were somehow Martha's fault. In fact swift remarriage for widowers after the death of a spouse was the norm rather than the exception, with the period in between often measured in months rather than years. There was no place for extended mourning in Puritan culture.

As usual with the Rainborowe women – with so many seventeenth-century women, in fact – Martha's voice remains unheard. No letters or journal or other writings of hers survive, no indication of how much she loved her new husband, or if she loved him at all. But the sparse and scattered references among the Winthrop papers suggest she was quickly accepted into her husband's extended family. John junior referred to her as 'my honoured mother', even though he was eleven years older than her. Stephen called her simply 'my mother' although judged by twenty-first-century standards, his relationship with Martha was even more complex, since while he was his stepmother's junior (by a whole two years) he was also her brother-in-law through his marriage to Judith.

Other members of the Winthrop circle mentioned Martha with respect, sometimes kindness. They sent her presents and invited John to bring her to them on visits. But in their eyes – and quite possibly, in her own – she was defined completely by her relationship with her husband.

If little is known of their married life together, rather more is known about its setting. The house they lived in was big by Boston standards, with a hall and parlour, study and kitchen on the ground floor; four chambers upstairs and two garrets; and a good-sized cellar. Architecturally, little had changed since the early 1630s: oak frames, clapboard walls and rooms grouped around massive chimney stacks of brick and stone were still the norm. In addition to the furniture that Martha brought to the marriage, the Winthrops had seven beds, ranging from a couple of truckle beds for servants which could be pushed out of sight when not in use, to an expensive down bed which stood in the parlour. They kept a gun in the entry – 'a harquebuz' – and there were plenty of other weapons scattered around the place: a musket and bandolier, two pistols, a short-barrelled French carbine and some old armour and swords. John kept a second carbine and a pair of bandoliers in his study, together with a brass pistol.

In the living hall there were six chairs, a table and a carpet to lay over it, and a cupboard for pewter, of which the Winthrops had at least thirty pieces, along with twenty tin plates and some ironware. The kitchen, which stood at the back of the house, was filled with the equipment which usually graced a seventeenth-century home in New and old England: kettles and brass pots, three-legged posnets, a pestle and mortar, iron pot-hangers set into the kitchen chimney, a skillet and three spits. John's study was more like a garden shed than a gentleman's library: although he kept his writing paper there, he also stored his tools – chisels, awls, adzes and axes – some medical equipment, including syringes and surgical saws; and a bewildering assortment of old hats, boots, shoes and stockings, 'a tufted velvet jerkin' and no fewer than six pairs of spectacles.[10] The inventory of John's belongings (but not Martha's) taken after his death again runs counter to the traditional image of the dour Puritan. John did have 'one old black suit', but he also owned satin doublets, a satin coat, a scarf made of cloth of gold, silk hose and caps of scarlet and velvet.[11] There was tapestry on their bed, and Martha had her own things to bring to the marriage – her striped bed-curtains, and the quilt of red and green silk.

The Boston in which the Winthrops spent their married life together had changed out of all recognition since Martha sailed into the Bay with her first husband twelve years earlier. The little cluster of buildings had turned into a sizeable town, home to nearly 250 families and their servants. There were stores and taverns and wine shops, eating houses and lodging houses and even the odd house of ill repute, unless that is being ungenerous to the inappropriately named Temperance Sweete, who was reprimanded by the court for 'having received into house and given entertainment unto disorderly company and ministering unto them wine and strong waters unto drunkenness'.[12]

Martha could pick her way along still unnamed streets down to Town Cove, where the waterfront was hidden beneath the timbers of dozens of new wharves. The spacious plots set out by the first settlers were being divided and built over, as the character of Boston changed from the headquarters of an agricultural economy to a centre of commerce. To the north, there were mills and they were building houses on reclaimed marshland. 'The town is full of good shops well furnished', reported one observer.[13] 'The chief edifice of this city-like town', said another, 'is crowded on the sea-banks, and wharfed out with great industry and cost, the buildings beautiful and large, some fairly set forth with brick, tile, stone and slate, and orderly placed with comely streets, whose continual enlargement presages some sumptuous city . . . This town is the very mart of the land.'[14]

With prosperity came confidence and a growing sense of independence. In 1648 the colony published *The Laws and Liberties of Massachusetts*, a handbook for magistrates which built on the earlier

Body of Liberties. Remarkable as that first code was, it had stopped
short of prescribing penalties for particular offences, except in
the case of its twelve capital crimes.* Ever since, Massachusetts
had wrangled over the need for more clarity, with John Winthrop
leading the fight for magistrates to retain their discretionary powers.
As far as he was concerned, God had given the few the ability
to rule the many, and through His word He had provided them
with sufficient guidance; trying to replace the rule of God with
the rule of man was to go against the scriptures. Winthrop also
continued to maintain that a flexible system of sentencing was
more just.

But he was overruled by the General Court, which with advice
from the church elders began compiling a code of laws in 1644.
The Laws and Liberties of Massachusetts, which took four years to
complete (and in which Winthrop seems to have played a major
role, notwithstanding his opposition to the idea), marked another
step away from dependence on shared cultural values with England.
'A commonwealth without laws', wrote Increase Nowell in the
'Epistle' to the *Laws,* 'is like a ship without rigging or steerage',
ignoring the fact that, in theory at least, New England already
had laws – the same laws which served old England.[15]

In itself the code of laws wasn't particularly revolutionary: it
prescribed punishments for twenty-five offences, ranging from
a ten-shilling fine for swearing, to death for being a Jesuit. It
also retained a degree of discretion: fornicators, for example,
might be fined or whipped or forced to marry, according to
what the magistrates found 'most agreeable to the word of
God'.[16] But it was an assertion of autonomy, a signal that although
it was only eighteen years old, Massachusetts was finding its
own identity.

Less positively, this determination to go its own way was
expressed in the colony's continuing repression of religious dissent.
Baptists were prosecuted; neighbouring colonies were reprimanded
for their leniency towards nonconformity; and when a synod of
elders met at Cambridge in 1648, tasked with examining church

---

* Idolatry, witchcraft, blasphemy, murder, killing in anger, killing through 'poisoning
or other such devilish practice', bestiality, sodomy, adultery, kidnapping, bearing
false witness, treason against 'our commonwealth'.

governance and organisation, they reaffirmed the exclusive and excluding nature of New England congregationalism:

> The doors of the churches of Christ upon earth, do not by God's appointment stand so wide open, that all sorts of people good or bad, may freely enter therein at their pleasure; but such as are admitted thereto, as members ought to be examined and tried first, whether they be fit and meet to be received into church society, or not.[17]

The repression of Protestant dissent continued to hurt New England's reputation at home. George Downing, John Winthrop's nephew, wrote that 'the law of banishment for conscience . . . makes us stink everywhere'.[18]

It also deterred Stephen Winthrop from going home. This wasn't a decision he took lightly: he went through a long process of prevarication and soul-searching, promising his father that he would be back in Boston soon, while becoming ever more deeply involved with the Parliamentarian cause. 'Your brother hath sent again for his wife', John had written wistfully to John junior in the autumn of 1645, when Stephen asked for Judith to join him in England, 'and it seemes means to stay in Engl. with his brother Rainsb[orowe].'[19] Stephen was open about the conflict he felt. 'I question not but providence will so work that I may see your face again', he told his father at one point; 'though I see a clear providence likewise at present in my stay here'.[20] Nehemiah Bourne made the same kinds of promises to Winthrop. 'I cannot but look westward', he said on one of his Newfoundland voyages.[21] It was only business and family matters that kept him away, he said. He'd be in Boston soon, he said. He never did go back.

Hugh Peter was always on the verge of returning, while becoming ever more deeply involved with the Independents and the army. Back in 1645 he had written to John Winthrop junior at Boston, 'desiring you to assure all that world that I am coming to you', and announcing that he was sending his mentally troubled wife Deliverance on ahead, 'for divers reasons'.[22] Deliverance went, but Hugh Peter stayed. He continued to promote New England congregationalism, writing approvingly to an English audience of 'those faithful, learned, godly brethren' on the other side of the Atlantic; although by 1647, as rumours of oppression began to spread, he was gently urging John Winthrop to check his intolerance towards dissent, and 'be tender towards those that hold Christ for the head, and would live quietly under your government . . . Let the magistrate and elders but devise a way to bring that about and you will have many friends here.'[23]

Peter returned to this theme again and again, urging Massachusetts to be more tolerant. Not in any inclusive, liberal twenty-first-century way: he never ceased to work for 'the utter ruin and extirpation of the Church of Rome'; he resisted plans to admit Jews into England; and he believed the only reason for entering into dialogue with both Jews and Muslims was to convert them to Christianity.[24] Those who advocated toleration – clergy like Peter, soldier-saints like Stephen Winthrop, godly merchants like Nehemiah Bourne – did so in the closer seventeenth-century sense of admitting difference between fellow Protestants. In another letter to Winthrop – a letter in which he yet again announced his imminent departure for New England, if only his health would hold and his business affairs would allow – Peter mourned his absence from 'sweet New England! And yet sweeter if division been not among you, if you will give any encouragement to those that are godly and shall differ.'[25]

In the spring of 1649 Peter took up the idea again, after his now-familiar protestation that he would give anything to be with his old friends. 'Be assured New England is a good country to be in, if you can be quiet among yourselves.'[26] By this time those friends had tired of caring for his fragile wife, and Deliverance had been shipped back to him: they were living apart, and Peter was wishing that he 'had never this wife so sent to me!'[27] But even her presence on one side of the Atlantic wasn't enough to send him to the other. And soon he was winding up his affairs in Salem and urging John Winthrop junior to abandon New England and come and live in London.

No one wanted to admit it. Not to themselves, and certainly not to the formidable Governor Winthrop. But for men in search of liberty, old England offered more. Hugh Peter and Stephen

Winthrop and Nehemiah Bourne and the others had come home. And the promised land was there to greet them.

John Winthrop's health had been poor over the summer of 1648. He was sick with a fever, although not sick enough to stay at home: in September he insisted on making a sixty-mile round trip from Boston to Ipswich, in Essex County, when none of the other magistrates were able to go. He improved over the autumn, presiding over the October session of the General Court at Boston, and handing down judgements on the usual range of issues. Every town was to obtain hounds as protection against wolves, and no other dog was to be kept without permission (unless it belonged to a magistrate). A citizen of Dover was to be prosecuted for professing anabaptism. Any beer-seller who harboured a drunk was to be fined £5.

But Winthrop was failing. He made the final entry in his journal in January 1649, a characteristic tale of divine wrath visited on innocence. A man from the Boston church had been working on the maintenance of a mill-dam one Saturday, and had neglected to stop when night fell, even though this meant he was breaking the injunction against working on the Lord's Day. The next evening the sinner's five-year-old daughter fell into a well and drowned: 'the father, freely in the open congregation, did acknowledge it the righteous hand of God for his profaning his holy day against the checks of his own conscience'.[28]

Winthrop's last surviving letter, written at the beginning of February to his son John, showed his mind still sharp, and his heart a little more generous. The ailing governor wrote proudly of Stephen's part in the campaign against the Scots, of Hugh Peter's exploits in Wales and brother-in-law Thomas Rainborowe's siege of Pontefract Castle. (He still didn't know that Thomas was dead.) The French 'stand for their liberty . . . The janissaries have slain their sultan.' And he was sending his son a rabbit. 'So with your mothers [i.e. Martha's] and mine own salutations and blessings to you all, in haste I rest your loving father.'[29]

In February he caught a cold, and it turned into a cough and a fever that he couldn't shake. From Salem, John Endicott reminded his old friend that 'we have not long to live here in this life, yet we shall here remain as long as our appointed times are set'.[30] A week later, on 14 March, Adam Winthrop wrote to his brother John in Connecticut to ask him to come to Boston. Their father had been in his bed for most of the past month, he said. He was weaker than Adam had ever seen him, too weak even to write a few lines. 'The Lord only knows the event.'[31]

The elders came to pray at Winthrop's bedside. At the Boston church, John Cotton led the congregation in prayers and fasting, and preached on Psalm 35, 'When they were sick, I humbled myself.' Winthrop had been as a friend, as a brother, 'as a mother, parent-like distributing his goods to brethren and neighbours at his first coming', said Cotton, 'and gently bearing our infirmities without taking notice of them'.[32]

If that last comment stretched the truth, now wasn't the time for the saints to quibble. On 26 March 1649 John Winthrop died peacefully in his bed, surrounded by friends and family and comforted by their prayers. After it was over, Rev. John Wilson sat in the Winthrop parlour and wrote to break the news to John junior, who was still in Connecticut. 'Our deep sorrow is not a little allayed by the consideration of God's merciful dealing with him in his sickness, and the manner of it', said Wilson.[33] The governor's death was a big thing; and Wilson, John Cotton and Richard Bellingham, who were all present, agreed that his funeral should wait a full week, so that John junior and anyone else would have time to reach Boston. A barrel and a half of powder were spent at the funeral, as the town and the colony saluted 'a man of great humility and piety, an excellent statesman . . . and of a public spirit'.[34]

John died intestate. He had revoked a will back in 1641 when he faced financial ruin because of his steward's dishonesty, and decided then to leave all 'to the most wise and gracious providence of the Lord'.[35] His estate, valued two weeks after the funeral, was worth just £103 10s. 11d. Martha and Adam were granted joint administration 'to pay so far as the estate will go'.[36]

Widowed for the second time in just over three years, Martha now had two small children to support. Joshua was still a babe in arms, fifteen weeks old when his father died; and as John Winthrop lay on his deathbed he 'did express his tender desires towards his wife and youngest child', and asked that any grant the colony might like to make in consideration of his long service should be given to Martha for Joshua's education and use – in itself an unusual request in an age and a culture which more often relied on male relatives or friends to administer a trust fund like that, rather than the widow.[37] A sum of £200 was awarded to Joshua – a great deal less than the £3,000 that Parliament awarded to Thomas Rainborowe's widow – and the General Court stipulated that if Joshua should die before he reached the age of twenty-one, then only one-third of the money should go to Martha, with the other two-thirds being given to Dean and Samuel Winthrop, 'they, as yet, having had no portions out of the governor's estate, nor like to have'.[38]

The Winthrop clan was kind enough to Martha, and she still had kin in New England: Increase and Parnell Nowell and mother-in-law Katherine Coytmore. The prenuptial trust meant she was financially secure; the estate she had brought to their marriage in 1647 remained her own instead of vanishing into the pockets of her husband's creditors.

But from scattered mentions in the sparse correspondence that survives, it looks as though the period following her husband's death wasn't free from financial problems. She was still owed money by her brother William, either a debt from his time in New England or more likely the remains of the £700 legacy left her by their father in 1642. John Leverett was in England and she appointed him as her attorney to extract the money from William, but without success. Stephen did his best to sort matters out, but he had no more luck than Leverett. 'The money my brother Raynborowe should pay for my mother will not be paid till he and his brother's widow are agreed', Stephen wrote. 'Their business is upon arbitration.'[39] Her other stepsons regarded her as a useful source of ready cash, and when her son by John Winthrop died in 1651, giving her a share in the £200 granted by the Massachusetts authorities for his future education, John junior moved quickly to borrow the money, offering a farm which he didn't quite own as security.

At the beginning of 1652 Martha married for a third time, and she married well. Nearly twenty years of trading in the 'very mart of the land' had made John Coggan, Boston's first shopkeeper, a wealthy man. At sixty-one Coggan owned a good deal of real estate in the colony, including four houses, two shops, a warehouse, a cornmill, an orchard and a farm.

It was a rapid courtship – so rapid that it makes John Winthrop's six months as a widower seem positively Victorian. The couple married on 10 March 1652, eight weeks after the death of Coggan's previous wife. God was just as quick to bless their union: Martha gave birth to a son nine months and five days later. They named him Caleb, after the figure in the Old Testament who was allowed to enter Canaan.

Surely there shall not one of these men of this evil generation see that good land, which I sware to give unto your fathers, Save Caleb the son of Jephunneh; he shall see it, and to him will I give the land that he hath trodden upon, and to his children, because he hath wholly followed the Lord.

Deuteronomy 1:35–6

29

Their Solitary Way

illiam Rainborowe's behaviour was growing ever more extreme. Still a major in Harrison's regiment of horse, in the months after the execution of Charles I he changed his troop's battle-standard to a vivid image of the king's decapitated head, blood still spurting from its neck, with the motto *Salus populi supreme lex*, 'Let the good of the people be the supreme law'. The junior officer who carried it, Cornet Wentworth Day, was a member of the Fifth Monarchists, a millenarian sect which believed the king's death was the prelude to Christ's Second Coming and the rule of the saints on earth. Their colonel, while a great deal more moderate, was nevertheless convinced that a day was coming soon when 'the powers of the world shall be given into the hands of the Lord and his saints'. As Harrison told a meeting of the General Council at Whitehall, 'this is the day, God's own day, wherein He is coming forth in glory in the world'.[1]

In May 1649 elements of Harrison's regiment were involved in a Leveller-inspired mutiny; it was put down by Cromwell, who surprised the mutineers as they were camped at Burford in Oxfordshire, had three of the ringleaders shot and gave 'a handsome cudgelling' to the rest.[2] Although Stephen Winthrop's troop had been one of those who joined in the mutiny, Stephen's military career was unaffected. William, however, was dismissed from the army, even though there is no evidence that he or his men mutinied. Presumably his extreme views and his sympathy for the Levellers made him a dangerous influence in the overheated aftermath of Burford.

William applied for a captaincy in the navy, but his application was vetoed by the Council of State. No reason was given, although there is little doubt that his extremism had something to do with it. And that extremism was being channelled in ever more curious directions. He joined the Ranters — if 'joined' is really the right word for a tendency rather than a religious sect, a vague association of ex-Baptists, ex-congregationalists, ex-everything.

The Ranters believed . . . well, what *did* they believe? According to their enemies, of whom there were many, this 'mad crew' was fond of nude dancing, rude songs, group sex, drinking and blaspheming.[3] They accepted 'no sacrament, no baptism, no duty, no obedience, no Devil, no hell'.[4] They refuted the idea of sin. They were 'libertines, who turn[ed] the grace of God into wantonness'.[5] Ranters were 'a people so dronish, that the whole course of their lives is but one continued scene of sottishness, their gestures filthy, their words obscene, and blasphemous, and all their deeds which they wretchedly glory in, impious, and horrid'.[6]

Unsurprisingly, there was a ready readership for the steady flow of pamphlets which purported to offer authentic and lurid descriptions of the Ranters in action, their 'damnable and diabolical opinions, their detestable lives and actions'.[7] Often with pictures.

Equally unsurprisingly, the Ranters themselves took a rather different view of their diabolical opinions and detestable lives. Believing that God is in all things, and all things are God, they rejected all formal worship, and dismissed the idea of sin. 'To the pure, all things are pure' was a favourite maxim. This pantheism, which was often coupled with an intensely personal experience of Christ, led to many of the excesses which the popular press dwelt on in such detail, including promiscuity, 'community of wives' and blasphemy. They believed that heaven was already here; there would be no day of judgement (although confusingly, many Ranters believed they were living through the Last Days); and all human-made laws and ordinances could, *should*, be disregarded.

Its subversive nature, its determination to destroy the social order and confound all the old certainties, meant that Ranterism lent itself naturally to radical political thinking, and after Burford several Ranter polemicists saw it as an extension of, and an advance upon, the Levellerism of John Lilburne and Thomas Rainborowe. 'I will overturn, overturn, overturn', proclaimed the Ranter preacher Abiezer Coppe, quoting Ezekiel 21:27. For Coppe, an ex-army chaplain, God Himself was a Leveller, coming, he announced, 'to Level in good earnest, to Level to some purpose, to Level with a witness, to Level the Hills with the Valleys, and to lay the Mountains low'.[8] The rich man was going to have to deliver up his riches, or Coppe's God would cut his throat. The old order was doomed: 'Howl, howl, ye nobles, howl ye rich men for the miseries that are coming upon you.'[9]

The revelations of Ranters like Coppe were so dramatic, their behaviour so bizarre, that the political implications of their teaching is sometimes forgotten. Essentially Coppe became a fool for God. He preached naked. He kissed the feet of beggars and cripples. He wandered the streets of London haranguing the wealthy, with bulging eyes, gnashing teeth and outstretched arms, proclaiming the 'notable day of the Lord' to them.

In the months following the mutiny at Burford, when their cause seemed lost in the army, a number of Levellers toyed with Ranterism, drawn to its message of revolution and rebellion. William Rainborowe became involved with Laurence Clarkson, a Lancashire tailor and one-time army preacher who had embraced and then discarded the Anglicans, the Presbyterians and the Baptists (he was 'dipped' in the moat of the Tower of London) before arriving in 1649 at pantheism and the Ranters. As Clarkson later recalled, he preached a distinctly libertarian message:

> There was no sin, but as man esteemed it sin, and therefore none can be free from sin, till in purity it be acted as no sin, for I judged that pure to me, which to a dark understanding was impure, for to the pure all things, yea all acts were pure.[10]

In the course of 1649 Clarkson gathered a group of like-minded disciples who wished, like him, to be made free. Some made free more than others: finding inspiration and justification in the Song of Solomon, he entertained a steady stream of women converts in his lodgings at Rood Lane in the City, 'which then were called *The Headquarters*'.[11] He preached that there was no such thing as property, no 'mine and thine', and therefore there could be no theft or cheating or lying; and that at death, the soul returned to become one with God. When he worried that he might have got this wrong, 'then a cup of wine would wash away this doubt'.[12] He occasionally tottered home to his long-suffering wife, who was raising their children in Suffolk.

William Rainborowe's involvement with this self-styled 'Captain of the Rant' dates from this Rood Lane period. William hosted meetings of Clarkson's followers and, according to rumour, played a full part in their various activities. He also helped to finance the publication in 1650 of Clarkson's somewhat opaque manifesto, *A Single Eye*, which set out to show 'what God is within, and what without; how He is said to be one, yet two; when two and not one, yet then one, and not two'.[13]

Now, this wasn't at all what the Independents had meant when they pressed for religious toleration. 1650 saw Parliament pass a spate of laws designed both to create a more godly society and at the same time to curb the excesses of the Ranters and the various other unorthodox sects springing up all over the place. There were Acts for the more frequent preaching of the Gospel in dissident parts of the country, for the better observation of the Lord's Day, for 'preventing of profane swearing and cursing' and, in August 1650, an Act against blasphemy and 'execrable opinions derogatory to the honour of God, and destructive to human society'. This last made it a crime for anyone to claim to be God or equal with God; or to suggest that adultery, swearing or drunkenness were holy; or to profess that 'unrighteousness in persons, or the acts of uncleanness, profane swearing, drunkenness, and the like filthiness and bruitishness, are not unholy and forbidden the Word of God'.[14] Penalties ranged from six months in gaol for a first offence, to banishment out of the country for a second. Specific concerns over the activities of the Ranters also led that summer to the formation of a parliamentary committee charged with the suppression of 'the obscene, licentious, and impious practices, used by persons, under pretence of liberty [or] religion'.[15]

Freedom had its limits.

And both Laurence Clarkson and William Rainborowe had exceeded them. Clarkson was arrested and hauled before the committee for suppressing licentious and impious practices, where he was interrogated about his behaviour – and the behaviour of others. Did he encourage adultery? He dodged the question, leading one of his interrogators to say it was a sad thing if honest men's wives might be deluded in this way; and another to reply 'he feared not his wife, she was too old'.[16]

'Did not Major Rainsborough, and the rest lie with other women?' Not that he knew, said Clarkson. They kept up the attack: referring to *A Single Eye*, 'Did not Major Rainsborough and these men [whose names had been found written into an almanack in Clarkson's possession] give you moneys to print this book?' What book? asked Clarkson. By his own account, he played with his adversaries, batting away their questions, confounding their arguments. The truth was less flattering: he confessed to 'making and publishing of the impious and blasphemous book, called, *A Single Eye*', and he implicated William.[17]

On 27 September Parliament passed an Act repealing a series of Elizabethan statutes aimed at recusants, which fined people for non-attendance at church and insisted on uniformity of worship. That same day, mindful of being criticised for being too liberal, the Commons decreed that Clarkson should be banished. All copies of *A Single Eye* were to be burned by the common hangman. And because of his support for Clarkson and the Ranters, William was dismissed as a JP for Middlesex and barred for the future from 'bearing or executing the office of a Justice of Peace' anywhere in the commonwealth.[18]

William and Clarkson were the only two named in the order, which was posted all over London and printed in the news-books. The severity of the sentences, declared *Mercurius politicus*, in a reference to the repeal of the recusancy laws, 'may serve to stop the slanderous mouths of those that publish abroad such vile reports of this *Commonwealth*, as if they intended to countenance impious and *licentious practices*, under pretence of *Religion* and *Liberty*'.[19] The sentence of banishment was never carried out, and Clarkson soon moved on to his next enthusiasm, astrology.

But William's outing as a Ranter put an end to his ambitions for any kind of public office. He retired to Higham Park in Northamptonshire, a Crown property with a tumbledown Great Lodge which he acquired in 1650, and which he subsequently sold for £5,498 15s. 2d., leading Royalist versifiers to sneer that 'Rainsborough nimble/sleighted his Thimble,/When Higham Park such profit did bring.'[20] It was from Higham that he wrote a long and rambling plea to the Admiralty commissioners in February 1653, asking for a chance to play his part in the war with the Dutch. He waited for the call, he said, 'not doubting but the same power if it call me by your honours will enable me (though a weak and unworthy Instrument) to answer your trust wth a mainfest faithfulness . . . I hope these few words may sufficiently speak my heart and remove all former apprehensions of my spirit.'[21]

It was no good. The Council of State vetoed his appointment again, doubting the sincerity of his conversion to orthodoxy. They were right. A couple of years later a list of Northamptonshire gentry who were known to be sympathetic towards Quakers fell into the council's hands. It included the name of 'Wm. Rainsborrow of Higham Park, whose brother was murdered.'[22]

Nehemiah Bourne had returned to his roots. In 1650 he attended a gathered church at Stepney, near where he was raised. It had been founded six years earlier by a group who wished, in the words of their covenant, 'to walk in all the ways of Christ held out unto them in the Gospel'.[23] The congregation was drawn from mariners' communities in East London – Wapping and Shadwell, Limehouse and Ratcliffe. Nehemiah's sister was a founder member with her husband, the Ratcliffe shipwright John Hoxton, uncle to the Rainborowes.

The Stepney meeting thrived. By the time Nehemiah attended – probably as a visitor, since there's no record of his admission – it had upward of 120 members. And the God they worshipped was a jealous God. In the spring of 1650 Mrs Browne of Limehouse, one of the first to be admitted to the Stepney meeting, was called to account by the congregation for her 'disorderly walking'. Were they accusing the woman of drunkenness? Immorality? Not a bit of it. They were upset because Mrs Browne dared to attend meetings at another gathered church, Coleman Street in the City, led by the Independent John Goodwin.

Mrs Browne did not care to be lectured by the other members of her church. She told them in no uncertain terms that she was not going to leave off going to hear Goodwin preach, and that the Stepney meeting had fallen into certain doctrinal errors, which she listed for their benefit.

Most of the members argued it was she who had fallen into error. Only Nehemiah spoke up to press for the more tolerant course: given that Mrs Browne was determined to keep listening to Goodwin, he said, why didn't Stepney simply grant her a dismission from their congregation so that she could seek admission to Coleman Street?

No one supported him. 'It was answered that if the church be slighted and offence given, there ought to be satisfaction given before any dismission be thought of.'[24] And by granting Mrs Browne leave to go to Coleman Street, Nehemiah's opponents said the meeting would effectively be condoning her low opinion of Stepney's theology.

Mrs Browne left anyway. And so did Nehemiah, although not – or not solely – because of the hard line on dissent adopted by the members of the Stepney meeting. In 1649 Parliament had begun a major review of the navy, building new ships and remodelling both the administration and the officer corps. Three new frigates were commissioned, and Nehemiah was thought of as a possible captain for one of them, but he was too involved with his Atlantic trading to spare the time for naval service. In January 1650 he came to the attention of the Committee of the Admiralty again when he returned from his latest New England voyage with news of a fierce skirmish with two Dutch warships, in which, it was said, 'he behaved very gallantly'.[25] The committee recommended him to the Generals of the Fleet, again for one of the new frigates, promising that 'we will endeavour to take him off from his merchant affairs. He . . . will do the state and yourselves both service and honour.'[26]

They were as good as their word. When the Commons received for their approval a list of captains to command Parliament's ships for the summer, Major Nehemiah Bourne (he still used the rank he'd had in Thomas Rainborowe's Eastern Association regiment back in 1644, and he kept it until his death half a century later) was assigned as captain of 'the Great Frigate at Woolwich'.[27] This was the 727-ton *Faithful Speaker*, launched from the yard at Woolwich in the final week of April, with a complement of 250 men and fifty guns, and named for Speaker William Lenthall. A second frigate being fitted out at Deptford was the *Valiant Fairfax*; the third was named the *President*. (The Royalist press helpfully suggested that more appropriate names would have been the *Perjury*, the *Covenants Breaker* and the *Pilate*.[28])

Nehemiah wasn't the only New Englander to hold a command in this new-modelled navy. Over the next couple of years, around thirty men with New England experience joined him. Thomas Graves gave up the transatlantic routes he had been sailing for nearly two decades to pursue a career in the navy. The man in charge of naval finances was Richard Hutchinson, brother-in-law of Anne, who had come back to England around the time of her murder in 1643. And his boss was the ex-governor of Massachusetts (and ex-disciple of Anne Hutchinson), Sir Henry Vane.

Hutchinson had links with the gathered church at Stepney, as did other leading naval officers. Some served as churchwardens or vestrymen. At least one, Edward Witheridge, had a similar career to Nehemiah's, in that he was a merchant-mariner who had settled in Boston, where he joined Cotton's church, before returning to England, attending at Stepney and joining Parliament's new navy. One suspects not only that the Stepney congregation was a tight community, but also that its strong maritime contacts and its links with the godly in New England stood it in good stead when it came to recruiting saints for the navy.

So did family. By the late spring of 1652, commercial rivalries between the Commonwealth and the Dutch Republic were poised to tip over into war, exacerbated by the passage the previous year of the first Navigation Act, which stipulated that English trade must be carried in English ships. Nehemiah was made captain of the forty-two-gun *Andrew*, and commander of a squadron of the summer fleet under Robert Blake. His brother John Bourne was captain of the *Assistance*, and a Bartholomew Bourne was serving as John's lieutenant. Hannah's brother Anthony Earning was captain of the *Reformation*. Thomas Graves was captain of the *President*.

When war with the Dutch did come, it was in that chaotic, confused way that wars have. In the middle of May a Dutch fleet in the Channel sailed close to the English coast in search of shelter from foul weather. The fleet encountered Nehemiah's squadron, which was patrolling in the Downs, and two officers went aboard to explain that their presence shouldn't be regarded as a hostile act.

Nehemiah wasn't convinced. As far as he was concerned, the behaviour of the Dutch was 'a high affront to this state, and a great provocation to us'.[29] He asked the Dutch officers why there was no sign of their admiral, Maarten Tromp, and they made matters worse by saying that Tromp wouldn't approach Nehemiah's squadron because he didn't want to strike his colours, the time-honoured acknowledgement of English sovereignty in the narrow seas.

> To which I returned him answer [reported Nehemiah], that we should expect nothing more nor less, but what they know to be the ancient right of this nation, and that would be expected not only here, but elsewhere in these seas wherever we met him . . . We had the strong God on our side, who would judge between the nations, and whether they intended war or peace, it did not signify much to me, but wished the hand of God might be upon that man, who should be first cause or ground of the breach between us.[30]

Whatever Tromp thought of this, he stayed put for the night. The next day, around noon, General Blake and the rest of the English fleet arrived to join Nehemiah's squadron off Goodwin Sands, and the Dutch set sail. Although they outnumbered the English by more than two to one, Nehemiah assumed they would head for home to avoid a confrontation; but Tromp made straight for Blake with flags flying. Blake fired one warning shot, a reminder to Tromp to strike his colours. When nothing happened, he fired a second. Then a third, which hit the Dutch ship and killed a crewman. Tromp responded with a broadside. Blake responded with another. The war had begun.

The Battle of Goodwin Sands, as it became known, was a muddled affair. It dragged on for five hours in the slow, stately, terrible way of naval battles until at dusk, having lost two ships in the fighting, Tromp withdrew. English casualties were relatively light, with no ship having more than a handful of fatalities, but the fleet sustained damage enough. 'Our rigging, masts, and sails [were] shot, most of us,' said Nehemiah, 'and many shot in our hulls, notwithstanding we have lost so few men.'[31]

His account of this opening engagement, which was sent in a letter to a merchant friend in London two days later, is interesting not just for its description of events, important though that is; or for Nehemiah's uncompromising attitude towards the Dutch, whom he regarded as at first full of 'insolent bravado', and then as cowards who had dishonoured themselves by running away from a much smaller fleet.

His words also show an uncompromising religious fervour, a confidence in divine approval. His letter is peppered with references to God's favour. The outcome of the battle is evidence 'that He is amongst us, and will appear in glory'. Nehemiah is 'very confident upon very safe grounds of faith, that [the Dutch] should be as driven stubble before the whirlwind of the Lord . . . This is the first of God's appearing for us by sea.' Although never in a majority, there was a substantial body of saints among the shipmasters of the new Commonwealth navy, with prominent Independents like Hugh Peter and Thomas Rainborowe's old chaplain, Thomas Brookes, active in recruiting them. In victory, they gloried in the knowledge that their providentialist God was on their side. In defeat, they searched their souls to find a reason for His deserting them. Nehemiah's brother John was dejected after a storm forced him back to harbour, fearing that God had abandoned him: 'it is not so easy a matter to live the life of faith' when things were going wrong, he wrote.[32] And when they were uncertain, they prayed for guidance, sometimes in surprisingly direct and innocent ways, as when, in the Channel in the early spring of 1653, Blake's fleet was hunting the Dutch in heavy fog. He summoned his officers and together they asked God to tell them where the enemy were. They found their answer in 2 Chronicles 20:16, 'Tomorrow go ye down against them: behold, they come up by the cliff of Ziz'. 'And no sooner did daylight dawn, but betwixt us and the shore we saw the enemy's fleet.'[33] God was an Englishman.

Nehemiah didn't know it at the time, but on the day he went into action at Goodwin Sands the Council of State made him rear admiral of the fleet under Blake, with William Penn, father of the founder of Pennsylvania, as vice admiral. Nehemiah was on active service in the *Andrew* throughout the summer campaign of 1652, which culminated in the English victory at the Battle of the Kentish Knock in September, where 'Major Bourne with the *Andrew* led on, and charged the Hollanders stoutly.'[34]

At the end of the year he changed careers again when the navy commissioners, who were responsible for the maintenance of the fleet, decided they needed to expand in order to meet the needs of war. In December they recruited three new commissioners: Nehemiah, Francis Willoughby and Edward Hopkins. All were New Englanders: Francis Willoughby had just come back from Charlestown, where he had known Nehemiah well enough to name his son after him (and his daughter after Hannah Bourne). Hopkins, who had been both governor and deputy governor of Connecticut before his return that year, was highly regarded in the colonies: John Winthrop had praised him as a man 'of great esteem for religion and wisdom'; and Edward Winslow, one of the Pilgrim Fathers, respected him as one 'that makes conscience of his words as well as his actions'.[35]

The ease with which the talented seventeenth-century gentleman could move from one discipline to another was impressive. Think of John Vanbrugh, morphing effortlessly (or so it seems) from tea-importer to soldier-spy to successful playwright, before becoming a builder of palaces. Or Christopher Wren, first an anatomist and an inventor, then an academic whose name was known all over Europe for his contribution to astronomy – and all this before, in his mid-thirties, he turned his thoughts to architecture.

They are the famous. Their stars burned bright. They take their place in every history of the century. But they're not the only ones to show a versatility, an adaptability which is all but lost in our own compartmentalised age of specialisms and specialisation. Nehemiah began his working life as a Wapping shipwright. On both sides of the Atlantic he built and owned ships, he traded across half the world. He fought as a soldier under Thomas Rainsborowe, as a naval commander under Blake. And now he had become a senior naval administrator. That's quite a career path. One might argue that the sea forms a common strand. But the skills are quite different. Imagine saying to an aeronautics engineer, 'You know about planes. Run an airline.'

Nehemiah took to his new role with enthusiasm. In February 1653 he was on the Thames and looking for men to press into service. When they proved hard to find in daylight, he surprised them in darkness: 'This morning about four o'clock', he reported to the Admiralty, 'I called the assistance of the constable and made a thorough search all over the town [of Gravesend], and very early sent away about fifty men.'[36] Still not satisfied, he took to the water and boarded boats and barges coming down from London before they could land, and their crews disperse. No doubt that didn't make him popular, but it certainly made him effective.

Over the next year the Committee of the Admiralty was bombarded with long letters from Nehemiah as he rode or sailed from London to the dockyards at Chatham, to Gravesend and Deal and Dover. The *Fairfax* has limped into the Downs, with 'masts much wounded, and the ship very much shattered'; he thinks it best to send her up to Chatham, because the yards at Portsmouth are too busy.[37] Locals are stripping cables, sails and anything else they can find from Dutch prizes moored at Dover; he searches houses in the town 'where I have found several hawsers, coils of rope, and sails, &c.' which the 'sharking people' freely confess to have taken, declaring they have done nothing wrong.[38] At Gravesend, one ship needs hammocks, another guns and stores. A third wants a surgeon. The press gangs are sending down unsuitable recruits, he complains, 'landsmen that I find were never at sea and others that are merely a burden to the service'.[39]

In April 1653, Cromwell expelled the MPs who remained in Parliament after Pride's Purge, the Rump. 'In the name of God, go!' he told them, bringing a company of musketeers into the House to help any who were still undecided. They were replaced by a nominated assembly selected by senior army officers for their godliness; but this assembly of saints proved too radical and in December it too was dissolved, and Cromwell was installed as Lord Protector of the realm, supported by a Council of State which was dominated by senior army officers.

These domestic political upheavals don't seem to have had much of an impact on Nehemiah. When the Rump was expelled, he was in the Thames Estuary making himself unpopular with the Newcastle coal fleet by pressing its crews. ('We were forced to spend forty or fifty shots before I could make them stay.'[40]) And when Cromwell threw away his principles and assumed the title of Lord Protector he was at Harwich on the east coast, casting insolent sailors into gaol and exulting at the 'great and immediate appearance of the Lord against the Dutch' in a storm which wrecked a good part of their fleet.[41]

There were casualties amongst the clan that year. Nehemiah's brother John was badly wounded in the head during the Battle of Portland; his lieutenant, Bartholomew Bourne, was killed in the same action. And after the Battle of Scheveningen in August, John Winthrop junior received a letter from a friend in England telling him that 'Mr Graves of Charlestown [is] slain.'[42] Now a rear admiral and in command of Nehemiah's old ship, the *Andrew*, Thomas Graves was one of several hundred Englishmen killed at Scheveningen, the last major battle of the First Dutch War. Graves 'of Charlestown', who had spent twenty years plying back and forth between the two Englands and had never quite managed to settle in either, was laid to rest eight days after the battle, when the battered fleet anchored at Aldeburgh in Suffolk. His widow Katherine, who had stayed in Charlestown when he came over, was granted £1,000 in compensation by Parliament: £300 for herself and £140 for each of the couple's five children. Quite a sum for a husband whose life was so separate from hers, so distant.

Stephen and Judith Winthrop continued to reassure their friends and families in New England that they would rather be there than in England. And yet they stayed. Stephen refused to sell his property in Massachusetts, on the understanding that he would be coming back. And yet they stayed. He constantly complained about the climate in England. 'The air is too moist for me, & breeds rheums & coughs', he told his brother John. If only he didn't feel so ill, 'I think I should come away immediately'.[43]

And yet they stayed.

They bought a pair of new houses in fashionable James Street in Westminster. They had a family: in the ten years after the deaths from smallpox of their two eldest, Judith gave birth to at least more five children, of whom three girls survived. And Stephen made a career. One reason for the Winthrops' reluctance to go back to Boston was the perception that the Massachusetts economy was still in a poor state. In fact it was recovering from the depression of the 1640s; but still as late as 1657 Stephen was expressing a hope that New England 'may have its times to flourish again, especial if they could get up some good manufactures. I hope the worst is past with them, & that subsistence will be easier gained hereafter.'[44]

But the main reason for their staying in old England was that for Stephen it was a land of opportunity. Roger Williams, who saw a lot of him when he was in London to lobby Cromwell over a patent to settle Providence Plantations, described the young officer as 'a great man for soul liberty'; but Stephen was never a political or religious radical like his brothers-in-law Thomas and William Rainborowe.[45] He was much more in the mould of Hugh Peter, whom he met often in the Whitehall corridors of power – a man who saw no contradiction between his genuine Puritanism and his equally genuine worldly ambition.

Stephen initially carved out a career in the New Model. When William's politics proved too much and he was ejected from Harrison's regiment of horse after the 1649 Leveller mutiny at Burford, Stephen remained. Within the year he was in Wales, filling William's place as Harrison's major and 'left with some horse to keep quiet these parts'.[46] The godly Harrison became more and more involved with the Fifth Monarchists – according to Roger Williams, who liked him, he was 'most high flown for the Kingdom of the Saints and the Fifth Monarchy' – until at the end of 1653 he was deprived of his military commission.[47] Once again Stephen stepped up, this time being promoted to colonel of the regiment. He was regarded as a safe man.

Which was why when Cromwell summoned Parliament in September 1656 (the second of his protectorate) Stephen was returned for the Scottish constituency of Banff and Aberdeen. He wasn't particularly active – his only significant contribution was to speak against members taking oaths – and when Parliament asked Cromwell to accept the title of king, Stephen was non-committal. 'What will be the issue I cannot tell,' he wrote to brother John, 'but it will soon be resolved for or against.'[48]

So it was. Many of Cromwell's old comrades in the army lobbied hard to prevent his accepting the crown, and although he was sorely tempted, he could not bring himself to do it. 'I would not seek to set up that which Providence hath destroyed and laid in the dust,' he said, 'and I would not build Jericho again.'[49]

One suspects Stephen would not have minded much either way. Within the parameters set by his faith and the victory of his side – parameters which took for granted the validity of Protestantism, Puritanism, Providentialism – he had little of Nehemiah's godly zeal and none of Thomas Rainborowe's passionate egalitarian republicanism. He was a moderate, a reminder that Stephen's 'side' was a spectrum, a holy alliance, a radiant cluster of dissidence and dissent and conflict.

Although Stephen was only in his thirties, he was frequently in poor health during the early 1650s. While his regiment was stationed in Scotland he was sent home because he was 'unfit to endure the field', said his commanding officer; 'I think he will hardly return again.'[50] He did return, but he was a martyr to his sciatica ('*zeatica*', he called it), which had been brought on by lying on the ground in wet fields when he was campaigning; and he made several trips to Bath in the mid-1650s to try and cure what he called his 'lameness'. His regiment was ordered back to London from Scotland in 1656, which might have been some relief; but he was no better, and for much of the winter he was bedridden and confined to his James Street house, where Judith gave birth to a boy in February. The baby didn't survive for very long.

In the summer of 1658 word reached John Winthrop junior in Boston that Stephen was very poorly indeed. There were even unconfirmed rumours 'that God hath taken him out of this life', John wrote to his son in London, 'which makes me sadly to bewail the loss of so dear a friend, and brother'.[51] Could the boy find out if the stories about his uncle were true?

They were. Stephen had been sick enough in May to make out his will: it was proved on 19 August. He left almost everything to Judith for her life, and then to his three daughters and 'such child or children as my said wife shall be now great with'. There were a few bequests – to his Winthrop nephews and nieces; to

Mary Rainborowe, 'daughter of my brother in law William Rainborowe' (this is the only evidence we have that Major William had a child); and £100 to the poor of Boston. In an exercise of filial devotion to the parents whose graves Stephen had never seen, he stipulated that in order to receive this legacy the inhabitants of Boston had to put up a monument 'for my deceased father and mother . . . of fifty pounds value at the least'.[52]

Two weeks later, while Judith still mourned her husband's death, there was another death, one which, unlike Stephen's, was destined to shake the world. At three o'clock in the afternoon of 3 September, Oliver Cromwell died at Whitehall. He had been ill for some time, and a chest infection turned into pneumonia. That night saw one of the fiercest storms in memory: Royalists said it was the Devil coming to take his soul down to hell.

A Land and Times Obscure

'The time is coming', wrote Nehemiah Bourne, when God 'will be jealous for his people, and will thrash the mountains of the world'.[1]

Nehemiah was writing in May 1659, a momentous time for the Commonwealth. Richard Cromwell, to whom his father had passed the title of Lord Protector as a king would hand on his crown, had been forced from office. The Rump Parliament, expelled by Oliver Cromwell back in 1653, had been restored. At a stroke fears which had been growing among republicans and those who still held to the Good Old Cause, fears that under 'Queen Dick' England would drift towards monarchism and the old system of rule by king, Lords and Commons, were put to rest.

Nehemiah was still a navy commissioner. He was still travelling between Harwich and London, complaining about government inefficiency and petty thefts from the stores and telling everyone who would listen how overworked and underpaid he was, while pursuing a few private enterprises of his own. He built a new drydock and shipwright's yard at Wapping, with stores for hemp, pitch and tar, and some workmen's houses; and continued to do a little trading on his own account, investing in ventures to New England and bringing back masts, which he was presumably able to sell to himself as a navy commissioner. No doubt he got a good price.

He retained his godliness and his republicanism, and by the late 1650s he had established close links with some of the senior officers in the army, to the extent that he was present at meetings at the Whitehall lodgings of Charles Fleetwood, commander-in-chief of the army, where the General Council decided to oust Richard Cromwell.

Nehemiah approved wholeheartedly of the army coup. As far as he was concerned, 'the cavaliers of Parliament' wanted a king. 'And what king think you?' he wrote in a letter to an unnamed friend in Boston. 'I can tell because I have good authority for it; this gentleman [Richard Cromwell], who they would have made so much haste to dress and set on horseback, was but to warm the saddle for another whom they better loved and liked.'[2] Charles Stuart was waiting in the wings – or more accurately, just across the English Channel. Now, to everyone's amazement, God had shown His hand and changed the government 'from monarchy to a free state and commonwealth . . . truly we are in some measure raised in our hopes that the Lord hath begun to breathe a spirit of life in dead bones'.[3]

His joy was short-lived. Within weeks, England was seething with rumours of a Royalist rising. The navy was ordered to sea to watch for signs of an invasion force, the army was mobilised, and garrisons in key towns across the country were strengthened in readiness.

The crisis was serious enough to propel William Rainborowe back into public life – and serious enough for the authorities to take him. On 19 July he was at the bar of the House of Commons, to present a petition from the Northamptonshire gentry asking that the militia be placed in safe hands. The House responded immediately by making him a 'Commissioner for the Militia in the County of Northampton', the first time he had been allowed to hold any public appointment since the Ranters and the scandal over the publication of *A Single Eye* nearly ten years earlier. Three weeks later he was made colonel of a regiment of horse in Northampton, and he set about buying guns for the coming struggle.

The regiment was never raised: William reported ruefully that a third of the Northamptonshire commissioners summoned to organise their forces didn't bother to turn up, and of those that did, more than half refused to swear the required oath to maintain the Commonwealth 'as it is declared by Parliament without a single person kingship or house of peers'.[4] This rather limited their part in the day's proceedings. But William was rehabilitated, for a moment.

The rumours had been true, and the expected risings came at the beginning of August, but a combination of good intelligence and the efficiency of the New Model Army proved too much for the small bands of disorganised and badly trained insurgents. Large numbers of them were rounded up before they could reach their prearranged muster points. Others got cold feet when they saw the extent of the military presence on the streets of their towns, and stayed at home. Only in the north-west, where warnings from fellow Royalists to abandon the rebellion didn't arrive in time, was there a serious challenge. Sir George Booth occupied Chester and set off for York with 4,000 men, assuming he would gather more supporters on his way. He was intercepted by John Lambert with a slightly larger force on 19 August, near Northwich in Cheshire. The insurgents scattered in the face of New Model cavalry and Booth tried to run for the Continent, only to be captured (while dressed as a woman, which caused no end of bad jokes in London) and taken to the Tower.

But although the Royalist insurrections hadn't led to a popular revolution, it was impossible to ignore the fact that there was a good deal of support in the country for the return of the king. While Lambert was marching north to meet Booth and his men, Nehemiah went on one of his regular trips to inspect the naval yard at Harwich. He found things falling apart – the stores were empty, a vessel was in such bad shape that she was about to sink in the harbour. Much worse than this, though, was the mood of the local people. They were 'embittered and malignant', he reported, 'and want nothing but opportunity and power to give trouble to the army'. Some of them were openly declaring for the king, and the governor of the town was doing nothing about it. The jubilation Nehemiah had felt only three months earlier was gone. Now, with a rising sense of panic, he wrote to the Admiralty, pleading with them 'to raise a company of the well-affected, to secure the town and port'.[5]

The autumn and winter saw confusion and chaos. In a repeat of the events of 1647–8, radical officers in the army petitioned for arrears of pay and a settlement of the relationship between the army and Parliament. The Rump sacked nine of the officers, including John Lambert, and demoted General Fleetwood. In reply, Lambert's troops occupied Westminster and expelled the Rump in September, only for it to be reinstated once more at the end of December as opposition to the military junta which replaced it grew, and the New Model – which as always held the key to power – broke in pieces. George Monck, a moderate Presbyterian and commander-in-chief of Commonwealth forces in Scotland, brought his 7,000-strong army south in support of Parliament, scattering Lambert's forces on the way and occupying London. Once more it seemed like the Last Days were here, that as regimes toppled and God prepared to thrash the mountains of the world, the 1,000-year reign of Christ on earth was about to begin. 'Come now, King Jesus!' cried the Fifth Monarchists.

They got a king. Just not the king they wanted.

The restoration of the monarchy in 1660 did indeed mark the End of Days for the Rainborowe clan, as it did for the Good Old Cause and, in a more literal sense, for forty-nine individuals who were judged to be guilty of 'execrable treason in sentencing to death, or signing the instrument for the horrid murder, or being instrumental in taking away the precious life of our late sovereign Lord Charles the first of glorious memory'.[6]

The psalm-singing Fifth Monarchist Thomas Harrison, colonel to both William Rainborowe and Stephen Winthrop, was one of the first to die. And he died well, with an unshaken belief in the rightness of his actions and sure that the restoration was a temporary setback. 'Where is your good old cause now?' jeered someone from the crowd as he was dragged to the scaffold. 'With a cheerful smile [Harrison] clapped his hands on his breast and said, Here it is, and I go to seal it with my blood.'[7] His last words on the ladder were 'By God I have leaped over a wall, by God I have

runn'd through a troop, and by my God I will go through this
death, and he will make it easy to me.'[8] God didn't. The regi-
cide's sentence was to be hanged, drawn and quartered. After
being half-hanged, he was taken down from the gallows still
conscious, 'and saw his bowels thrown into the fire'.[9] According
to one account, he was *still* conscious when the third part of the
sentence was being carried out, and struggled with the executioner
as he was being dismembered.

Three days later it was Hugh Peter's turn. Peter, who was in
ill health and who hadn't taken much part in public affairs since
the fall of Richard Cromwell, hadn't signed Charles I's death
warrant and wasn't on the original list of those exempted from
pardon. But he was hated – for his close relationship with
Cromwell, his demagogic sermons to the New Model, his support
for the king's execution. There were also rumours that he had
been the masked executioner who separated Charles I's head
from his body. In June the new Parliament, which was dominated
by Royalists and Presbyterians, resolved that 'Hugh Peter be
excepted out of the Act of General Pardon and Oblivion.'[10] He
was tried at the Old Bailey on 13 October, the day that Harrison
died, on a charge of 'compassing and imagining the death of
the king'.[11] The verdict was a foregone conclusion – Peter made
a half-hearted defence, with none of his previous flair for rhetoric
– and on 16 October he went to the scaffold, accompanied by
John Cook, who had prosecuted the king, and Thomas Harrison's
head, which was placed on Cook's sledge as a memento mori.
Nice touch.

Accounts of Peter's death are contradictory, a confusion driven
partly by the determined assault on his character by the Royalist
press, and partly by the fact that the crowd was cheering so loudly
that no one could hear his last words. He was said to have smiled
at the last, saying 'This is a good day. He is come that I have long
looked for.' What is clear is that the crowds rejoiced at his death.
'When his head was cut off, and held up aloft upon the end of
a spear, there was such a shout, as if the people of England had
acquired a victory.'[12]

The retribution continued for years. John Lambert and Henry
Vane were spared death, on the grounds that neither had signed
the king's death warrant. Lambert spent the rest of his life – he

died in 1684 – languishing in various island prisons; but Charles II's government had second thoughts about sparing Vane, who was beheaded on Tower Hill on 14 June 1662. For some, even death offered no escape: the corpses of Oliver Cromwell, Henry Ireton, who had died on the Irish campaign back in 1651, and two others, Colonel Thomas Pride and John Bradshaw, who had presided over Charles I's trial, were disinterred, hanged, decapitated and cast into a pit.

Some regicides did manage to escape. They plea-bargained. They fled to the Continent, although that didn't guarantee their safety: John Lisle was assassinated in Lausanne by Royalist agents in 1664. And in an act of self-serving treachery that still taints his name, George Downing, nephew of John Winthrop, one of the first Harvard graduates and a one-time chaplain in the New Model Army, masterminded the kidnapping of three regicides in the Netherlands, including his ex-colonel, John Okey. They were brought back to England and executed in 1662. 'In New England,' wrote an eighteenth-century governor of Massachusetts, 'it became a proverbial expression to say of a false man who betrayed his trust, that he was an arrant George Downing.'[13]

New England offered sanctuary to three of the regicides. John Dixwell, who had been undistinguished until he signed the king's death warrant, remained undistinguished, living quietly under the name of James Davids in New Haven until his death in 1689. The exploits of the other two, Edward Whalley and his son-in-law William Goffe, have become the stuff of legend. Whalley, the colonel replaced by Thomas Rainborowe during the siege of Worcester, and the godly Goffe, who at the Putney debates kept reminding his fellow officers of the need for prayer, arrived in New Haven in July 1660 and went on the run, chased by two Royalist agents brandishing warrants from the king. Sympathisers, including the minister John Davenport and the colony's governor, hid them in their homes, in cellars and cabins in the forest, in a cave. They eventually settled in Hadley, Massachusetts, where the most famous of many stories about them is set. During the vicious Indian wars of 1675–8 the townspeople of Hadley were gathered in their meeting house to pray when they were surrounded by a band of hostile Wampanoag. They panicked.

Suddenly, and in the midst of the people there appeared a man of a very venerable aspect, and different from the inhabitants in his apparel, who took the command, arranged, and ordered them in the best military manner, and under his direction they repelled and routed the Indians, and the town was saved. He immediately vanished, and the inhabitants could not account for the phenomenon, but by considering that person as an Angel sent of God upon that special occasion for their deliverance.[14]

Much later they discovered the Angel was Goffe.

In the heady 1790s, when the United States of America was revelling in its new-found independence and revolution in France seemed to promise liberty, equality and fraternity across the western world, Americans saw the story of Goffe and Whalley in simple terms, with their ancestors welcoming fugitives from tyranny to the land of the free. 'All New-England were their friends', wrote one historian in 1794. 'They did not view them as traitors, but as unfortunate sufferers in the noble cause of civil liberty, prostrated by the Restoration, and again lost and overwhelmed in a return and irresistible inundation of tyranny.'[15]

And there's some truth in that. But as with the war, the colonies adopted a cautious line towards the Restoration. To begin with, they weren't at all sure that monarchy was going to stick; they held off from proclaiming Charles II as king until they were. (They had before them the example of poor John Eliot, minister for Roxbury, whose pro-republican and long-delayed *Christian Commonwealth* had been published with impeccably bad timing, just as the Commonwealth collapsed.) They were also anxious, as always, about the prospect of English interference in their affairs. It came in 1662, in the form of an instruction from Charles II. Far from heralding a return to arbitrary tyranny, Charles made a series of demands for religious toleration and political freedoms. Everyone should be allowed to follow the Anglican liturgy if they wished; and 'all persons of good and honest lives and conversations' should be admitted to Communion and their children to baptism. All freeholders should be able to vote in the election of officials, 'though of different persuasions concerning church government'.[16]

New England reacted as it always had done to unpalatable royal commands. It ignored them and hoped they'd go away.

And it remained a bastion of godliness, a haven for the saints. To veterans William Rainborowe and Nehemiah Bourne, New England – even a New England which still set its face against toleration – offered a more palatable alternative to old England, where scores were being settled, dissent was being stamped out and placemen were being insinuated into public life at every level. Nehemiah lost his job as a navy commissioner and went back to the transatlantic trade full-time. William ended up in gaol: his response to the Restoration was to try and sell the guns he had bought for his militia regiment in Northampton, forty cases of pistols; and when the authorities heard what he was up to, he was arrested at his London house in Stepney and thrown into the Gatehouse on suspicion of treason. He spent January 1661 in gaol, and was released on his own bond for £500 on 7 February.

And then both William and Nehemiah went back to New England. As for when they went over, or how long they stayed, that belongs in its due place.

First, though, Martha, for whom the year 1660 also proved to be the end of days. Martha's third husband John Coggan had died in April 1658, leaving her to raise their five-year-old son Caleb alone. Her Charlestown brother-in-law Increase Nowell, on whom she had counted for support in the past, was gone. She was still only forty-one, with a personal fortune of over £1,000 and a life-interest in a good part of Coggan's shops and farms. She expected to marry again.

But no one asked her. At least, no one among the community's leaders, no one to rank with Thomas Coytmore or John Winthrop or John Coggan. There was a farmer, 'a mean man'. And loneliness, a need for male company, a sense that time was passing, led her to encourage this nameless farmer. Only when things had gone too far did she have second thoughts. She grew depressed.

And suddenly she was dead.

The Boston magistrates were told of her death at a meeting on 24 October 1660. It was 'not without suspicion of poison'.[17] In New Haven, Rev. John Davenport heard the story from a man who had heard it from a man in the Bay. 'When she reflected upon what she had done, and what a change of her outward condition she was bringing herself into,' he reported to John Winthrop junior, 'she was discontented, despaired, and took a great quantity of ratsbane.'[18] Everyone believed Martha had taken her own life, a terrible thing then, as it is now. Worse, because the law showed no mercy to the victim. As it happened, just a week earlier the Massachusetts General Court had condemned suicide as a wicked and unnatural practice, and ordered that anyone found to have taken their own life was to be buried by the common highway, and a cartload of stones laid upon the grave 'as a brand of infamy, and as a warning to others to beware of the like damnable practices'.[19] But the Boston magistrates didn't do that. Instead they simply ordered that Martha be given a decent burial. They gave this woman who had been at the heart of the colony's life almost since its birth, they gave her the benefit of the doubt. God have mercy on her soul.

And now the story of the Rainborowe clan breaks in pieces. Their movements appear and disappear, flashes of light half-glimpsed out of the corner of an eye. Judith Winthrop and her children vanish. Where did they go? Her name crops up here and there in legal documents as she tries to sell Stephen's New England property. Decades later one of her daughters is shifted around London from parish to parish with her own children, a pauper that no one wants.

Edward Rainborowe, the baby of the family, who has not figured at all in this story, appears now, only to drift in and out of sight. He's a young naval officer in the last years of the Commonwealth, serving aboard Nehemiah Bourne's old ship, the *Speaker*. By the 1670s he has been in New England, where he was described as 'an intelligent gentleman' with a good knowledge of the Dutch colony of New Netherland; and is living in Knightsbridge, having acquired 1,500 acres of land in Rhode Island Colony that once belonged to Stephen Winthrop.[20]

Nehemiah takes his family back to Boston in 1662; but he can't settle. He's back in London by 1670, importing New England timber. When his patient wife Hannah dies in 1684, seven years before his own end, the inscription on her tomb in the dissenters' burial ground at Moorfields gives a hint of her strength. She has been 'a most suitable companion to him in various and extraordinary paths of divine providence by sea, and land, at home, and in remote parts'.[21]

And Major William Rainborowe? The last glimpse we have of ranting, radical revolutionary William is in 1673, in Boston. His nephew, Thomas's son, is with him. Other than that, all we hear is that 'Major Rainborowe has a thousand pounds in money lying by him, which I perceive he knows not well what to do with.' John Winthrop junior's son asks his father whether they should borrow it if they can get a good rate of interest.[22]

And with that, William vanishes.

So is this where my search for the Rainborowes ends? With a phial of ratsbane and a sad old man clutching his moneybags? I've lost sight of them through their last years. I know I have. I can't find them any more and I probably never will. But to remember only this dying fall, this sadness, is to lose sight of something more important. The Rainborowes mattered. Not only in the way that every life matters, but because they were there at a moment when the world changed. And they helped to change it. They forged links between continents which are still strong today. They fought for a liberty that no one had dreamed possible. For a brief moment they made the world their own, and if they were destined never to enter the promised land, then at least they forged the way.

After all this time, I still don't know the Rainborowes and their clan, Thomas and William and Nehemiah and the rest. Their hearts stay just out of reach. If I'm honest, I'm not even sure I like them, with their hard mix of Puritanism and politics, their ruthless pursuit of personal profit.

But in that strange way the past has of offering confusion when you look for certainties, of taking conflicting emotions and binding them close together, the Rainborowes have made me love them. Now that they're gone and my own search for their promised land has ended in a fade to grey, their passion, their cries for justice, their lust for adventure loom larger than ever. I wish I'd known them.

Notes

Chapter 1

1 Allen B. Hinds (ed.), *Calendar of State Papers Relating to English Affairs in the Archives of Venice*, vol. 21, Longmans, Green & Co. (1916), 280.

2 Knolles, 1,508. The narrative of the *Sampson*'s encounter with the Knights of St John seems to have been written by Roe himself; he mentions it in a letter to Viscount Grandison written from Livorno on 18 September 1628, which is reprinted in Richardson. The original narrative is lost, but a copy was printed in the 4th edition of Knolles' *Historie of the Turkes*, 1,508–11.

3 In 1618 Rainborowe was offered £25 by the Levant Company as a reward for his good service against pirates. He asked to be made a member of the Company instead.

4 Knolles, 1,508.

5 Richardson, 827.

6 Ibid.

7 Knolles, 1, 509.
8 Ibid.
9 Richardson, 827.
10 Quoted in Strachan, 281.

Chapter 2

1 John Stow, *The Survey of London*, J. M. Dent & Sons (1940), 113.
2 Ibid., 375.
3 Ibid., 376.
4 G. P.V. Akrigg, 'England in 1609', *Huntingdon Library Quarterly*, vol. 14, no. 1 (November 1950), 79.
5 London return of seamen, watermen and fishermen in 1629, in Andrews, 224. These figures are unlikely to be entirely accurate, but they provide a reasonable if rough guide.
6 http://www.trinityhouse.co.uk/th/about/history.html
7 Harris, nos. 191–2.
8 Ibid., no. 184.
9 Ibid., no. 294.
10 Hatton, 1, 302.
11 Ibid.
12 TNA: PROB 11/150/224.
13 Widdowes, preface.
14 Ibid.
15 Hill and Frere, 175.
16 *CSPD*, 20 October 1626.
17 Clarke, 158.
18 Ibid.
19 Ibid., 159.
20 Ibid.
21 Sedgwick, dedication.
22 Ibid., 107.
23 Gouge, 511.
24 TNA: PROB 11/146/28.
25 Elizabeth Jocelin, *The Mothers Legacie to her Unborne Childe* (1624), 26–7.
26 Downame, 329.
27 Nichols, 'To the Reader'.

28 Gouge, 537.
29 TNA: PC 2/38/591, 26 November 1628.
30 Anon., *The Great Messenger of Mortality*, 1.

Chapter 3

1   'Specimen of the first Writ of Ship-money' in Gardiner (1899), 106.
2   Ibid., 105.
3   TNA: SP 16/270/65.
4   Manwaring and Perrin 1, 230.
5   TNA: SP 16/302/124.
6   Ibid.
7   TNA: SP 16/311/138.
8   Manwaring and Perrin 1, 248.
9   Ibid., 236.
10 Ibid., 237.
11 *Portland MSS*, vol. 3, 35.
12 Ibid.
13 Manwaring and Perrin 1, 242.
14 *Portland MSS*, vol. 3, 38.
15 TNA: SP 16/337/1.
16 Ibid.
17 Ibid.
18 Ibid.
19 Ibid.
20 *CSPD*, 1635 (undated)
21 Ibid., 2 September 1636.
22 Harris, no. 261.
23 *CSPD*, 2 September 1636.
24 Ibid., 4 August 1636.
25 Ibid., December 1636.
26 Ibid.
27 Ibid., *CSPD*, 28 November 1636.
28 Ibid., 4 December 1636.
29 TNA: SP 16/349/63.
30 Ibid.
31 Ibid.
32 Ibid.

33 Dunton, 3.
34 TNA: SP 94/39/195.

Chapter 4

1   Quoted in Andrews, 176.
2   TNA: SP 16/369/190.
3   *CSPD*, 10 July 1637.
4   TNA: SP 71/13/8.
5   TNA: SP 16/369/206.
6   Dunton, 9.
7   Ibid., 15–16.
8   TNA: SP 16/369/190.
9   Dunton, 15.
10 TNA: SP 71/13/15.
11 Roberts (1638), 77.
12 TNA: SP 71/13/21.
13 Dunton, 19–20.
14 TNA: SP 16/369/212.
15 TNA: SP 71/13/25.
16 TNA: SP 71/13/21.

Chapter 5

1   TNA: SP 16/369/214
2   Africanus, 68.
3   Ibid., 69.
4   Ogilby, 165.
5   Ibid., 166.
6   TNA: SP 16/369/215.
7   TNA: SP 16/368/4.
8   Burrell, 2.
9   *CSPD*, 2 October 1637.
10 TNA: SP 71/1/154.
11 Ibid.
12 Loomie, 230.
13 Knowler, 124.
14 Davenant, 2.

15 G. Thorn Drury (ed.), *The Poems of Edmund Waller,* vol. I (1901), 'Of Salle' [sic.], 14.
16 Knight, i.
17 *CSPD,* 20 June 1636.
18 Ibid., 22 June 1636.
19 Morgan, 676.
20 TNA: SP 16/379/162.
21 Ibid.
22 Ibid.
23 Perrin, 156.
24 Ibid., 215.
25 Ibid.
26 Ibid., 165.
27 Glover, 8.
28 *CSPD,* 2 March 1638.
29 Davies, 25–6.
30 Perrin, 167.
31 *CSPD,* 15 August 1638.
32 Ibid.

Chapter 6

1 Council for Virginia.
2 Bradford, 62.
3 Kingsbury, 74.
4 TNA: PRO, CO 1/4/57.
5 Kingsbury, 38.
6 *WJ* I, 194.
7 A point made by Carla Gardina Pestana, whose excellent *The English Atlantic in an Age of Revolution 1640–1661,* Harvard University Press (2007) I have pillaged for the following section.
8 Codignola, 79.
9 Hening, 123.
10 Winthrop (1838), 7, 45.
11 Ibid., 47.
12 Hutchinson (1865), I, 53.
13 *WJ* I, 152.

14   *RGCMB* 1, 66.

15   Hutchinson (1865), 1, 54.

16   Wood, 51.

17   Ibid., 52.

18   Ibid.

19   *WP* 3, 168.

20   Anon., *A Proportion of Provisions Needfull for Such as Intend to Plant themselves in New England, for one whole year. Collected by the Adventurers, with the advice of the Planters.*

21   *Englands Oaths. Taken by all men of Quality in the Church and Common-wealth of England*, 2.

22   Quoted in Chaplin (1964), 49.

23   'Richard Mather's Journal', in Young, 448–9.

24   Wood, 50.

25   Ibid.

26   Jonah 2:5.

Chapter 7

1   'Autobiography of the Rev. John Barnard,' *Collections of the Massachusetts Historical Society*, 3rd series, vol. 5 (1836), 209.

2   *WJ* 1, 200.

3   Josselyn, 7.

4   Ibid., 9.

5   Ibid., 11. Richard Mather, whose 1635 crossing took him past the Newfoundland Banks in mid-July, noted that 'it was a very cold wind, like as if it had been winter, which made some to wish for more clothes': 'Richard Mather's Journal', in Young, 465.

6   Josselyn, 11.

7   Ibid.

8   Cressy calls this 'Puritan osmosis syndrome'. *Coming Over*, on which I have drawn heavily for parts of this chapter, is still the best account of the practical process of migration.

9   Josselyn, 20.

10   Cotton Mather, 1, 221.

11   'Early Records of Charlestown', in Young, 375–6.

12   'Roger Clap's Memoirs', in Young, 348–9.

13   Jameson, 66.

14   Ibid., 68.
15   Noble and Cronin, 2, 81.
16   Boston Record Commissioners, *Charlestown*, 20.
17   Jameson, 211.
18   Ibid., 68.
19   *RGCMB* 2, 233.

Chapter 8

1   *WJ* 1, 176.
2   Ibid.
3   Cotton Mather, 2, 440.
4   *RGCMB* 1, 168.
5   Fiske, 145.
6   The phrase is Andrew Delbanco's, in his *The Puritan Ordeal* (1989), 96; I owe the reference to Cave, 519.
7   Captain John Mason, 'Brief History of the Pequot War', reprinted in Orr, 39.
8   *WJ* 1, 220.
9   Ibid., 231.
10   *WP* 3, 435.
11   Adams, 274, 290.
12   Ibid., 336.
13   'The Winthrop Papers', *Collections of the Massachusetts Historical Society*, 4th series (1863), 473.
14   H. McGiffert (ed.), *God's Plot: Puritan Spirituality in Thomas Shepard's Cambridge*, University of Massachusetts Press (1994), 51.
15   Quoted in DNB John Cotton.
16   *CSPD*, 12 December 1626.
17   *WJ* 1, 62.
18   Bell, 48.
19   Ibid., 49.
20   Ibid., 52.
21   Lechford, 150–1.
22   Budington, 184.
23   Weld, 19.
24   John Cotton, *A coppy of a letter of Mr Cotton of Boston, in New England*, 5.
25   *WJ* 1, 107.

26   *WP* 3, 167. I owe this quote – and much else – to Rutman.
27   Shepard (1660), Part 2, 200.

Chapter 9

1   *WJ* 1, 260.
2   Oliver Ayer Roberts, *History of the Military Company of the Massachusetts* (1895), vol. 1, 10.
3   Charlestown Town Records, quoted in Budington, 195.
4   TNA: PROB 11/146/28.
5   Chaplin, 'Nehemiah Bourne', 40.
6   *WJ* 1, 272.
7   *WP* 4, 154–5.
8   Ibid.
9   Ibid.
10   Ibid., 214.
11   Ibid.
12   G. A. Raikes (ed.), *The Ancient Vellum Book of the Honourable Artillery Company* (1890), vii.
13   Clarendon, 1, 230.
14   *WP* 4, 214.
15   *LJ*, 10 March 1629.
16   Ibid., 13 April 1640.
17   Ibid.
18   *CJ*, 17 April 1640.
19   *LJ*, 24 April 1640.
20   Clarendon, 1, 237.
21   *CSPD*, 20 April 1640.
22   Clarendon, 1, 298–9.
23   Ibid., 253.
24   *CJ*, 21 November 1640.
25   Ibid., 30 October 1641.
26   *CSPD*, 19 June 1640.
27   Ibid., 22 June 1640.
28   *CJ*, 10 December 1640.
29   Ibid., 12 December 1640.
30   Raithby, 134–5.
31   *CJ*, 25 August 1641.
32   Ibid., 9 September 1641.

33   Ibid.

34   Ibid., 22 November 1641.

35   TNA: PROB 11/189/79.

36   *CSPD*, 16 February 1642.

Chapter 10

1   *RGCMB* 1, 87.

2   *The Freeman's Oath* (1639). This broadside was produced by Stephen and Matthew Daye on the colony's first printing press in Cambridge.

3   Lechford, 58.

4   *WJ* 1, 122.

5   *RGCMB* 1, 118.

6   Ibid., 157. The paper ballot didn't extend to the conduct of the Court, where a show of hands remained the accepted method of voting on motions or points of dispute.

7   Ibid., 302.

8   Lechford, 69.

9   Peter (1660), 3.

10   Ward, *The simple cobler* [sic] *of Aggawam in America*, 67.

11   Noble and Cronin, 2, 104.

12   Ibid., 62.

13   Ibid., 121.

14   *WJ* 1, 283.

15   Ibid.

16   *RGCMB* 1, 108.

17   *WP* 3, 76; *RGCMB* 1, 88.

18   *WP* 4, 477, 473.

19   *RGCMB* 1, 147.

20   Cotton, *An Abstract of the Lawes of New England*, 10–11.

21   Winthrop (1853), 1, 388–9.

22   *WJ* 2, 3. Winthrop was in some financial difficulties at the time, and he later claimed to welcome the chance to look to his own affairs. Even more welcome was a subscription, amounting to nearly £500, to help him extricate himself from the muddle he was in (caused by his bailiff, who had run up debts of £2,500 without Winthrop's knowledge); and a grant of 3,000 acres of land to his wife Margaret.

23   *Times*, 10 December 1856.

24   Lechford, 60.

25   Ibid., 61.

26   *WJ* 2, 36.

27   Whitmore, 55.

28   Ibid., 33.

29   Ibid.

30   Ibid., 43.

31   Ibid., 47.

32   Ibid., 53.

33   Ibid.

34   W. F. Poole, quoted in Dean, 65.

35   Cahn, 110.

Chapter 11

1   *WJ*, 2, 31.

2   Quoted in Rutman, 184.

3   Increase Mather, 5.

4   *WJ* 2, 19.

5   *RGCMB*, 1, 304.

6   *WP* 4, 285.

7   *WJ* 2, 31.

8   Ibid., 23.

9   Boston Record Commissioners (1881), 58.

10   Ibid., 59.

11   *RGCMB* 1, 341.

12   Ibid., 337.

13   This brief account owes a great deal to Ian Friel's illuminating Gresham College lecture on 'Elizabethan Merchant Ships and Shipbuilding' http://www.gresham.ac.uk/lectures-and-events/elizabethan-merchant-ships-and-shipbuilding

14   Manwaring and Perrin 2, 153.

15   George Waymouth, *The Jewell of Artes* (1604), Add MSS 19889, f.135; quoted in Oppenheim, 186.

16   *WJ* 2, 70.

17   For Coytmore's will see *New England Historical and Genealogical Register*, vol. 7 (1853), 32.

18 Ibid.
19 Ibid.
20 Ibid.
21 Roberts (1638), 112.
22 *WJ* 2, 92.
23 Ibid., 93.
24 Aspinwall, 395–6.

Chapter 12

1   Quoted in Bagwell, 1, 343.
2   Anon., *A Bloody Battell: or the Rebels Overthrow*, 6, 1.
3   Anon., *Bloody Newes from Norwich*, 5.
4   Sir John Leeke to Sir Edmund Verney, 10 January 1642; BL M636/4.
5   *CJ*, 11 February 1641.
6   *A Declaration of both Houses of Parliament, Concerning the Affairs of Ireland*, 6.
7   Anon., *Remonstrans Redivivus*, 4.
8   *WJ* 1, 310.
9   Firth and Rait, 9.
10 Ibid.
11 Peter (1642), 23, 3, 24.
12 Ibid., 4.
13 Ibid., 5.
14 Ibid., 6.
15 Quoted in Bagwell, 2, 38.
16 Peter (1642), 11.
17 Clanricarde, 207.
18 Ibid.
19 Peter (1642), 12.
20 Ibid., 13.
21 Clanricarde, 223.
22 Ibid., 224.
23 Peter (1642), 16.
24 Ibid., 20.
25 Ibid., 21.
26 Clanricarde, 265.

Chapter 13

1   Hooke, 9.
2   *WP* 4, 334.
3   Hutchinson (1795), 1, 118.
4   'Articles of Confederation between the Plantations', in David Pulsifer (ed.), *Records of the Colony of New Plymouth*, vol. 9 (1859), 3. I owe this quote to Carla Gardina Pestana, *The English Atlantic*, 33.
5   Quoted in Stearns, 168–9.
6   *Speciall Passages And Certain Informations from Severall Places*, 6–13 December 1642, 153.
7   Dobson, 3.
8   *WP* 4, 366.
9   Ibid., 21.
10 *WJ* 1, 121.
11 *WP* 4, 84.
12 *RGCMB* 1, 276.
13 *CJ*, 17 June 1643.
14 Ibid.
15 *The Parliament scout*, 20–7 June 1643, 3.
16 *Certaine Informations from severall parts of the Kingdome*, 19–26 June 1643, 5.
17 'The Solemn League and Covenant', in Gardiner (1899), 268–9.
18 Laing, 2, 90.
19 *WP* 4, 444.
20 Anon., *Hulls Managing of the Kingdomes Cause*, 21; 'T.V.' 5; Sir John Meldrum to Speaker Lenthall, 14 October 1643, in Powell and Timings, 94.
21 Anon., *Hulls Managing of the Kingdomes Cause*, 19.
22 Powell and Timings, 95.
23 Ibid.
24 Anon., *Hulls Managing of the Kingdomes Cause*, 20.
25 Powell and Timings, 95.
26 Anon., *Hulls Managing of the Kingdomes Cause*, 22.
27 *Portland MSS* 1, 139.
28 'T.V.', 6.
29 Anon., *Hulls Managing of the Kingdomes Cause*, 21.

30 Bruce and Masson, 72.
31 Ibid., 72–3.
32 Ibid., 13.
33 Suffolk Record Office, HD 36/A/132

Chapter 14

1 Israel Stoughton to John Stoughton, *Proceedings of the Massachusetts Historical Society*, vol. 5 (1860–1862), 138.
2 *RGCMB* 1, 135.
3 Sir Nicholas Stoughton, 'History of the Stoughton Family', BL Add. MS. 6174.
4 *WJ* 2, 253.
5 'Abstracts of the Earliest Wills Upon Record in the County of Suffolk, MS.', *New England Historical and Genealogical Register*, vol. 4 (1850), 51.
6 Ibid.
7 Ibid.
8 Ibid.
9 Preface to John Norton, *The Answer to the Whole Set of Questions of the Celebrated Mr William Appolonius* (1648).
10 Hooke, 16.
11 Quoted in Trease, 141.
12 Bruce and Masson, 79; TNA: SP 16/503/56. I owe both of these quotes to Holmes, 198.
13 Laing, 2, 229.
14 Bruce and Masson, 73.
15 Ibid., xxiv.
16 Ibid., 72.
17 Baxter, 45–6.
18 Dobson, 3.
19 Goodwin, 7.
20 Ibid., 8.
21 Parker, 3–4.
22 Simeon Ash and William Rathband, 'To the Reader', in Ball.
23 Cromwell, *Writings*, 1, 287.
24 *Clarke Papers* 1, 287; Bourne, 6.
25 Hugh Peter in Richard Mather, foreword.
26 *RGCMB* 2, 85.

27 *WJ* 2, 235.
28 Winthrop (1644), preface.
29 Ibid., 66, 64.
30 Edwards (1644), 289.
31 Edwards (1646), Part 1, 147–8; quoted in Moore, 125.
32 Williams, *Bloudy Tenent*, 2–3.
33 Williams, *Mr Cotton's Letter*, 1.
34 *WP* 5, 13.
35 Hutchinson (1795), 1, 437.
36 'Documents Relating to Hugh Peters', *New England Historical and Genealogical Register*, vol. 39 (1885), 373.
37 Shepard (1645) 3.

Chapter 15

1   Gardiner (1883), 2.
2   Ibid.
3   *CSPD* 1644–5, 25 November to 6 January.
4   Ibid.
5   Gardiner (1883), 2.
6   Vicars (1644), 322.
7   Ibid.
8   Vicars (1645), 203.
9   *Weekly Intelligencer*, 10–17 December 1644, 1.
10 *A Diary, or an Exact Journall*, 5–12 December, 5.
11 *London Post*, 10 December 1644, 2.
12 *Perfect Occurrences of Parliament*, 6–13 December 1644, 5.
13 Vicars (1646), 76.
14 *WJ* 2, 258.
15 Rushworth (1721), 6, 8.
16 *CI*, 11 December 1644.

Chapter 16

1   *LI*, 11 April 1646.
2   John Vernon, *The Young Horse-man, or, The Honest Plain-dealing cavalier* (1644), 8.
3   Noble's *Memoirs*, quoted in Mastin, 153.
4   Cromwell, *Good Newes Out of the West* (1645), 4.

5   Sprigg, 45.
6   Fairfax et al. (1645), 2.
7   Walker, 130–1.
8   Elton, 176.
9   Foard, 265.
10 Clarendon, 5, 184–5.
11 'The Copie of a Letter sent from a Gentleman of publike employment in the late service neere Knaseby', in *An Ordinance of the Lords and Commons assembled in Parliament* (17 June 1645), 4.
12 *Perfect Occurrences of Parliament*, 30 May–6 June 1645, 1. I owe this quote to Gentles (1991), 107.
13 *Moderate Intelligencer*, 12–19 June 1645, 125.
14 Baxter, 54.
15 Stearns, 250–1.
16 Lilburne (1645), 6.
17 Sprigg, 322.
18 Ibid., 69.

Chapter 17

1   Ibid., 70.
2   Ibid., 72.
3   Ibid., 73.
4   Ibid., 74.
5   *Portland MSS* 1, 242.
6   Sprigg, 85.
7   Quoted in Wildman, 172.
8   Sprigg, 86.
9   Ibid.
10 Ibid., 88.
11 Sprigg, 89.
12 http://mshed.org/explore-contribute/themes/transforming/transforming-places-of-conflict/bristol's-civil-war-defences/
13 Rushworth, *Storming Bristoll*, 18. At the same time the troops were given six shillings apiece for their bravery at Bridgwater; this no doubt contributed to their shouts of joy.
14 Rushworth, *Storming Bristoll*, 4–5.
15 Ibid., 9

16 Ibid., 16.
17 Ibid., 17.
18 Ibid., 18.
19 Ibid., 20.
20 Cromwell, *Lieut: Generall Cromwells Letter*, 5.
21 Ibid., 7.
22 Sprigg, 121.
23 Ibid., 125–6.
24 Ibid., 125.

Chapter 18

1 *WJ* 2, 249.
2 Vives, 368.
3 Quoted in Conger, 29.
4 Ibid., 34.
5 1 Timothy 5:11, 13.
6 Aspinwall, 46.
7 *WJ* 2, 260.
8. *RGCMB* 2, 149.
9 Ibid., 260–1.
10 Shepard (1645), 2.
11 *RGCMB* 2, 135.
12 *WJ* 2, 256.
13 Aspinwall, 394.
14 *WP* 5, 62–3.
15 Ibid., 70.

Chapter 19

1 Ibid.
2 Peter, *Gods Doings*, 37–8.
3 Ibid., 33.
4 Ibid., 'Epistle Dedicatory'.
5 Ibid., 41.
6 Edwards (1646), first and second parts, 50.
7 Peter, *Gods Doings*, 24.
8 Cary, 1, 8–9.
9 Ibid., 9.

10   Rushworth (1721), 6, 276.

11   Quoted in Bund, 183.

12   Bund, 189.

13   Sprigg, 284.

14   Baxter, 55.

15   Ibid., 56.

16   Bund, 191.

17   Ibid., 192. All of them except Sir William Russell, a local man who had taken Worcester for the king back in November 1642. Thomas explicitly exempted Russell from the articles of surrender, something which delayed a decision by the defenders. In the end Russell said he would walk out and surrender himself if it meant saving the city; and Thomas gave assurances that he would be used as a gentleman. He was heavily fined, but he escaped with his life.

18   Peter, *Last Report*, 4.

19   Cary, 1, 138.

20   *CJ*, 11 November 1646.

21   Prynne (1659), 9.

22   *WP* 5, 98.

23   Ibid, 244.

24   Aspinwall, 367.

25   *WJ* 2, 317.

26   *WJ* 2, 318.

27   Ibid.

28   Ibid.

29   *WP* 4, 357.

30   *WP* 1, 355.

31   *WJ* 2, 327; *WP* 1, 227.

32   *WP* 1, 355.

33   *WP* 5, 173.

34   Ibid., 216.

35   Ibid., 203.

36   Ibid., 180.

37   Ibid., 220.

38   *RGCMB* 2, 234.

39   Ibid., 233.

Chapter 20

1 *WP* 5, 138.
2 Ibid., 129.
3 *CJ*, 29 March 1647.
4 Clarendon, 5, 76; *LJ*, 30 March 1647.
5 Anon., *The Apologie of the Common Souldiers*, 3.
6 Anon., *A New Found Strategem*, 1.
7 *Clarke Papers* 1, 34.
8 Ibid., 38.
9 Ibid., 44.
10 Ibid., 48.
11 Ibid., 65.
12 Ibid., 66.
13 Anon., *A Vindication of A Hundred Sixty seven Commission Officers*, 6.
14 *CJ*, 23 April 1647.
15 Ibid.
16 *LJ*, 12 May 1647.
17 *CJ*, 28 May 1647.
18 Cary, 1, 222.

Chapter 21

1 *Perfect Diurnall*, 31 May–7 June 1647, 12.
2 *WP* 5, 62.
3 Ibid., 174.
4 Rushworth (1721), 6, 139.
5 *CJ*, 8 June 1647.
6 Abbott, 1, 460.
7 *CJ*, 14 June 1647.
8 Anon., *A Humble Remonstrance*, 2.
9 Anon., *A Remonstrance of the Shee-Citizens of London*, title page.
10 *Clarke Papers* 1, 182.
11 Rushworth (1721), 6, 653.
12 *A Continuation of Certain Speciall and Remarkable Passages*, 30 July–6 August 1647, 5.
13 Rushworth (1721), 7, 752.

14 Gardiner (1893), 3, 346.
15 Ibid.
16 Berkeley, 35.
17 Ibid.
18 Ibid., 35–6.
19 Tibbutt, 84.
20 Ibid.
21 Ibid., 89.
22 Anon., *The Intentions of the Armie*, 6.
23 Tibbutt, 89.
24 Batten, 2.
25 Ibid.
26 Tibbutt, 91.
27 Lilburne (1646), 9, 8.
28 Lilburne, *Two Letters*, 1; Lilburne, *The Juglers Discovered*, 1.
29 *WP* 5, 175.
30 Ward, *A Religious Retreat*, 7, 12.
31 Peter (1647), 4.
32 Ibid., 7.
33 Ibid., 9.
34 Ibid., 11.
35 Anon., *The Case of the Armie Truly Stated*, 2.
36 Ibid., 15.

Chapter 22

1 *Clarke Papers* 1, 244.
2 Ibid., 245.
3 Ibid., 247.
4 Ibid., 227–8.
5 Ibid., 238.
6 Ibid., 242.
7 Ibid., 244.
8 Ibid., 246.
9 Ibid.
10 Ibid.
11 Ibid., 247.
12 Ibid., 265.
13 Ibid., 255.

14   Ibid., 256–7.
15   *OED*, citing Clarendon MSS 2638, newsletter of 1 November 1647.
16   *Clarke Papers* 1, 287.
17   Ibid., 286.
18   Ibid., 287.
19   Ibid., 287–8.
20   Ibid., 290.
21   Ibid., 291.
22   Ibid., 299.
23   Ibid., 300.
24   Lilburne, *Rash Oaths Unwarrantable*, 54.
25   *Clarke Papers* 1, 301.
26   Ibid., 303.
27   Ibid.
28   Ibid., 309.
29   Ibid., 309, 310.
30   Ibid., 311.
31   Ibid.
32   Ibid., 320.
33   Ibid., 325.
34   Ibid., 323.
35   Ibid., 328.
36   Ibid., 330.
37   Ibid., 329.
38   Ibid., 330.
39   Ibid., 338.
40   Ibid., 335.
41   Ibid., 346.
42   Ibid., 367.

Chapter 23

1   Tibbutt, 95.
2   Ibid, 96.
3   Ibid.
4   *Clarke Papers* 1, 367.
5   Ibid., 374.
6   Ibid., 351.

7   Ibid., 398.
8   Ibid., 380.
9   Ibid., 383.
10 Ibid., 407.
11 Ibid., 402.
12 Ibid., 317.
13 Ibid., 416.
14 Ibid., 441.
15 Ibid., 411.
16 Quoted in Gardiner (1893), 3, 248.
17 Quoted in *DNB*, Robert Hammond.
18 *Clarke Papers* 1, 417.
19 Ibid.
20 Rushworth (1647), 2.
21 Ibid., 4.
22 Anon., *A Full Relation of The Proceedings at the Rendezvous*, 16.
23 *LJ*, 16 November 1647.
24 *Mercurius elencticus*, 12–19 November 1647, 4.
25 *The Kingdomes Weekly Intelligencer*, 16–23 November 1647, 2.
26 *LJ*, 16 November 1647.
27 Anon., *A Full Relation of The Proceedings at the Rendezvous*, 4.
28 *The Justice of the Army Against Evill-Doers Vindicated* (1649), 6.
29 *LJ*, 16 November 1647.
30 *Mercurius elencticus*, 12–19 November 1647, 8.
31 Quoted in Gentles (1991), 226.

Chapter 24

1   Rushworth (1721), 2, 943.
2   *LJ*, 27 December 1647.
3   Birch, 1, 97.
4   *LJ*, 16 November 1647.
5   *CJ*, 10 December 1647.
6   *LJ*, 22 December 1647.
7   Ibid., 28 December 1647.
8   *CJ*, 1 January 1648.
9   Berkeley, 70.
10 Powell and Timings, 312.

11   G. Bate, *Elenchus motuum nuperorum in Anglia* (1685), 86.
12   Powell and Timings, 313.
13   Ibid., 314.
14   Ibid., 315.
15   Carter, 12.
16   *CSPD*, 23 May 1648.
17   Powell and Timings, 328.
18   *The Kingdomes Weekly Intelligencer*, 23–30 May 1648, 3.
19   Anon., *A declaration from the City of London*.
20   Powell and Timings, 328.
21   Ibid., 329.
22   Ibid.
23   *CSPD*, 20 May 1648.
24   *WP* 5, 174–5.
25   Powell and Timings, 331.
26   Carter, 52–3.
27   Ibid., 53.
28   Powell and Timings, 334.
29   *Mercurius bellicus*, 30 May–6 June 1648.
30   Quoted in Jones (2005), 108.
31   Lisle et al.
32   Powell and Timings, 334.
33   Ibid., 341.
34   Gardiner (1893), 3, 384.
35   Powell and Timings, 303.
36   Batten, 3.
37   Powell and Timings, 354.
38   Ibid., 353–4.
39   Ibid., 354.

Chapter 25

1   Clarendon, 6, 62.
2   *WP* 5, 280.
3   Ibid., 266.
4   Quoted in Jones (2005), 108.
5   *The Parliament-kite*, 17–24 August 1648, 5.
6   *The Moderate intelligencer*, 3–10 August 1648, 4.
7   Ibid., 27 July–3 August 1648, 11–12.

8   Carter, 166.
9   Ibid., 171.
10 Ibid.
11 Whitelock, 2, 388.
12 *The Kingdomes weekly intelligencer*, 22–29 August 1648, 4.
13 Carter, 178.
14 Quoted in Stearns, 321.
15 *WP* 5, 281.
16 Carter, 182–3.
17 Fairfax (1648), 2.
18 Ibid., 4.
19 Whitelock, 2, 394.
20 *Clarke Papers* 2, 35.
21 Ibid.
22 Ibid., 36.
23 Ibid., 37.
24 Ibid., 39.
25 Fairfax (1648), 1.
26 Anon., *The Triumph of Loyalty*, 1.
27 Carter, 201.
28 Quarles, 9.
29 Anon., *The Triumph of Loyalty*, 17.
30 Anon., *The Cruell Tragedy Or Inhumane Butchery, of Hamor and Shechem*, 15.
31 'Philocrates', 77.
32 Anon., *Colonell Rainsborowes Ghost*.
33 Whitelock, 2, 413; Rushworth (1721), 7, 1,279.

Chapter 26

1   Longstaffe, 100.
2   Paulden, 11.
3   Ibid., 14.
4   Rushworth (1721), 7, 1,294–5.
5   Bodleian Tanner MSS 57/2/378.
6   Ibid.
7   Ibid.
8   Surtees, 94.
9   *The Moderate*, 31 October–7 November 1648, 4.

10   Rushworth (1721), 7, 1,300.
11   Paulden, 15.
12   Ibid., 16.
13   Ibid.
14   Ibid., 17.
15   Anon., 'A Letter from Doncaster', 5.
16   Ibid.
17   Smith, 3.
18   Ibid., 4.
19   Ibid., 6.
20   Rushworth (1721), 7, 1,316.
21   Ibid., 7, 1, 318.
22   *The true informer or Monthly mercury*, 7 October–8 November 1648, 20.
23   Surtees, 100.
24   *The Moderate*, 7–14 November 1648, 6.
25   Anon., *Severall Petitions Presented to His Excellency the Lord Fairfax* (1648), 8.
26   *The Moderate*, 14–21 November 1648, 161–2.
27   Ibid., 161.
28   Rushworth (1721), 7, 1337.
29   *Mercurius pragmaticus*, 31 October–14 November 1648, 5.
30   Anon., 'A Letter from Doncaster', 6.
31   *The Moderate*, 31 October–7 November 1648, 8.
32   Ibid..
33   Anon., *A Directory for The Publique Worship of God*, 35.
34   Ibid.
35   *Mercurius melancholicus*, 14–21 November 1648, 4.
36   *Mercurius pragmaticus*, 14–21 November 1648, 4.
37   *Mercurius elencticus*, 15–22 November 1648, 503.
38   Ibid., 504.
39   *Mercurius pragmaticus*, 14–21 November 1648.
40   Brooks, 23.
41   Ibid., 4–5.
42   Ibid., 7.
43   Ibid., 8.
44   Ibid., 20–1.
45   Ibid., 15.
46   Ibid., 14.

47 Ibid., 12–13.
48 Ibid., 23.

Chapter 27

1   Alleyn.
2   Anon., *A New Elegie in Memory of the Right Valiant, and most Renowned Souldier, Col. Rainsborough.*
3   Anon., *In Memoriam Thomae Rainsbrough, Pro Populo, & Parliamento, Chiliarchae Fortissimi.*
4   *Mercurius impartialis*, 5–12 December 1648, 3.
5   *Mercurius melancholicus*, 14–21 November 1648, 5.
6   Anon., *Colonell Rainsborowes Ghost*, 1.
7   Anon., *The Famous Tragedie of King Charles I*, 24.
8   Ibid., 26.
9   Ibid., 37.
10 Ibid., 38.
11 Ibid., 39.
12 'J.T.'
13 Ibid.
14 Rushworth (1721), 7, 1, 327.
15 *The Moderate*, 14–21 November 1648, 163.
16 Prynne (1648), 5.
17 Verax, 50.
18 Finch, 166.
19 Howell, 4, 1,070.
20 Ibid., 1082.
21 Ibid., 1128.
22 Ibid., 1139.
23 *Surtees*, 107.
24 Howell, 4, 1,257–8.
25 Ibid., 1,264.
26 Ibid., 1,267.
27 *WP* 5, 305.
28 Ibid., 322.
29 Lilburne (1649), 10–11.
30 Anon., *A Full and Exact Relation of the Horrid Murder committed upon the Body of Col. Rainsborough* (1648), 4.
31 Bodleian Tanner MS 57/411.

32 *CJ.*, 26 December 1648.
33 *CJI*, 6 June, 20 July 1649; ibid., 22 June 1650.

Chapter 28

1 *WP* 5, 206.
2 Ibid., 203.
3 Ibid., 204.
4 Edwards (1646), Part 3, 81–2.
5 *WP* 5, 266.
6 Ibid., 311.
7 Cotton Mather, *Elizabeth in her Holy Retirement. An essay to prepare a pious woman for her lying in* (1710), 6–7.
8 Quoted in Nancy Schrom Dye, 'History of Childbirth in America', *Signs*, vol. 6, no. 1 (autumn 1980), 99.
9 *WP* 5, 290.
10 Ibid., 336.
11 Ibid., 334.
12 Quoted in Rutman (1965), 190.
13 Maverick, 15.
14 Jameson, 70.
15 Massachusetts, *Lawes*, foreword.
16 Ibid., 23.
17 Quoted in Wall, 227.
18 *WP* 5, 42.
19 Ibid., 114.
20 Ibid., 203.
21 Ibid., 243.
22 Ibid., 30.
23 Ibid., 147.
24 Anon., *A Declaration of the Gallant Service*, 3.
25 *WP* 5, 158.
26 Ibid., 320.
27 Ibid., 357.
28 *WJ* 2, 355.
29 *WP* 5, 312.
30 Ibid., 317.
31 Ibid., 319.
32 Cotton Mather, 1, 119.

33 *WP* 5, 325.
34 'Diary of John Hull', *Transactions and Collections of the American Antiquarian Society*, vol. 3 (1857), 173.
35 Winthrop (1853), 2, 440.
36 *WP* 5, 337.
37 *RGCMB* 3, 161.
38 Ibid.
39 *WP* 6, 49.

Chapter 29

1   *Clarke Papers* 2, 185.
2   Fairfax et al. (1649), 4.
3   Anon., *The Ranters Reasons Resolved to Nothing*, 2.
4   Reading, 6.
5   'R.F.', 4.
6   Anon., *The Ranters Religion*, 2.
7   Ibid., 1.
8   Coppe, *A Fiery Flying Roll*, 2.
9   Coppe, *A Second Fiery Flying Roule*, 19.
10 Claxton (1660), 25.
11 Ibid., 26.
12 Ibid., 27.
13 Claxton (1650), title page.
14 *An Act Against several Atheistical, Blasphemous and Execrable Opinions* (1650).
15 *CJ*, 14 June 1650.
16 Claxton (1660), 31.
17 England and Wales, Parliament, 'Upon Report from the Committee for suppressing licentious and impious practices', 27 September 1650.
18 Ibid.
19 *Mercurius politicus*, 26 September–3 October 1650, 287.
20 Thomas Joy, *A Loyal Subjects Admonition* (undated, probably 1660).
21 William Rainborowe to Richard Salwey, 28 February 1653, National Maritime Museum MS AGC/12/1.
22 *CSPD*, 19 December 1655.
23 'A Booke for Church Affaires at Stepny', Tower Hamlets Local History Library and Archives, W/SMH/A/1/1, 1.

24 Ibid., 192.
25 *CSPD*, 18 January 1650.
26 Ibid.
27 *CJ*, 2 March 1650
28 *Mercurius elencticus*, 22–29 April 1650, 7.
29 Bourne, 4.
30 Ibid.
31 Ibid., 7.
32 Quoted in Bernard Capp, *Cromwell's Navy*, Oxford University Press (1989), 300.
33 Gardiner and Atkinson, 4, 94.
34 Ibid., 2, 282.
35 Chaplin (1964), 69; *WP* 4, 453.
36 Gardiner and Atkinson, 4, 58.
37 Ibid., 112.
38 Ibid., 146.
39 Ibid., 346.
40 Ibid., 348.
41 Ibid., 6, 186.
42 *WP* 6, 346.
43 Winthrop et al. (1882), 8, 218, 214.
44 Ibid., 218.
45 *WP* 5, 193–4.
46 Winthrop et al. (1882), 8, 210.
47 Quoted in Firth and Davies, 1, 189.
48 Winthrop et al. (1882), 8, 217.
49 *Speeches of Oliver Cromwell*, ed. I. Roots, Dent (1989), 137.
50 Quoted in Firth and Davies, 1, 191.
51 Winthrop et al. (1882), 8, 46.
52 TNA: PROB 11/280/17.

Chapter 30

1 *Clarke Papers* 3, 217.
2 Ibid., 211.
3 Ibid., 216–17.
4 Firth and Rait, 1,272.
5 *CSPD*, 18 August 1659.
6 England and Wales, Sovereign, *A Proclamation to Summon the*

Persons Therein Named, who Sate, Gave Judgment, and Assisted in that Horrid and Detestable Murder . . .

7   Ludlow, 215.

8   Anon., *The Speeches and Prayers of Some of the Late King's Judges* (1660), 10.

9   Firth, 2, 305.

10   *CJ*, 18 June 1660.

11   Stearns, 416.

12   *Mercurius publicus*, 15–22 October 1660, 678.

13   Hutchinson (1795), 1,107n.

14   Stiles, 109.

15   Ibid., 112.

16   Hutchinson (1795) 1, 204.

17   'Abstracts of the Earliest Wills in Suffolk'; *New England Historical and Genealogical Register*, vol. 31 (1877), 107.

18   Davenport, 337.

19   *RGCMB* 4, 432.

20   Waters, 1, 170–1.

21   Chaplin (1964), 151.

22   Winthrop et al. (1882), 8, 394.

List of Abbreviations

BL: British Library.

CJ: Journal of the House of Commons vols. 1–12 (1802–3).

Clarke Papers: The Clarke Papers (ed. C. H. Firth), 4 vols., Camden Society (1891–1901).

CSPD: Calendar of State Papers, Domestic Series, Her Majesty's Stationery Office (1856–1972).

DNB: Dictionary of National Biography.

LJ: Journal of the House of Lords, vols. 1–20 (1832–4).

RGCMB: Records of the Governor and Company of the Massachusetts Bay in New England (ed. Nathaniel B. Shurtleff), 5 vols. (1853–4).

TNA: The National Archives, UK.

WJ: John Winthrop, *Winthrop's Journal 1630–1649* (ed. James Kendall Hosmer), 2 vols., Charles Scribner's Sons (1908).

WP: Winthrop Papers (eds. Worthington C. Ford, Stewart Mitchell, Allyn Bailey Forbes, Malcolm Freiberg), 6 vols., Massachusetts Historical Society (1929–92).

Bibliography

Abbott, Wilbur Cortez (ed.), *The Writings and Speeches of Oliver Cromwell*, 4 vols., Harvard University Press (1937–47).

Adams, Charles Francis (ed.), *Antinomianism in the Colony of Massachusetts Bay, 1636–1638* (1894).

Adamson, J. H. and Folland, H. F., *Sir Harry Vane: His Life and Times 1613–1662*, Bodley Head (1973).

Adamson, J., 'The English Nobility and the Projected Settlement of 1647', *Historical Journal*, vol. 30 (1987), 567–602.

Adamson, John (ed.), *The English Civil War: Conflicts and Contexts, 1640–49*, Palgrave Macmillan (2009).

Africanus, Leo, *A Geographical Historie of Africa*, trans. John Pory (1600).

Alleyn, Thomas, *An Elegie upon The Death of that Renowned Heroe Coll. Rainsborrow* (1648).

Andrews, K. R., *Ships, Money and Politics*, Cambridge University Press (1991).

Anon., *A Bloody Battell: or the Rebels Overthrow* (1641).

Anon., *A declaration from the City of London . . . also a message concerning Prince Charles, read in the House of Lords, from Sir Thomas Dishington* (27 May 1648).

Anon., *A declaration of the gallant service performed by the thrice worthy and faithfull minister of the Gospell of Jesus Christ, Mr Hugh Peters* (1646).

Anon., *A Full Relation of The Proceedings at the Rendezvous of that Brigade of the Army that was held in Corkbush field in Hartford . . .* (1647).

Anon., *A Humble Remonstrance of the Representations of Divers Moderate, and peaceable Citizens of London, to both Houses of Parliament* (1647).

Anon., 'A Letter from Doncaster', *Packets of Letters from Scotland, and the North parts of England*, no. 34 (7 November 1648), 4–6.

Anon., *A New Elegie in Memory of the Right Valiant, and most Renowned Souldier, Col. Rainsborough* (1648).

Anon., *A New Found Strategem framed in the old forge of Machivilisme . . .* (1647).

Anon., *A Proportion of Provisions Needfull for Such as Intend to Plant themselves in New England, for one whole year. Collected by the Adventurers, with the advice of the Planters* (1630).

Anon., *A Remonstrance of the Shee-Citizens of London* (1647).

Anon., *A Vindication of A Hundred Sixty seven Commission Officers That are come off from the Army* (1647).

Anon., *Bloody Newes from Norwich . . .* [to which] *is added the last bloody Newes from Ireland* (1641).

Anon., *Colchester's Teares: Affecting and Afflicting City and Country* (1648).

Anon., *Colonell Rainsborowes Ghost: or, A true Relation of the manner of his Death . . .* (1648).

Anon., *Hulls Managing of the Kingdomes Cause* (1644).

Anon., *In Memoriam Thomae Rainsbrough, Pro Populo, & Parliamento, Chiliarchae Fortissimi* (1648).

Anon., *Remonstrans Redivivus: or An Accompt of the Remonstrance and Petition, Formerly presented by divers Citizens of London . . .* (1643).

Anon., *The Apologie of the Common Souldiers of his Excellencie Sir Tho. Fairfaxes army* (1647).

Anon., *The Case of the Armie Truly Stated* (1647).

Anon., *The Cruell Tragedy Or Inhumane Butchery, of Hamor and Shechem* (1648).

Anon., *The Famous Tragedie of King Charles I* (1649).

Anon., *The Great Messenger of Mortality* (1600).

Anon., *The Intentions of the Armie* (1647).

Anon., *The Justice of the Army Against Evill-Doers Vindicated* (1649).

Anon., *The Ranters Reasons Resolved to Nothing* (1651).

Anon., *The Ranters Religion* (1650).

Anon., *The Speeches and Prayers of Some of the Late King's Judges* (1660).

Anon., *The Triumph of Loyalty: or The Happinesse of a Suffering Subject* (1648).

Armstrong, Maurice W., 'Religious Enthusiasm and Separatism in Colonial New England', *Harvard Theological Review*, vol. 38 (1945), 111–40.

Aspinwall, William, *A Volume relating to the Early History of Boston containing the Aspinwall Notarial Records*, Boston Municipal Printing Office (1903).

Bagwell, Richard, *Ireland Under the Stuarts and During the Interregnum*, Longmans, Green and Co., 3 vols. (1909–16).

Bailyn, Bernard, *The New England Merchants in the Seventeenth Century*, Harper Torchbook (1964).

Ball, John, *A Tryall of the New-Church Way in New-England and in Old* (1644).

Barber, Sarah, *A Revolutionary Rogue: Henry Marten and the English Republic*, Sutton (2000).

Barnard, John, 'Autobiography of the Rev. John Barnard', *Collections of the Massachusetts Historical Society*, 3rd series, vol. 5 (1836), 177–242.

Batten, William, *A Declaration of Sir William Batten, Late Vice-Admiral for the Parliament* (1648).

Baxter, Richard, *Reliquiae Baxterianae* (1696).

Bell, Susanna, *The Legacy of a Dying Mother to her Mourning Children* (1673).

Berkeley, Sir John, *Memoirs of Sir John Berkley* [*sic*] (1699).

Birch, Thomas (ed.), *A Collection of the State Papers of John Thurloe*, 7 vols. (1742).

Boston Record Commissioners, *A Report of the Record Commissioners containing Charlestown Land Records, 1638–1802* (1883).

Boston Record Commissioners, *Second Report of the Record Commissioners of the City of Boston; containing the Boston Records, 1634–1660, and the Book of Possessions* (1881).

Bottigheimer, Karl S., 'English Money and Irish Land: The "Adventurers" in the Cromwellian Settlement of Ireland', *Journal of British Studies*, vol. 7 (1967), 12–27.

Bourne, Nehemiah, *The Copy of a Letter from the Reare-Admiral of the English Fleet for the Common Wealth of England* (1652).

Bradford, William, *Of Plymouth Plantation* (ed. Samuel Eliot Morison), Alfred A. Knopf (2006).

Brady, Andrea, 'Dying with Honour: Literary Propaganda and the Second English Civil War', *Journal of Military History*, vol. 70 (2006), 9–30.

Breen, Louise A., 'Religious Radicalism in the Puritan Officer Corps: Heterodoxy, the Artillery Company, and Cultural Integration in Seventeenth-Century Boston', *New England Quarterly*, vol. 68 (1995), 3–43.

Brook, Benjamin, *The Lives of the Puritans*, 3 vols. (1813).

Brooks, Thomas, *The Glorious Day of the Saints' Appearance* (1648).

Bruce, John and Masson, David (eds.), *The Quarrel Between The Earl of Manchester and Oliver Cromwell*, Camden Society (1875).

Budington, William I., *The History of the First Church, Charlestown* (1845).

Bund, J. W. Willis, *The Civil War in Worcestershire, 1642–1646*, Simkin, Marshall, Hamilton, Kent & Co. (1905).

Burrell, Andrewes, *To the Right Honourable, The High Court of Parliament, The Humble Remonstrance of Andrewes Burrell Gent. For a Reformation of Englands Navie* (1646).

Bushnell, Edmund, *The Compleat Ship-Wright*, 5th edition (1688).

Cahn, Mark D., 'Punishment, Discretion, and the Codification of Prescribed Penalties in Colonial Massachusetts', *American Journal of Legal History*, vol. 33, no. 2 (April 1989), 107–36.

Carlin, Norah, 'Leveller Organization in London', *Historical Journal*, vol. 27 (1984), 955–60.

Carter, Matthew, *A Most True and exact Relation of That as Honourable as unfortunate Expedition of Kent, Essex, and Colchester* (1648).

Cary, Henry (ed.), *Memorials of the Great Civil War in England from 1646 to 1652*, 2 vols. (1842).

Cave, Alfred A., 'Who Killed John Stone? A Note on the Origins of the Pequot War', *William and Mary Quarterly*, 3rd Series, vol. 49, no. 3 (July 1992), 509–21.

Chaplin, W. R., 'Nehemiah Bourne', *Publications of the Colonial Society of Massachusetts*, vol. 42 (1964), 28–155.

Chaplin, W. R., 'William Rainsborough (1587–1642) and his Associates of the Trinity House', *Mariners' Mirror*, vol. 31 (1945), 178–97.

Cholmley, Hugh, *The Memoirs of Sir Hugh Cholmley* (1787).

Clanricarde, Ulick de Burgh, Earl of, *The Memoirs and Letters of Ulick, Marquis of Clanricarde* (1757).

Clarendon, Edward, Earl of, *The History of the Rebellion and Civil Wars in England*, 8 vols. (1826).

Clarke, Samuel, *The Lives of Thirty-two English Divines Famous in their Generations for Learning and Piety* (1677).

Claxton [Clarkson], Laurence, *A Single Eye* (1650).

Claxton [Clarkson], Laurence, *The Lost Sheep Found* (1660).

Codignola, Luca, *The Coldest Harbour of the World: Simon Stock and Lord Baltimore's Colony in Newfoundland, 1621–1649*, trans. Anita Weston, McGill-Queen's University Press (1988).

Conger, Vivian Bruce, *The Widows' Might: Widowhood and Gender in Early British America*, New York University Press (2009).

Coppe, Abiezer, *A Fiery Flying Roll* (1649).

Coppe, Abiezer, *A Second Fiery Flying Roule* (1649).

Cotton, John, *A coppy of a letter of Mr Cotton of Boston, in New England* (1641).

Cotton, John, *An Abstract or the Lawes of New England, As they are now established* (1641).

Council for Virginia, *By His Majesties Councell for Virginia. Whereas upon the returne of Sir Thomas Dale Knight . . .* (1617).

Cressy, David, *Coming Over: Migration and Communication between England and New England in the Seventeenth Century*, Cambridge University Press (1987).

Cromwell, Oliver, *Good News Out of the West* (1645).

Cromwell, Oliver, *Lieut: Generall Cromwells Letter To The House of Commons, of All the Particulars of taking the City of Bristoll* (1645).

Cromwell, Oliver, *The Writings and Speeches of Oliver Cromwell*, ed. Wilbur Cortez Abbott, 4 vols., Harvard University Press (1937–47).

Davenant, William, *Britannia Triumphans: A Masque* (1637) [1638].

Davenport, A. Benedict (ed.), *A History and Genealogy of the Davenport Family* (1851).

Davies, Robert (ed.), *The Life of Marmaduke Rawdon of York*, Camden Society (1863).

Davis, J. C., 'The Levellers and Democracy', *Past and Present*, no. 40 (July 1968), 174–80.

Dean, John Ward, *A Memoir of the Rev. Nathaniel Ward* (1868).

Dobson, Edward, *XIV Articles of Treason and other Misdemeanours* (1643).

Donagan, Barbara, *War in England 1642–1649*, Oxford University Press (2010).

Downame, John, *Guide to Godlinesse* (1622).

Dunton, John, *A True Journal of the Salley Fleet* (1637).

Edwards, Thomas, *Antapologia* (1644).

Edwards, Thomas, *Gangraena* (1646).

Ellis, M. F. H., 'The Channel Islands and the Great Rebellion', *Bulletin of the Société Jersiaise*, vol. 13 (1937), 191–246.

Elton, Richard, *The Compleat Body of the Art Military*, 2nd edn. (1659).

England and Wales, Parliament, *A Declaration of both Houses of Parliament, Concerning the Affairs of Ireland* (1641) [1642].

England and Wales, Parliament, *Upon Report from the Committee for suppressing licentious and impious practices* (1650).

England and Wales, Sovereign, *A proclamation to summon the persons therein named, who sate, gave judgment, and assisted in that horrid and detestable murder . . .* (1660).

Englands Oaths. Taken by all men of Quallity in the Church and Common-wealth of England (1642).

Fairfax, Thomas et al., *Three Letters, From the Right Honourable Sir Thomas Fairfax, Lieut. Gen. Crumwell [sic] and the Committee residing in the Army* (1645).

Fairfax, Thomas, *A Letter From his Excellency the Lord Fairfax Generall of the Parliaments Forces . . . Concerning the surrender of Colchester* (1648).

Fairfax, Thomas et al., *A Full Narative [sic] of All the Proceedings betweene His Excellency the Lord Fairfax and the Mutineers* (1649).

Fairfax, Thomas, *Original Memoirs of Sir Thomas Fairfax* (1810).

Finch, Heneage, *An Exact and most Impartiall Accompt of the Indictment, Arraignment, Trial, and Judgment (according to Law) of nine and twenty Regicides* (1660).

Firth, C. H. (ed.), *The Memoirs of Edmund Ludlow*, 2 vols. (1894).

Firth, C. H. and Rait, R. S. (eds.), *Acts and Ordinances of the Interregnum, 1642–1660*, 3 vols. (1911).

Firth, C. H. and Davies, Godfrey, *The Regimental History of Cromwell's Army*, 2 vols., Oxford University Press (1940).

Firth, C. H., *Cromwell's Army: A History of the English Soldier During the Civil Wars, The Commonwealth and the Protectorate*, Greenhill Books (1992).

Fiske, John, *The Beginnings of New England* (1898).

Foard, Glenn, *Naseby: The Decisive Campaign*, Pen & Sword (2004).

'G. W.', *Respublica Anglicana or the Historie of the Parliament in their late Proceedings* (1650).

Gardiner, S. R., *History of the Great Civil War, 1642–1649*, 5 vols. (1893).

Gardiner, S. R. (ed.), 'Letter from the Earl of Manchester', *Camden Miscellany* 8 (1883), 1–3.

Gardiner, S. R. (ed.), *The Constitutional Documents of the Puritan Revolution 1625–1660* (1899).

Gardiner, S. R. and Atkinson, C. T. (eds.), *Letters and Papers relating to the First Dutch War*, 6 vols., Navy Records Society (1899–30).

Gentles, Ian, 'The New Model Officer Corps in 1647', *Social History*, vol. 22 (1997), 127–44.

Gentles, Ian, *The New Model Army in England, Scotland and Ireland, 1645–1653*, Blackwell (1991).

Glover, George, *The Arrivall and Intertainements of the Embassador Alkaid Jaurer Ben Abdella* (1637).

Goodwin, John, *A Reply of two of the Brethren to A.S.* (1644).

Gouge, William, *Of domesticall duties* (1622).

Gregg, Pauline, *Free-Born John: The Biography of John Lilburne*, Phoenix Press (2000).

Harris, G. G. (ed.), *Trinity House of Deptford Transactions, 1609–35: London Record Society*, vol. 19 (1983).

Hatton, Edward, *A New View of London*, 2 vols. (1708).

Hebb, David Delison, *Piracy and the English Government, 1616–1642*, Scolar Press (1994).

Hening, William Waller (ed.), *The Statutes at Large; Being a Collection of all the Laws of Virginia*, vol. 1 (1809).

Hensman, E. W., 'The East Midlands and the Second Civil War, May to July, 1648', *Transactions of the Royal Historical Society*, 4th series, vol. 6 (1923), 126–59.

Hill, G. W. and Frere, W. H. (eds.), *Memorials of Stepney Parish* (1890–1).

Historical Manuscripts Commission, *The Manuscripts of His Grace the Duke of Portland*, vols. 1 and 3 (1891–4).

Holmes, Clive, 'Colonel King and Lincolnshire Politics, 1642–1646', *Historical Journal*, vol. 16 (1973), 451–84.

Holmes, Clive, *The Eastern Association in the English civil war*, Cambridge University Press (1974).

Hooke, William, *New Englands Teares, for Old Englands Feares* (1641).

Hotten, J. C. (ed.), *The Original Lists of Persons of Quality . . . Who Went From Great Britain to the American Plantations 1600–1700* (1874).

Howell, T. B. (ed.), *A Complete Collection of State Trials*, vol. 4 (1816).

Hutchinson, Lucy, *Memoirs of the Life of Colonel Hutchinson*, 2 vols. (1885).

Hutchinson, Thomas (ed.), *The Hutchinson Papers*, Publications of the Prince Society, 2 vols. (1865).

Hutchinson, Thomas, *The History of Massachusetts, from the first settlement thereof in 1628, until the year 1750*, 2 vols. (1795).

'J.T.', *An Elegie Upon the Honourable Colonel Thomas Rainsbrough, butchered at Doncaster Sunday the 29. Octob. 1648*.

Jameson, J. Franklin (ed.), *Johnson's Wonder-Working Providence*, Charles Scribner's Sons (1910).

Jones, Phil, *The Siege of Colchester 1648*, Tempus (2003).

Jones, Whitney R. D., *Thomas Rainborowe (c. 1610–1648)*, Boydell Press (2005).

Josselyn, John, *An Account of Two Voyages to New-England, Made during the years 1638, 1663* (1865).

Kennedy, D. E., 'The English Naval Revolt of 1648', *English Historical Review*, vol. 77 (1962), 247–56.

Kingsbury, Susan Myra (ed.), *Records of the Virginia Company*, vol. 4, Library of Congress (1935).

Kishlansky, Mark A., 'What Happened at Ware?', *Historical Journal*, vol. 25 (1982), 827–39.

Knight, Francis, *A relation of seaven yeares slaverie under the Turkes of Argeire* (1640).

Knolles, Richard, *The Generall Historie of the Turkes*, 4th edition (1631).

Knowler, William (ed.) *The Earl of Strafforde's Letters and Dispatches*, vol. 2 (1740).

Kupperman, Karen Ordahl (ed.), *America in European Consciousness 1493–1750*, University of North Carolina (1995).

Kupperman, Karen Ordahl, 'Definitions of Liberty on the Eve of Civil War: Lord Saye and Sele, Lord Brooke, and the American Puritan Colonies', *Historical Journal*, vol. 32 (1989), 17–33.

Laing, D. (ed.), *The Letters and Journals of Robert Baillie*, 3 vols. (1842).

Lechford, Thomas, *Plain Dealing, or News from New England*, J. K. Wiggin & Wm. Parsons Lunt (1867).

Lilburne, John, *A More full Relation of the great Battell fought betweene Sir Tho: Fairfax, and Goring, on Thursday last, 1645* (1645).

Lilburne, John, *The Free-mans Freedom Vindicated* (1646).

Lilburne, John, *The Juglers Discovered* (1647).

Lilburne, John, *Rash Oaths Unwarrantable* (1647).

Lilburne, John, *The Second Part of England's New-Chaines Discovered* (1649).

Lilburne, John, *Two Letters Writ by Lieut. Col. John Lilburne . . . to Col. Henry Martin, a Member of the House of Commons, upon the 13 and 15 of September, 1647* (1647).

Lindley, Keith, 'Irish Adventurers and Godly Militants in the 1640s', *Irish Historical Studies*, vol. 29 (1994), 1–12.

Lisle, Thomas, et al., *The Declaration of the Navie . . . With their Resolutions upon turning out Colonell Rainsbrough from being their Commander, May 28th 1648* (1648).

Longstaffe, W. Hylton Dyer (ed.), 'A Journal of the First and Second Sieges of Pontefract Castle, 1644–1645, by Nathan Drake', *Miscellanea*, Publications of the Surtees Society, vol. 37 (1861), 1–125.

Loomie, Albert J. (ed.), *Ceremonies of Charles I: The Note Books of John Finet 1628–1641*, Fordham University Press (1987).

Ludlow, Edmund, *A Voyce from the Watch Tower: Part Five, 1660–1662*, ed. A. B. Worden, Camden Society, 4th series, 21 (1978).

MacCormack, J. R., 'The Irish Adventurers and the English Civil War', *Irish Historical Studies*, vol. 10 (1956), 21–58.

Manwaring, G. E. and Perrin, W. G. (eds.), *The Life and Works of Sir Henry Mainwaring*, Navy Records Society, 2 vols. (1920–2).

Massachusetts, *The Book of the General Lawes and Libertyes Concerning the Inhabitants of the Massachusetts* (1648).

Massachusetts Historical Society, *Winthrop Papers*, eds. Worthington C. Ford, Stewart Mitchell, Allyn Bailey Forbes, Malcolm Freiberg, 6 vols. (1929–92).

Mastin, John, *The History and Antiquities of Naseby* (1792).

Mather, Cotton, *Magnalia Christi American*, 2 vols. (1820).

Mather, Increase, *A Brief Relation of the State of New England from the Beginning of that Plantation to this Present Year, 1689* (1689).

Mather, Richard, *Church-Government and Church-Covenant Discussed* (1643).

Maverick, Samuel, *A Briefe Discription of New England and the Severall Townes therein*, D. Clapp (1885).

Mendle, Michael (ed.), *The Putney Debates of 1647: The Army, the Levellers and the English State*, Cambridge University Press (2001).

Mercurius bellicus.

Mercurius elencticus.

Mercurius impartialis.

Mercurius melancholicus.

Mercurius pragmaticus.

Merritt, J. F., 'Puritans, Laudians, and the Phenomenon of Church-Building in Jacobean London', *Historical Journal*, vol. 41 (1998), 935–60.

Moderate Intelligencer.

Moore, Susan Hardman, *Pilgrims: New World Settlers and the Call of Home*, Yale University Press (2007).

Morgan, John, *A Complete History of Algiers* (1731).

Morgan, John, *Godly Learning: Puritan Attitudes towards Reason, Learning and Education, 1560–1640*, Cambridge University Press (1988).

Morrison, Hugh, *Early American Architecture*, Dover (1987).

Morton, A. L., *The World of the Ranters*, Lawrence & Wishart (1979).

Murphy, Elaine, 'Atrocities at Sea and the Treatment of Prisoners of War by the Parliamentary Navy in Ireland, 1641–1649', *Historical Journal*, vol. 53 (2010), 21–37.

Nichols, Josias, *An Order of Houshold [sic] Instruction* (1596).

Noble, John and Cronin, John Francis (eds.) *Records of the Court of Assistants of the Colony of the Massachusetts Bay*, 3 vols. (1901–28).

Ogilby, John, *Africa* (1670).

Oppenheim, M., *A History of the Administration of the Royal Navy* (1896).

Orr, Charles (ed.), *History of the Pequot War* (1897).

Parker, Thomas, *The True Copy of a Letter* (1644).

Parliament-kite.

Paulden, Thomas, *Pontefract Castle. An Account How it was Taken: And how General Rainsborough was Surprised in his Quarters at Doncaster, Anno 1648* (1702).

Peacock, Edward, 'Notes on the Life of Thomas Rainborowe', *Archaeologia*, vol. 46, pt. 1 (1880), 9–64.

Perrin, W. G. (ed.), *The Autobiography of Phineas Pett*, Navy Records Society 51 (1918).

Pestana, Carla Gardina, *The English Atlantic in an Age of Revolution 1640–1661*, Harvard University Press (2004).

Pestana, Carla Gardina, 'The Problem of Land, Status, and Authority: How Early English Governors Negotiated the Atlantic World', *New England Quarterly*, vol. 78 (2005), 515–46.

Peter, Hugh, *A True Relation of the Passages of Gods Providence in a Voyage for Ireland* (1642).

Peter, Hugh, *A Word for the Armie. And Two Words to the Kingdome. To Cleare the One, And Cure the Other* (1647).

Peter, Hugh, *Gods Doings, and Mans Duty, Opened in a Sermon* (1646).

Peter, Hugh, *Mr Peters Last Report of the English Wars* (1646).

Peter, Hugh, *The Case of Mr Hugh Peters, Impartially Communicated to the View and Censure of the Whole World* (1660).

'Philocrates', *The Loyall Sacrifice: presented In the Live and Deaths of those two Eminent-Heroick Patterns . . . Sir Charls Lucas and Sir George Lisle* (1648).

Powell, J. R. and Timings, E. K. (eds.), *Documents Relating to the Civil War 1642–1648*, Navy Records Society (1963).

Prestwich, John, *Prestwich's Republica, or, A Display of the Honours, Ceremonies and Ensigns of the Common-Wealth* (1787).

Prynne, William, *A Brief Necessary Vindication of the Old and New Secluded Members* (1659).

Prynne, William, *A True and Ful Relation of the Officers and Armies Forcible Seising of Divers Eminent Members of the Commons House* (1648).

Purkiss, Dianne, *The English Civil War: A People's History*, Harper Press (2006).

Quarles, John, *Fons Lachrymarum* (1648).

'R. F.', *The Ranters Principles & Deceits* (1654).

Raithby, John (ed.), *The Statutes that Passed into Law under Charles I and Charles II* (1819).

Reading, John, *The Ranters Ranting* (1650).

Reid, Legh W., 'The English Ancestry of the Hoxtons of Maryland and Virginia', *Virginia Magazine of History and Biography*, vol. 60 (1952), 115–68.

Richardson, Samuel (ed.), *Sir Thomas Roe's Negotiations with the Grand Signor* (1740).

Roberts, Lewes, *The Merchants Mappe of Commerce* (1638).

Roberts, Oliver Ayer, *History of the Military Company of the Massachusetts*, 4 vols. (1895–1901).

Rushworth, John, *A True Relation of the Storming Bristoll* [*sic*] (1645).

Rushworth, John, *Historical Collections of Private Passages of State*, 8 vols. (1721).

Rushworth, John, *Remonstrance From His Excellency Sir Thomas Fairfax, and His Councell of Warre* (1647).

Rushworth, John, 'The Copie of a Letter sent from a Gentleman of publike employment in the late service neere Knaseby', *An Ordinance of the Lords and Commons assembled in Parliament* (17 June 1645).

Rutman, Darrett B., 'Governor Winthrop's Garden Crop: The Significance of Agriculture in the Early Commerce of Massachusetts Bay', *William and Mary Quarterly*, 3rd series, vol. 20 (1963), 396–415.

Rutman, Darret B., *Winthrop's Boston: Portrait of a Puritan Town 1630–1649*, University of North Carolina Press (1965).

Sachse, William L., 'The Migration of New Englanders to England, 1640–1660', *American Historical Review*, vol. 53 (1948), 251–78.

Salmon, Marylynn, 'The Legal Status of Women in Early America: A Reappraisal', *Law and History Review*, vol. 1 (1983), 129–51.

Scott, David, 'The "Northern Gentlemen", the Parliamentary Independents, and Anglo-Scottish Relations in the Long Parliament', *Historical Journal*, vol. 42 (1999), 347–75.

Sedgwick, Richard, *A Short Summe of the Principall Things Contained in the Articles of our Faith . . .* (1624).

Shepard, Thomas, *New Englands Lamentation for Old Englands Present Errours* (1645).

Shepard, Thomas, *The Parable of the Ten Virgins* (1660).

Shurtleff, Nathaniel B., *A Topographical and Historical Description of Boston* (1871).

Smith, John, *The Innocent Cleared: or, The Vindication of Captaine John Smith, Capt. Lieutenant under Colonell Rainsborough* (1648).

Speciall Passages And certain Informations from Severall Places.

Sprigg[e], Joshua, *Anglia rediviva, Englands Recovery* (1647).

St George, Robert Blair, 'Bawns and Beliefs: Architecture, Commerce, and Conversion in Early New England', *Winterthur Portfolio*, vol. 25 (1990), 241–87.

Stearns, Raymond Phineas, *The Strenuous Puritan: Hugh Peter 1598–1660*, University of Illinois (1954).

Stiles, Ezra, *A History of Three of the Judges of King Charles I* (1794).

Strachan, Michael, '*Sampson's* Fight With Maltese Galleys, 1628', *Mariner's Mirror*, vol. 55 (1969), 281–9.

'T. V.', *Good and true Newes from Bedford . . . Together with another Letter from the Lion, a Ship in service for the Parliament resident now at Hull* (1643).

The Kingdomes weekly intelligencer.

The Parliament scout.

The true informer or Monthly mercury.

Thornton, John Wingate, *The Historical Relation of New England to the English Commonwealth* (1874).

Tibbutt, H. G. (ed.), 'The Tower of London Letter-Book of Sir Lewis Dyve, 1646–47', *Publications of the Bedfordshire Historical Record Society*, vol. 38 (1958), 49–96.

Tinniswood, Adrian, *Pirates of Barbary: Corsairs, Conquests and Captivity in the 17th-Century Mediterranean*, Jonathan Cape (2010).

Trease, G., *Portrait of a Cavalier: William Cavendish, first Duke of Newcastle*, Macmillan (1979).

Ulrich, Laurel Thatcher, 'John Winthrop's City of Women', *Massachusetts Historical Review*, vol. 3 (2001), 19–48.

Underdown, David, 'Party Management in the Recruiter Elections, 1645–1648', *English Historical Review*, vol. 83 (1968), 235–64.

Underdown, David, 'The Independents Reconsidered', *Journal of British Studies*, vol. 3 (1964), 57–84.

Underdown, David, 'The Parliamentary Diary of John Boys, 1647–8', *Bulletin of the Institute of Historical Research*, vol. 39 (1966), 161–4.

Underdown, David, *Somerset in the Civil War and Interregnum*, David & Charles (1973).

Verax, Theodorus [Clementine Walker], *Anarchia Anglicana: or the History of Independency*, Part II (1661).

Vicars, John, *Gods Arke Overtopping the Worlds Waves* (1645).

Vicars, John, *Jehovah-jireh God in the Mount* (1644).

Vicars, John, *The Burning-Bush not Consumed* (1646).

Vives, Juan Luis, *A Very Fruitfull and Pleasant Booke Called the Instruction of a Christian Woman* (1540).

Walker, Edward, *Historical Discourses Upon Several Occasions* (1705).

Wall, Robert Emmet, Jr., *Massachusetts Bay: The Crucial Decade, 1640–1650*, Yale University Press (1972).

Ward, Nathaniel, *A Religious Retreat Sounded To A Religious Army, By one that desires to be faithful to his Country, though unworthy to be named* (1647).

Ward, Nathaniel, *The Simple Cobler [sic] of Aggawam in America* (1647).

Waters, Henry F., *Genealogical Gleanings in England*, 2 vols., New England Historic Genealogical Society (1907).

Webb, T. W. (ed.), *Military Memoir of Colonel John Birch*, Camden Society (1873).

Weisberg, K. Kelly, '"Under Greet Temptations Heer" – Women and Divorce in Puritan Massachusetts', *Feminist Studies*, vol. 2 (1975), 183–93.

Weld, Thomas, *An Answer to W. R. His Narration* (1644).

Wertz, Richard W. and Dorothy C., *Lyin-in: A History of Childbirth in America*, The Free Press (1977).

Wheeler, James Scott, *The Irish and British Wars 1637–1654: Triumph, Tragedy, and Failure*, Routledge (2002).

Whitelock, Bulstrode, *Memorials of the English Affairs*, 4 vols. (1853).

Whitmore, William H., *A Bibliographical Sketch of the Laws of the Massachusetts Colony From 1630 to 1686* (1890).

Widdowes, Giles, *The Schysmatical Puritan* (1630).

Wildman, W. B., *A Short History of Sherborne* (1902).

Williams, Roger, *Mr Cotton's Letter Lately Printed, Examined and Answered* (1644).

Williams, Roger, *The Bloudy Tenent of Persecution, for Cause of Conscience* (1644).

Winthrop, John, 'A Modell of Christian Charity', *Collections of the Massachusetts Historical Society*, 3rd series (1838), 31–48.

Winthrop, John, *A Short Story of the Rise, Reign, and Ruin of the Antinomians* (1644).

Winthrop, John, *The History of New England from 1630 to 1649*, ed. James Savage, 2 vols. (1853).

Winthrop, John, *Winthrop's Journal 1630–1649*, ed. James Kendall Hosmer, 2 vols., Charles Scribner's Sons (1908).

Winthrop, John et al., 'The Winthrop Papers', *Collections of the Massachusetts Historical Society*, 4th series (1863).

Winthrop, John et al., 'The Winthrop Papers (continued)', *Collections of the Massachusetts Historical Society*, 5th series (1882).

Wood, William, *New Englands Prospect* (1634).

Wyman, Thomas Bellows, *The Genealogies and Estates of Charlestown*, 2 vols. (1879).

Young, Alexander (ed.), *Chronicles of the First Planters of the Colony of Massachusetts Bay* (1846).

Acknowledgements

I am keenly aware that any historian who tries to straddle the Atlantic can end up with wet feet. If that is true of me, the fault is all mine. But many people and institutions have done their best to keep me from falling in the water. I want to thank staff at the British Library, The National Archives of the UK, the London Library, the Bodleian Library and Tower Hamlets Local History Library and Archives. I am particularly grateful to Captain Richard Woodman FRHistS FNI, who was kind enough to show me material from his forthcoming official history of the Corporation of Trinity House; to Bath Spa University and especially to Dr Kristin Doern of BSU's School of Humanities and Cultural Industries, for making my research a great deal easier than it might have been; to Dan Franklin of Jonathan Cape and Lara Heimert of Basic Books, for their support and encouragement; to my agents, Felicity Bryan and George Lucas, for enriching my life in so many ways.

And last, first, always, I'm grateful to Helen. She knows why.

Index

Rainborowe, Margery (*née* Jenney) (wife
of Major William Rainborowe) 119,
257, 258, 259
Rainborowe, Martha (mother of Captain
William Rainborowe) 9, 14, 17
Rainborowe Martha (later, Coytmore;
Winthrop; Coggan) (daughter of
Captain William Rainborowe): birth
11; marries Thomas Coytmore 11, 22,
23, 59; childhood 17; father's will and
57, 68; children 59, 123, 187–8, 302–3;
choice to emigrate to America 61;
choice of Massachusetts Bay Colony
and 62–3; family in America 64, 80;
settles in Charlestown 64, 75–6, 77, 79,
80; preparations for voyage to America
65, 68, 69, 70; voyage to America
71–5; introduction to realpolitik of
New England religious life 80, 81; first
year in New England 85, 86; admitted
to full communion at Charlestown
church 86–90, 106; land 109–10;
husband's will and 123; Stephen
Winthrop and 138, 139; death of
husband and 190–1; marries John
Winthrop 206–7, 301, 302; John
Winthrop's children and 303–4; death
of John Winthrop and 310–11; marries
John Coggan 311–12; death of John
Coggan and 336; death 336–7
Rainborowe, Mary (daughter of Major
William Rainborowe) 328
Rainborowe, Reynold (son of Captain
William Rainborowe) 11, 22, 57
Rainborowe, Samuel (son of Captain
William Rainborowe) 11, 17, 18, 19
Rainborowe, Thomas (father of Captain
William Rainborowe) 9–10, 14, 31
Rainborowe, Colonel Thomas (son of
Captain William Rainborowe) 326,
327; siege commander in English Civil
War xix, 161–3, 165, 168, 175–86, 199,
200–2, 265–77; man of advanced
political views xix–xx, 159, 166, 227,
235–40, 295; speech in favour of
universal male suffrage, 1647 xix–xx,
235–40, 295; radical New Englanders
fight for in English Civil War xx,
148–66, 167, 319, 322, 323; parentage
11; date of birth 11; childhood 17;

Levant merchant 22, 104, 130;
marriage 46; children 46; father's will
and 57, 58; Irish Adventure/Adventure
for Irish Lands, involvement in, 1642
128, 129, 130, 131, 132, 133, 134, 139,
143, 298; financial difficulties due to
Irish Adventure 139; parliamentarian
navy, joins, 1643 139–40, 141, 143, 145;
Swallow, command of 139; *Lion*,
command of 139–40, 141, 143, 145;
sails to aid beleaguered town of Hull,
1643 141–2; handed the command of
an infantry battalion at Hull, 1643 143,
144–5; taken prisoner by Royalists at
Hull, 1643 144–6; leaves navy and
joins Meldrum's army, 1643 145–6;
raises own infantry regiment for
Eastern Association 146, 147;
recruitment to army and 147, 168;
Marston Moor battle, takes no part in
151; convinced God himself is
involved in workings of humankind
on a daily basis 154; portrait/
appearance 158–9; connection with
New Englanders influences political
views 159, 166; Crowland, role in
siege of, 1644 161–3, 165; return of
New Englanders in regiment to New
England 163–6; New Model Army,
becomes colonel of new infantry
regiment in, 1645 166; spends spring,
1645 in Abingdon training new
regiment 167; Gaunt House, role in
taking of, 1645 168; Naseby, role in
battle of, 1645 167, 169–73; West
Country campaign, role in, 1645
174–86; Bridgwater, role in siege of,
1645 175–6, 177–8, 265; Sherborne,
role in siege of, 1645 178–80;
Nunney, role in siege of, 1645 178,
181; Bristol, role in siege of, 1645
180–5; Berkeley Castle, role in siege
of, 1645 185–6; Tiverton, possibility of
involvement of fighting at, 1645 186;
Corfe Castle, role in siege of, 1645
186; Oxford, blockade of 186, 199;
Woodstock Manor, role in siege of,
1646 199; camps outside walls of
Oxford, 1646 199; Worcester siege, role
in, 1646 200–2, 334; Hugh Peter